# ISAIAH 40–66

The texts in Isaiah 40–66 are widely admired for their poetic brilliance. Situating Isaiah within its historic context, Katie M. Heffelfinger explores its literary aspects through a lyrically informed approach that emphasizes key features of the poetry and explains how they create meaning. Her detailed analysis of the text's passages demonstrates how powerful poetic devices, such as paradox, allusion, juxtaposition, as well as word and sound play, are used to great effect via the divine speaking voice, as well as the personified figures of the Servant and Zion. Heffelfinger's commentary includes a glossary of poetic terminology that provides definitions of key terms in non-technical language. It features additional resources, notably "Closer Look" sections, which explore important issues in detail, as well as "Bridging the Horizons" sections that connect Isaiah's poetry to contemporary issues, including migration, fear, and divided society.

Katie M. Heffelfinger is Deputy Director and Lecturer in Biblical Studies and Hermeneutics at the Church of Ireland Theological Institute. She is the author of *I Am Large, I Contain Multitudes: Cohesion and Conflict in Second Isaiah* (2011).

# NEW CAMBRIDGE BIBLE COMMENTARY

GENERAL EDITOR: Ben Witherington III

HEBREW BIBLE/OLD TESTAMENT EDITOR: Bill T. Arnold

EDITORIAL BOARD
Bill T. Arnold, *Asbury Theological Seminary*
James D. G. Dunn, *University of Durham*
Michael V. Fox, *University of Wisconsin-Madison*
Robert P. Gordon, *University of Cambridge*
Judith M. Gundry, *Yale University*

The New Cambridge Bible Commentary (NCBC) aims to elucidate the Hebrew and Christian Scriptures for a wide range of intellectually curious individuals. While building on the work and reputation of the Cambridge Bible Commentary popular in the 1960s and 1970s, the NCBC takes advantage of many of the rewards provided by scholarly research over the last four decades. Volumes utilize recent gains in rhetorical criticism, social scientific study of the Scriptures, narrative criticism, and other developing disciplines to exploit the growing advances in biblical studies. Accessible jargon-free commentary, an annotated "Suggested Readings" list, and the entire *New Revised Standard Version* (NRSV) text under discussion are the hallmarks of all volumes in the series.

PUBLISHED VOLUMES IN THE SERIES
*The Pastoral Epistles*, Scot McKnight
*The Book of Lamentations*, Joshua A. Berman
*Hosea, Joel, and Amos*, Graham R. Hamborg
*1 Peter*, Ruth Anne Reese
*Ephesians*, David A. deSilva
*Philippians*, Michael F. Bird and Nijay K. Gupta
*Acts*, Craig S. Keener
*The Gospel of Luke*, Amy-Jill Levine and Ben Witherington III
*Galatians*, Craig S. Keener
*Mark*, Darrell Bock
*Psalms*, Walter Brueggemann and William H. Bellinger, Jr.
*Matthew*, Craig A. Evans
*Genesis*, Bill T. Arnold
*The Gospel of John*, Jerome H. Neyrey
*Exodus*, Carol Meyers
*1–2 Corinthians*, Craig S. Keener
*James and Jude*, William F. Brosend II
*Judges and Ruth*, Victor H. Matthews
*Revelation*, Ben Witherington III

# Isaiah 40–66

**Katie M. Heffelfinger**
*Church of Ireland Theological Institute*

Shaftesbury Road, Cambridge CB2 8EA, United Kingdom

One Liberty Plaza, 20th Floor, New York, NY 10006, USA

477 Williamstown Road, Port Melbourne, VIC 3207, Australia

314–321, 3rd Floor, Plot 3, Splendor Forum, Jasola District Centre, New Delhi – 110025, India

103 Penang Road, #05-06/07, Visioncrest Commercial, Singapore 238467

Cambridge University Press is part of Cambridge University Press & Assessment, a department of the University of Cambridge.

We share the University's mission to contribute to society through the pursuit of education, learning and research at the highest international levels of excellence.

www.cambridge.org
Information on this title: www.cambridge.org/9781107166059

© Cambridge University Press & Assessment 2024

This publication is in copyright. Subject to statutory exception and to the provisions of relevant collective licensing agreements, no reproduction of any part may take place without the written permission of Cambridge University Press & Assessment.

First published 2024

*A catalogue record for this publication is available from the British Library.*

*Library of Congress Cataloging-in-Publication Data*
NAMES: Heffelfinger, Katie M., author.
TITLE: Isaiah 40 - 66 / Katie Heffelfinger, Church of Ireland Theological Institute, Dublin.
OTHER TITLES: Isaiah fourty - sixty-six
DESCRIPTION: Cambridge, United Kingdom ; New York, NY, USA : Cambridge University Press, 2024. | Series: New Cambridge Bible commentary | Includes bibliographical references and indexes.
IDENTIFIERS: LCCN 2023028757 | ISBN 9781107166059 (hardback) | ISBN 9781316617304 (paperback)
SUBJECTS: LCSH: Bible. Isaiah XL-LXVI–Criticism, interpretation, etc.
CLASSIFICATION: LCC BS1520 .H45 2024 | DDC 224/.107–dc23/eng/20230831
LC record available at https://lccn.loc.gov/2023028757

ISBN 978-1-107-16605-9 Hardback
ISBN 978-1-316-61730-4 Paperback

Cambridge University Press & Assessment has no responsibility for the persistence or accuracy of URLs for external or third-party internet websites referred to in this publication and does not guarantee that any content on such websites is, or will remain, accurate or appropriate.

*To my parents, with love and admiration*

# Contents

| | |
|---|---|
| *List of Supplementary Sections* | page xi |
| *Preface* | xiii |
| *A Word about Citations* | xv |
| *List of Abbreviations* | xvii |

| | |
|---|---|
| 1 INTRODUCTION | 1 |
| Key Aspects of a Poetic Approach | 2 |
| Important Contexts for Reading Isaiah 40–66 | 5 |
| About the Audience(s) | 6 |
|    Historical Context and Isaiah 40–55 | 8 |
|    Historical Context and Isaiah 56–66 | 10 |
| Isaiah 40–66 and Other Biblical Voices | 11 |
| Meaning(s) and Isaiah 40–66 | 13 |
| 2 SUGGESTED READING | 15 |
| Commentaries | 15 |
| Literary Studies | 16 |
| Compositional Studies | 17 |
| History, Trauma, Exile, and Migration Studies | 18 |
| Other Relevant Monographs, Articles, and Essays | 19 |
| 3 COMMENTARY | 21 |
| Isaiah 40:1–31 | 21 |
| Isaiah 41:1–7 | 34 |
| Isaiah 41:8–20 | 42 |
| Isaiah 41:21–29 | 60 |
| Isaiah 42:1–4 | 65 |
| Isaiah 42:5–9 | 69 |
| Isaiah 42:10–13 | 74 |

| | |
|---|---|
| Isaiah 42:14–20 | 79 |
| Isaiah 42:21–25 | 84 |
| Isaiah 43:1–21 | 89 |
| Isaiah 43:22–28 | 97 |
| Isaiah 44:1–5 | 102 |
| Isaiah 44:6–22 | 105 |
| Isaiah 44:23 | 114 |
| Isaiah 44:24–28 | 115 |
| Isaiah 45:1–8 | 121 |
| Isaiah 45:9–25 | 126 |
| Isaiah 46:1–13 | 138 |
| Isaiah 47:1–15 | 145 |
| Isaiah 48:1–11 | 157 |
| Isaiah 48:12–22 | 161 |
| Isaiah 49:1–13 | 167 |
| Isaiah 49:14–50:3 | 175 |
| Isaiah 50:4–11 | 186 |
| Isaiah 51:1–8 | 193 |
| Isaiah 51:9–16 | 200 |
| Isaiah 51:17–52:12 | 205 |
| Isaiah 52:13–53:12 | 215 |
| Isaiah 54:1–17 | 231 |
| Isaiah 55:1–13 | 238 |
| Isaiah 56:1–8 | 247 |
| Isaiah 56:9–57:21 | 255 |
| Isaiah 58:1–14 | 267 |
| Isaiah 59:1–21 | 274 |
| Isaiah 60:1–22 | 283 |
| Isaiah 61:1–11 | 295 |
| Isaiah 62:1–12 | 302 |
| Isaiah 63:1–6 | 308 |
| Isaiah 63:7–64:12 | 319 |
| Isaiah 65:1–25 | 328 |
| Isaiah 66:1–24 | 341 |
| | |
| *Glossary of Poetic Terminology* | 355 |
| *Author Index* | 359 |
| *Scripture Index* | 363 |
| *Subject Index* | 375 |

# Supplementary Sections

| | |
|---|---:|
| A Closer Look: The Voice of Comfort | 33 |
| A Closer Look: The Coastlands and the Creator of the Cosmos | 40 |
| A Closer Look: Cyrus the Persian | 41 |
| Bridging the Horizons: "God's Sovereign Choice" | 50 |
| Bridging the Horizons: Isaiah 40–66 and Human Migration | 55 |
| A Closer Look: The Servant and His "Songs" | 68 |
| A Closer Look: The Majestic Divine Speaker | 73 |
| A Closer Look: The Final Form and the Former Things | 77 |
| A Closer Look: Indictment, Sarcasm, and Rhetorical Questions | 88 |
| Bridging the Horizons: On Loving Poetry and Poetry's Loves | 119 |
| A Closer Look: A God Who Hides Himself | 136 |
| A Closer Look: Jacob-Israel and the Exiles | 143 |
| A Closer Look: Daughter Zion and Daughter Babylon | 152 |
| A Closer Look: City as Woman in the Ancient Near East | 155 |
| A Closer Look: A Covenant People | 174 |
| A Closer Look: Lady Zion and the Suffering Servant, the Rhetorical Power of Juxtaposition | 184 |
| Bridging the Horizons: Fear Not | 199 |
| Bridging the Horizons: Seeing Jesus and Seeing the Servant Today | 224 |
| A Closer Look: Zion and the Audience | 238 |
| A Closer Look: The Reforestation Imagery of Isaiah 40–66 in the Context of the Book of Isaiah | 245 |
| A Closer Look: From Servant to Servants | 253 |
| A Closer Look: "Third Isaiah" as "Under-Rated" Poet | 264 |
| Bridging the Horizons: "Third Isaiah" and the Divided Society | 292 |
| Bridging the Horizons: Isaiah 56–66 and the New Testament | 313 |
| A Closer Look: Conflicted Commands and Competing Contentions in the Memory Motif | 338 |
| A Closer Look: Birth and Breastfeeding Imagery in Isaiah 40–66 | 351 |

xi

# Preface

It has been a joy, a privilege, and a challenge to give myself to the work of this commentary over the last number of years. Isaiah 40–66 contains some of the most startling and captivating words of Scripture, and their resonances, despite nearly countless scholarly engagements with them, are ultimately inexhaustible. This brief commentary represents my attempt to capture some of the delight of this poetry for my readers. A single volume of this size could never hope to grapple with all of the potential meanings or even with every word of the text. That is not its aim. It is my hope that this poetic work with Isaiah 40–66 makes clear the richness with which this text repays close attention and that, in so doing, it might motivate readers to continue the journey of reading it closely themselves.

My sincere thanks are due to a number of people and organizations without whom this work would not be complete. Sabbatical leave during the Autumn semester of 2018 enabled significant drafting work to be completed. I am grateful to the Representative Church Body of the Church of Ireland for making my sabbatical possible and to the Loyola Institute at Trinity College Dublin for the generous allocation of office space. My colleagues and students at the Church of Ireland Theological Institute have provided immense encouragement and practical support. In this regard, I am particularly grateful to Maurice Elliott, Patrick McGlinchey, Bridget Nichols, Lynda Levis, Jane Kelly, Daphne Metcalfe, and Hazel Connor. I am grateful to Shai Held, Michael Spence, Patricia Tull, and Brent Strawn for helpful feedback on drafted material and to the Trinity College Dublin Biblical Studies Seminar for group engagement with an early portion of a draft. Bill Arnold has provided excellent counsel as series editor, and I am grateful for his insight and encouragement. Beatrice

Rehl from Cambridge University Press has been attentive, helpful, and gracious, for which I am genuinely appreciative.

My family ground my writing in the joy of shared living, and I cannot imagine undertaking this work without the love and support of my husband and daughter. My parents forged the home in which I first grew into the faith, and their love and support over my lifetime have been an invaluable undergirding to all that I have done. It is as a testimony to their commitment to each other and to the life of faith that I dedicate this volume to them.

# A Word about Citations

All volumes in the *New Cambridge Bible Commentary* (NCBC) include footnotes, with full bibliographical citations included in the note when a source is first mentioned. Subsequent citations include the author's initial or initials, full last name, abbreviated title for the work, and date of publication. Most readers prefer this citation system to endnotes that require searching through pages at the back of the book.

The Suggested Reading lists, also included in all NCBC volumes after the Introduction, are not a part of this citation apparatus. Annotated and organized by publication type, the self-contained Suggested Reading list is intended to introduce and briefly review some of the most well-known and helpful literature on the biblical text under discussion.

A WORD ABOUT TRANSLATIONS

Throughout this commentary, NRSV$^{ue}$ is the primary biblical translation used, as is standard in the NCBC series. The text given at the opening of the discussion of each poem is NRSV$^{ue}$ and only departs from that translation for aspects of lineation, paragraphing, and stanza divisions. Each of these departures is discussed in the footnotes. Where the commentary's discussion quotes a biblical text, the translation is NRSV$^{ue}$ unless either discussed as an alternative or proposed translation or offered as a "gloss" of the transliterated Hebrew text. Glosses are typically marked using the abbreviation i.e. and juxtaposed to the transliterated Hebrew text.

# Abbreviations

| | |
|---|---|
| AB | *Anchor Bible* |
| BBR | *Bulletin for Biblical Research* |
| BDB | Brown, F., S. R. Driver, and C. A. Briggs. *A Hebrew and English Lexicon of the Old Testament.* Oxford, 1907. |
| BHS | *Biblia Hebraica Stuttgartensia.* Edited by K. Elliger and W. Rudolph. Stuttgart, 1983. |
| *BSac* | *Bibliotheca sacra* |
| CC | Continental Commentaries |
| ConBOT | Coniectanea biblica: Old Testament Series |
| Eng. | English |
| FOTL | The Forms of the Old Testament Literature |
| *HALOT* | Koehler, L., W. Baumgartner, and J. J. Stamm, *The Hebrew and Aramaic Lexicon of the Old Testament.* Study Edition. Two Volumes. Leiden, 2001. |
| HBM | Hebrew Bible Monographs |
| *HBT* | *Horizons in Biblical Theology* |
| Heb. | Hebrew |
| *HTR* | *Harvard Theological Review* |
| *IB* | *Interpreter's Bible* |
| ICC | International Critical Commentary |
| JBL | *Journal of Biblical Literature* |
| JPS | Jewish Publication Society |
| JSOT | *Journal for the Study of the Old Testament* |
| JSOTSup | Journal for the Study of the Old Testament: Supplement Series |
| *JTI* | *Journal of Theological Interpretation* |
| MT | Masoretic Text (Codex Leningradensis as represented in *BHS*) |
| NA[27] | *Novum Testamentum Graece*, Nestle-Aland, 27th ed. |

| | |
|---|---|
| NET | New English Translation |
| *NIB* | *The New Interpreter's Bible* |
| NRSV | New Revised Standard Version |
| NRSV$^{ue}$ | New Revised Standard Updated Edition |
| OTL | Old Testament Library |
| *PIBA* | *Proceedings of the Irish Biblical Association* |
| SBLDS | Society of Biblical Literature Dissertation Series |
| *SCJR* | *Studies in Christian-Jewish Relations* |
| *SJT* | *Scottish Journal of Theology* |
| *TynBul* | *Tyndale Bulletin* |
| *VT* | *Vetus Testamentum* |
| VTSup | Vetus Testamentum Supplements |
| WBC | Word Biblical Commentary |
| *ZAW* | *Zeitschrift für die alttestamentliche Wissenschaft* |

# 1 Introduction

Into the apparent divine silence of the exile, a poetic voice sounds: "Comfort, O comfort my people, says your God" (Isa 40:1). The chapters that follow are filled with voices. The prophetic poet, the Servant, and Zion all have something to say. But throughout, the dominant voice is that of Israel's God. This divine first-person speech conveyed by the prophetic text soothes as well as rages. It offers vivid images of coming restoration and of estranging wrath. At times the contrast between passages pulls the reader in opposite directions, producing an almost irreconcilable tension.[1] At other points, the words seem so overlapped with earlier passages that it is as though the text is doubling back upon itself.[2] These features are elements of Isaiah 40–66's poetic style. As poems, the texts of Isaiah 40–66 convey their message more through vivid word pictures, juxtapositions, and emotional encounters than through an argument about ideas.

This commentary will argue that Isaiah 40–66 proclaims its message above all else *poetically*. Shifts and disjunctions, distinctive voices, emotional turbulence, and piling up of metaphors are the primary means by which these chapters proclaim their prophetic message. A strategy that tries to make sense of these features by flattening them into a single storyline or a logically driven argument will reduce rather than enhance

---

[1] For example, the audience are commanded both "Remember the former things" (46:9) and "Do not remember the former things" (43:18). See also Francis Landy, "Spectrality in the Prologue to Deutero-Isaiah," in *The Desert Will Bloom: Poetic Visions in Isaiah* (eds. A. Joseph Everson and Hyun Paul Kim; Atlanta: Society of Biblical Literature, 2009), 152. On "intractable problem" as drawn from literary theory, see Katie M. Heffelfinger, *I Am Large, I Contain Multitudes: Lyric Cohesion and Conflict in Second Isaiah* (Leiden: E. J. Brill, 2011), 67–69.

[2] For example, Zion's restoration in chapters 49 and 54 reuses and modifies words and images.

2                                                          *Introduction*

our appreciation of the message the ancient prophetic text conveys.[3] Instead, what is needed is an approach that treats these poetic features as conveying and carrying the meaning of the text. Such an approach is what this commentary intends to offer.

## KEY ASPECTS OF A POETIC APPROACH

A poetically informed approach allows our expectations about what a text might mean and how it might convey that meaning to be significantly influenced by the awareness that the text is poetic. It has been common in the history of interpretation for other factors to heavily influence our expectation about the meaning of Isaiah 40–66. One factor that often plays a significant role in determining what sort of meaning we might expect to find has been the knowledge that the text is prophetic. If one expects that Israel's prophets urge Israel to take particular action, then it is not difficult to associate them with orators.[4] Such an association leads one to expect that prophetic texts should be read for their argument and that the main interpretive goal is to determine what action the audience is being urged to adopt.[5] On the other hand, the notion that Israel's prophets spoke to historical audiences in specific historical circumstances can orient readers to the events that were occurring during the time in which they worked. Such details can also potently shape the expectations of readers and lead historical events to become a significant focus.[6] The historical events of the exile and return do, indeed, make an impact upon these poems and will be taken into account in what follows. However, knowing what historical

---

[3]   On the general "readerly tendency ... to read for plot," see J. Cheryl Exum, *Song of Songs: A Commentary* (OTL; Louisville: Westminster John Knox, 2005), 42. Examples of plot-oriented readings include Joseph Blenkinsopp, *Isaiah 40–55* (AB 19A; New York: Doubleday, 2002), 349; and Klaus Baltzer, *Deutero-Isaiah* (Hermeneia; trans. Margaret Kohl; Minneapolis: Fortress Press, 2001), 19, on Isaiah 52:13–53:12; and John L. McKenzie, *Second Isaiah* (AB 20; Garden City, NY: Doubleday, 1968), 15–17,on Isaiah 40.

[4]   Richard J. Clifford, *Fair Spoken and Persuading* (New York: Paulist, 1984), 4, applies the label "orator" to Second Isaiah.

[5]   Examples include Clifford, *Fair Spoken and Persuading* (1984), see especially pp. 4–5; and Yehoshua Gitay, *Prophecy and Persuasion: A Study of Isaiah 40–48* (Bonn: Linguistica Biblica, 1981), see especially pp. 26–27.

[6]   For example, K. Baltzer, *Deutero-Isaiah* (2001), 30, dates Second Isaiah later than the dominant position of scholarship (450–400 BCE) and offers a correspondingly distinct interpretation of the work's aims (pilgrimage to Jerusalem).

# Key Aspects of a Poetic Approach

events these texts were spoken into does not exhaust the significance of what they proclaim in that setting. Therefore, while I do not deny that prophecy and history are each appropriate in their own way, I argue that prophetic poetry creates its own expectations.[7] These expectations are certainly not incompatible with historical audiences and are not irreconcilable with a public speaker. However, attention to poetic prophecy with specific attention to its poetic character does shape expectation in significant ways.

It will be important, then, to clarify what sort of expectations about meaning poetry creates in the reader. Throughout this commentary, I will take meaning to be "the projection of a possible and inhabitable world."[8] Interpretation explores and exposes that world to the mind of the reader. Interpretation offers that possible world as the context for the audience's response. Interpreting a poetic text involves paying particular attention to the poetic features of the text and considering them to carry and convey the text's meaning. It also means actively resisting assumptions about meaning that do not belong to the text's "world."

One of the most significant things that is largely absent from Isaiah 40–66's "world" is a narrative or discursive structure. That is, these poems do not present either a "story" or an "argument." Rather they are best conceived of as offering an experience or an encounter. These poems are a series of nonnarrative poems arranged into a larger whole. Their world is illuminated by careful attention to the features that they share with other nonnarrative poems, especially lyric poems.[9] For this reason, the type of interpretation undertaken in this commentary might be helpfully described as a lyrically informed poetic approach.

Individual texts exhibit particular preferences for poetic features, and any approach to interpretation should be adapted to the needs of the text in question. However, it is possible to enumerate a few general features of

---

[7] See further Katie M. Heffelfinger, "Persuasion, Poetry and Biblical Prophets," *PIBA* 43–44 (2021): 38–53.

[8] Paul Ricoeur, *The Rule of Metaphor: Multi-disciplinary Studies of the Creation of Meaning in Language* (trans. Robert Czerny; Buffalo: University of Toronto Press, 2000), 92.

[9] For further defense and explanation of this claim, see K. M. Heffelfinger, *I Am Large* (2011), 36–81.

4                                                      *Introduction*

what I mean by a lyrically informed poetic approach to Isaiah 40–66. These will be employed throughout the commentary.

1. A lyrically informed poetic approach to Isaiah 40–66 will draw attention to the experience and encounter produced by the text. Jonathan Culler's description of lyric as seemingly the "utterance of a voice" applies quite potently to Isaiah 40–66, where the overwhelming dominance of the divine speaking voice, especially in 40–55, is a primary unifying factor in an otherwise fractious series of poems.[10] Throughout, this commentary will aim to expose the encounter the text produces for its reader and particularly to highlight the tone of the speaking voice and the emotions it both elicits and describes.

2. The tension mentioned in the opening paragraph of this introduction is a tension at the heart of Isaiah 40–66. A poetically informed reading will not attempt to harmonize between wrath and comfort or between paradoxical and juxtaposed commands and imageries. Rather, the apparently irreconcilable tensions within the text and expressed by its speaking voices are vital to the way these poems create a possible world for their readers. Their mode of poetic persuasion depends upon sharp shifts between opposing emotions and possibilities. By setting these sharply into relief through contrast, the poetry produces urgency and orients its audience toward the attitudes and actions it urges them to inhabit. So, a poetic approach to these chapters will involve highlighting the tensions and contradictions and illustrating the ways that meaning is produced by juxtaposing them.

3. A lyrically informed poetic approach to Isaiah 40–66 will involve unpacking the meaningful significance of the poems' literary artistry. It is important to bear in mind that poetic texts of all types, and especially those that employ features common to lyric poems, exploit the richness and ambiguity of language. Poetry revels in allusion, sound play, metaphor, and double entendre. For the poet, openness and uncertainty about words and images are not problems to be overcome but possibilities to be exploited. Poetry produces its impact on the reader at least in part by exulting in the uncertainty and mutability of

[10] Jonathan Culler, *Literary Theory: A Very Short Introduction* (New York: Oxford University Press, 1997), 75.

*Important Contexts for Reading Isaiah 40–66*

5

language.[11] The words, sounds, and rhythms of poetry unfold the world of the poem. It is not that these "ornaments" can be translated into a meaning that exists separately from them. Rather, the poetic voice utters rhythms, sound, and syllables that "systematically infect and affect thought."[12] A lyrically informed poetic approach will not merely observe poetic features such as wordplay, sound play, juxtaposition, parataxis (see Glossary of Poetic Terminology), metaphor, and repetition. Rather, it will consider these the primary modes of poetic meaning-making and will treat them as the way the poetry expresses its message. As Roy F. Melugin insightfully pointed out, "In poetry the forms and images are at least as important as the thought. By means of these the poet calls into being certain feelings and attitudes and associations which are not, strictly speaking 'thoughts.'"[13]

Isaiah 40–66 is not a seamless and harmonious text. It does not move by a sequence of logical argumentation toward an obviously urged action. Successful receipt of the message of these prophecies will involve experience and encounter. It will result in a transformation of attitudes and emotions. It cannot be replaced by a distillation of the cognitive content of the message. Rather, these chapters open up possible worlds into which the audience is invited.

## IMPORTANT CONTEXTS FOR READING ISAIAH 40–66

While this commentary is intentionally focusing on the poetic techniques that Isaiah 40–66 uses to make meaning, context is not unimportant to its work. The intended historical audience of these chapters plays an important role in shaping the message that the prophetic poets offer to them. Their expectations, attitudes, and historical circumstances all make an imprint on these poems. That is, these prophetic poems are not spoken into a void. In order to interpret them, we need to consider the historical context in which their audiences lived. In addition, we should consider the

---

[11] See further Katie M. Heffelfinger, "Truth and Hidden Things: Reading Isaiah 45:9–25 as Scripture," in *A New Song. Biblical Hebrew Poetry as Jewish and Christian Scripture* (eds. Stephen D. Campbell, Richard G. Rohlfing Jr., and Richard S. Briggs; Bellingham, WA: Lexham Press, 2023), 159–160.

[12] J. Culler, *Literary Theory* (1997), 80.

[13] Roy F. Melugin, *The Formation of Isaiah 40–55* (New York: Walter de Gruyter, 1976), 78.

6                                                                    *Introduction*

biblical context that these poems were spoken into since the prophetic poets responsible for these chapters were very fond of quoting from and alluding to other biblical texts.

ABOUT THE AUDIENCE(S)

Since 1892, the year Bernhard Duhm published his influential work, commentaries on these chapters seem obliged to take a position on how many separate historical periods the canonical book of Isaiah addresses.[14] The suggestion that Isaiah could well be divided into at least two historical sections is older than Duhm's work but this date is considered a watershed moment in the history of Isaiah scholarship, and one that introduced the possibility of a third section.[15] A historical division between chapters 39 and 40 is largely uncontroversial.[16] At this point, the figure of the prophet Isaiah of Jerusalem disappears, as does his historical context of the eighth century and the narratives about him. Babylon, which had been a looming but not yet realized threat in Isaiah 39, is already the oppressor at whose hand Israel has suffered by chapter 40.[17]

Chapters 56–66, however, have been much more heavily debated. These chapters do seem, on balance, to be somewhat later than Isaiah 40–55, but not significantly so. As Brooks Schramm observes, "the majority view dates Isaiah 56–66 to the early restoration period."[18] He warns, however, "Given the almost total lack of historical references in Isaiah 56–66, a good

---

[14]   See Marvin A. Sweeney, *Isaiah 40–66* (FOTL; Grand Rapids: William B. Eerdmans, 2016), 11–13, on Duhm's indebtedness to earlier thinking.

[15]   See the helpful summary of the history of this discussion in H. G. M. Williamson, "Isaiah: Book of," in *Dictionary of the Old Testament Prophets* (eds. Mark J. Boda and J. Gordon McConville; Downers Grove, IL: IVP, 2012), 366–371; as well as Ewe Becker, "The Book of Isaiah: Its Composition History," in *The Oxford Handbook of Isaiah* (ed. Lena-Sofia Tiemeyer; New York: Oxford University Press, 2020), 39–40.

[16]   James Muilenburg, "The Book of Isaiah, Chapters 40–66: Introduction, and Exegesis," in *Ecclesiastes, The Song of Songs, Isaiah, and Jeremiah* (*IB*; ed. George Arthur Buttrick; Nashville: Abingdon Press, 1956), 382, calls this division "widely accepted." See the helpful discussion of H. G. M. Williamson, "Isaiah: Book of" (2012), 370.

[17]   The word "Babylon" does not appear in chapter 40. However, it is explicitly referenced in 43:14; 47:1; 48:14; and 48:20 and the destruction by the Babylonians and ensuing exile of Jerusalem's inhabitants is the most obvious referent of the language of Jerusalem having "served her term" and that "her penalty is paid" (40:2).

[18]   Brooks Schramm, *The Opponents of Third Isaiah: Reconstructing the Cultic History of the Restoration* (JSOTSup 193; Sheffield: Sheffield Academic, 1995), 21.

*About the Audience(s)* 7

measure of restraint is in order" while assigning a tentative date of 538–400.[19] There is something of a change in the circumstances of the addressees and a shift in the style of the prophetic proclamation marked by both continuity and discontinuity. The prophetic poetry largely continues, using many of the same techniques and favorite images that Isaiah 40–55 employed, though with new features and tendencies.[20] The prophetic poetic style of this section exhibits some distinctive features of its own (see further A Closer Look: "Third Isaiah" as an "Under-Rated" Poet). One contextual difference is that in these latter chapters, the exiles seem to have returned to Judah. Some "gathering" of the LORD's people has already happened (56:8) and there are references to the house of the LORD (56:5, 7), which would seem to imply that there is an expectation that the temple is to be rebuilt.

So, discussion of the historical audience means paying attention to at least two historical contexts. First, Isaiah 40–55 seems primarily to address Judeans who are living in exile in Babylon. It commands them to "Go out from Babylon" (48:20) and displays particular interest at various points in Babylon's imminent fall as well as familiarity with its practices.[21] Frequent allusion to Lamentations, which is most probably a text from the community who remained behind in Jerusalem,[22] need not necessarily overturn the arguments in favor of a likely exilic audience for Isaiah 40–55. It seems that there was contact between the exiles and those who remained behind, and the reuse and reapplication of texts is entirely possible between these

---

[19]  B. Schramm, *Opponents of Third Isaiah* (1995), 52.
[20]  See the helpful overview of similar literary techniques in Benjamin D. Sommer, *A Prophet Reads Scripture: Allusion in Isaiah 40–66* (Stanford: Stanford University Press, 1998), 187–192.
[21]  See further discussion in K. M. Heffelfinger, *I Am Large* (2011), 91–92. A contrasting opinion is available in Lena-Sofia Tiemeyer, *For the Comfort of Zion: The Geographical and Theological Location of Isaiah 40–55* (VTSup 139; Leiden: Brill, 2011), 2, who argues for a "Judahite provenance" for Isaiah 40–55. While it seems likely that the exiles are a primary audience of these chapters for the reasons detailed above, they may not be the exclusive audience. The poems could potentially resonate with other communities of Judeans in the time period including those remaining in Judah. See the discussion in John Goldingay and David Payne, *Isaiah 40–55* (ICC; London: T&T Clark, 2006), 1:33, and their helpful note of caution that "the traditional critical view that the poet worked in Babylon is probably right."
[22]  See, e.g., F.W. Dobbs-Allsopp, *Lamentations* (IBC; Louisville: John Knox, 2002), 4.

8         *Introduction*

communities.[23] A second context is that of Isaiah 56–66. The exiles have returned to Judah and the audience are undergoing the difficult period of rebuilding. Isaiah 40–55 and 56–66 do not have entirely distinct audiences but overlapping ones whose background includes a significant historical shift.

In addition, while this commentary is not focused on historical authorship claims and intentionally reads the text as it finally stands (see A Closer Look: The Final Form and the Former Things), it is important to note the scholarly consensus that the final form of chapters 40–66 is the result of a long process, which seems likely to have involved multiple authorial hands.[24] Chapters 56–66, in particular, are frequently regarded as composed of poems drawn together from different authors.[25] Thus, the audience of the final form of the book is somewhat distinct from the audience of each of the larger units.[26] However, it seems that one of the features of the final form of Isaiah is that it preserves the distinctive earlier voices of the book and relates them together without flattening them (see A Closer Look: The Final Form and the Former Things and A Closer Look: "Third Isaiah" as "Under-Rated" Poet). For this reason, this commentary will journey through the poems with attention to the audience(s) they appear to present within each larger unit's own world. That means that for Isaiah 40–55 the primary attention is to an audience of exiles and for Isaiah 56–66 the community facing the challenges of return.

## Historical Context and Isaiah 40–55

Scholars have claimed that the Judean exiles prospered in Babylon and that one of the difficulties for the prophetic poet of Isaiah 40–55 was to convince the exiles to depart a relatively comfortable life in Babylon.[27] However,

---

[23]  See, e.g., Carol A. Newsom, "Response to Norman K. Gottwald, 'Social Class and Ideology in Isaiah 40–55,'" *Semeia* 59 (1992): 75; and K. M. Heffelfinger, *I Am Large* (2011), 93.

[24]  See the introductory discussion in H. G. M. Williamson, "Isaiah: Book of" (2012), 366–371.

[25]  Joseph Blenkinsopp, *Isaiah 56–56* (AB 19B; London: Doubleday, 2003), 54–60, provides an overview of scholarly discussion.

[26]  See the helpful discussion of a Second Temple period audience in Goldingay and Payne, *Isaiah 40–55* (2006), 1:35.

[27]  See, for example, the description in R. J. Clifford, *Fair Spoken* (1984), 13.

# About the Audience(s)

Daniel L. Smith-Christopher has convincingly argued that there are good reasons to doubt that the exiles' experience was a largely positive one. His reasons include the testimony of the exiles themselves in their literature, which periodically uses the language of slavery to describe their condition, and the reports the Neo-Babylonians make of their own treatment of displaced peoples.[28]

It would be hazardous indeed to attempt a full reconstruction of the objective facts of the exiles' experience in Babylon. We lack sufficient evidence for this historical period to carry out such a task without a great deal of uncertainty and speculation.[29] However, the important reality that makes an impact on how we understand the prophetic poet's message to this population is their own perspective on their exile as represented in this text. That perspective comes through clearly in the cited speech of the audience and in the allusions the prophetic poet makes to other biblical texts that seem to represent the audience's perspective.

Personified figures who represent the audience of Isaiah 40–55 speak only three times in the whole of these fifteen chapters. One of these, the "we" speech of Isaiah 53 is less an indicator of their attitude toward their exile than an example of what attitude the prophet urges them to adopt.[30] The other two, however, are remarkably similar to one another, and the way they appear in the text makes it clear they are the perspective of the audience that the prophetic poet aims to transform. Each time (40:27; 49:14) a figure closely associated with the audience (Jacob, Zion) has their former speech cited directly and refuted. In each case, the charge is that they have been abandoned or neglected by the LORD. In each case, the poetry forcefully and emphatically denies this claim.

These embedded quotations of the audience's speech are the most significant indicators of their own perspective. They combine with and express the concerns voiced in the book of Lamentations, as will be discussed below. They are an audience who are uneasy about their

---

[28]  See Daniel L. Smith Christopher, *A Biblical Theology of Exile* (Minneapolis: Fortress Press, 2002), 65–68. On the use of the term "displacement," see J. Ahn, "Exile," in *Dictionary of the Old Testament Prophets* (eds. Mark J. Boda and J. Gordon McConville; Nottingham: InterVarsity Press, 2012), 198.

[29]  See, e.g., J. Blenkinsopp, *Isaiah 40–55* (2002), 101; and the discussion in K. M. Heffelfinger, *I Am Large* (2011), 85–86.

[30]  This passage will be discussed in greater detail in the commentary on it.

relationship with their God. Their trust in the LORD has been undermined by their experience of exile. They fear that the LORD has abandoned, forgotten, or neglected them. This is the emotional world that the prophetic poet seeks to transform in Isaiah 40–55. The raging and consoling of the divine voice, its overwhelming and constant presence, and its majestic tone together produce an emotionally charged encounter that directly answers the audience's spoken fears about the LORD's absence, rejection, and apparent untrustworthiness. The contrast between righteous indignation and consolation in the divine speaking voice produces a tension that creates urgency for the audience to accept the divine offer of comfort and restoration. The poetry wrestles through competing perspectives and emotions swirling around the reconciliation between the exiles and God in whom they had placed their trust. It urges the audience to accept the offered reconciliation and does so by juxtaposing the threat that looms if they reject such comfort with vivid depictions of the promised restoration.

## Historical Context and Isaiah 56–66

The historical details of the audience's circumstances in Isaiah 56–66 are similarly murky.[31] It appears that some have returned to Jerusalem (56:8; 62:10), and an influx of worshippers and other returnees is anticipated (56:8; 60:4–13; 62:10; 66:20). In places, the city seems yet to be rebuilt (e.g., 62:1, 7; 64:10–12). For these reasons, this commentary agrees with the many scholars who tentatively date these chapters to an early period in the return.[32]

The poetic technique of citation and refutation of audience speech continues in these chapters, and here a variety of perspectives and issues emerge. The "potential" speech of foreigner and eunuch highlight concerns over inclusion within the worshipping community (56:3). The cited speech of those who appear to represent the leaders of the returned community undermines their authority by presenting them as pursuing drunkenness and their own gain (56:12). The same themes appear in the next cited speech in these chapters in which the people voice a complaint that their

---

[31] See Jacob Stromberg, *Isaiah After Exile: The Author of Third Isaiah as Reader and Redactor of the Book* (Oxford: Oxford University Press, 2011), 7, who writes that "a fully satisfying reconstruction of the social-historical situation . . . remains elusive."

[32] See B. Schramm, *Opponents of Third Isaiah* (1995), 51–52.

fasting is disregarded by the LORD (58:3). The refutation is that their fast days are self-serving and therefore unacceptable to the LORD. In a similar way to the "we" speech of Isaiah 53, which placed "confessional" words on the audience's lips, Isaiah 59:9–15 are poetic lines spoken by the "we" of the text that express the reality of the transgression and injustice that are thematic in these chapters. Thus, each of these "citations" of audience speech, in its own way, points to a context in which those who have returned face the struggle of being a restored people in a restored land. They struggle to act justly toward one another. They struggle to distribute power and they struggle to determine who is to be included in the community of those restored. Into these struggles of restoration, the prophet speaks. While Isaiah 40–55 employed its poetically persuasive means to move its entire exilic audience toward a reconciling encounter with the LORD, Isaiah 56–66 differentiates between groups within its audience apparently urging them into the group characterized by faithfulness to the LORD (see A Closer Look: "Third Isaiah" as "Under-Rated Poet").

## ISAIAH 40–66 AND OTHER BIBLICAL VOICES

The prophetic poetic voice of these chapters is not a voice that emerges from out of nowhere. Instead, the poetic voice echoes, modifies, and answers back to a range of other biblical voices. This important poetic technique of allusion relates the message of these poems to previous tradition and the audience's own experiences but also highlights the distinctive message of the new poem by juxtaposing the new expression with the remembered one in the audience's mind.[33]

One important literary context for Isaiah 40–66 is the context given to it by the final form of the book of Isaiah in the Hebrew canon (see A Closer Look: The Final Form and the Former Things). That is, the book itself prompts us to read Isaiah 40–66 as intimately related to Isaiah 1–39.[34]

---

[33] B. Sommer, *A Prophet Reads Scripture* (1998), 158.
[34] Brevard S. Childs has been particularly influential in this regard. See, e.g., his comments on reading the whole of Isaiah in Brevard S. Childs, *Isaiah* (OTL; Louisville: Westminster John Knox, 2001), 3, 443–444; See also B. Schramm, *Opponents of Third Isaiah* (1995), 43, 79–80; Katie M. Heffelfinger, "Isaiah 40–55," in *The Oxford Handbook of Isaiah* (ed. Lena-Sofia Tiemeyer; New York: Oxford University Press, 2020), 116 and A Closer Look: The Final Form and the Former Things.

12                                                                    *Introduction*

And, indeed, there are common themes, vocabulary, and motifs that run through the whole of the material, and there are echoes of earlier material in the exilic and postexilic portions of the book. Perhaps most importantly, the consistent themes of the LORD's exalted status, judgment of wrongdoing, and orientation toward future deliverance run from the beginning to the end of Isaiah as a whole.[35]

While Isaiah 1–39 certainly provides important canonical and theological context for Isaiah 40–66, I would argue that the most significant biblical voice in shaping the message of many of these poems is the book of Lamentations. I am not alone in connecting these chapters with Lamentations. I have been convinced of Lamentations' relevance by the insightful studies of Tod Linafelt and of Patricia Tull.[36] Chapters 40–55, with their opening announcement of comfort, directly answer the demand Lamentations makes that the LORD should act as Zion's comforter.[37] Throughout these poems, the divine voice claims the role of comforter, declaring it emphatically. The pervasive, overwhelming, and unifying divine voice breaks the long silence that ran through Lamentations and continues beyond it as the book "is left opening out into the emptiness of God's nonresponse."[38] Thus, the apparent divine silence of exile, which I mentioned in the opening lines of this introduction, is an idea that comes particularly from Lamentations, and it is a silence that Second Isaiah seems intentionally shaped to answer.[39]

---

[35]  See also K. M. Heffelfinger, "Isaiah 40–55" (2020) 119–120.
[36]  Tod Linafelt, *Surviving Lamentations: Catastrophe, Lament, and Protest in the Afterlife of a Biblical Book* (London: University of Chicago Press, 2000); Patricia Tull Willey, *Remember the Former Things: The Recollection of Previous Texts in Second Isaiah* (SBLDS 161; Atlanta: Scholars Press, 1997). See also Norman K. Gottwald, "Social Class and Ideology in Isaiah 40–55: An Eagletonian Reading," *Semeia* 59 (1992): 43–57; and C. A. Newsom, "Response to Norman K. Gottwald" (1992): 73–78.
[37]  Adele Berlin, *Lamentations* (OTL: Louisville: Westminster John Knox, 2002), 48; see also K. M. Heffelfinger, *I Am Large* (2011), 98–100.
[38]  T. Linafelt, *Surviving Lamentations* (2000), 60. Linafelt, and others, note that God never speaks in Lamentations. As Tod Linafelt "Surviving Lamentations," *Horizons in Biblical Theology* 17 (1995): 51, says "The voice of YHWH never sounds in the book of Lamentations."
[39]  See T. Linafelt, *Surviving Lamentations* (2000), 74; and Katie M. Heffelfinger, "'I Am He, Your Comforter': Second Isaiah's Pervasive Divine Voice as Intertextual 'Answer' to Lamentations' Divine Silence," in *Reading Lamentations Intertextually* (eds. Heath A. Thomas and Brittany N. Melton; LIBOTS 714; London: T&T Clark, 2021). See also M. A. Sweeney, *Isaiah 40–66* (2016), 31, who claims that "Lamentations ... may well have posed the questions that chs. 40–55 and 56–66 are designed to answer."

*Meaning(s) and Isaiah 40–66*

13

But it is not just the speech of the divine voice that points to Lamentations. Both Lady Zion and the Servant as personified figures echo the motifs of Daughter Zion and "the man" of Lamentations.[40] The Isaian poetic prophet takes up these metaphors and builds upon them in developing the poetic message of raging comfort to the exiles (see further A Closer Look: Lady Zion and the Suffering Servant, the Rhetorical Power of Juxtaposition).

First Isaiah and Lamentations are the most significant of Isaiah 40–66's biblical source texts for this commentary's work, but they are by no means the only ones. This prophetic poetry draws richly on the traditions of the past and redeploys them in distinctive ways. Throughout this commentary, I will draw attention to this poetic technique as it both explains and illuminates the prophetic poetry's message.

## MEANING(S) AND ISAIAH 40–66

Read poetically, these passages offer a possible world where the audience are invited into a transformative encounter with a series of voices, most prominently the LORD's. These encounters work imagistically and affectively to reorient the audience and to redirect their allegiances. In the exilic context, the poems work together through the juxtaposition of speaking tones in the LORD's voice and by contrasting two compelling personifications. Lady Zion embodies the audience's suffering while the Servant embraces obedience and transformation. The juxtaposed encounters with these personifications draw the audience away from attachment to their complaint into embrace of the reconciliation and relationship being offered by the divine voice (see A Closer Look: Lady Zion and the Suffering Servant, the Rhetorical Power of Juxtaposition).

In the postexilic texts, juxtaposition evokes a possible world of clashing faithful and rebellious responses.[41] Here the prophetic poetry forges resonance and appeal, drawing its audience into identity with the servants, an identity that embraces the "way" of the LORD as opposed to their own. Contrasting fear and repulsion reinforce this aim, driving the audience

---

[40] See P. Tull Willey, *Remember the Former Things* (1997), 211–219; and A Closer Look: The Servant and His Songs.

[41] See also M. A. Sweeney, *Isaiah 40–66* (2016), 21.

away from the behaviors and attitudes depicted as their own way.[42] By merging Zion, her children, and the Servant's shared appeal into the servants, Isaiah 56–66 reengages the divine-human relationship for the returnees in a new context (see A Closer Look: From Servant to Servants).

The final poems of the book of Isaiah draw together the themes of the book as a whole. Any accounting for the message should take account of the way Isaiah 56–66 gathers together motifs from Isaiah 1–39 along with Isaiah 40–55 to produce a vision of ultimate restoration that is the final movement along a trajectory of warning, punishment and reconciliation[43] (see further A Closer Look: "Third Isaiah" as "Under-Rated Poet" and A Closer Look: The Final Form and the Former Things). In this way, the accumulated impact of Isaiah's emotional encounters offers a possible world that cannot ultimately be reduced to a claim but is best captured in a poetic vision that holds together mercy and justice, wrath and reconciliation, divine initiative and human faithfulness (see A Closer Look: "Third Isaiah" as "Under-Rated Poet").

This short summary of the messages of Isaiah 40–66 is no substitute for the encounters that the poems themselves offer. Their work ultimately persuades by reshaping the imagination, by realigning hope, and by recalibrating the heart (see Bridging the Horizons: On Loving Poetry and Poetry's Loves). Exposing the possible worlds offered by the emotion, experience, and encounter of each poem is the task of the commentary that follows.

---

[42] See also M. A. Sweeney, *Isaiah 40–66* (2016), 21, on the rhetorical impact of "differentiation between the fates of the righteous and the wicked."

[43] Cf. M. A. Sweeney, *Isaiah 40–55* (2016), 17, and especially 24–25 on the relationship of "the interplay between judgment and restoration" to the history of the eighth to fourth centuries.

# 2 Suggested Reading

COMMENTARIES

Commentaries on Isaiah 40–66 are an overwhelming abundance and only a selection can be included here. James Muilenburg's commentary is a landmark in scholarship on Isaiah 40–66 and is still immensely valuable for its literary attentiveness. More recent work on Isaiah 40–55 by John Goldingay and David Payne is insightful and gives comprehensive coverage to the range of scholarship on these chapters along with detailed discussion of its own translation decisions. Joseph Blenkinsopp's two volumes similarly provide both thoroughly engaged commentary and detailed translation discussion for Isaiah 40–55 and 56–66 respectively. Brevard Childs contributes insightful readings and occupies an important place in the move toward reading these chapters within the context of the book of Isaiah.

Alter, Robert. *The Hebrew Bible: A Translation with Commentary.* Volume 2 Prophets *Nevi'im.* New York: W. W. Norton & Company, 2019.

Baltzer, Klaus. *Deutero-Isaiah.* Hermeneia. Translated by Margaret Kohl. Minneapolis: Fortress Press, 2001.

Blenkinsopp, Joseph. *Isaiah 40–55.* Anchor Bible 19A. New York: Doubleday, 2002.

Blenkinsopp, Joseph. *Isaiah 56–66.* Anchor Bible 19B. New York: Doubleday, 2003.

Childs, Brevard S. *Isaiah.* Old Testament Library. Louisville: Westminster John Knox, 2001.

Goldingay, John, and David Payne. *Isaiah 40–55.* International Critical Commentary. 2 vols. New York: T&T Clark, 2006.

McKenzie, John L. *Second Isaiah*. Anchor Bible 20; Garden City, NY: Doubleday, 1968.

Muilenburg, James. "The Book of Isaiah, Chapters 40–66: Introduction, and Exegesis." Pages 381–773 in *Ecclesiastes, The Song of Songs, Isaiah, and Jeremiah*. Vol. 5 of *Interpreter's Bible*. Edited by George Arthur Buttrick. Nashville: Abingdon, 1956.

Sweeney, Marvin A. *Isaiah 40–66*. The Forms of the Old Testament Literature. Grand Rapids: William B. Eerdmans Publishing Company, 2016.

Watts, John D. W. *Isaiah 34–66*. Word Biblical Commentary 25. Rev. ed. Grand Rapids: Zondervan, 2005.

Westermann, Claus. *Isaiah 40–66*. Old Testament Library. Translated by David M. G. Stalker. Philadelphia: Westminster Press, 1969.


LITERARY STUDIES

Literary sources listed here are of several types. Approaches to reading biblical poetry have played an important role in this commentary. Alter, Dobbs-Allsopp, Berlin, and Kugel fall into that category. Alter's work occupies a seminal place in the field of literary studies of biblical texts and his *Art of Biblical Poetry* offers a readable and engaging introduction. Berlin and Kugel each play important roles in the development of thinking about biblical poetry and, in particular, parallelism. Dobbs-Allsopp has been a primary figure in recent studies of biblical poetry and his work *On Biblical Poetry* merits a place as a central key text in ongoing work in this area. Couey and James' edited volume presents a series of readings of biblical poems along with a useful introduction by the editors. Mullins presents an accessibly written, engaging invitation to reading biblical texts from a literary, and especially poetic, perspective.

In addition, this category of the suggested reading list includes works that offer literary readings of Isaiah 40–66 or portions thereof. Key readings that consider these chapters' literary relationships with other biblical texts and have made essential contributions to the argument of this commentary include the works of Linafelt, Tull Willey, and Sommer.

Alter, Robert. *Art of Biblical Poetry*. New York: Basic Books, 1985.

Berlin, Adele. *The Dynamics of Biblical Parallelism*. Revised and Expanded. Grand Rapids: Eerdmans, 1985.

*Compositional Studies* 17

Couey, J. Blake, and Elaine T. James, eds. *Biblical Poetry and the Art of Close Reading*. Cambridge: Cambridge University Press, 2018.

Dobbs-Allsopp, F. W. *On Biblical Poetry*. Oxford: Oxford University Press, 2015.

Kugel, James L. *The Idea of Biblical Poetry: Parallelism and Its History*. Baltimore: Johns Hopkins University Press, 1981.

Linafelt, Tod. *Surviving Lamentations: Catastrophe, Lament, and Protest in the Afterlife of a Biblical Book*. Chicago: University of Chicago Press, 2000.

Mullins, Matthew. *Enjoying the Bible: Literary Approaches to Loving the Scriptures*. Grand Rapids: Baker, 2021.

Tull Willey, Patricia. *Remember the Former Things: The Recollection of Previous Texts in Second Isaiah*. Society of Biblical Literature Dissertation Series 161. Atlanta: Scholars Press, 1997.

Sommer, Benjamin D. *A Prophet Reads Scripture: Allusion in Isaiah 40–66*. Stanford: Stanford University Press, 1998.

COMPOSITIONAL STUDIES

Discussion of the history of these chapters' composition has been a dominant interest of the field of biblical studies for many years. Roy Melugin is an important figure in the turn toward consideration of the relationship of Isaiah's parts to the whole of the book. Williamson's detailed and convincing study argues for a dominant role for Isaiah 40–55 in the formation of the whole book and has commanded wide-ranging influence in the field. Rendtorff's proposal develops an insightful argument about the role of Isaiah 56–66 to the overall formation of the book. Mettinger stands as a turning point in the treatment of the Servant Songs.

Hays, Christopher B. "The Book of Isaiah in Contemporary Research." *Religion Compass* 5, no. 10 (2011): 549–566.

Melugin, Roy F. *The Formation of Isaiah 40–55*. Beihefte zur Zeitschrift für die alttestamentliche Wissenschaft 141. New York: Walter de Gruyter, 1976.

Mettinger, Tryggve N. D. *A Farewell to the Servant Songs: A Critical Examination of an Exegetical Axiom*. Scripta Minora; Lund: Royal Society of Letters, 1983.

Stromberg, Jacob. *Isaiah after Exile: The Author of Third Isaiah as Reader and Redactor of the Book.* Oxford: Oxford University Press, 2011.

Rendtorff, Rolf. "The Composition of the Book of Isaiah." Pages 146–169 in *Canon and Theology: Overtures to an Old Testament Theology.* Translated by Margaret Kohl. Minneapolis: Fortress Press, 1993.

Rendtorff, Rolf. "Isaiah 56:1 as a Key to the Formation of the Book of Isaiah." Pages 181–189 in *Canon and Theology: Overtures to an Old Testament Theology.* Translated by Margaret Kohl. Minneapolis: Fortress Press, 1993.

Williamson, H. G. M. *The Book Called Isaiah: Deutero-Isaiah's Role in Composition and Redaction.* Oxford: Clarendon Press, 1994.


HISTORY, TRAUMA, EXILE, AND MIGRATION STUDIES

This category includes works that shed light on important factors in the ancient context of Isaiah 40–66.

Ahn, John. "Exile." Pages 196–204 in *Dictionary of the Old Testament Prophets.* Edited by Mark J. Boda and J. Gordon McConville. Nottingham: InterVarsity Press, 2012.

Berges, Ulrich. "Trito-Isaiah and the Reforms of Ezra/Nehemiah: Consent or Conflict?" *Biblica* 98, no. 2 (2017): 173–190.

Boase, Elizabeth, and Christopher G. Frechette, eds. *Bible through the Lens of Trauma.* Atlanta: SBL Press, 2016.

Briant, Pierre. *From Cyrus to Alexander: A History of the Persian Empire.* Translated by Peter T. Daniels. Winona Lake, IN: Eisenbrauns, 2002.

Day, Peggy L. "The Personification of Cities as Female in the Hebrew Bible: The Thesis of Aloysius Fitzgerald, F.S.C." Pages 283–302 in *Reading From This Place: Social Location and Biblical Interpretation in Global Perspective.* Volume 2. Edited by Fernando F. Segovia and Mary Ann Tolbert; Minneapolis: Fortress Press, 1995.

Fried, Lisbeth S. "Cyrus the Messiah? The Historical Background to Isaiah 45:1." *Harvard Theological Review* 95, no. 4 (2002): 373–393.

Halvorson-Taylor, Martien A. *Enduring Exile: The Metaphorization of Exile in the Hebrew Bible.* Vetus Testamentum Supplements 141. Leiden: Brill, 2011.

Lim, Bo H. "Exile and Migration: Toward a Biblical Theology of Immigration and Displacement." *The Covenant Quarterly* 74 (2016): 3–15.

Markl, Dominik. "The Babylonian Exile as the Birth Trauma of Monotheism." *Biblica* 101, no. 1 (2020): 1–25.

Schramm, Brooks. *The Opponents of Third Isaiah: Reconstructing the Cultic History of the Restoration.* Journal for the Study of the Old Testament: Supplement Series 193. Sheffield: Sheffield Academic Press, 1995.

Smith-Christopher, Daniel L. *A Biblical Theology of Exile.* Minneapolis: Fortress Press, 2002.

Stulman, Louis, and Hyun Chul Paul Kim. *You Are My People: An Introduction to Prophetic Literature.* Nashville: Abingdon, 2010.

OTHER RELEVANT MONOGRAPHS, ARTICLES, AND ESSAYS

Beuken, Willem A. M. "The Main Theme of Trito-Isaiah 'The Servants of YHWH.'" *Journal for the Study of the Old Testament* 47 (1990): 67–87.

Brettler, Marc, and Amy-Jill Levine. "Isaiah's Suffering Servant: Before and After Christianity." *Interpretation: A Journal of Bible and Theology* 73, no. 2 (2019): 158–173.

Clifford, Richard J. *Fair Spoken and Persuading: An Interpretation of Second Isaiah.* New York: Paulist Press, 1984.

Kaminsky Joel, and Anne Stewart. "God of All the World: Universalism and Developing Monotheism in Isaiah 40–66." *Harvard Theological Review* 99, no. 2 (2006): 139–163.

Lynch, Matthew J. "Zion's Warrior and the Nations: Isaiah 59:15b–63:6 in Israel's Zion Traditions." *Catholic Biblical Quarterly* 70 (2008): 244–263.

Sawyer, John F. A. *The Fifth Gospel: Isaiah in the History of Christianity.* Cambridge: Cambridge University Press, 1996.

Schmidt, Uta. "Servant and Zion: Two Kinds of Future in Isaiah 49." Pages 85–91 in *"My Spirit at Rest in the North Country" (Zechariah 6.8): Collected Communications to the XXth Congress of the International Organization for the Study of the Old Testament, Helsinki 2010.* Beiträge zur Erforschung des Alten Testaments und des antiken Judentum 57.

Edited by Hermann Michael Niemann and Matthias Augustin. Oxford: Peter Lang, 2011.

Tull, Patricia K. "Who Says What to Whom: Speakers, Hearers, and Overhearers in Second Isaiah." Pages 157–168 in *Partners with God: Theological and Critical Readings of the Bible in Honor of Marvin A. Sweeney.* Edited by Shelley L. Birdsong and Serge Frolov. Claremont: Claremont Press, 2017.

# 3 Commentary

ISAIAH 40:1–31

> [1] Comfort, O comfort my people,
>     says your God.
> [2] Speak tenderly to Jerusalem,
>     and cry to her
> that she has served her term,
>     that her penalty is paid,
>     that she has received from the LORD's hand double for all her sins.[1]
>
> [3] A voice cries out:[2]
>     "In the wilderness prepare the way of the LORD,
>     make straight in the desert a highway for our God.
> [4] Every valley shall be lifted up,
>     and every mountain and hill be made low;
> the uneven ground shall become level,
>     and the rough places a plain.
> [5] Then the glory of the LORD shall be revealed,
>     and all people shall see it together,
>     for the mouth of the LORD has spoken."

---

[1] I am deviating from the lineation printed in NRSV[ue] here. The final line is a triplet in which each line begins with *kî* (i.e., "for"). This triple repetition, along with the elongated final line, marks the end of the stanza.

[2] NRSV[ue] appears to treat this line as independent, not including it in the couplet that follows. I am treating it as an integral part of the triplet. The same type of clause appears in verse 6, and there it is clearly the first line of a couplet.

# Commentary

$^6$ A voice says, "Cry out!"
And I said, "What shall I cry?"
All flesh is grass,
their constancy is like the flower of the field.
$^7$ The grass withers; the flower fades,
[[when the breath of the LORD blows upon it;
surely the people are grass.
$^8$ The grass withers; the flower fades]];
but the word of our God will stand forever.

$^9$ Get you up to a high mountain,$^3$
O Zion, herald of good news;
lift up your voice with strength,
O Jerusalem, herald of good news,
lift it up, do not fear;
say to the cities of Judah,
"Here is your God!"

$^{10}$ See, the Lord GOD comes with might,$^4$
and his arm rules for him;
his reward is with him,
and his recompense before him.
$^{11}$ He will feed his flock like a shepherd;
he will gather the lambs in his arms,
and carry them in his bosom,
and gently lead the mother sheep.

$^{12}$ Who has measured the waters of the sea in the hollow of his hand
and marked off the heavens with a span,
enclosed the dust of the earth in a measure,
and weighed the mountains in scales
and the hills in a balance?

---

3    I am treating this as a small stanza of its own, given its distinctive addressee. The paragraphing marks in the MT support such a division.

4    I am treating v. 10 as the beginning of a new stanza. This stanza begins the unit vv. 10–17 as described in the commentary below. The parallel patterning of vv. 10 and 15 is important to the structuring of this section, and the stanza breaks reflect these elements.

*Isaiah 40:1–31*

<sup>13</sup> Who has directed the spirit of the LORD,
    or as his counselor has instructed him?
<sup>14</sup> Whom did he consult for his enlightenment,
    and who taught him the path of justice?
    [[Who taught him knowledge,
    and showed him the way of understanding?[5]

<sup>15</sup> Even the nations are like a drop from a bucket,
    and are accounted as dust on the scales;
    see, he takes up the isles like fine dust.
<sup>16</sup> Lebanon would not provide fuel enough,
    nor are its animals enough for a burnt offering.]]
<sup>17</sup> All the nations are as nothing before him;
    they are accounted by him as less than nothing and emptiness.

<sup>18</sup> To whom, then, will you liken God,
    or what likeness compare with him?
<sup>19</sup> An idol? – A workman casts it,
    and a goldsmith overlays it with gold
    and casts for it silver chains.
<sup>20</sup> As a gift one chooses mulberry wood
    – wood that will not rot –
then seeks out a skilled artisan
    to set up an image that will not topple.
<sup>21</sup> Have you not known?[6]
    Have you not heard?

---

[5] The lineation here reflects the patterning of the line in Hebrew. The first and final lines are parallel to one another with forms of the verb *bîn* and the related noun *tĕbûnâ*, and the central two lines are parallel to one another, employing identical forms of the verb here translated "taught" *wayĕlammĕdēhû*. This chiastic structure (See "chiasm" in Glossary of Poetic Terminology), alongside the long couplet in v. 12, draws attention to the central contrast it frames in v. 13, between the LORD *wĕ'îš* (i.e., "and a man") as discussed in the commentary below. NRSV<sup>ue</sup>'s translation "as his counselor" for *wĕ'îš 'ăṣtô* omits explicit reference to a "man" here.

[6] NRSV<sup>ue</sup> creates a stanza break here and at v. 24. I read all of this as one stanza as it appears to speak in the same voice to the same audience. The short stanza beginning at v. 25 mirrors this one in its opening, offering a parallel beginning to the stanza spoken in the divine voice.

24                                         *Commentary*

Has it not been told you from the beginning?
      Have you not understood from the foundations of the earth?[7]
[22] It is he who sits above the circle of the earth,
      and its inhabitants are like grasshoppers,
who stretches out the heavens like a curtain,
      and spreads them like a tent to live in,
[23] who brings princes to naught,
      and makes the rulers of the earth as nothing.
[24] Scarcely are they planted, scarcely sown,
      scarcely has their stem taken root in the earth,
when he blows upon them, and they wither,
      and the tempest carries them off like stubble.[8]

[25] To whom, then, will you compare me, or who is my equal?
      says the Holy One.[9]
[26] Lift up your eyes on high and see:
      Who created these?
He who brings out their host and numbers them,
      calling them all by name;
because he is great in strength,
         mighty in power,
         not one is missing.

[27] Why do you say, O Jacob,
      and assert, O Israel,
"My way is hidden from the LORD,
      and my right is disregarded by my God"?
[28] Have you not known?
      Have you not heard?[10]

---

[7]   My lineation departs from that of NRSV[ue] here. A pair of shorter couplets is preferable here as it reflects the parallelism indicated in the four line-initial occurrences of the interrogative with negative particle *hălô '*.

[8]   NRSV[ue] marks v. 24 as an independent short stanza. I have treated it instead as directly tied to the princes imagery immediately preceding.

[9]   My lineation here follows the accent marks of the Hebrew text. Additionally, elsewhere in the poem the attribution via "says" is its own line, see 40:1.

[10]   The lineation here departs the NRSV[ue] and mirrors that of v. 21. See the discussion of the reasoning for that lineation above.

*Isaiah 40:1–31*

> The LORD is the everlasting God,
>> the Creator of the ends of the earth.
> He does not faint or grow weary;
>> his understanding is unsearchable.
> [29] He gives power to the faint,
>> and strengthens the powerless.
> [30] Even youths will faint and be weary,
>> and the young will fall exhausted,
> [31] but those who wait for the LORD shall renew their strength;
>> they shall mount up with wings like eagles;
> they shall run and not be weary;
>> they shall walk and not faint.

In the wake of an apparent extended exilic silence, the incomparable God of Israel speaks.[11] A majestic tone and cosmic imagery contrast sharply with the repeated withering descriptions of the human audience. This encounter both offers comfort and forces the audience to see themselves as they truly are in contrast to the sovereign divine speaker. It introduces the motif of comfort but does so in a way that hints at the vacillations of tone between rage and soothing which will come from the voice offering comfort (see A Closer Look: The Voice of Comfort).

Comfort, commanded in the opening line, will become thematic in the chapters that follow.[12] The LORD will claim the title of Comforter ("he who comforts you, " 51:12) and repeated announcements point to comfort

---

[11] See the discussion of silence in Introduction. The final form of the book of Isaiah presents Hezekiah's reign in chapter 39 just before this announcement a significant amount of time later and is silent about the period falling between these two moments. See Francis Landy, "Spectrality in the Prologue to Deutero-Isaiah," in *The Desert Will Bloom: Poetic Visions in Isaiah* (eds. A. Joseph Everson and Hyun Paul Kim; Atlanta: Society of Biblical Literature, 2009), 136; and Patricia K. Tull, "Who Says What to Whom: Speakers, Hearers, and Overhearers in Second Isaiah," in *Partners with God: Theological and Critical Readings of the Bible in Honor of Marvin A. Sweeney* (eds. Shelley L. Birdsong and Serge Frolov; Claremont: Claremont Press, 2017), 162. See also Louis Stulman and Hyun Chul Paul Kim, *You Are My People: An Introduction to the Prophetic Literature* (Nashville: Abingdon, 2010), 55, who also describe "silence between chapter 39 and chapter 40."

[12] See F. Landy, "Spectrality" (2009), 136–137; and Joseph Blenkinsopp, *Isaiah 40–55* (AB 19A; New York: Doubleday, 2002), 179, who calls comfort a "leitmotif." Robert Alter, *The Hebrew Bible: A Translation with Commentary* (Vol. 2 Prophets; New York: W.W. Norton, 2019), 748, calls this the "the key word ... [which] sounds the great theme of Second Isaiah's prophecies."

from the LORD (49:13; 51:3; 52:9; 57:18; 66:13). The beginning points of that motif, here, appear carefully crafted to overturn Lamentations' complaint that Zion had no comforter (Lam 1:2, 9, 17, 21). As the divine voice breaks the silence accorded it by Lamentations, it does so emphatically with a double imperative. The word itself (*nḥm*, "comfort") can mean both comfort and a change of mind.[13] Here, it is possible that the prophet allows an element of irony to appear in a potential double meaning. From the apparent perspective of the audience, a resolve to offer comfort would indeed be a change of mind on the part of Israel's God. However, the audience's perspective will be called into question in what follows.

Relational imagery surrounds the opening words of comfort and helps to clarify their meaning. This is the comfort of renewed relationship.[14] Lamentations' depiction of Zion as comforterless drew upon widow and abandoned woman imagery. She appeared as one who looked to her lovers but found no one to comfort her (Lam 1:2). Here, the opening lines make a clear connection of relationship between those being comforted and the divine speaker. It is "my people" whose comfort is commanded by "your God" (v. 1).[15] The distinctive phrase translated "speak tenderly" by the NRSV[ue] (*dabběrû 'al-lēb*, i.e., "speak upon the heart") appears, in a range of grammatical inflections, in family and marital contexts in the Hebrew Bible (Gen 34:3 Shechem and Dinah; Gen 50:21 Joseph and his brothers; Ruth 2:13 Ruth and Boaz; Judg 19:3 the Levite and his concubine; Hosea 2:16 the LORD and Israel). There is an intimacy about this speaking, and its pairing with the command to comfort points to a comfort that takes the form of renewed and restored relationship.[16] There is also a juxtaposition here between "my people" to whom comfort is being offered and Jerusalem/Zion to whom tender speech is to be offered. These are not the same figures. Indeed, as the series of poems proceeds, the audience, associated with Jacob and my people, will be treated as Zion's children. However, here in the opening lines, we see the close connection between

---

[13]   See, e.g., Isa 57:6 where the NRSVue has "relent". HALOT 1:688–689, lists both "comfort" and "regret" among meanings of the verb. See F. Landy, "Spectrality" (2009), 136. On "comfort" and Lamentations, see further Introduction.

[14]   See Stephen A. Geller, "A Poetic Analysis of Isaiah 40:1–2," *HTR* 77 (1984): 416.

[15]   See further S. A. Geller, "Poetic Analysis" (1984), 415, on the significance of "my people" and "your God."

[16]   See further F. Landy, "Spectrality" (2009), 138–139; and S. A. Geller, "Poetic Analysis" (1984), 416, on the parallels for and discussion of the phrase "speak to the heart."

*Isaiah 40:1–31*

the audience and the city, represented by the family metaphor of mother and children (see A Closer Look: Zion and the Audience).

The voice of the LORD, shattering the divine silence depicted in Lamentations, does not speak in isolation. Unattributed voices join in. Yet this is not a conversation but the juxtaposition of unnamed voices. The idea that these lines are spoken in a "heavenly court," or "Divine Council," is a common one.[17] However, there is no scene, no narrative, and no interaction between the divine voice and these voices. Contrast and catchword links are the keys to the relationship between these lines. Verse 6 hints at conversation, but it is not a full-fledged dialogue. Rather, there is an exchange of a line each. Blenkinsopp rightly calls the Divine Council approach, "not well founded."[18] Neither is this passage best treated as a "prophetic call" given its poetic and allusive quality and almost complete lack of attention to a figure clearly identifiable as the "prophet."[19]

The pointed ambiguity of these unnamed speakers contrasts sharply with the "says your God" of the opening lines. Here "a voice cries out," another speaks, and the repeated sounds of these words (*qôl qôrē'*, v. 3; *qôl 'ōmēr qĕrā'*, v. 6) create a veritable echo chamber and reinforce these voices' ephemerality.[20] They are fleeting and undeveloped, matching their description of the people, and in sharp contrast to the divine voice whose speaking opened the poem and whose word "stand[s] forever" (v. 8). The poetry highlights this contrast through repetition and sound play. From the outset of a series of poems that will be dominated and held together by the loquaciousness of the divine speaker, all other voices are relativized through the contrast between the power of divine speech and the fleeting nature of humanity.

Two stanzas begin with the announcement of an anonymous speaking voice (vv. 3 and 6). Each concludes with a reference to the word of the LORD (vv. 5 and 8). The first of these stanzas emphasizes the cosmic glory

---

[17] See, e.g., John Goldingay and David Payne, *Isaiah 40–55* (ICC; London: T&T Clark, 2006), 1:80.

[18] J. Blenkinsopp, *Isaiah 40–55* (2002), 179. See, similarly, R. Alter, *Hebrew Bible* (2019), 748.

[19] However, it is noteworthy that Stephen A. Geller, "Were the Prophets Poets?," *Prooftexts* 3 (1983): 218, offers a reading that accounts for the poetics of this passage while considering it a "call."

[20] See Francis Landy, "The Ghostly Prelude to Deutero-Isaiah," *Biblical Interpretation* 14, 4 (2006): 358. P. K. Tull, "Who Says What" (2017), 163, comments on the "ambiguities" of these voices.

28                                                            *Commentary*

of the LORD by commanding and pronouncing the transformation of geographic features. Like the opening imperatives of 40:1, these are plural and their addressee unspecified. The ambiguity persists, leaving the emphasis not on the addressee but on the majesty of the God whose "glory" is "revealed" (v. 5). The rough edges of the landscape are smoothed away and flattened before the glory of Israel's God. The repetition of "every" (v. 4) and "all" (v. 5) (*kol*) highlights the singularity of the glorified LORD. Everything else, each valley, each hill, all people blend into the now homogenized landscape. They, like the voices whose sound they echo through near homonyms (*kol, qôl*), are unnamed beside the particular and glorified deity.[21]

The following stanza (vv. 6–8) further intensifies the reduction of the human role. While "all flesh" (v. 5) (*kol-bāśār*) joined in observing the divine glory in the newly flattened landscape, here "all flesh" (*kol-habāśār*, i.e., "all the flesh," v. 6) are likened to mere grasses. Grasses link by synecdoche (see "synecdoche" in Glossary of Poetic Terminology) to the hills and valleys, as they often form a tiny part of that landscape. The poetry drives the point home through repetition and patterning. The poetic pair grass and flowers appears in a parallelistic couplet expressing the unnamed voice's sense of the nature of humanity (v. 6). These lines draw attention to themselves through their sound (*kol-habāśār ḥāṣîr wĕkol-ḥasdô kĕṣîṣ haśśādeh*).[22] Once this metaphor of "the people are grass" is firmly established, the poet elaborates the contrast between this image for humanity and the nature of the LORD. Each of the remaining verses of the stanza begins with a line that repeats the refrain "the grass withers; the flower fades" (vv. 7 and 8) again repeating the concentration of *ṣ*, *b*, and *ḥ* sounds from v. 6. In each case, the line stands in direct contrast to the image of the deity in the following line. The first of these (v. 7) gives the LORD's breath as the cause of the fleeting nature of the humans/grasses. The second positions the LORD's word as the exact opposite of that fleeting nature.[23] In each case, the breath and the word hearken

---

[21]   Claus Westermann, *Isaiah 40–66* (trans. David M. G. Stalker; OTL; Philadelphia: Westminster Press, 1969), 40.

[22]   See further J. Goldingay and D. Payne, *Isaiah 40–55* (2006), 1:82.

[23]   Cf. F. Landy, "Spectrality" (2009), 148–149; and R. Alter, *Hebrew Bible* (2019), 749.

*Isaiah 40:1–31* 29

back to the mouth of the LORD, which spoke in v. 5 and there reinforced the divine glory.[24]

This is not a logical discourse on the difference between the divine and the human; rather it is a pastiche of voices and images, offering the same emphasis from different angles. Throughout, the impression grows that the glory of the divine speaker towers over all else.

The poetry intensifies the encounter by directly addressing the audience in the following heavily patterned unit (vv. 10–17). Here, couplet/triplet-initial repetition divides the unit into three sections. The first and last sections form an inclusio (see "inclusio" in Glossary of Poetic Terminology) with repetitions of *hinnēh* (i.e., look! v. 10 a, b; cf. NRSV[ue], "See") and *hēn* (v. 15 a, b).[25] The first of these sections emphasizes the strength and might of the LORD who is coming juxtaposed immediately with a gentle pastoral image.[26] The "arm" (*zĕrōaʿ*) of the LORD is a common motif in cosmic battle imagery within the Hebrew Bible. Here it "rules for him" in a context filled with language of "might" and "reward" (v. 10). However, this same word, "arm," is what gathers the lambs in the following verse, a context replete with images of provision and gentleness.[27] The poetry leaves these images side by side, allowing their contrasting associations to develop a growing sense of paradox. It is as though the "Comfort, O comfort my people" peeks out for a moment through the celebration of the cosmic grandeur of the LORD. Both must be held in tension, for it is the incomparable creator who offers gentle restoration.[28]

A sequence of rhetorical questions raises the emotional pitch still further. Through them the unidentified speaker implies that the audience should already know the incomparability of the LORD. Rhetorical

---

[24]   See S. A. Geller, "Were the Prophets Poets?" (1983), 215–216, on the way the poetry "highlights another major ambiguity" (215) in its pairing of breath and word in this context.

[25]   See further J. Goldingay and D. Payne, *Isaiah 40–55* (2006), 1:106.

[26]   See R. Alter, *Hebrew Bible* (2019), 750.

[27]   See F. Landy, "Spectrality" (2009), 158 and cf. J. Blenkinsopp, *Isaiah 40–55* (2002), 186–187, who notes the association of shepherding imagery with rulers.

[28]   As S. A. Geller, "Poetic Analysis" (1984), 419, puts it regarding v. 2: "It is precisely the hint of *ribh* that reminds Israel that God's sympathy is an act of grace. She has no claim against him. It is not that in an excess of rage (Isa 54:7–8) he allowed her to suffer excessively and now owes her a reward (40:10). On the contrary, her punishment was doubly deserved. It is this knowledge, borne by the negative covenantal nuance that allows the divine sympathy to appear as an expression of love."

30  *Commentary*

questions appear throughout chapters 40–55, frequently with edges of indictment and sarcasm (see A Closer Look: Indictment, Sarcasm, and Rhetorical Questions). Rhetorical questions pepper the remainder of this poem (vv. 12–14, 18–19, 21, 25, 27–28a).

The first series of rhetorical questions, introduced by the repetition of "who" (vv. 12, 13) and "whom" (v. 14), points to the unfathomable glory of the creator God. This series continues the tight poetic patterning indicated by the structure (look – who – look) of verses 10–15. Here, verses 12 and 14 are long and chiastically structured (see "chiasm" in Glossary of Poetic Terminology), creating a central pivot of the significantly shorter v. 13. Right at the center of the pivot, the two figures being contrasted are named for the only time in the series of rhetorical questions. Everywhere else in vv. 12–14 they are "who" or "he." Here, in immediate juxtaposition, are the LORD and a man (v. 13), driving home the point of the series of rhetorical questions: no human should dare to tell God what God should and should not do. The language of justice (v. 14) and associated ideas (balance vv. 12, 15; and scales v. 12) pair up with repetitive language of enlightenment, knowledge, and understanding (v. 14). These imageries – justice, knowledge, and the incomparability of the LORD – will pervade the remainder of the poem.

The lines that follow circle back and come at the same ideas and images reiterating and intensifying their emotional charge.[29] Nations (v. 17) and idols (v. 19) are quickly rejected as comparison partners and the theme of knowledge reappears with a more strident tone. The questions "Have you not known? Have you not heard?" (v. 21) form a near refrain, reappearing in v. 28. While the NRSV[ue] translates these two verses identically, the Hebrew shows slight variation in phrasing. In its second iteration, the refrain becomes less tightly parallel, breaking the chain of anticipated phrasing and drawing attention to the phrase that might reasonably be translated "surely you have not heard?"[30] Vivid imagery of the cosmic

---

[29]  See Benjamin D. Sommer, "Prosody and Preaching: Poetic Form and Religious Function in Biblical Verse," in *A New Song: Biblical Hebrew Poetry as Jewish and Christian Scripture* (eds. Stephen D. Campbell, Richard G. Rohlfing Jr., and Richard S. Briggs; Bellingham, WA: Lexham Press, 2023), 126–130 on circularity as poetic technique.

[30]  This translation is my own. For another option that takes account of the differentiation between v. 21 and v. 28 see John D. W. Watts, *Isaiah 34–66* (rev. ed.; WBC 25; Grand Rapids: Zondervan, 2005), 85. The movement is from a consistent pattern of *hălô'*

# Isaiah 40:1–31

creator's majesty stands juxtaposed with an expansion of the "people are grass" metaphor. Participles present the divine nature in stark contrast to the human inhabitants of that creation. The poet plays with sound as the "circle" (*ḥûg*) upon which the mighty LORD "sits" (*hayyōšēb*) stands dramatically alongside the "grasshoppers" (*ḥāgab*) image for the earth's inhabitants (NRSV[ue] "and its inhabitants," Heb. *wĕyōšĕbêhā*).[31] The language of formlessness (*tōhû*, NRSV[ue] "naught," v. 23), which already appeared in v. 17 for the nations, here places the nations in the realm of cosmic uncreatedness (see Gen 1:2 where NRSV[ue] translates *tōhû wābōhû* as "complete chaos"). Goldingay and Payne's description of the prophet's point is apt. They write, "human forms of government and ordered life do not constitute order but anti-order, negation and darkness rather than light and value."[32] The creator God, the incomparable, unfathomable one, both creates and uncreates (vv. 22–23).[33] When the "people are grass" image reappears, the repetition of "scarcely" (*'ap*) creates a sense of quickening and a pair of couplets expands the image of dissolution and dispersion at the blast of the LORD's breath (v. 24).[34]

While it has been potentially unclear who is addressing the audience up to this point, v. 25 is clearly in the divine voice.[35] Again rhetorical questions showcase the incomparability of the LORD (vv. 25–26). The address intensifies as now the addressees themselves are pointedly asked about their own speech (v. 27).[36] Their charge that their "way is hidden" and that justice (NRSV[ue] "right") has been overlooked by God has already been overwhelmed by the powerful accumulation of images of divine knowledge, might, and justice. These images work to refute the audience even

---

followed by a verb in the imperfect (v. 21) to *hălō'* followed by a verb in the perfect paralleled by *'im-lō'* and a verb in the perfect (v. 28).

[31] J. Goldingay and D. Payne, *Isaiah 40–55* (2006), 1:120, refer to this sound play as "a double wordplay."

[32] J. Goldingay and D. Payne, *Isaiah 40–55* (2006), 1:109. See also J. Blenkinsopp, *Isaiah 40–55* (2002), 183.

[33] F. Landy, "Spectrality" (2009), 149, comments similarly regarding vv. 7–8.

[34] Repetition of "scarcely" (*'ap*) conveys additional meaning through word play with *'ap* meaning "nose," the location of breath and "anger," e.g., Isa 48:9. See *HALOT*, 1:76.

[35] J. Goldingay and D. Payne, *Isaiah 40–55* (2006), 1:122, treat the divine voice's expression of the rhetorical question from v. 18 as an indicator that "the passage works toward a climax."

[36] C. Westermann, *Isaiah 40–66* (1969), 58, points to these cited words of the audience as indicating the "real feelings of the prophet's hearers."

32            *Commentary*

before their own charge is acknowledged.[37] Thus, the potency of their charge is eliminated before it is even expressed. The refrain "have you not known" recasts the hearer's mind to that which has preceded, a litany of cosmic power, creative energy, ability to uncreate, and foreknowledge. The audience's charge falls flat, subsumed as an embedded quotation, and overwhelmed not only by refutation but also by the emotional freight of the profoundly humbling imagery of divine grandeur.[38]

The poem, however, does not end with indictment. The final lines return to the opening announcement of comfort and place the contrast between divine majesty and human weakness at the center of that comfort. The final lines signal the end of the poem with a chaistically shaped repetition of the verbs "faint" and "weary" (vv. 28, 31). The LORD is characterized as the one who never wearies, consistent with the imagery throughout the poem. Humans, on the other hand, as has been the consistent message of the poem, tire, "weary," and "fall exhausted" (v. 30). On either side of this central assertion of human frailty are parallel claims that the LORD gives "strength" (vv. 29, 31) and enables those who depend upon him to "not be weary" and "not faint" (v. 31). Central to this final poetic unit is the juxtaposition of human weakness and divine strength. It is the LORD's power that makes the difference.

This poem announces comfort, but it is not a gentle comfort that simply affirms that all will be well. This is comfort with a central core of divine might. The cosmic creator of the universe is both powerful approaching comforter and powerful, majestic, all-knowing potential destroyer. Comfort, in these final lines, comes from recognizing the limits of human understanding and strength and receiving renewed and restored relationship with the cosmic creator God, the only one who can provide strength.

---

[37]   P. K. Tull, "Who Says What" (2017), 165, says of Jacob here, "his words indict himself." C. Westermann, *Isaiah 40–66* (1969), 48, notes that the complaint of v. 27 "is implicitly challenged from v. 22 onwards." See also Ulrich F. Berges, *The Book of Isaiah: Its Composition and Final Form* (HBM 46; trans. Millard C. Lind; Sheffield: Sheffield Phoenix, 2012), 318–319, on this theme.

[38]   The delineation of voices in vv. 27–31 regains much of the poem's opening ambiguity. Potentially, the divine voice explicitly announced at v. 25 continues speaking and refers to itself in the third person as is not uncommon in these chapters (see, e.g., 40:1 "your God") and has occurred in v. 26. However, the ambiguity leaves open the possibility that another of the unnamed voices of this poem takes up the divine perspective and speaks here. In either case, the audience's complaint is refuted from the perspective of and in keeping with the preceding refutation by the divine voice.

# A Closer Look: The Voice of Comfort

The opening and closing sections of the poem, which offer promises of restoration and provision can easily give the reader the impression that this poem focuses on uplifting its audience. But the contrast between these lines and the central sections is a powerful poetic technique. The audience are not primarily those who will mount up on wings like eagles, or those who receive comfort from the mouth of the Lord in this poem. Rather, they are the ones who wither like grass (vv. 6–8), who do not know and do not understand (v. 21), who cannot possibly produce a good comparison partner for God (vv. 17–18, 25), and wrongly charge the one from whom justice comes (vv. 13–14) with injustice (v. 27). The contrast is double. It is between both what the people could be and are, and what they are and what the LORD is. In neither comparison does the people's current state fare well.

This opening poem sets up the central tension of the coming series of poems (chapters 40–55). The offer of comfort comes from one who expresses anger, aggravation, and power. It comes to a people who are weak, failing, and faltering and who express a sense of neglect and rejection from God. Reconciliation between these two moves through vacillations in the tone of the divine speaker, but the central contrast between the creator God and the people remains.[39]

A CLOSER LOOK: THE VOICE OF COMFORT

Comfort flows thematically through Isaiah 40–66. It is a focal point of Isaiah 40–55[40] and appears several times in 56–66 as well, notably in the final depictions of restoration (e.g., Isa 66:11, 13). But comfort is more than a theme or focus of attention in these chapters, it is one of the main ways the divine voice speaks. Like the other major tones of the divine speaking voice (see A Closer Look: The Majestic Divine Speaker and A Closer Look: Indictment, Sarcasm, and Rhetorical Questions), a comforting tone can be observed in the poetry's features. Important signals that the divine voice in these chapters is speaking comfort can be seen in exhortations not to be

---

[39] See P. K. Tull, "Who Says What" (2017), 168.
[40] See, e.g., J. Blenkinsopp, *Isaiah 40–55* (2002), 179, who calls comfort a "leitmotif." His comments here are on the appearance in Isaiah 40's opening words and their relevance for introducing 40–48, though he notes occurrences in 49 and 52 as well.

afraid (e.g., 41:10, 13, 14), in offers of future care and support (e.g., 43:2; 54:11–14; 65:20–22), in direct address often alongside a term that connects the addressee in relationship to the speaker (e.g., "O Jacob my servant," 44:1), in family imagery (e.g., "offspring," "sons," "daughters," 43:5–6; "mother," 66:13; "wife," 54:6), and use of the term "comfort" (e.g., 40:1; 54:11; 57:18; 66:13).[41] Embrace of divinely offered comfort in the form of reconciliation is one of the main persuasive aims of the poems.[42] They seek to overturn audience attitudes through attitudes of their own. By not only claiming the title comforter ("he who comforts you," 51:12), but speaking comfortingly, the divine voice enacts its aim to comfort the audience. That is, it offers a comforting encounter. Importantly, this tone is not the only tone that the divine voice speaks in. Rather, by juxtaposing this comforting tone with the others, the appeal of comfort is intensified.[43]

ISAIAH 41:1–7

Listen to me in silence, O coastlands;
>     let the peoples renew their strength;
let them approach, then let them speak;
>     let us together draw near for judgment.[44]
² Who has roused a victor from the east,
>     summoned him to his service?
He delivers up nations to him
>     and tramples kings under foot;
he makes them like dust with his sword,
>     like driven stubble with his bow.
³ He pursues them and passes on safely,
>     scarcely touching the path with his feet.
⁴ Who has performed and done this,
>     calling the generations from the beginning?
I, the LORD, am first,
>     and will be with the last.

---

[41]  See details of these features in K. M. Heffelfinger, *I Am Large* (2011), 178–181.
[42]  K. M. Heffelfinger, *I Am Large* (2011), 276.
[43]  K. M. Heffelfinger, *I Am Large* (2011), 276.
[44]  NRSV[ue] marks a stanza break here. I have treated this short poem as a single unit.

# Isaiah 41:1–7

<sup>5</sup> The coastlands have seen and are afraid;
>    the ends of the earth tremble;
>    they have drawn near and come.
<sup>6</sup> Each one helps the other,
>    saying to one another, "Take courage!"
<sup>7</sup> The artisan encourages the goldsmith,
>    and the one who smooths with the hammer encourages the one
>        who strikes the anvil,
> saying of the soldering, "It is good,"
>    and they fasten it with nails so that it cannot be moved.

In this short poem, which closely echoes the poem it follows, the divine voice expresses its sovereignty to a new group of addressees. The tone continues to magnify the cosmic creator and the shape of this poem places that message in the center of an ironic invitation to "the ends of the earth." These, who are invited to "renew their strength," attempt, in their fear, to strengthen themselves.

While the named addressees of this poem are the "coastlands" (see A Closer Look: The Coastlands and the Creator of the Cosmos), it seems most likely that this is an address meant to be "overheard" by the primary audience of these chapters, the "my people" of chapter 40's opening lines.[45] The coastlands, who appear in a parallel construction with "the ends of the earth" (41:5), imply the inhabitants of far-off lands. By addressing these distant peoples through the personification of their homelands, the divine voice reinforces its own cosmic significance. That the God now speaking to the exilic audience can command far-off land masses builds upon the preceding poem's cosmic creator depiction.

The opening address to the "coastlands" (41:1) sets up their ironic response (41:5–7) in words heavily overlapped with the closing lines of Isaiah 40. There the addressees were offered a vision of what it might look like to depend upon the strength that the LORD provides, to "renew their strength" (*yaḥălîpû kōaḥ*) (40:31). Here, in Isa 41:1, "the peoples" parallel to the "coastlands" are invited to "renew their strength" (*yaḥălîpû kōaḥ*). It is not necessary to emend the text to eliminate the repetition.[46] Repetition and overlapping of

---

[45]   See J. Blenkinsopp, *Isaiah 40–55* (2002), 196, who comments similarly.
[46]   Contra C. Westermann, *Isaiah 40–66* (1969), 62.

36　　　　　　　　　　　　　　　　　　　　　　　　　　　　　　　*Commentary*

phrases are typical of Second Isaian style and in this instance are a means by which the indicting tone of this passage is intensified.[47] The repetition heavily colors the opening words "Listen to me in silence" (*haḥărîšû*, i.e., "be still"). While the term does typically connote verbal quiet (e.g., Gen 34:5, "Jacob held his peace"), it can mean inactivity as in Exod 14:14 where Moses tells the people "The LORD will fight for you, and you have only to keep still." Here, immediately following the announcement that those who "wait for the LORD" will "renew their strength," the invitation to the coastlands to be still and "renew their strength" seems to imply not just verbal silence but the kind of dependence upon the creator described in the preceding poem. That such an invitation is ironic is not yet clear,[48] though it is hinted at in the words offered for them to say, "let us draw near together for judgment" (41:1).[49] It is only in the resumption of the coastlands motif later in the poem that the resonance with this opening invitation shows those who respond to have misunderstood the source of strength.

The coastlands reappear in v. 5 in a heavily patterned triplet that intensifies the image through repetition and development. The patterning and repetition underscore the terrifying quality of their encounter with the divine speaker and the LORD's agent. The opening three-word line plays with the similar sounding terms see (*rā'û*) and fear (*yîrā'û*) and thereby calls attention to its return to the coastlands theme. Such sound play also closely connects the two activities. Those who see are afraid. These far-off, personified land-masses were invited to "renew their strength." Instead, they "have seen and are afraid." The central section of the triplet echoes and emphasizes this fearfulness noting that "the ends of the earth tremble." Fear comes before approach in the sequencing of this triplet and it receives heavy emphasis dominating the first two-thirds of the triplet. The word used for their approach further reinforces the echo of the poem's opening verse. They draw near (*qārbû*), with the poetic voice reiterating what the

---

[47]　See J. D. W. Watts, *Isaiah 34–66* (2005), 99, for defense of a similar assessment.

[48]　Jerome T. Walsh, "Summons to Judgement: A Close Reading of Isaiah XLI 1–20" *VT* XLIII.3 (1993): 359, in his comments on v. 5 similarly observes that the invitation here "is shown to be ironic."

[49]　Many scholars (e.g., C. Westermann, *Isaiah 40–66* [1969], 63), treat this passage as the first of a "series of trial speeches." However, while the language is from the legal realm, it seems best to regard these as features that flavor the poetry, rather than formal categories. See J. Blenkinsopp, *Isaiah 40–55* (2002), 196; and B. S. Childs, *Isaiah* (2001), 317.

*Isaiah 41:1–7*                                                                       37

people were instructed to invite themselves to do: "draw near." However, in the earlier occurrence that drawing near was "for judgment" (41:1).

Judgment is what the reader has begun to recognize as imminent for these addressees. However, their actions, as depicted in the poem, appear to enact more obviously the "together" of "let us together draw near for judgment." The together language produces a contestational tone as Shalom Holtz points out.[50] While Holtz appears to take these words as a continuation of the invitation to judgment in the divine voice, and I take them as suggested audience speech, Holtz's insight that "together" here refers to adversaries rather than allies still obtains and resonates ironically with the imagery of strengthening one another in vv. 6–7.[51] Here the emphasis is on their teamwork with one helping another.[52] Their attention is devoted to strengthening one another. Their admonition "Take courage" (*ḥăzāq*, i.e., be strong, v. 6), employs the same word as is used to describe their mode of speech to each other (NRSV[ue] "encourages," *wayĕḥazzēq* 41:7), as well as what they do to their creation "with nails" to ensure its stability (NRSV[ue] "fasten," *wayĕḥazzēqhû* 41:7).[53] This heavy repetition of a word for strength points back to the poem's opening line's invitation to these people to "renew their strength" (*yaḥălîpû kōaḥ*). The strength they seek is not that which comes from waiting upon the LORD. Instead, they seek strength in "help" from each other and from the materials with which they work. Their trembling, their enactment of the activity that was to bring them to judgment, and the seeking of strength rather than waiting for divinely offered strength are each poetic indicators of the negative depiction the poem offers of these figures' response.[54]

The artisan imagery is another indication of the dubious nature of the strength these figures seek. The "artisan" (*ḥārāš*), the "goldsmith" (*ṣōrēp*),

---

[50]  Shalom E. Holtz, "The Case for Adversarial *yaḥad*," *VT* 59 (2009): 213–214. Holtz's comments hint at this irony.

[51]  S. E. Holtz, "The Case" (2009), 213.

[52]  J. D. W. Watts, *Isaiah 34–66* (2005), 103–104, is similar.

[53]  See also M. A. Sweeney, *Isaiah 40–66* (2016), 71 who refers to the repetitive use of the verb here as "word play."

[54]  J. Goldingay and D. Payne, *Isaiah 40–55* (2006), 1:153, treat these lines as "narrative, describing reactions to the challenge of vv. 1–4." While verbal forms typically associated with narrative appear here, a shift to narrative is not necessary as poetic features continue, as Goldingay and Payne's comments recognize (see their comments on "parallelism within v. 5a" [p. 151] and comments about colometry, pp. 151–152)

38                                                                    *Commentary*

and the "one who smooths with the hammer" appear without introduction. Their juxtaposition with the images already present in the poem suggests that they are to be associated with the inhabitants of the "coastlands" and the "ends of the earth." However, these are not entirely new figures in Second Isaiah's world. These terms appear as types of idolmakers in Isaiah 40. There the "artisan" (in 40:19 NRSV[ue] translates the term "workman," both *ḥārāš*) "casts" the "idol" and the "goldsmith" (*ṣōrēp*) "overlays it" (40:19).[55] The disparagement of idols in Isaiah 40 and the ringing rebuttal of their attempt at a "likeness," highlights the futility of this attempt at corporate self-strengthening. These figures, who cannot produce anything resembling an adequate likeness for the LORD, also cannot produce anything like the "strength" (*kōaḥ*) the LORD provides, despite their attempts at being strong (*ḥāzaq*).[56]

Between the invitation to "renew their strength" and this self-strengthening response, the central portion (41:2–4) of the poem focuses on the divine speaker and again does so in a mode that echoes the preceding poem. The overwhelming might of the one who offers such strengthening and the powerful descriptors employed underscore the futility of the craftspeople's attempts to strengthen their creation with "nails" (41:7). The rhetorical question "Who?" opens vv. 2 and 4 and keeps the whole description of the coming whirlwind of militaristic conquest anchored to divine causation (compare 40:12–14). The LORD is proclaimed as the one who "roused" the champion figure (41:2) and as the one who has "performed and done this" (41:4). Even the lines employing a militaristic metaphor retain this focus on the LORD as the source of what is coming. The NRSV[ue]'s translation "victor from the east" implies a military figure and the lines that follow repeatedly refer to this figure in personalized ways, for example, "him," "his" (41:2, 3).

This figure "from the east" (41:2), hinting as it does at a military conqueror, carries connotations of Cyrus the Persian (see A Closer Look: Cyrus the Persian). However, it is important to note that no such explicit reference is made here, though the poet certainly knows that name and will

---

[55]   J. T. Walsh, "Summons to Judgement," 359, also notes the connection between these figures and those in Isa 40.

[56]   For further comments on the irony of this passage, see B. S. Childs, *Isaiah* (2001), 318; and J. D. W. Watts, *Isaiah 34–66* (2005), 103–104.

*Isaiah 41:1–7*   39

use it later (44:28; 45:1).[57] Here the language is simply of righteousness (Heb. *ṣedeq*, i.e., "righteousness"), though it is heavily personified. The emphasis lies not on this figure, who is not even named, but instead on the one who raises him up.[58] The poetry builds intensity through the rhetorical question "Who" and active verbs "roused," "summoned," "delivers up," whose subject is the implied answer to "who" but is not named. The subject of the verbs becomes less clear as the actions become less about causation and more about militaristic sounding action (e.g., "tramples," "pursues them," 41:2, 3), and the actions move out of the realm of expected actions of a military victor toward a sweeping force "scarcely touching the path with his feet" (41:3).

The distinction between the divine source of strength and the one the LORD raises up seem unclear in these verses, mirroring the text's own question "who" until the divine voice answers the question resoundingly in the climactic couplet of this section of the poem: "I, the LORD, am first, and will be with the last" (41:4). The placement and the phrasing of this couplet combine to give it heavy emphasis in the poem's movement. It stands just outside the envelope created by the resumption of the "who" question. This structure subsumes the description to the question about who brought him to prominence. That question receives its answer in dramatic form as the poem suddenly reveals that the speaker is none other than Israel's God who has brought all this about. The couplet's heavy emphasis on the speaker's own self also draws attention and reinforces the claim. The first-person pronoun appears twice in the couplet, both opening it as a self-predication of the divine name "I (*'ănî*), the LORD" and closing it as an emphatic self-declaration (*'ănî-hû'*, i.e., "I am he," v. 4; cf. NRSV[ue]).[59]

---

[57] As C. Westermann, *Isaiah 40–66* (1969), 64, observes, this "hint . . . is quite in keeping with his style of writing."

[58] Cf. R. Alter, *Hebrew Bible* (2019), 752, who translates "who has stirred up victory from the east" and comments that "this translation understands the reference to be to God, not to a king whom God is using as his instrument." Alter does go on to connect "the historical event in view" with Cyrus and his comment highlights the focus of the poem on the LORD here. Whether "victor" or "victory" is the translation, the emphasis is not on a human king but on the LORD.

[59] Both J. Blenkinsopp, *Isaiah 40–55* (2002), 197; and J. Goldingay and D. Payne, *Isaiah 40–55* (2006), 1:149, comment on the significance of this self-declaration with Goldingay and Payne noting that it "implicitly answer[s] . . . the rhetorical question."

40 Commentary

Through irony and contrast this poem dramatically underscores the invitation to the audience to draw their strength from dependence upon the LORD (40:31). As they "overhear" its address to the inhabitants of far-off lands, they are shown the folly of attempts at self-strengthening and hear, in the majestic voice that commands the coastlands, the reliable might of their God.

A CLOSER LOOK: THE COASTLANDS AND THE CREATOR OF
THE COSMOS

The image of the coastlands (*'iyyîm*, also translated in NRSV[ue] as "islands") appears frequently in Isaiah 40–66. So much so, that it might be considered part of the distinctly exilic and postexilic Isaian vocabulary. This term occurs twelve times in Isaiah 40–66. Of the thirty-six total occurrences in the Hebrew Bible, the canonical book of Isaiah contains nineteen, while the next largest number is in Ezekiel, which uses the term nine times. As a poetic image, this recurrent term has the impact of magnifying the reach of the divine speaker's claims. From its appearance in the first chapter (40:15) to its appearance in the last chapter (66:19), the language of the coastlands conveys the breadth of divine sovereignty. Far-off lands are like dust before the creator (40:15). They are commanded by both the divine voice (41:1) and the Servant (49:1). They hope (51:5) and fear (41:5). They wait (51:5; 60:9) and they are invited to offer praise (42:10). They will be the audience for declarations of divine glory (66:19). Throughout, they convey that which is at the furthest limit. They are the embodiment of the "ends of the earth," with which they stand in parallel (41:5). It is not necessary to propose specific locations.[60] Instead, the parallelism repeatedly presents this image as one of cosmic distance and, as a poetic image, demands no specific localized referent. It magnifies the reach of the divine speaker by portraying God as addressing the most distant peoples imaginable. As a personification of the imaginable limits of the world, the coastlands imply an audience composed of their

---

[60] Cf. Gene R. Smillie, "Isaiah 42:1–4 in Its Rhetorical Context," *BSac* 162 (2005): 59, who connects the image to "Philistia, Phoenicia (Tyre/Sidon), Lebanon, Syria" and regards the coastlands as a "synecdoche for people on the fringes outside of but near to the community of God's people."

inhabitants.[61] As a poetic device, they exhibit the splendor of the Creator God who calls earth into being and who thus can command the landscape of its furthest reaches.

## A CLOSER LOOK: CYRUS THE PERSIAN

Cyrus appears by name twice in Second Isaiah (44:28 and 45:1). Despite the small number of actual references, he has exerted considerable influence on the interpretation of these chapters. Westermann, for example, calls "the oracle concerning Cyrus ... the pivot on which all that is said in this book turns."[62] He has been used as a point of reference for determining the approximate date at which these chapters were composed.[63] He has also been suggested by some as the identity of the "servant."[64] However, Cyrus functions in the poetry as one specific example of the LORD's power. The focus at each occurrence of his name is on the LORD's activity and use of Cyrus to carry out God's purposes (see explicitly 44:28). Perhaps one reason for Cyrus' use in this regard is the attention he must draw for the audience due to his importance in the exiles' own situation.

Biblical texts know Cyrus as the Persian king who allowed the exiles to return home and who commanded (Ezra 1:3, parallel 2 Chron 36:23) and subsidized the rebuilding of the temple (Ezra 3:7, 6:4).[65] Broader ancient Near Eastern history knows him as a Persian king who rose to prominence and conquered the known world (Media, Lydia, Neo-Babylonia) in a

[61]  See further J. Goldingay and D. Payne, *Isaiah 40–55* (2006), 1:107.

[62]  C. Westermann, *Isaiah 40–66* (1969), 10. See also Antti Laato, *The Servant of YHWH and Cyrus: A Reinterpretation of the Exilic Messianic Programe in Isaiah 40–55* (ConBOT 35; Stockholm: Almqvist & Wiksell, 1992), 12; and U. F. Berges, *The Book of Isaiah* (2012), 318–321.

[63]  See, e.g., J. Blenkinsopp, *Isaiah 40–55* (2002), 93; R. Clifford, *Fair Spoken* (1984), 9; and C. Westermann, *Isaiah 40–66* (1969), 3.

[64]  See J. D. W. Watts, *Isaiah 34–66* (2005), 117, who describes multiple servant figures including a "second servant" who "is the Persian authority in the persons of Cyrus, Darius, and Artaxerxes." J. Blenkinsopp, *Isaiah 40–55* (2002), 210, treats Cyrus as the servant in his discussion of Isaiah 42:1–9.

[65]  See Pierre Briant, *From Cyrus to Alexander: A History of the Persian Empire* (trans. Peter T. Daniels; Winona Lake, IN: Eisenbrauns, 2002), 46. Notably, Briant comments that "Doubts persist about the authenticity of these quotations" and "while the measures ascribed to Cyrus appear legitimate as a whole, contradictions and uncertainties regarding certain details of the royal decrees and their exact chronology still remain" (47).

42                                                                          Commentary

relatively short period of time (roughly 550–530).[66] His conquest of Babylon is described in Persian-influenced sources that present the event as swift, nonviolent, and the welcome of a liberator by the Babylonians.[67] However, there are good reasons to suspect this portrayal. It seems almost indisputable that the entrance of Cyrus to Babylon was enabled by previous military victories over the Babylonians, such as the capture of "Sippar. . . days before they entered Babylon."[68] Similarly, it is telling that the documents produced during the Persian reign in Babylon (e.g., Cyrus Cylinder) present precisely "the image that Persian propaganda itself would have portrayed."[69] Cyrus stands within history as the figure who should be credited with conquering the Neo-Babylonian Empire and instigating the period of Persian control over the ancient Near East. Cyrus died just nine years after the fall of Babylon and the Persian Empire as experienced by the returnees is largely that of his successors.[70]

ISAIAH 41:8–20

[8] But you, Israel, my servant,[71]
    Jacob, whom I have chosen,
    the offspring of Abraham, my friend;

---

[66]  P. Briant, *From Cyrus* (2002), 13.
[67]  See Piotr Michalowski, "The Cyrus Cylinder," in *The Ancient Near East: Historical Sources in Translation* (ed. Mark W. Chavalas; Oxford: Blackwell, 2006), 426–430; and Bill T. Arnold, "Chronicle 7: The Nabonidus Chronicle," in *The Ancient Near East: Historical Sources in Translation* (ed. Mark W. Chavalas; Oxford: Blackwell, 2006), 418–420.
[68]  David Vanderhooft, "Cyrus II, Liberator or Conqueror? Ancient Historiography concerning Cyrus in Babylon," in *Judah and the Judeans in the Persian Period* (ed. Oded Lipschits and Manfred Oeming; Winona Lake, IN: Eisenbrauns, 2006), 360. P. Briant, *From Cyrus* (2002), 41, similarly refers to the Babylonian Chronicle's recording of "an initial battle won by Cyrus at Opis on the Tigris, dated 10 October 539," as support for his claim that it is "unlikely that Babylonia could have fallen without resistance."
[69]  P. Briant, *From Cyrus* (2012), 41. See also Amélie Kuhrt, "The Cyrus Cylinder and Achaemenid Imperial Policy," JSOT 25 (1983): 83–97; and J. Blenkinsopp, *Isaiah 40–55* (2002), 94.
[70]  P. Briant, *From Cyrus* (2012), 34, treats the death of Cyrus "in Central Asia (530)" as one of only "two events" in his life that can be "precisely dated."
[71]  The shift to direct address to the audience indicates a new poem.

*Isaiah 41:8–20*

43

⁹ you whom I took from the ends of the earth,
  and called from its farthest corners,
saying to you, "You are my servant,
  I have chosen you and not cast you off";
¹⁰ do not fear, for I am with you;
  do not be afraid, for I am your God;
I will strengthen you; I will help you;
  I will uphold you with my victorious right hand.

¹¹ All who are incensed against you
  shall be ashamed and disgraced;
those who strive against you
  shall be as nothing and shall perish.
¹² You shall seek those who contend with you,
  but you shall not find them;
those who war against you
  shall be as nothing at all.
¹³ For I, the LORD your God,
  hold your right hand;
it is I who say to you,⁷²
  "Do not fear, I will help you."

¹⁴ Do not fear, you worm Jacob,
  you maggot Israel!
I will help you, says the LORD;
  your Redeemer is the Holy One of Israel.
¹⁵ I will make of you a threshing sledge,
  sharp, new, and having teeth;
you shall thresh the mountains and crush them,
  and you shall make the hills like chaff.
¹⁶ You shall winnow them, and the wind shall carry them away,
  and the tempest shall scatter them.
Then you shall rejoice in the LORD;
  in the Holy One of Israel you shall glory.

---

⁷²  My lineation here departs from NRSV^ue. Treating the announcement of speech and what is said as parallels produces a more balanced couplet.

44                                                                                    *Commentary*

<sup>17</sup> When the poor and needy seek water,
      and there is none,
      and their tongue is parched with thirst,
I the LORD will answer them,
      I the God of Israel will not forsake them.
<sup>18</sup> I will open rivers on the bare heights
      and fountains in the midst of the valleys;
I will make the wilderness a pool of water
      and the dry land springs of water.
<sup>19</sup> I will put in the wilderness the cedar,
      the acacia, the myrtle, and the olive;
I will set in the desert the cypress,
      the plane and the pine together,
<sup>20</sup> so that all may see and know,
      all may consider and understand,
that the hand of the LORD has done this,
      the Holy One of Israel has created it.

In this encouraging poem, the audience encounters the divine speaker who urges them toward a dramatic emotional transformation from trembling targets of human strife to chosen, strengthened, and helped divine servants. Their powerful defender promises presence, the total elimination of that which troubles them, and a superabundant quenching of thirst. They are repeatedly commanded to abandon their fear in recognition of the help that is at hand from the powerful creator who has spoken the previous poems. Imagery for human adversaries lays heavy emphasis on their impending irrelevance, while striking images for the audience command attention. Together these elements produce a vision of the transition from judgment to restoration.

The way the divine speaker addresses the audience emphasizes relationship, grounding the command to abandon fear in the promise of divine presence and help. Twice in this declaration of who the audience are, the divine voice will proclaim "my servant" (v. 8, v. 9) and "chosen" (v. 8, v. 9), calling attention to the personal connection between speaker and audience. Each time the two designations "my servant" and "chosen" are repeated, a third term is used, differing between the two occurrences. These look both backwards "the offspring of Abraham, my friend" (v. 8) and forwards

*Isaiah 41:8–20*                                                                 45

"I have ... not cast you off" (v. 9). In this poetic retelling to the exiles of
who they are, the text recalls the ancient memory that the LORD had made
a covenant promise to Abraham. Blenkinsopp helpfully points to "the
importance of living within a tradition after the profound discontinuity
attendant on the destruction of the nation state."[73] Here the ancient
promise to Abraham is brought into the audience's own experience. That
ancient choosing is a continuing aspect of their experience. They have not
been rejected (see Bridging the Horizons: "God's Sovereign Choice").

Their chosenness sharply contrasts with the imagery of the preceding
poem. Here the divine voice recounts its own action in strengthening
(*heḥĕzaqtîkā*, i.e., "I strengthened you," NRSV[ue] "I took," v. 9) the audience
"from the ends of the earth" and calling them "from its farthest corners"
(v. 9). This image is familiar from the preceding poem's description of the
trembling "coastlands" (v. 5). The juxtaposition and contrast with the
preceding poem's imagery and language highlights the reassurance being
offered here. Now the divine voice who had spoken ironically and whose
calling evoked a terrified response speaks to Jacob-Israel offering help and
protection, precisely as it indicates that they have been called out of the
place where fearsome trembling had been (41:5).

The poetry entices the audience away from their fearfulness by combining its contrast between the audience and the coastlands with the important poetic technique of repetition. The divine voice repeats its prohibition
against fear in vv. 10, 13, and 14. In verse 10, the offer of comfort grows in
intensity as the parallel commands move from the familiar, and frequently
repeated in Isaiah 40–55, "do not fear" (*'al-tîrā'*) to the much less common
"do not be afraid" (*'al-tištā'*).[74] The reason intensifies alongside it, moving
from "I am with you" to the more expansive "I am your God" (v. 10). This
affirmation that the LORD is "your God" echoes the opening announcement of comfort in Isaiah 40, a speech whose comfort came in part
through the expression of that relationship – that "my people" were

---

[73]  J. Blenkinsopp, *Isaiah 40–55* (2002), 200. See also J. Goldingay and D. Payne, *Isaiah
      40–55*, (2006), 1:160, on the importance of patriarchal figures in the exiles'
      current conditions.
[74]  *tištā'* is very likely related to the root *št'* (see *HALOT*, 2:1671; J. Blenkinsopp, *Isaiah
      40–55* [2002], 199, also reads the verb this way). If so it is a verb that occurs only twice in
      the Hebrew Bible. Both occurrences are in Isaiah 41 (41:10 and 41:23). In 41:23, it occurs
      in parallel with the word for fear here but in the reverse order creating a mirror image of
      this occurrence.

46    *Commentary*

addressed by "your God" (40:1). Repeatedly and emphatically, the reason the audience can let go of their fear is because of the LORD (v. 10). It is their being chosen by the LORD and the LORD's powerful action on their behalf that justify reassurance. The amount of emphasis upon and repetition of this theme points to the centrality of fear in the exiles' experience. Their fearfulness and sense of abandonment are what the poetry of Isaiah 40–55 works to transform (See Introduction: About the Audience(s) and Bridging the Horizons: Isaiah 40–66 and Human Migration).

A third way the poetry works to reestablish the audience's confidence in the LORD is through direct contrast between the LORD and those the audience fears. The "victorious right hand" (v. 10) of God introduces a militaristic image in which "those who war against you" (v. 12) are no match for the divine might. The divine speaker justifies the irrelevance of the audience's enemies by claiming to "hold" (*maḥăzîq*, i.e., strengthen) their "right hand" (v. 13). The cosmic mismatch between the LORD's strength and their human enemies finds expression in the contrast the poetry arranges between these figures. In Hebrew, the clause indicating the downfall of these adversaries precedes the reference to them each time. This construction points to the poem's much more intense focus upon their becoming "as nothing," than upon the depiction of these figures and the trouble they cause. They are presented each time as what might woodenly be rendered "the men of your" (Heb. *'anšê*) dispute (v. 11; cf. NRSV[ue] "Those who strive against you"), strife (v. 12; cf. NRSV[ue] "those who contend with you"), and battle (v. 12; cf. NRSV[ue] "those who war against you").

The contrast between these human beings and "your God" (v. 13) is abrupt when the poem reverses the order of clauses, placing "For I, the LORD, your God" first in the couplet that follows. The juxtaposition of a very human depiction of the adversaries with the divine speaker promising strength evokes the earlier poems' indications of the cosmic significance of the LORD's strength (e.g., 40:21–26). The poetic structure works to convince the exiles that they should not fear these ones who "shall be as nothing" (vv. 11, 12) and will be unable to be found (v. 12) but should, rather, place their trust in the one who speaks the command "do not fear" (v. 13).

Further developing the shift away from "receiving from the LORD's hand double for all her sins" (40:2) into a new reality, together the worm

*Isaiah 41:8–20*                                                                 47

(v. 14), the threshing sledge (v. 15), the watering of the wilderness (v. 18), and the reforestation (v. 19) motifs draw on imagery already familiar in the full book of Isaiah to offer a definitive turn from judgment against Israel to the visitation of that judgment upon her enemies. Just as the preceding stanzas contrasted the audience's chosenness with the coming elimination of those who trouble them, these next stanzas reinforce that idea by juxtaposing images that are already familiar to illustrate a dramatic turning of divine judgment. Having discounted human enemies as a source of fear, the poem shifts its attention away from them. The people who troubled the audience cannot be found in vv. 14–16. The audience deploys its new strength against geographic features rather than people (v. 15) and experiences the transformation from receipt of divine wrath to restoration.

The title "worm Jacob" draws attention to itself and its judgment associations by interrupting the repetition of the refrain "Do not fear" and "I will help you" (v. 14). Especially given the poem's emphasis up to this point upon the chosenness of and particular protection afforded to the audience by the divine voice, this attribution "worm Jacob" shocks the reader with its strikingly negative emotional impact.[75] This is not a term of "endearment."[76] Instead, the contrast between the context of comfort and the primary sense of "worm" is one of the poetic effects of the imagery. Small and apparently insignificant, worms appear in association with the dead and with judgment elsewhere in Isaiah (14:11; 66:24).[77] As Philip Stern points out, the worm figure conveys "blind dwellers in darkness" and notes that the passage presents "transformation of the puny eating machine, Worm Israel, into one mighty set of teeth."[78] In the immediate aftermath of the divine voice's announced intention to make "those who war against you . . . as nothing at all," the attribution "worm Jacob" hints at the worm that benefits from the carnage of battle.

---

[75]    See further J. Blenkinsopp, *Isaiah 40–55* (2002), 201.

[76]    This is the claim of J. Muilenburg, "Isaiah 40–66" (1956), 5:457.

[77]    These are the only two other occurrences of the term in the book of Isaiah. See J. Blenkinsopp, *Isaiah 40–55* (2002), 201, on "death and decay" as well as "insignificance" as implications. See also J. T. Walsh, "Summons to Judgement" (1993), 366.

[78]    Philip Stern, "The 'Blind Servant' Imagery of Deutero-Isaiah and Its Implications," *Biblica* 75 (1994): 226.

48                                                                    *Commentary*

While hardly a flattering image, the idea that the exiles benefit from the coming warfare, seems apt.

The threshing of the mountains motif intimates judgment and here the audience are not just beneficiaries but implements of divine justice.[79] "Mountains" and "hills" as well as threshing appear in judgment contexts earlier in the canonical book (see 2:12–13; 21:10; and 27:12–13). Connections to judgment are also created by the poet's use of a rare term "threshing sledge" (*môrāg*, v. 15). "Threshing sledge" occurs only two other times in the Hebrew Bible and both of the other two are parallel accounts of the same incident in the life of David, in which he seeks to end divine punishment brought about by his undertaking a census which incurred divine wrath (2 Sam 24:22 and 1 Chron 21:23).[80] These elements of larger context grant the image a strong connection with divine judgment. If divine judgment is conveyed here, the "nothing" (vv. 11, 12) to which the audience's enemies are to be turned finds a strong echo in the chaff into which the hills are to be transformed.[81] Divine judgment is enacted through the audience figured as an agricultural tool that reaps a harvest that obliterates solid and apparently permanent features of the landscape. They are given a glimpse of what the cosmic creator's power can do through them.

This intensely reassuring poem has focused its attention on the strength and might of the divine speaker who stands on the audience's side. In the final stanza, the expression of reassurance turns to dramatic provision, the lavish watering of a parched landscape. Here, the poetic speaker turns away from direct address and refers to those who receive abundant provision as "them" (41:17), and the promise is that the LORD will not forsake them.[82] Combined with the "everyone who thirsts" invitation of Isa 55:1, this turn

---

[79]  See further J. T. Walsh, "Summons to Judgement" (1993), 366.

[80]  Against J. T. Walsh, "Summons to Judgement" (1993), 357, who acknowledges that *môriggîm* in the stories about David and *môrāg* here are "related etymologically" but indicates that they do not necessarily "refer to the same agricultural implement," differentiation between the only occurrences of these forms is not compelling.

[81]  Scholars including C. Westermann, *Isaiah 40–66* (1969), 77; and B. S. Childs, *Isaiah* (2001), 320, read these references to the threshing of the mountains as referring to geographic features between the exiles and their homeland. While return to Judah could be an element of what the poem implies, this reading potentially overlooks the judgment connotations detailed above as well as the poetic contrast between solid mountains and ephemeral chaff.

[82]  Interestingly, C. Westermann, *Isaiah 40–66* (1969), 80, uses the language of encounter to describe this passage stating, "Israel encounters this God and the power that he has."

*Isaiah 41:8–20*

from "you" to the less specific "them" hints at a vision of restoration in which those who benefit from God's judgment of the audience's enemies is broader than themselves.

The imagery of vv. 17–20 further reinforces the turn from judgment to consolation by drawing on images of judgment in the book of Isaiah's earlier chapters. Watering of the landscape will be a recurrent motif in Isaiah 40–55 (see e.g., 41:17–18; 43:19–20; 44:3–4, but cf. the parching imagery in 42:15; 44:27; and 50:2) but it is not new in the sequence of the final form of the book of Isaiah (see 30:25–26 and 35:1–2, 6–7).[83] Thirst is answered, not with just enough water to drink, but with water that pours out of the landscape ("fountains in the midst of the valleys," v. 18) and that transforms the barren wasteland into a place where a variety[84] of trees grow (see A Closer Look: The Reforestation Imagery in Isaiah 40–66 in the Context of the Book of Isaiah). Destruction of trees and occasionally the burning of trees had been a motif of judgment in Isaiah's eighth-century prophecies (see especially 2:12–13; 6:12–13; 9:18–19).[85] While the preceding poem had the coastlands see and fear (41:5), here the transformation of the desert serves as a signal, ensuring that those who "see" may "know" the power of Israel's God (v. 20). Drawing on the imagery of judgment already familiar in Isaian prophecy, this poem underscores the transition from

[83] J. Goldingay and D. Payne, *Isaiah 40–55* (2006), 1:179, also connect this passage to Isa 35. While Isa 35 comes before Isa 41 in the sequence of the final book of Isaiah, it is a matter of discussion and debate whether Isa 35 predates Isa 41 in composition and whether the author of Isa 40–55 influenced its composition or editing. See H. G. M. Williamson, *The Book Called Isaiah: Deutero-Isaiah's Role in Composition and Redaction* (Oxford: Clarendon, 1994), 211–215, for a summary of this discussion and a viewpoint that leads to Isa 35 alluding to Isa 40–55, rather than the other way around (see esp. p. 215 n. 62). For the purposes of poetic interpretation of the final form of the book, this distinction does not lessen the impact of the echo of Isa 35 here.

[84] J. Goldingay and D. Payne, *Isaiah 40–55* (2006), 1:183, claim that the significance of the list is that it "expresses totality."

[85] Kristen Nielsen, *There Is Hope for a Tree: The Tree as Metaphor in Isaiah* (JSOTSup 65; trans. Christine and Frederick Crowley; Sheffield: JSOT Press, 1989), 84, says "*fire* ... appears several times in Isaianic imagery" (emphasis original). While I agree with Bradley J. Spencer, "The 'New Deal' for Post-exilic Judah in Isaiah 41,17–20," *ZAW* 112 (2000): 583–597, that the absence of "travel imagery" (586) and the lack of reference to trees in passages that allude to the Exodus (585) undermine interpretations that see the provision of trees as indicating shade for the exiles' return home (588–589), I am not convinced by Spencer's argument that the tree imagery here relates to building (589) and find a reversal of judgment as described above more satisfactory as it accounts not only for a property of trees but also for the use of this imagery in the larger book of Isaiah.

50                                                              *Commentary*

judgment to restoration, depicting the judgment shifting to Israel's enemies
and the emergence of a richly wooded forest as an illustration of the ending
of the burning wrath of God.

BRIDGING THE HORIZONS: "GOD'S SOVEREIGN CHOICE"[86]

The theme of God's specially chosen people appears repeatedly in Isaiah
40–66 (e.g., 41:8, 9; 43:20; 45:4; 49:7; 65:9, 15, 22). These chapters stress that
God has chosen Israel,[87] a motif that resonates throughout the Hebrew
Bible.[88] This concept of Israel's election is an important claim that has
implications for interpretation of this text, for ethics, and for theology.

Election is an expression of the enduring covenant between God and the
people Israel. Out of God's own freedom and love,[89] God has chosen
Abraham's family from all the peoples of the earth, to be God's own special
people, God's "treasured possession" (Exod 19:5–6; see also Deut 7:6; 14:2;
26:18). Deuteronomy 7:7–11 emphasizes both that the LORD's choice of
Israel emerges from divine love and that it is a permanent commitment
that is grounded in the LORD's own faithfulness. That is, as the Apostle
Paul writes about Israel's election, "they are beloved for the sake of their
ancestors, for the gifts and the calling of God are irrevocable"
(Rom 11:28–29).[90]

However, Christian thinking has not always accepted Paul's expression
of the permanence of God's choice of Israel.[91] Supersessionism claims that

---

[86]  This phrase appears in Mark D. Nanos, "'The Gifts and Calling of God Are Irrevocable'
      (Romans 11:29): If So, How Can Paul Declare that 'Not All Israelites Truly Belong to
      Israel' (9:6)?," *SCJR* 11.1 (2016): 13.
[87]  J. Kaminsky and A. Stewart, "God of All the World: Universalism and Developing
      Monotheism in Isaiah 40–66," *HTR* 99:2 (2006): 139–163.
[88]  Joel S. Kaminsky, "Reclaiming a Theology of Election: Favoritism and the Joseph Story,"
      *Perspectives in Religious Studies* 31.2 (2004): 135.
[89]  Michael Wyschogrod, *The Body of Faith: God in the People Israel* (London: Jason
      Aronson, 1996), 58.
[90]  See, e.g., R. W. L. Moberly, "A Chosen People," in *Old Testament Theology: Reading the
      Hebrew Bible as Christian Scripture* (Grand Rapids: Baker Academic, 2013), 44; and Shai
      Held, "Does God command genocide in the book of Joshua?" (review of L. Daniel Hawk
      *The Violence of the Biblical God: Canonical Narrative and Christian Faith*), *Christian
      Century*, July 23, 2019, www. christiancentury.org/review/books/does-god-command-
      genocide-book-joshua.
[91]  M. D. Nanos, "The Gifts and Calling of God Are Irrevocable" (2016), 1–17, examines
      Paul's argument closely and highlights the ways in which translation and interpretive
      decisions have impinged upon reception of Paul's message.

Bridging the Horizons: "God's Sovereign Choice"

the church has taken the place of the people of Israel in God's purposes.[92] It is sometimes called "replacement theology" or "displacement theology."[93] This teaching has been widespread in Christian history and has had an undeniably significant impact on the formulation of Christian doctrine.[94] The extrication of this idea from Christian theology is a monumental task but a vital and necessary one.[95]

Supersessionism has been explicitly rejected by a number of Christian denominations.[96] It raises vital questions about the nature of Christian understandings of the covenant faithfulness of God. As the 2016 Resolution adopted by the United Methodist Church puts it, "We believe that just as God is steadfastly faithful to the biblical covenant in Jesus Christ, likewise God is steadfastly faithful to the biblical covenant with the Jewish people, and no covenantal relationship is invalidated by the other."[97] Additionally, supersessionism undermines the Christian claim to worship God as revealed in the Hebrew Bible, because, as Soulen observes, "While it may be possible to imagine a god who is indifferent to the existence of the Jewish people, it is impossible to so imagine the God of the Hebrew

---

[92] R. Kendall Soulen, *The God of Israel and Christian Theology* (Minneapolis: Fortress, 1996), 2. Soulen's work analyzes the history of supersessionism while rejecting it and proposing an alternative.

[93] R. K. Soulen, *God of Israel* (1996), 12–13, uses the term "theology of displacement" as a synonym for supersessionism. See also Commission for Religious Relations with the Jews, "'The Gifts and the Calling of God Are Irrevocable' (Rom 11:29) A Reflection on Theological Questions Pertaining to Catholic-Jewish Relations on the Occasion of the 50th Anniversary of 'Nostra Aetate'" (No. 4), 2.17, www.christianunity.va/content/unitacristiani/en/commissione-per-i-rapporti-religiosi-con-l-ebraismo/commissione-per-i-rapporti-religiosi-con-l-ebraismo-crre/documenti-della-commissione/en.html, which uses the phrase "replacement theory" to gloss supersessionism.

[94] R. K. Soulen, *God of Israel* (1996), 3.

[95] R. K. Soulen, *God of Israel* (1996), 3.

[96] See, e.g., Commission for Religious Relations with the Jews, "The Gifts and the Calling of God Are Irrevocable"; and The United Methodist Church, "Book of Resolutions: United Methodist Guiding Principles for Christian-Jewish Relations," www.umc.org/what-we-believe/united-methodist-guiding-principles-for-christian-jewish-relations.

[97] The United Methodist Church, "Guiding Principles for Christian-Jewish Relations," under Heading 4 "Christians and Jews are bound to God though biblical covenants that are eternally valid."

Scriptures, the God of Israel."[98] Thus, Christian theology when tainted by supersessionism is self-contradictory.[99]

Christians must reject supersessionism not least because of the results of this disastrously damaging doctrine. As the statement on this matter from the Presbyterian Church (USA) puts it, "The long and dolorous history of Christian imperialism, in which the church has often justified anti-Jewish acts in the name of Jesus, finds its theological basis in this teaching."[100] The implications of this doctrine have been poisonous in the extreme and have implicated Christian theology in atrocious acts of violence. These results alone are reason enough for its wholesale rejection.[101]

---

[98] R. K. Soulen, *God of Israel* (1996), 4. See also Commission for Religious Relations with the Jews, "The Gifts and the Calling of God Are Irrevocable," 2.17, which observes that "the Church unequivocally professes, within a new theological framework, the Jewish roots of Christianity. While affirming salvation through an explicit or even implicit faith in Christ, the Church does not question the continued love of God for the chosen people Israel. A replacement or supersession theology which sets against one another two separate entities, a Church of the Gentiles and the rejected Synagogue whose place it takes, is deprived of its foundations."

[99] R. K. Soulen, *God of Israel* (1996), 4.

[100] "A Theological Understanding of the Relationship between Christians and Jews" General Assembly *Minutes* 1987, www.presbyterianmission.org/wp-content/uploads/christiansjews1.pdf.

[101] Importantly, rejection of a theology of displacement does not mean that Jews and Christians do not differ on essential and important commitments, not least their understanding of the nature, person, and work of Jesus Christ. Respectful and mutually enriching dialogue requires honest engagement with difficult issues. The United Methodist Church, "Guiding Principles for Christian-Jewish Relations," under point 5, while affirming its commitment to proclamation of its understanding of the salvific significance of Jesus, states, "We bear our Christian witness in a state of humility since we cannot know fully the way in which God's Spirit will work, nor can we know in whom the Spirit will be made manifest." Appropriately, Commission for Religious Relations with the Jews, "The Gifts and the Calling of God Are Irrevocable," 5.37, following its interaction with Paul's argument in Romans 9–11 (5.36), in its statement regarding "the highly complex theological question of how Christian belief in the universal salvific significance of Jesus Christ can be combined in a coherent way with the equally clear statement of faith in the never-revoked covenant of God with Israel," concludes in a parallel vein to the Apostle's own invocation of divine mystery (Rom 11:25, 33), stating, "Here we confront the mystery of God's work." For detailed work with this passage, see M. D. Nanos, "The Gifts and Calling of God" (2016). A different perspective on these issues, including the relevant insight that the idea of covenant requires attention to the several covenants in Scripture, including Abrahamic, Mosaic and Noachic, is that of Benedict XVI, "Grace and Vocation without Remorse: Comments on the Treatise *De Iudaeis*," *Communio* 45 (2018): 181–182. Notably, "The Abrahamic covenant is described as universal and unconditional" (181).

*Bridging the Horizons: "God's Sovereign Choice"* 53

A conscious turn away from supersessionism and the remnants of its influence in Christian thinking has important implications for the interpretation of Isaiah 40–66 as well as for doing theology and living faith in light of this text. First, and most obviously, it means that Christians are not entitled to overlook the text's natural reference to God's ongoing promises to Israel in their interpretation of these chapters (e.g., 54:10). For Isaiah 40–66, Israel refers primarily to the exilic and postexilic Judean community and this meaning must play a prominent role in any interpretation of the text's historical meaning and an any application of it. It is true that some of the latest written chapters in this book explicitly envision the inclusion of some gentiles within the community and as enjoying blessings from the LORD (e.g., 56:3–8).[102] However, these verses in no way envision a removal of those promises from the people of Israel.[103] Bearing these natural emphases of the text in mind is a key aspect of faithful interpretation of references to Israel and to the nations in Isaiah 40–66.[104]

Second, the biblical concept of election removes divine love from the realm of abstraction. As Kaminsky puts it, "God's special love for Israel reveals God's ability to connect to humans in a much more profound and intimate way than the assertion that God has a generic and equal love for all humans."[105] Election grounds God's love in the concrete and particular.[106] It is God's choice of a biological family, a particular one, grounded in a concrete history.[107] By highlighting the real, particular love that God has for one human family, election reminds believers that God's love is not an abstract generalization and connects it intimately to the lived realities of human existence. In addition, Israel's own testimony about its election repeatedly emphasizes the freedom and surprise of this choice. The God of Israel explicitly did not choose a nation that was strong and mighty (Deut 7:7).[108] Instead, the emphasis of the Hebrew Bible is on God's choice, which can open the door to "astonished wonder at the unpredictable gift of

---

[102] See J. Kaminsky and A. Stewart, "God of All the World" (2006), 159–162.
[103] J. Kaminsky and A. Stewart, "God of All the World" (2006), 159.
[104] See, e.g., the exegetical impact of this idea in J. Kaminsky and A. Stewart, "God of All the World" (2006), 144, where the theme of the nations underscores the LORD's sovereignty.
[105] J. S. Kaminsky, "Reclaiming and Theology of Election" (2004), 143.
[106] M. Wyschogrod, *The Body of Faith* (1996), 61.
[107] M. Wyschogrod, *The Body of Faith* (1996), 58.
[108] See R.W.L. Moberly, "A Chosen People" (2013), 43–45.

54                                                                                      *Commentary*

love"[109] and invite an appreciation of divine "grace."[110] It invites Christian readers to embrace God's choice of the blessing of "difference and mutual dependence."[111] God has chosen Israel, but as Wyschogrod has pointed out, this does not mean that others are not loved.[112] It means that they are loved by a God who loves in a real and concrete way rather than in abstraction. And, it means that they can learn to receive blessing through rejoicing in the "blessing of an other."[113]

Finally, Christians who embrace the doctrine of Israel's election find that their understanding of the nature of God's loving choice can be dramatically altered. It is not at all uncommon for Christian theologians to read God's calling of Abraham in Gen 12 and the statement there that "in you all the families of the earth shall be blessed" (Gen 12:3) as a statement of God's purposes in calling Abraham and his family. However, this is a reading that has been appropriately critiqued as "instrumental."[114] Rather than viewing God's choice of Israel as derived from God's having "fallen in love" with Abraham,[115] an instrumental approach sees God's choice of Israel as a means to an end.[116] But this colors God's loving embrace of humanity with utilitarian motives. The biblical witness is that God chooses Israel out of love. As Moberly comments "It is an end in itself."[117] Such a theology has the power to undercut the subtle ways in which contemporary society and theology may incline us to view ourselves and one another through the lenses of utility. Humans are not simply "usefulness" to God and the

---

[109] R. W. L. Moberly, "A Chosen People" (2013), 45.
[110] R. W. L. Moberly, "A Chosen People" (2013), 52.
[111] R. K. Soulen, *The God of Israel* (1996), 116.
[112] M. Wyschogrod, *The Body of Faith* (1996), 64.
[113] The phrase is from R. K. Soulen, *The God of Israel* (1996), 117. See J. S. Kaminsky, "Reclaiming" (2004), 143–145, for articulation of how Joseph's rivalry with his brothers is resolved in their acceptance of Jacob's favoritism and an analysis of how this story articulates a theology of election.
[114] See both R. W. L. Moberly, "A Chosen People" (2013), 46–47; and Joel S. Kaminsky, "Election Theology and the Problem of Universalism," *Horizons in Biblical Theology* 33 (2011): 40.
[115] M. Wyschogrod, *The Body of Faith* (1996), 63.
[116] See the insightful rebuttal of instrumentalization given by Shai Held, *The Heart of Torah: Essays on the Weekly Torah Portion: Leviticus, Numbers, and Deuteronomy* (Vol. 2; Philadelphia: Jewish Publication Society, 2017), 333–334 n. 23 who, commenting on Deuteronomy, articulates the distinction between "God's concern for other peoples" and the idea that "Israel's election is *for the sake of* other peoples."
[117] R. W. L. Moberly, "A Chosen People" (2013), 46.

*Bridging the Horizons: Isaiah 40–66 and Human Migration* 55

election of a people for the sake of love itself enshrines this idea within our understanding of the nature of the God of Israel.

Those who embrace Israel's chosenness and God's permanent commitment to the covenant with Abraham may find in it an affirmation that the love with which God loves human beings is reliable and steadfast, that it is particular, concrete, and concerned with the realities of real lived human experience. They find that divine love forces them to face hard truths about themselves, and they discover that God loves human beings for their own sake, not for what God can gain from them. This concept of election is a doctrine that has much to commend it, not only for the sake of better interpretation of Isaiah 40–66 on its own terms but also for the living of a life of faith in the world.

## BRIDGING THE HORIZONS: ISAIAH 40–66 AND HUMAN MIGRATION

A context of massive human uprooting and movement is something our contemporary situation shares with the exilic period.[118] The experiences of forced migrants in our moment invite readers to envision relevant connections between the ancient text and our contemporary world. More than that, the "primary task" that Louis Stulman and Hyun Chul Paul Kim name for readers in this context is "to hear those voices of pain and acknowledge the wreckage of dejected communities stripped of power, prestige, and purpose."[119] That is, recognition of the resonance between ancient and modern contexts invites a particular form of active listening to both ancient and contemporary voices.

I do not suggest that contemporary experiences can be read into ancient texts as though a shared experience of migration overcomes vast cultural and time differences. Indeed, as Bo H. Lim points out, both ancient and modern experiences of migration are "diverse" and "To flatten the

---

[118] This point is well made by John Ahn and Frank Ritchel Ames, "Introduction," in *The Prophets Speak on Forced Migration* (eds. Mark J. Boda, Frank Ritchel Ames, John Ahn, and Mark Leutcher; Atlanta: SBL, 2015), 3, who comment "Even the most cursory glance at events regularly reported in the contemporary media reveals the pervasiveness of this theme and the depth of its impact upon local and distant communities and cultures, and the same can be said of the ancient sixth to third centuries BCE."

[119] Louis Stulman and Hyun Chul Paul Kim, *You Are My People: An Introduction to Prophetic Literature* (Nashville: Abingdon, 2010), 54.

experiences and texts of migration into one uniform category is not merely an act of intellectual dishonesty; it is an unwillingness to listen to the distinct message of particular texts and a disregard for the unique ways people are impacted by migration."[120] Careful listening to the particular experiences of those who have been forced to migrate in our own time may suggest possibilities for inquiry into areas and themes within the text that we might not otherwise have noticed, and resonance between the words of the ancient text and the experiences of contemporary migrants may open up possibilities for dialogue, empathy, and action among readers in both migrating and receiving cultures.[121]

The primary audience of Isaiah 40–55 referred to throughout this commentary as "exiles" (see About the Audience[s] in the Introduction) seem best understood in terms of the categories articulated by John Ahn as having experienced "Purposive Forced Migration."[122] That is, their migration was "physically at the hands of a dominant power."[123] War and its traumas are indisputably part of the exilic experience of migration, and "written prophecy is at the same time disaster literature *and* survival literature."[124] These contexts are vital interfaces between the ancient text and its own world, as well as between contemporary readers and our own world.

Trust is an essential human concern and one that invites attentive listening from Isaiah 40–66's readers. It is a quality that "is indispensable for human life and society" and is helpfully defined as "one's willingness to be vulnerable to others, based on the expectation that one will not be harmed or exploited."[125] Scholarship on contemporary refugee experience highlights that "trauma and exposure to war were significant in shaping trust among refugees in resettlement and that this impacted participants'

---

[120] Bo H. Lim, "Exile and Migration: Toward a Biblical Theology of Immigration and Displacement," *The Covenant Quarterly* 74 (2016): 7.

[121] See, e.g., C. A. Strine, "The Study of Involuntary Migration as a Hermeneutical Guide for Reading the Jacob Narrative," *Biblical Interpretation* 26 (2018): 485–498, who amply demonstrates that awareness of issues faced by involuntary migrants can illumine emphases in biblical texts.

[122] J. Ahn, "Exile," in *Dictionary of the Old Testament Prophets* (eds. Mark J. Boda and J. Gordon McConville; Nottingham: InterVarsity Press, 2012), 200.

[123] B. H. Lim, "Exile and Migration" (2016), 8. Lim is drawing on the theoretical work of Ahn in this context.

[124] L. Stulman and H. C. P. Kim, *You Are My People* (2010), 8.

[125] Ryan Essex, Erika Kalocsányiová, Nataliya Rumyantseva, and Jill Jameson, "Trust Amongst Refugees in Resettlement Settings: A Systematic Scoping Review and Thematic Analysis of the Literature," *Journal of International Migration and Integration* 23 (2022): 544.

fundamental outlook on the world."[126] While the audience of Isaiah 40–55 are not "refugees" as this term is used and defined in contemporary scholarship,[127] they are forcibly displaced people who have experienced war and trauma. Their own literature expresses "mistrust" and the repeated injunctions by the divine voice, "Fear not" seem to answer a perception that the world in which the exiles live is inherently unpredictable (see also Bridging the Horizons: Fear Not). That is, trust and its absence are features of the exiles' experience.[128]

These experiences are brought closer to contemporary readers by the experiences of people within our own world who have been forced to migrate. Trust is inherently "relational" and varies for individual people from context to context and relationship to relationship depending on a large number of complex factors.[129] If trust is "damaged" in many migration experiences,[130] and if it is vital to personal and societal good,[131] then one desire shaped in engaged listeners might be to support and facilitate trust. Members of receiving cultures might seek first to examine themselves to see whether their attitudes and assumptions are trust-worthy. That is, do they not seek their own ways and aim instead for the avoidance of harm and active resistance to the exploitation of others (cf. 58:1–14). Second, in recognition that "mistrust" can be "a survival mechanism,"[132] they might practice not expecting trust even while seeking to merit it.

---

[126] R. Essex, E. Kalocsányiová, N. Rumyantseva, and J. Jameson, "Trust Amongst Refugees" (2022), 562.

[127] See J. Ahn, "Exile" (2012), 202–203.

[128] E. Valentine Daniel and J. Chr. Knudsen, "Introduction," in *Mistrusting Refugees* (eds. E. Valentine Daniel and John Chr. Knudsen; London: University of California Press, 1995), 2, offer the definitional insight that "the capacity to trust needs to be underwritten by the capacity to tame chance, especially the chance of being hurt." The absence of that sense of capacity resonates with the exilic situation and parallels the observation of R. Essex, E. Kalocsányiová, N. Rumyantseva, and J. Jameson, "Trust Amongst Refugees" (2022), 543, on contemporary refugee experience where "A major theme was the fundamental need in resettlement for a restoration of lost or damaged trust." See also L. Stulman and H. C. P. Kim, *You Are My People* (2010), 55.

[129] R. Essex, E. Kalocsányiová, N. Rumyantseva, and J. Jameson, "Trust Amongst Refugees" (2022), 559.

[130] R. Essex, E. Kalocsányiová, N. Rumyantseva, and J. Jameson, "Trust Amongst Refugees" (2022), 565.

[131] R. Essex, E. Kalocsányiová, N. Rumyantseva, and J. Jameson, "Trust Amongst Refugees" (2022), 544.

[132] R. Essex, E. Kalocsányiová, N. Rumyantseva, and J. Jameson, "Trust Amongst Refugees" (2022), 561.

Both past and future play vivid roles in Isaiah 40–66. Not only are contradictory commands given about what the exilic audience should do with their memories (43:18; 46:9), there is a thematic interest in both the "former things" (e.g., 41:22; 42:9; 43:9, 18; 46:9; 48:3; 65:17) and "things to come" (41:22) (see further A Closer Look: Conflicted Commands and Competing Contentions in the Memory Motif). These themes seem intimately tied in their original historical context to the experience of forced migration. That is, the exilic audience of Isaiah 40–55 find themselves in circumstances radically different from their past and not of their own choosing. For a community experiencing a radical level of disconnect between the security of their past and their own present experience, it appears that reflection and remembrance are important tasks. As Stulman and Kim put it, "Prophetic meaning-making is candid about the deep ruptures of life."[133]

Memory is a vital and a complex theme in these chapters and one that expresses and embodies the challenges of living hopefully in a world of overwhelming change.[134] Complex poetry, such as we encounter in Isaiah 40–66, that does not smooth out the difficulties has the potential to build in its readers tolerance for the complex experiences, memories, and histories of those whose stories they have yet to hear as well as their own.[135] As Sheringham and Taylor highlight, "Individuals who have been forced to migrate are neither an un-storied human mass lacking agency, nor purely noble individual exiles whose lives follow a heroic narrative, but people with lives as contradictory and complex as those who have not been displaced."[136] Openness to hear testimonies and experiences without flattening or categorizing them and without seeking to use them for our own purposes is a capacity vital for real welcome and one that patience with ancient, complex, and conflicted texts might helpfully build (see further Bridging the Horizons: On Loving Poetry and Poetry's Loves).

---

[133] L. Stulman and H. C. P. Kim, *You Are My People* (2010), 13 (original bold type omitted).
[134] See L. Stulman and H. C. P. Kim, *You Are My People* (2010), 66–67.
[135] See K. M. Heffelfinger, "Truth and Hidden Things," in *A New Song: Biblical Hebrew Poetry as Jewish and Christian Scripture* (eds. Stephen D. Campbell, Richard G. Rohlfing Jr., and Richard S. Briggs; Bellingham, WA: Lexham Press, 2023), 172–173.
[136] Olivia Sheringham and Helen Taylor, "On Stories, Storytelling, and the Quiet Politics of Welcome," *ACME: An International Journal for Critical Geographies* 21.3 (2022): 289.

*Bridging the Horizons: Isaiah 40–66 and Human Migration* 59

Finally, the issues of nationalism and identity come to the fore throughout Isaiah 40–66, but perhaps especially in chapters 56–66. Much has been made by commentators of the text's interest in Zion,[137] as well as the concerns about inclusion of the "foreigner."[138] Each of these motifs works to create identity and to modify the audience's allegiances and self-understanding toward an allegiance to the LORD. These issues of allegiance and particularly of a nationalized identity are also issues of our own place and time. In both the United States and Europe, documented rises in social division and dissent accompany discussion of contemporary migration,[139] including what has been called "a concerning rise in nationalism and xenophobia."[140] Like loss of trust, division and suspicion are elements of loss of relationship. Interconnectedness can be built across lines of apparent division through patient and attentive listening to the "stories [others] ... want to share"[141] (see also Bridging the Horizons: "Third Isaiah" and the Divided Society). It is not strictly the "content of the

---

[137] See, e.g., the helpful summary of scholarly discussion of Zion in Isaiah in Matthew J. Lynch, "Zion's Warrior and the Nations: Isaiah 59:15b–63:6 in Israel's Zion Traditions," *CBQ* 70 (2008): 244, as well as his comments on "the nations" in Isaiah 40–55 and 56–66 (246 n. 7).

[138] See, e.g., the reference that Christophe Nihan, "Ethnicity and Identity in Isaiah 56–66," in *Judah and the Judeans in the Achaemenid Period: Negotiating Identity in an International Context* (eds. Oded Lipschits, Gary N. Knoppers, and Manfred Oeming; Winona Lake, IN: Eisenbrauns, 2011), 69, makes to scholarship on this issue in Isa 56–66.

[139] On "Europe and ... the United States," see Daniel Vega Macías, "The COVID-19 Pandemic on Anti-immigration and Xenophobic Discourse in Europe and the United States," *Estudios Fronterizos* 22 (2021), 2. On Ireland in early 2023, see Patrick Freyne, "Refugees Welcome: 'Chanting "Get Them Out"' to the Most Vulnerable. What Does That Achieve?," *Irish Times*, January 28, 2023, www.irishtimes.com/life-style/people/2023/01/28/local-community-groups-step-up-opposition-to-those-protesting-about-refugees-in-their-areas/. On the political situation in Austria and Hungary respectively, see Elżbieta M. Goździak and Izabella Main, "European Norms and Values and the Refugee Crisis: Issues and Challenges," in *Europe and the Refugee Response: A Crisis of Values?* (eds. Elżbieta M. Goździak, Izabella Main, and Brigitte Suter; London: Routledge, 2020), 2–3, www.taylorfrancis.com/books/e/9780429279317.

[140] See Kathleen M. Roche, Bernhard Streitwieser, and Seth J. Schwartz, "A Call for Research on Immigrant and Refugee Youth amidst the Global Rise in Xenophobia and Nationalism," *International Journal of Intercultural Relations* 90 (2022): 166. See also Lydia Ayame Hiraide, "Ambivalent Borders and Hybrid Culture: The Role of Culture and Exclusion in Historical European Discourses of Migration," *Journal of European Studies* (2022): 9, who notes, "As Europe entered the twenty-first century, we saw an extraordinary resurgence of xenophobic nationalism across the continent."

[141] O. Sheringham and H. Taylor, "On Stories, Storytelling, and the Quiet Politics of Welcome" (2022), 297.

60  Commentary

stories," the details of experiences, that have the potential to dissolve divisions but the creative activity of forging spaces of "between-ness,"[142] generative mutuality, and the profound "welcome" of offering the reciprocal possibilities of both knowing and being known.[143] Patient, empathetic, and honest openness to real, active, and engaged hearing of those voices that wish to speak is a capacity that can be lived out in concert with Isaiah's poetry, a capacity it can build in its readers if they will practice it, and a capacity that can be a starting point for ethical response to the struggles of those migrating and those receiving them in our time and place.

## ISAIAH 41:21–29

[21] Set forth your case, says the LORD;
    bring your proofs, says the King of Jacob.
[22] Let them bring them,
    and tell us what is to happen.[144]

---

[142] "Betweenness" as I am using it here is the terminology of Iain McGilchrist, *The Master and His Emissary: The Divided Brain and the Making of the Western World* (expanded ed.; London: Yale University Press, 2019). See especially page 93 for definitional discussion and differentiation between focus on "how" and "what." McGilchrist describes this kind of knowing as involved in forging connection between human beings, or in his terms "promot[ing] cohesion" (123), and as having "no ulterior purpose, no aim in view, and [being] ... non-acquisitive" (445). These values seem inherently relevant to the discussion of "trust" above. Similarly focussed on "community cohesion" are the comments of Kye Askins, "Being Together: Everyday Geographies and the Quiet Politics of Belonging," *ACME: An International E-Journal for Critical Geographies* 14.2 (2015): 473, who examines a "befriending scheme" for Refugees and Asylum Seekers in England and emphasizes "radical openness to the simultaneity of difference and similarity" and the "*potential to shift* how we see and how we feel about our others" (emphasis original).

[143] As Nick Gill, "The Suppression of Welcome," *Fennia* 196.1 (2018): 90, notes "scholars who have studied welcome emphasise its emotional and relational character." Importantly, attention to "care" in recent work highlights the need to pay attention to balances of power and agency between participants; see K. Askins, "Being Together" (2015), 472; and Jonathan Darling, "The Fragility of Welcome – Commentary to Gill," *Fennia* 196.2 (2018), 221–222, who describes a particular form of welcome that "was arrived at here through considerable hard work on the one hand, from both the volunteers and the asylum seekers who together created an environment in which all could feel safe, and considerable trial and error on the other."

[144] The lineation in the NRSV[ue] treats "what is to happen" as its own line, breaking a phrase between lines. I have preferred to treat the whole clause as a line here.

# Isaiah 41:21–29

Tell us the former things, what they were,
  so that we may consider them
and that we may know their outcome
  or declare to us the things to come.
²³ Tell us what is to come hereafter,
  that we may know that you are gods;
do good, or do harm,
  that we may be afraid and terrified.
²⁴ You, indeed, are nothing,
  and your work is nothing at all;
  whoever chooses you is an abomination.

²⁵ I stirred up one from the north, and he has come,
  from the rising of the sun he was summoned by name.
He shall trample on rulers as on mortar,
  as the potter treads clay.
²⁶ Who declared it from the beginning, so that we might know,
  and beforehand, so that we might say, "He is right"?
There was no one who declared it,
  none who proclaimed,¹⁴⁵
  none who heard your words.
²⁷ I first have declared it to Zion,
  and I give to Jerusalem a herald of good tidings.
²⁸ But when I look there is no one;
  among these there is no counselor
  who, when I ask, gives an answer.
²⁹ No, they are all a delusion;
  their works are nothing;
  their images are empty wind.

Without warning or explanation, the divine voice's tone shifts dramatically, producing an ironic encounter for the audience to overhear between the LORD and that which is "nothing at all."¹⁴⁶ This ironic invitation is

---

¹⁴⁵ NRSV^ue treats this as a couplet. The three-part parallelism here argues in favor of a triplet.

¹⁴⁶ Contra C. Westermann, *Isaiah 40–66* (1969), 86, it is precisely the meaninglessness of an exchange with that which is "non-existent" through which the poem creates its ironic

heavily interlaced with the language of the preceding poem, even as it differs sharply from it in its emotion and addressee. While the divine voice sarcastically invites the gods of the nations to offer "proofs" v. 21), the unit as a whole presents itself as a "proof" to the audience that they can trust themselves to the promised restoration and provision offered by the LORD.

Legal language opens the poem, as the first in a series of commands invites unspecified hearers to bring a "case" (*rîb*, v. 21) and to offer "proofs" (v. 21). While the tone is certainly disputatious and contestational, the legal imagery does not develop into a full-blown courtroom dynamic. Legal imagery does indeed add elements of dispute to this poem. However, it is not purely legal but heavily ironic poetry.[147] Instead, the "case" (*rîb*, v. 21) echoes the preceding poem's reference to "those who strive against you" (Heb. *'anšê rîbekā*, 41:11).[148] In that context the strivers were to become "as nothing" (*kĕ'ayin*, 41:11 ) and "those who war against you" like "nothing at all" (*kĕ'epes*, 41:12), employing the same words for nonexistence used in this poem's charge to the "gods" (v. 23) that they are "nothing" (*mē'ayin*, 41:24) and "nothing at all" (*mē'āpe'*, 41:24).[149]

The poem's structure heavily emphasizes the charge of "nothing"-ness against the addressees. They remain unnamed throughout the poem and it first becomes clear that the poem addresses other "gods" with the charge of their nonexistence in v. 23. Picking up the chain, "nothing" and "nothing at all" that appeared in vv. 11 and 12, the poem's two units end with parallel triplets that employ and exploit the sound of these terms. The first triplet (41:24) moves through the charges of being "nothing" (*mē'ayin*, 41:24), and their work being "nothing at all" (*mē'āpe'*, 41:24), to the charge that "whoever chooses you is an abomination" (41:24). The second triplet (41:29) no longer directs the charge at the "gods" but instead appears to refer to the same non-addressees in the third person calling them "a delusion" (*'āven*, 41:29), which by sound play sounds very close to

---

rhetorical power. B. S. Childs, *Isaiah* (2001), 321, similarly treats "The ploy of a trial" as a "rhetorical device."

[147] Contra C. Westermann, *Isaiah 40–66* (1969), 83.

[148] J. Goldingay and D. Payne, *Isaiah 40–55* (2006), 1:193, observe the repetition.

[149] The present text likely contains a textual error and should be read *me'epes* here following the critical apparatus in BHS. See also J. Blenkinsopp, *Isaiah 40–55* (2002), 204; and J. Muilenburg, "Isaiah 40–66" (1956), 5:461. The strong parallelism with the final triplet of the poem which uses *'epes* further supports this reading.

*Isaiah 41:21–29*

"nothing" (*'ayin*), naming their "works" as "nothing" (*'epes*, 41:29) and insisting that "their images are empty wind," a compelling image with overtones of the emptiness that preceded creation (41:29). The wording here is *rûaḥ wātōhû* (i.e.,"wind and formlessness"), phrasing that hints at both the *tōhû wābōhû* "formless void (NRSV)" (cf. "complete chaos" NRSV[ue]) of the earth and the *rûaḥ* "wind" of God present there (Gen 1:2).

All of this emphasis on the "nothing"-ness of the apparent addressees lends a highly ironic tone to the poem. Here the divine speaker, who has promised not only to do great things for the exiles but that "all may see and know ... that the hand of the LORD has done this" (41:20), indicts those who ought to fail to terrify the exiles (41:23) for being and doing "nothing at all." This invective against "nothing" is placed into the exiles' hearing, underscoring the invitation to trust the LORD's comfort offered by the previous poem by undermining the reality of that which they fear.

The irony produced by the situation of a disputation with "nothing" carries through in the charges they are invited to bring. The ability to know what will happen, and to correctly declare it, is a prerogative that belongs only to the LORD in Isaiah 40–66 and is offered as proof of deity. The language "fulfills the prediction of his messengers" (44:26) confirms rather than detracts from this idea as the prediction comes ultimately from the one sending the message, that is, the LORD.[150] Here, the invitation is to either tell what was, "the former things," or what will be, "the things to come" (41:22).[151] The implication is that those being addressed can do neither. In other words, they can declare absolutely nothing.[152] Similarly, they are invited to "do good, or do harm" (41:23). Again, the implication is that they can do neither of these things and so can do nothing.[153] Together

---

[150] See C. Westermann, *Isaiah 40–66* (1969), 85; and Muilenburg, "Isaiah 40–66" (1956), 5:460.

[151] Contra C. Westermann, *Isaiah 40–66* (1969), 85, who sees the "former things" here as referring to correct interpretation of the past; and J. Blenkinsopp, *Isaiah 40–55* (2002), 203, who translates the "former things" reference, "Declare what is to happen in advance," it seems best to read the "former things" and the "things to come" in parallel with "do good, or do harm." That is, each pair implies the whole range of things that could be declared or done and the inability of the "gods" to do or say anything underscores their nothingness.

[152] J. Muilenburg, "Isaiah 40–66" (1956), 5:460.

[153] Against J. Goldingay and D. Payne, *Isaiah 40–55* (2006), 1:197, the idea that the gods are invited to do "something beneficial for their people and/or calamitous for their foes" requires reading beyond the text's own presentation, rests on a different reading of v. 22

64                                                                    *Commentary*

these ironic invitations to say something and to do something appear designed to undermine the exiles' fear. The heavily sarcastic "do good, or do harm, that we may be afraid and terrified" closely echoes "do not fear, for I am with you; do not be afraid, for I am your God" (41:10) of the previous poem.[154] As noted there, a common word for be afraid (*tîra '*) is paired with a term for fear that occurs only twice in the Hebrew Bible (*tišta '*), in 41:10 and 41:23. Their order is inverted between the two occurrences with the rarer term appearing first in 41:23. Just before the poem's first unit closes with its insistence upon the nothingness of these adversaries in v. 24, the poem directs the hearers' attention back to the command not to be afraid through this repetition of the rare word for fear.

The poem's second unit takes up a parallel theme, emphasizing the gods' inability to declare what will be and the contrast this produces between these nonentities and the LORD. While the poem has been dominated by imperatives, commanding the ironic non-addressees to do or declare something, the second unit opens with the LORD declaring God's own completed actions: "I stirred up" (41:25). Here the text alludes again (see 41:2) to the warrior who will be named later in the series of poems.[155] However, the emphasis in this context is not on revealing the identity of the instrument that God will use but rather on the LORD's ability to declare and carry it out. The divine voice insists that none other has made this known but that the LORD has already offered a herald (41:27).[156] In direct contrast to what the divine voice insists that the gods cannot do in any instance, the LORD offers a specific example of what Israel's God has already achieved.

In this short poetic unit, the divine voice disputes with an apparent source of the exiles' fear. They are offered the opportunity to overhear a sarcastic and ironic rebuttal of their fearfulness of that which does not

---

than I have defended above, and overlooks the contrast with the depiction of the LORD in Isa. 45:7. There "I make weal and create woe" parallels "light" and "darkness" and each of these appear designed to convey totality.

[154] J. Blenkinsopp, *Isaiah 40–55* (2002), 206, also refers to this couplet as "sarcastic."

[155] See also J. Blenkinsopp, *Isaiah 40–55* (2002), 206.

[156] B. S. Childs, *Isaiah* (2001), 322, makes an interesting link between this fulfilment and Isaiah 13 "which is redactionally located within First Isaiah." Matthew Seufert, "Isaiah's Herald," *Westminster Theological Journal* 77 (2015): 266, notes of the LORD that "The Herald . . . vindicates him as the God who speaks."

*Isaiah 42:1–4*                                                                                          65

exist, has no power, and cannot tell, much less influence, the future. The emphatic claim is that there is nothing to fear from these nonentities.

## ISAIAH 42:1–4

> ¹ Here is my servant, whom I uphold,
>>    my chosen, in whom my soul delights;
> I have put my spirit upon him;
>>    he will bring forth justice to the nations.
> ² He will not cry or lift up his voice
>>    or make it heard in the street;
> ³ a bruised reed he will not break,
>>    and a dimly burning wick he will not quench;
>>    he will faithfully bring forth justice.
> ⁴ He will not grow faint or be crushed
>>    until he has established justice in the earth,
>>    and the coastlands wait for his teaching.

In this short poem, the divine voice presents a figure who will convey one of Second Isaiah's important rhetorical strategies, the Servant, interweaving this motif with other Second Isaian imageries and tying the Servant's role heavily to justice. This is not the hearers' first encounter with "the Servant." They were addressed as the servant of the LORD in 41:8–9. However, here the personification takes shape significantly, as the divine voice announces this figure, speaking of him in the third person.

The introduction of the personified Servant in Isaiah 42 ties the servant image closely to the exilic audience and offers it as an image for them to inhabit.[157] This passage's close relationship to the use of servant imagery in Isaiah 41:8–9 conveys this connection and constrains its interpretation in important ways (see A Closer Look: The Servant and His "Songs"). In Isaiah 41, the divine voice addresses the audience directly as "my servant" (ʿabdî), naming them as Israel and Jacob in parallel lines and stressing that the LORD has "chosen" (root bḥr) them, repeating the claim

---

[157]  See B. S. Childs, *Isaiah* (2001), 325; and J. Goldingay and D. Payne, *Isaiah 40–55* (2006), 1:213, for arguments connecting Israel and the Servant here.

66　　Commentary

in both verses 8 and 9.[158] The same language appears in 42:1, where the divine voice presents "my servant" ('*abdî*) and describes him as "my chosen" (*bĕḥîrî*).[159] By using the same terms, the poetry creates connections that closely tie the Servant figure to the audience.

The heavy emphasis of this poem is on the Servant's commission to produce "justice" (*mišpāṭ*, 42:1, 3, 4).[160] Twice the divine voice claims that the servant is to "bring forth justice" (42:1, 3) and the poem concludes by indicating that his work will continue "until he has established justice" (42:4).[161] Given the apparent close association of the Servant with Jacob-Israel, it is noteworthy that justice (*mišpāṭî*, i.e., "my justice"; cf. NRSV[ue] "my right") is precisely what Jacob had complained that the LORD had overlooked in his case (40:27).[162] If the beginning points of the audience being invited to see themselves as the personified Servant emerge in this poem, it is telling that the work of that figure is to bring about the thing that Jacob has complained of lacking. It is as if the audience are given a different perspective on the injustice they have suffered. They are invited to see themselves, acting through God's strength and spirit (42:2), as the ones tasked with producing the justice they require.

The personification develops through poetic imagery that evokes rather than stating a transparent claim.[163] The depiction carries overtones of distress and danger, yet the Servant who is vulnerable to these things does not inflict them. The Servant is one who will not "cry out" "in the street," perhaps alluding to, and reversing, the exhortation in Lamentations to

---

[158] Tryggve N. D. Mettinger, *A Farewell to the Servant Songs: A Critical Examination of an Exegetical Axiom* (trans. Frederick H. Cryer; Lund: CWK Gleerup, 1983), 10, notes the connection.

[159] Ulrika Lindblad, "A Note on the Nameless Servant in Isaiah XLII 1–4" *VT* XLIII (1993): 116.

[160] C. Westermann, *Isaiah 40–66* (1969), 95, also notes the recurrence of "justice" and "bring forth." For a helpful rebuttal of resistance to reading the commissioned one as Jacob-Israel here, see U. Lindblad, "A Note," 116.

[161] J. Blenkinsopp, *Isaiah 40–55* (2002), 210, connects justice with "a ruler," supporting his claim that Cyrus is envisioned here. However, such a reading requires overlooking the strong connections to 41:8–9 and the explicit reference to Jacob-Israel there. Blenkinsopp does comment that "Much of what is said in these verses could also be said of Israel either projecting an ideal Israel or an Israel in the guise of one of the great figures from its past" (211).

[162] B. S. Childs, *Isaiah* (2001), 324, observes that the presentation of the Servant in 42 forms part of the divine reply to Israel's charge concerning justice in 40:27.

[163] See C. Westermann, *Isaiah 40–66* (1969), 93.

*Isaiah 42:1–4*

Zion to "cry out" "for the lives of your children, who faint for hunger at the head of every street" (Lam 2:19).[164] The two verbs used here for what the Servant will not do, "cry out" (*yiṣ'aq*) and "lift up" (*yiśśā'*), are each used in Lamentations 2 as imperatives to Zion. She is commanded to "Cry aloud" (*ṣā'aq*, 2:18) and to "Lift" her hands (*śĕ'î*, 2:19). The language of the "street" is the same in both Lam 2:19 (*ḥûṣôt*, i.e., "streets") and Isa 42:2 ("in the street" *baḥûṣ*).[165] The "wick" and the "reed," which will be spared any damage in the Servant's work for justice, appear as vulnerable figures.[166] Each is described in ways that emphasize their already beleaguered status.[167] They are "bruised" (*rāṣûṣ*) and "dimly burning" (*kēhāh*) (42:3). Paradoxically, the same language is used of the Servant himself. He will not "grow faint" (*yikheh*) or "be crushed" (*yārûṣ*) until his commission is completed (42:4).[168]

In this very brief interlude, the divine voice offers a glimpse of the Servant.[169] The figure will develop in prominence and in attractiveness to the audience as the poems progress. For now, the figure stands as one who "delights" the LORD, who is given God's "spirit" and who will continue his work until he brings about the very thing that Jacob has claimed is missing from his experience: justice. Yet the depiction may not be entirely attractive to the exilic audience, interacting as it does with images of weakness

---

[164] Though he does not connect the passage to Isa 41, B. D. Sommer, *A Prophet Reads Scripture* (1998), 128–130, argues that Isa 40–66 alludes to Lam 2:13–19 elsewhere. If that is the case, the evidence that the poet knew the passage from Lamentations increases the likelihood of a genuine allusion here.

[165] Regarding "street," J. Goldingay and D. Payne, *Isaiah 40–55* (2006), 1:216, note "the term's prominence in Lamentations" in support of their claim that it "denotes the place of judgment."

[166] Hyun Chul Paul Kim, "An Intertextual Reading of 'A Crushed Reed' and 'A Dim Wick' in Isaiah 42.3," *JSOT* 83 (1999): 113–124, offers intertextual evidence for reading the reed and wick as referring to Egypt and Babylon respectively. Kim reads their vulnerability here as elements of polemic expressing "Israel's hope of impending doom upon the enemy nations" (120).

[167] J. Goldingay and D. Payne, *Isaiah 40–55* (2006), 1:218, observe that these images are "elsewhere figures for people who might seem strong but are actually weak."

[168] See C. Westermann, *Isaiah 40–66* (1969), 96; and J. Muilenburg, "Isaiah 40–66" (1956), 5:466, on repetition. G. R. Smillie, "Isaiah 42:1–4" (2005), 57, helpfully notes the impact of sound on verse 3 as well as the repetition of these terms with reference to the servant in verse 4.

[169] While I disagree with his conclusions about the servant imagery, Smillie, "Isaiah 42:1–4" (2005) is correct to highlight "the author's artistic ability to delay" (50) and to reject approaches that disregard the author's apparent preference to "prolong ambiguity" (51).

68 Commentary

and vulnerability. These elements connect with their recent experience and offer a vision of the LORD's ability to use them to bring about justice.

### A CLOSER LOOK: THE SERVANT AND HIS "SONGS"

Perhaps one of the most well-known figures in Isaiah 40–55 is the Servant of the LORD, or the "Suffering Servant." Scholars have described four passages from Isaiah 40–55 as the "Servant Songs" and have made numerous attempts to assign this figure to a particular historical person.[170] This approach can be conclusively rejected.[171] The Servant figure is best understood as a personification that the poetry employs to convince the audience to embrace the comfort the LORD offers. The Servant as a personification embodies that which the poems invite their audience to become.[172] Such an approach fits well with those passages that describe the Servant (e.g., 42:1–4), those that present the Servant as speaking (e.g., 49:1–13), and those that refer to the Servant in connection with Israel (e.g., 41:8–9).

Frequently, the divine voice addresses the exiles as Jacob and Israel. The address "you" commonly accompanies these Jacob-Israel attributions (e.g., 41:8; 41:14; 43:1, 22) tying them firmly to the audience. Servant language within Isaiah 40–55 first appears in association with Jacob-Israel.[173] In Isaiah 41:8, the divine voice calls them, "you, Israel, my servant, Jacob, whom I have chosen." Indeed, the majority of the references to "servant" in Isaiah 40–55 refer to Jacob-Israel and through them to the exilic audience, as Mettinger has demonstrated.[174]

---

[170] In his rejection of an individual interpretation, T. N. D. Mettinger, *Farewell* (1983), 45, lists among the figures scholars have proposed and who we can now safely eliminate from contention: "the prophet himself, Duhm's unknown teacher of the Law, Isaiah, Uzziah, Hezekiah, Josiah, Jeremiah, Ezekiel, Job, Moses, Jehoiachin, Cyrus, Sheshbazzar, Zerubbabel, Meshullam, Nehemiah, and Eleazar."

[171] T.N.D. Mettinger, *Farewell* (1983), offers a full and insightful rebuttal of the theory of four songs that were added to the text by another hand and refer to a servant figure distinct from that appearing elsewhere in the book.

[172] Cf. M. A. Sweeney, *Isaiah 40–66* (2016), 201, who describes the Servant as "Israel personified" and "the model for Isaiah's audience to emulate."

[173] J. L. McKenzie, *Second Isaiah* (1968), LII, refers to the Servant as "an ideal figure" and calls the Servant "what Israel is to become" (LV). J. Muilenburg, "Isaiah 40–66" (1956), 5:453, calls the Servant "the chief characterization of the covenant people."

[174] T.N.D. Mettinger, *Farewell* (1983), 30. Of nineteen verses in Isaiah 40–55 that employ the noun "servant," seven make explicit identification with Jacob-Israel.

*Isaiah 42:5–9* 69

However, these references are not the elements of Second Isaiah's servant imagery that have captured the imagination of readers. The personification of the Servant, as illustrated especially in Isaiah 49:1–13 and 52:13–53:12, stands as a particularly powerful poetic trope. Patricia Tull has compellingly offered the insight that the Servant develops the "man" of Lamentations 3 and that this figure stands alongside another poetic figure, personified Zion (see A Closer Look: Lady Zion and The Suffering Servant, the Rhetorical Power of Juxtaposition].[175] The Servant, particularly through his association with Jacob-Israel, offers an idealized response to the divine announcement of comfort. This figure embodies testimony to the LORD's power and deliverance (e.g., 49:13). He imitates and reflects the power and majesty of the divine speaker (e.g., 49:5; 50:8–9). He offers a response to the conditions of exile that embraces the transition from nonresistance to suffering (53:7) to glorification and restoration by God's hand (53:12). The Servant exemplifies, through vivid poetic personification, the transformation that the poetry aims to enact upon its audience. He expresses and enacts that which the poems invite them to become.

ISAIAH 42:5–9

⁵ Thus says God, the LORD,
     who created the heavens and stretched them out,
     who spread out the earth and what comes from it,
who gives breath to the people upon it
     and spirit to those who walk in it:
⁶ I am the LORD; I have called you in righteousness;
     I have taken you by the hand and kept you;
I have given you as a covenant to the people,
     a light to the nations,
       ⁷ to open the eyes that are blind,

---

[175] P. Tull Willey, *Remember the Former Things* (1997), 211–219. Uta Schmidt, "Servant and Zion: Two Kinds of Future in Isaiah 49," in *"My Spirit at Rest in the North Country" (Zechariah 6.8): Collected Communications to the XXth Congress of the International Organization for the Study of the Old Testament, Helsinki 2010* (BEATAJ 57; eds. Hermann Michael Niemann and Matthias Augustin; Oxford: Peter Lang, 2011), 89, considers the rhetorical power of the Servant personification, and also raises the issue of the juxtaposition of the Servant and Zion (91).

70                *Commentary*

> to bring out the prisoners from the dungeon,
>> from the prison those who sit in darkness.
> [8] I am the LORD; that is my name;
>> my glory I give to no other,
>> nor my praise to idols.
> [9] See, the former things have come to pass,
>> and new things I now declare;
> before they spring forth,
>> I tell you of them.

This short poetic unit conveys the majesty and reliability of the divine speaker through its glorifying tone and its orderly patterning. Within this structure, the exiles hear their own commission placed firmly within the plan and purpose of this glorious and trustworthy divine speaker.[176]

The poem divides into three sub-units, whose poetic form conveys the orderliness of their speaker. The opening unit develops the claim that the LORD is speaking using participles that extol the divine speaker. This mode of speech is common to the divine voice in Isaiah 40–55 and is one of the features that conveys its majesty (see A Closer Look: The Majestic Divine Speaker). Here the participles focus on the LORD's status as creator and move through modes of expansion.[177] The opening triplet employs three participles, the last two of which convey ideas of "stretching out." The poetic form reflects the grandness of scale implied in one who "stretched out" (v. 5) the skies and "spread out the earth" (v. 5). Parallelism expands upon the idea, leaving the verbal form gapped (see "gapping" in Glossary of Poetic Terminology) to create space for reference to the produce of the earth. The couplet that follows in this participial glorification of the divine speaker is even more expansive, allowing the verb "who gives" to govern a double reference to people (v. 5).

The refrain "I am the LORD," which marks the beginning of the second and third units, divides the speech that has been so expansively introduced into two sections. Each of these units is doubly marked, by both the refrain and by the closure of the unit before. In each case, the preceding unit is

---

[176] J. Blenkinsopp, *Isaiah 40–55* (2002), 211, also reads this poem as "addressed ... to the congregation."

[177] B. S. Childs, *Isaiah* (2001), 326, notes that the "language resonates of Genesis 1 and the Psalter."

# Isaiah 42:5–9

closed by a single participle for the beneficiaries of divine giving ("those who walk in it," v. 5 and "those who sit in darkness," v. 7). These are the only times in this poem that the participles have human referents.

The second unit places the addressees' commission firmly within the context of divine control and purpose. The divine voice retains all the activity to its own self, employing active verbs that convey the certainty and firmness of the LORD's control. These verbs simultaneously link this calling to the calling made to Jacob-Israel directly and through the Servant personification. The verbs "I have called" (v. 6; cf. 41:9), "I have taken" (v. 6; cf. 41:9, 13), "[I have] kept" (v. 6; cf. 49:8), and "I have given" (v. 6; cf. 42:1; 49:8) emphasize the LORD's agency emphatically and repeatedly. The stress laid upon the divine prerogative in "I am the LORD" and in the opening participles extolling the speaker continues in the insistence that this calling is accomplished by the "I" that is speaking.

At the same time, these verbs forge links with other passages that use these same verbs, especially Jacob-Israel's call in 41:8–9, the introduction of the personified Servant figure in 42:1–4, and the poem spoken in that Servant's voice in 49:1–13. It is impossible to ignore the virtually identical statements of purpose given to the audience here and spoken by the Servant in 49:8 (NRSV[ue] "and kept you; I have given you as a covenant to the people" 42:6; NRSV[ue] "I have kept you and given you as a covenant to the people" 49:8). The Hebrew that these words translate is identically phrased.[178] In this way, the series of poems strongly correlates this commission with the Servant, but 42:6–7 is equally overlapped with the call to Jacob-Israel in 41:8–9.[179] Thus, the series of poems moves through

---

[178] See U. Lindblad, "A Note" (1993), 118–119, on this and additional connections between these passages.

[179] I have treated 42:1–4 and 42:5–9 as separate but closely juxtaposed poems, as verse 5 announces a new divine pronouncement ("Thus says the LORD") and shifts significantly in the tone with which it addresses its audience (see, e.g., J. Blenkinsopp, *Isaiah 40–55* [2002], 211, who treats them as "conjoined passages [that] ... form a *literary* unit" emphasis original). Whether or not one reads 42:1–4 as a distinct poem, it is not clear that such a close association with the Servant as introduced in 42:1–4 should be carried into 42:5–9, as Servant language is not explicit in these later verses, and it is not untypical of Second Isaian style to shift referent within poems. In any case, the language of verses 6–7 is equally overlapped with a passage that does not directly reference the Servant figure (41:8–9) and with the Servant's own declaration (49:8) as detailed above. This argues against sole identification with the Servant introduced in Isaiah 42:1–4.

72                                                                        *Commentary*

assurance to the exiles that they have been called and chosen (41:8–9), to introduction of the personification of their idealized response (42:1–4) (see A Closer Look: The Servant and His "Songs"), to a commission grounded in the creator's purpose that hints at an association between the exiles and the Servant figure, to the Servant's own expression of his commission and its place in God's purposes (see further the discussion of Isa 49:1–13).[180]

The poems do not build a narrative of the exiles' identification with the Servant figure. Rather, they offer juxtaposed images that tie the addressees ever closer to the response the poetry aims to evoke in them. This response is embodied in the personification of the ideal response, the Servant.

This poem is not really about the audience, though the central section addresses them directly. Its apparent aim is to place them firmly within the context of the creator God's total control of all that is and all that will be and to express the glory and majesty of the God who speaks. The final structured section of the poem returns to the theme of divine activity and purpose from which the central section never really departed. The refrain of divine self-reference intensifies here doubling back again with the emphatic assertion "that is my name." The divine voice insists on its dramatic distinction from those it previously decried as "nothing" (41:24). In direct contrast to the nonentities who cannot tell either what has been or what will be (41:22–23), the LORD claims that God's own statements about what would be, have been (42:9), and that the "new things" it announces will certainly be (42:9).

Pervading this poem is the overwhelming majesty of the divine voice who gives all that exists. While "to give" (Hebrew *ntn*) is an undeniably common verb in Hebrew, its pervasiveness in this short poem indicates that the poet conveys meaning through its repetition. This verb appears in each of the three sections of the poem and its function progresses alongside the poem's imagery. In the opening expression of the creator's grandeur, the verb appears as the participle "who gives" (*nōtēn*, v. 5) governing the

---

[180] The factors outlined above regarding overlap between this addressee, Jacob-Israel and the personified Servant argue in favor of taking the exiles themselves as the addressees of this poem. See, e.g., J. Goldingay and D. Payne, *Isaiah 40–55* (2006), 1:226. Against K. Baltzer, *Deutero-Isaiah* (2001), 125, who, in his examination of vv. 1–9 sees the parallels with 41:8–16 as indicating two "installation accounts" and therefore two servants, it is not at all untypical of either poetic style in general, nor of Second Isaian style in particular, to double back on the same theme. The same Servant is implied here as in chapter 41.

# A Closer Look: The Majestic Divine Speaker

double and expanded reference to humans. Their very "breath" and its parallel "spirit" are presented as given by the LORD. When the addressees' own task appears, it is the audience themselves who are now "given" (*wĕ'ettenka*, v. 6) by the divine hand to be a covenant people (see A Closer Look: A Covenant People).[181] Finally, the glory of the LORD, which is central to the tone of this poem, is precisely what the LORD will not "give" (*'ettēn*, v. 8) to another. Just as the final verse draws together the certainty of God's claims in the past with the declarations the LORD makes for the future, so these verbs move from characteristic activity ("who gives"), to action with the audience as its object ("I give you"), to certain future ("I will [not] give"). Each of these – the very substance of human life, the purpose through which the audience will bring benefit to others, and the majesty that must be for God alone – are within the power of the LORD alone to give.

## A CLOSER LOOK: THE MAJESTIC DIVINE SPEAKER

A magnanimous self-assurance pervades the speech of the divine voice in Isaiah 40–66,[182] whether speaking comfort or wrath. At times the poetry offers a glimpse of this majestic tone purely on its own (e.g., 42:5–9). Participles glorifying the divine voice at times interrupt the transition from announcement of divine speech to the content of that speech, lending a sense that the poetry itself is offering a hymn to the speaker (e.g., 42:5; 43:1; 44:2, 24–28; 56:8).[183] These participles may be accompanied by references to past actions such as creation or deliverance and with assured promises about the future. Confidence in the divine speaker's own ability to carry out what is promised is repeatedly announced (e.g., 43:11; 44:26; 45:23; 46:11; 55:11; 56:1; 60:22)[184] and the divine voice announces its own presence with

---

[181] The NRSV[ue] translates "I have given." Each of the verbs following "I have called you" are presented in the MT as imperfect (incomplete action) verbs. In context incomplete action seems probable, though the consonants could support either reading; cf. the suggested emendation in *BHS*, 739.

[182] Preferred techniques for conveying majesty in the divine voice shift somewhat from chapter 56 onwards, but overall the tone continues to be relevant. See further description of this tone and its markers in K. M. Heffelfinger, *I Am Large* (2011), 186–189, where it is referred to as "Majestically Supreme Confidence."

[183] See, e.g., J. Muilenburg, "Isaiah 40–66" (1956), 5:390. See also Theodore M. Ludwig, "The Traditions of the Establishing of the Earth in Deutero-Isaiah," *JBL* 92.3 (1973): 346, 348.

[184] Interestingly, these last two turn to assurances about time.

74 *Commentary*

exuberant majesty (e.g., "I am the Lord," 43:11, 15; 45:5, 6, 18; 48:17; 51:15; 60:22), often accompanied by the glorifying participles (e.g., 43:15–17; 45:7; 48:17; 51:15; 61:8). Interestingly, as the Servant takes up his commission, his speech increasingly takes on these features and they contrast ever more sharply with Zion's tone. In its juxtaposition with the Servant and Zion in Isaiah 40–55, the majestic confidence of the divine voice works both to encourage audience trust and to magnify the force of both the danger of threatened wrath and the reliability of comfort offered. Throughout Isaiah 40–66, it expresses and conveys the Isaian commitment to a vision of the LORD that is grand, awe-inspiring, and worthy of ultimate reverence. Thus, the majestic tone of the divine speaker enhances and expands the rhetorical aims of the poems, urging the audience to trust this confident, majestic divine speaker.

ISAIAH 42:10–13

[10] Sing to the LORD a new song,
> his praise from the end of the earth!
Let the sea roar and all that fills it,
> the coastlands and their inhabitants.
[11] Let the desert and its towns lift up their voice,
> the villages that Kedar inhabits;
let the inhabitants of Sela sing for joy,
> let them shout from the tops of the mountains.
[12] Let them give glory to the LORD
> and declare his praise in the coastlands.
[13] The LORD goes forth like a soldier;
> like a warrior he stirs up his fury;
he cries out; he shouts aloud;
> he shows himself mighty against his foes.

This brief exhortation to praise sits juxtaposed to the divine voice's insistence that the LORD alone merits praise. In words that echo God's claim in verse 8, "my glory I give to no other, nor my praise to idols," regions representing the whole of the created world, and particularly those against whom destruction has been promised, are invited to "give glory to the LORD and declare his praise" (v. 12). While the passage interrupts the

*Isaiah 42:10–13* 75

apparent stream of speech in the divine voice (42:5–9 and 42:14–20), its appearance here is heavily interwoven with the images that both precede and follow, and it creates links between these speeches of the divine voice and earlier texts to which it seems to intend to refer. These links with earlier passages underscore the trustworthiness of the divine speaker, especially through commanding unlikely worshippers to praise.

The opening call to praise has a broad reach, inviting praise "from the end of the earth" (v. 10). The lines that follow give various expressions to the idea of the "end of the earth," fleshing it out in a couplet each referring to sea (v. 10), desert (v. 11), and mountains (v. 11).[185] Each of these expand upon the idea and could simply be giving extravagant voice to the call for praise to come from everywhere. However, the chain sea, desert, mountain, and particularly the references to Kedar and Sela,[186] draw the hearer's attention to the truth of the claims already made about the LORD. These claims have evoked this praise, particularly the LORD's ability to announce and bring about the "former things" (42:9).

Kedar and Sela do not simply imply "the most obscure and remote places."[187] Instead, they represent particular enemies of Israel about whom the LORD had spoken "former things" (see A Closer Look: The Final Form and the Former Things).[188] These peoples are now called to praise. Isaiah 42's call to the sea, the desert, and the mountains seems designed to echo the series of oracles from Isaiah 21 where destruction is proclaimed for Edom (Seir) and Kedar. There Edom (Seir rather than Sela – See Gen 32:3;

---

[185] C. Westermann, *Isaiah 40–66* (1969), 103–104, comments on the expansiveness of the call to praise.

[186] The patterning of the lines draws additional attention to the named tribe (Kedar) and town (Sela). Their precision already stands out in a context of sweeping geographical reference. The language of habitation is heavily repeated in these lines and patterned as a participle, "coastlands and their inhabitants" (*yōšĕbêhem*), a finite verb, "villages that Kedar inhabits" (*tēšēb*), and a participle, "the inhabitants of Sela" (*yōšĕbê*) of the same verb.

[187] J. Muilenburg, "Isaiah 40–66" (1956), 5:471.

[188] That Sela and Kedar represent enemies of the audience is clear. See J. Goldingay and D. Payne, *Isaiah 40–55* (2006), 1:239. See, for example, the invective at the end of Psalm 137. Some scholars read "Sela" in the final line of that poem as containing a double reference, both to a "rock" and to "Sela," the Edomite town whose name means rock, e.g., Mitchell Dahood, *Psalms III: 101–150* (AB17A; New York: Doubleday, 1970), 274. Sela, translated "clefts of the rock" by the NRSV[ue], appears within Jeremiah's oracle concerning Edom (Jer 49:7–22), in a chapter that also directly references Kedar (Jer 49:28). Obadiah reflects difficulties with Edom in the exilic period (see, e.g., Paul R. Raabe, *Obadiah* [AB24D; London: Doubleday, 1996], 51).

2 Kgs 14:7; and 2 Chron. 25:12) and Kedar appear together in a series of oracles against "the wilderness of the sea" (21:1–10), which announces the fall of Babylon; "concerning Dumah" (21:11–12), which includes the reference to Seir; and "concerning the desert plain" (21:13–17), which proclaims the coming destruction of Kedar.[189] However, now these places that were to be destroyed are called to offer "praise" (42:10, 12) and to "shout for joy" (42:11). The things the LORD has proclaimed have "come to pass" (42:9), including their destruction. Edom and Kedar are both objects of prophecies of destruction from the preexilic oracles against the nations, and each experiences destruction prior to the time of this poem, making their destruction "former things" that have occurred.[190] Now "new things" are announced (42:9). The poet has paired calls to praise with regions that call to mind an oracle concerning the fall of Babylon (21:1–10), an oracle that employs laboring woman imagery (which will reappear in 42:14) and threshing and winnowing imagery (which has just been used in 41:15–16). Seir and Kedar faced judgment and destruction. Now they appear to function as witnesses to the reality of Israel's God when they offer praise to the one who declared their destruction. Perhaps most significantly, their testimony supports the accuracy of the oracle that is foremost in the exiles' minds and concern, the fall of Babylon. If the nations against whom the LORD had proclaimed destruction can sing a "new song" (42:10) of praise to the LORD who proclaims "new things" (42:9), then the exiles can trust that the LORD who promises deliverance and comfort will fulfil the divine word.[191]

The final lines of this short poem seem to support such a reading. Divine warrior imagery offers a depiction of the LORD as one who is equipped to

---

[189] J. Muilenburg, "Isaiah 40–66" (1956), 471, observes that Kedar is referenced in 21:16 but does not comment significantly on this connection.

[190] P. R. Raabe, *Obadiah* (1996), 54–55, draws on textual and archaeological evidence to indicate that Edom fell during Nabonidus' reign. He suggests 533, which is prior to the time to which this poem was addressed. Regarding Kedar, see M. Patrick Graham, "Kedar," *NIDB* (ed. Katharine Doob Sakenfeld et al.; Nashville: Abingdon, 2008), 3:488, who describes "attacks" by Nebuchadnezzar and "control" by Nabonidus. Interestingly, a positive turn in Kedar's standing appears initiated by Cyrus' victories according to M. P. Graham, "Kedar" (2008), 3:488.

[191] B. S. Childs, *Isaiah* (2001), 327, observes how the passage "involve[s] the reader ... in rendering praise."

# A Closer Look: The Final Form and the Former Things

fulfil the promised destruction of Jacob's enemies.[192] This is God who merits praise not only from Israel but from the whole world. This is the LORD who will not only not share praise with idols but who evokes praise even from the enemies of God's own people.

## A CLOSER LOOK: THE FINAL FORM AND THE FORMER THINGS

The poetic approach undertaken in this commentary is primarily a final form approach. That is, it is largely concerned with interpreting the work as it stands in the shape we have received it within the canon. The final form of the book is without clear markers of transitions between the commonly recognized historical sections, a fact that should be taken into account in this matter.[193] Whatever the history of these sections, it does seem that those responsible for finally compiling the book of Isaiah implied it should be read as a whole. However, as noted in the Introduction, and as widely acknowledged by scholars, the book of Isaiah itself is the product of a long history. Similarly, the component sections have undergone some editing and adaptation, both within themselves and in the process of drawing them together.[194]

Two authors who write about how the final form of the book of Isaiah has come together have each at various points influenced the work of this commentary. Each of them takes account of the complexity of the book's history, particularly that of Isaiah 1–39.[195] First, it is apparent that some form of Isaiah 1–39 has had a significant impact on the thinking and message of Isaiah 40–55. H. G. M. Williamson sees Second Isaiah as

---

[192] See further J. Goldingay and D. Payne, *Isaiah 40–55* (2006), 1:241, on militaristic imagery.

[193] Rolf Rendtorff, "Isaiah 56:1 as a Key to the Formation of the Book," in *Canon and Theology* (trans. and ed. Margaret Kohl; Minneapolis: Fortress, 1993), 182, points to the impact of unmarked transitions.

[194] This study of the formation of the book over time and the various stages at which it was edited is referred to as "redaction criticism." For a helpful overview of recent scholarship on Isaiah including recent redaction criticism, see Christopher B. Hays, "The Book of Isaiah in Contemporary Research," *Religion Compass* 5.10 (2011): 549–566.

[195] H. G. M. Williamson, *Book Called Isaiah* (1994), 27, comments "there is widespread agreement (which I fully share) that the first part of Isaiah developed over an extended period of time, reaching well down into the post-exilic era." Rolf Rendtorff, "The Composition of the Book of Isaiah," in *Canon and Theology* (trans. and ed. Margaret Kohl; Minneapolis: Fortress, 1993), 168, discusses the possibility that there never was an independent form of Isaiah 1–39.

78                                                                    *Commentary*

intentionally building upon and connecting his ministry to the work of Isaiah of Jerusalem as conveyed in an early version of Isaiah 1–39, what he refers to as "the literary deposit of First Isaiah."[196] Williamson's approach treats the author of Isaiah 40–55 as having access to an early version of Isaiah 1–39 but also as having been involved in editing and shaping the earlier prophetic work as he incorporated it into the growing book that included his own work. In this approach, the author of Isaiah 40–55 plays a dominant role in shaping the whole.[197] Williamson's observations are pertinent, and it does seem at times that chapters 40–55 allude intentionally and meaningfully to passages that now stand within the final form of Isaiah 1–39. Most significantly, Isaiah 40–55 takes the LORD's ability to announce "the former things"[198] as evidence of the LORD's sole deity (e.g., 46:8–10) and draws upon things announced in Isaiah 1–39 to support this claim (e.g., allusion to Isaiah 21 in Isaiah 42).

Second, it appears that the prophetic figure responsible for Isaiah 56–66 also played a constructive role in producing the final form of the book of Isaiah. Rolf Rendtorff sees both a significant disjunction between First and Second Isaiah and evidence of themes that are worked through the whole.[199] Rendtorff's analysis insightfully highlights distinctions in word usage between Isaiah 1–39 and 40–55 that illuminate the work of the postexilic prophet in drawing them together in the final book. As Rendtorff compellingly shows, and as discussion of chapters 56–66 will repeatedly bear out, the prophetic poet responsible for these chapters, which appear last in the book, was a masterful synthesizer of previous texts (see A Closer Look: "Third Isaiah" as "Under-Rated" Poet) and has certainly played a significant role in the shaping of the final version of the book of Isaiah.[200]

---

[196]  H. G. M. Williamson, *Book Called Isaiah* (1994), 28. See also R. E. Clements, "Beyond Tradition-History: Deutero-Isaianic Development of First Isaiah's Themes," *JSOT* 31 (1985): 101.

[197]  H. G. M. Williamson, *Book Called Isaiah* (1994), 240–241. In this matter R. Rendtorff, "Composition" (1993), 167, agrees.

[198]  On the former things, see H. G. M. Williamson, *Book Called Isaiah* (1994), 113.

[199]  R. Rendtorff, "Isaiah 56:1" (1993), 188; and R. Rendtorff, "Composition" (1993), 150–151. While Rendtorff argues that chapters 1–39 and 40–55 developed independently and only came together when the final section of the book was added, he places less emphasis on this detail than on the impact on the final form, R. Rendtorff, "Isaiah 56:1" (1993), 187.

[200]  The analysis of H. G. M. Williamson, *Book Called Isaiah* (1994), 20, is self-consciously concerned with the earlier phase of construction of Isaiah 1–55, and as such he sets

*Isaiah 42:14–20*

Thus, each of the exilic and postexilic phases of the book's development make an important impact on interpretation. Rendtorff's analysis takes Isaiah 56–66's postexilic audience as the final audience of the book when taken as a whole.[201] This commentary appreciates that insight and its important implications for the meaning of the book but also recognizes, as both Williamson and Rendtorff do, that Isaiah 40–55 is a cohesive section that played a very significant role in the shaping of the whole.[202] As such, it can be read in terms of its exilic audience alongside the final form and final section's interest in the postexilic audience. Without obliterating the tension that the exilic voice leaves on some matters, the chronologically final postexilic voice of Isaiah 56–66 draws together the testimonies of Isaiah of Jerusalem and the exilic voice who seems to have intentionally connected his own ministry to the eighth-century prophet's "former things." As such, in its final form, the book of Isaiah, despite being a product of multiple prophetic poets and historical periods, stands as a meaningful whole. Drawing together warnings set in a preexilic context with final restoration visions, the final form of the book of Isaiah presents a vision of God's mercy, and humanity's continual need for repentance, in a world that is neither entirely dominated by judgment or restoration but reflects both.

## ISAIAH 42:14–20

[14] For a long time I have held my peace;
    I have kept still and restrained myself;
now I will cry out like a woman in labor;
    I will gasp and pant.
[15] I will lay waste mountains and hills
    and dry up all their herbage;
I will turn the rivers into islands
    and dry up the pools.

---

Isaiah 56–66 outside the boundaries of his study, though he does indicate that further editing at this stage was likely.

[201] R. Rendtorff, "Isaiah 56:1" (1993), 186.

[202] H. G. M. Williamson, *Book Called Isaiah* (1994), 24–26; R. Rendtorff, "Composition" (1993), 167.

80                                                                    *Commentary*

<sup>16</sup> I will lead the blind
    by a road they do not know;
by paths they have not known
    I will guide them.
I will turn the darkness before them into light,
    the rough places into level ground.
These are the things I will do,
    and I will not forsake them.
<sup>17</sup> They shall be turned back and utterly put to shame –
    those who trust in carved images,
who say to cast images,
    "You are our gods."

<sup>18</sup> Listen, you that are deaf,
    and you that are blind, look up and see!
<sup>19</sup> Who is blind but my servant
    or deaf like my messenger whom I send?
Who is blind like my dedicated one
    or blind like the servant of the LORD?
<sup>20</sup> He sees many things, but he does not observe them;
    his ears are open, but he does not hear.[203]

The tone of this poem is dark with glimmers of light. In it the divine voice expresses the intention to give voice to things thus far held in restraint. Not surprisingly, given the juxtaposition between comfort and anger elsewhere in the series of poems, the resolve to bring an end to the period of having "kept still" results in the expression of both ominous imagery and promises of comfort. The encounter it offers confronts the audience, forcing them to face the reality of their position before God, both in its danger and in its promise.

    The opening image is an arresting one. In stark contrast to three actions of restraint depicting what has been ("held my peace," "kept still,"

---

[203] While I recognize the juxtaposition between warrior imagery (v. 13) and the laboring woman imagery (v. 14) as highlighted by Katheryn Pfisterer Darr, "Like Warrior, like Woman: Destruction and Deliverance in Isaiah 42:10–17," *CBQ* 49 (1987): 564, I have treated v. 14 as beginning a new poem. The break between poems is indicated by the shift to first person speech. This observation does not necessarily eliminate the relevance of juxtaposed images at the end and beginning of adjacent poems in the final form of the text.

*Isaiah 42:14–20* 81

"restrained myself"), the divine voice issues a stream of impending actions beginning with "cry out like a woman in labor" (42:14). Such an image is evocative on a number of levels. Applied by the divine voice to itself here, it conveys a productive bringing forth, pain, and a process that once begun cannot be halted.[204]

Here, the poetry juxtaposes an image of the divine warrior who "cries out" and is "mighty against his foes" (42:13) directly with this self-description that claims "I will cry out like a woman in labor" (42:14). Masculine and feminine gendered comparisons for the deity stand together here with the divine voice expressing the feminine one (see A Closer Look: Birth and Breastfeeding Imagery in Isaiah 40–66). The immediately following verbs "I will gasp and pant" tilt the force of the image toward pain and struggle and perhaps suggest the source of the desiccation imagery. That is, the divine breath that elsewhere withers things and dries them up (e.g., 40:7), here blasts after being pent up.[205] This image of the LORD bringing forth the promised comfort presents that comfort as far from simple. This is a restive poem that expresses difficulty in the promised reconciliation.

An allusion frames the impact upon the landscape and the people. This allusion ties this poem's imagery to the opening promise of comfort in Isaiah 40. There "every mountain and hill (*kol-hār wĕgibâ*)" was to be "made low" and "the uneven ground (*he ʿāqōb*) ... level (*lĕmîšôr*)" (40:4).[206] Here the LORD will "lay waste mountains and hills (*hārîm ûgĕbāʿôt*)" (42:15) and "turn ... the rough places into level ground

---

[204] See K. P. Darr, "Like Warrior" (1987), 564. On both the "unstoppable" nature of labor and its inherent danger in the ancient world see also Claudia Bergmann, "'Like a Warrior' and 'Like a Woman Giving Birth': Expressing Divine Immanence and Transcendence in Isaiah 42:10–17," in *Bodies, Embodiment, and Theology in the Hebrew Bible* (eds. S. Tamar Kamionkowski and Wonil Kim; London: T&T Clark, 2010), 47. A number of prophetic texts employ childbirth imagery to depict physical, mental, or emotional anguish. See, e.g., Isa. 13:8; 21:3; Jer. 49:22. J. L. McKenzie, *Second Isaiah* (1968), 44, says the image of childbirth "is elsewhere applied to those who are suffering fear or pain, but not to Yahweh." While Darr's insightful analysis helpfully connects the imagery in this case to the divine breath and its desiccating impact, this aspect of the imagery does not necessarily negate the elements of pain in the image, as Darr's comments seem to imply (see K. P. Darr, "Like Warrior," [1987], 567). As poetic imagery, the motif is capable of carrying both the powerful desiccation sense and the connotations of restiveness I am pointing to here.

[205] See further K. P. Darr, "Like Warrior, Like Woman" (1987), 568–569.

[206] J. Goldingay and D. Payne, *Isaiah 40–55* (2006), 1:247, also note this connection.

82               *Commentary*

(*lĕmîšôr*)" (42:16). The poetry plays with words for drying in these lines. The verb "I will lay waste" (*'aḥărîb*) means both "reduce to ruins" and "dry up."[207] While the destructive meaning makes sense with reference to mountains and hills, the images that follow employ "I will dry up" (*'ôbîš*), which finds sound play resonance in "utterly put to shame" (*yēbāšû bōšet*, 42:17). Violence and destructiveness against the mountains are not new in these poems (see 41:15), however, drying up does appear as a change (see 41:18).[208] The imagery conveys God's power to utterly transform whatever appears so that desert becomes oasis and oasis, desert. Especially through the resonance with "shame" later in the poem and the violence of "lay waste," these coming transformations of the landscape gain fearsome intonations.

Even the claim "I will lead the blind by a road they do not know" is unclear in its emotional tenor. It carries implications of exile and of enforced confusion, but the tension within this reference to the blind ultimately resolves in the expectation of guidance and comfort. It sits between a tumultuous transformation of the physical world and a promise to "turn ... darkness ... into light" (42:16) and to "not forsake them" (42:16). The translation "lead" perhaps implies gentle guidance, but the Hebrew verb could plausibly be translated "I will make them walk" (*wĕhôlaktî*; cf. NRSV[ue] "I will lead") and is, at times, used of taking people where they would not wish to go including into exile (e.g., Deut 28:36; Jer 32:5).[209] In Lamentations, the "man" who speaks says the LORD has "driven and brought" (*nāhag wayyōlak*) him "into darkness without any light" (Lam 3:2). If Isaiah 42 alludes to Lamentations here, it carries the implications of desperation and struggle there and ultimately resolves them in promise. The darkness is about to be transformed into light (42:16) and the people will not find themselves abandoned (42:16).

However, the attitude of gentle promise is short lived in this poem. An invective against idolators stands juxtaposed to this promise of guidance

---

[207] *HALOT*, 1:349.

[208] C. Westermann, *Isaiah 40–66* (1969), 107, notes this contrast with the imagery of Isaiah 41.

[209] J. Goldingay and D. Payne, *Isaiah 40–66* (2006), 1:247, note that the term "can also refer to a negative transition, such as being led *into* exile and darkness (e.g., Jer 32.5; Lam 3.2)." K. Baltzer, *Deutero-Isaiah* (2001), 146, reads the image in terms of "solicitude for the blind." This range of potential meanings supports my claim that the emotional import of the image is potentially ambiguous.

*Isaiah 42:14–20*                                                                                    83

and it recolors the tone of the divine voice. Here, the emphatic "utterly put to shame" recalls the desiccation of the landscape through sound play and reminds the exiles that those who ascribe deity to idols are angering the God whose creative power includes the power to dry up (42:15).

The dark tone continues as ironic commands demand that the deaf "Listen" and the blind "look up and see" (42:18). As Blenkinsopp comments regarding vv. 18–25, "The argumentative or disputatious tone is certainly in evidence here."[210] Here the divine voice directly addresses the audience. The exiles who would have heard themselves referenced as the "blind" who were to be brought on a way "they do not know" (42:16) now hear themselves commanded to do precisely what they cannot.[211] The heavy repetition of blind and deaf in the rhetorical questions of these lines convey aggravation and hint at divine judgment. The "servant" here is Jacob-Israel (see A Closer Look: The Servant and His "Songs") and the final line points to the judgment against Israel when Isaiah of Jerusalem was called (see A Closer Look: The Final Form and the Former Things).[212] There the divine voice sent Isaiah to proclaim the message "Keep listening, but do not comprehend; keep looking, but do not understand" (6:9).[213] The final couplet of the poem reinforces the sense that the audience is still blind and deaf in the way Isaiah of Jerusalem proclaimed. They are able to see but cannot. They are able to hear but do not.[214]

The audience stands indicted as the poem closes. They have heard God give voice to what has been held back "For a long time" (42:14). The aggravation at their inability to see what God is doing goes back "a long time" echoing the judgment against them in Isaiah of Jerusalem's day. They have heard the potentially destructive wrath of God depicted and they have been confronted with the fate of those who trust in idols.

---

[210]  J. Blenkinsopp, *Isaiah 40–55* (2002), 218.

[211]  C. Westermann, *Isaiah 40–66* (1969), 109, indicates a sense of "paradox" in the commands, as do J. Goldingay and D. Payne, *Isaiah 40–55* (2006), 1:257.

[212]  John Goldingay, "Isaiah 42.18–25," *JSOT* 67 (1995): 52.

[213]  H. G. M. Williamson, *Book Called Isaiah* (1994), 47, endorses a connection between Isaiah 6 and Isaiah 42 and 43, noting that "the hardening passage in Isaiah 6 seems to have exerted particular influence on Deutero-Isaiah" (51). On this connection, see also R. E. Clements, "Beyond Tradition-History" (1985), 103. J. D. W. Watts, *Isaiah 34–66* (2005), 131; J. Goldingay, "Isaiah 42.18–25" (1995), 51, who sees connection to Isaiah 6 as pointing to "a hidden promise"; and P. Stern, "Blind Servant" (1994), 227.

[214]  See J. Goldingay, "Isaiah 42.18–25" (1995), 50, on having eyes and ears that "receive sound and light waves" as "necessary but not . . . sufficient."

84

There has been a glimmer of possibility in the promise to lead the blind and to give light. These images stand together in the poem, and it does not reconcile them or smooth over the roughness between them. Rather, the audience is left to experience an encounter with God that offers a vision of anger both restrained and expressed alongside images of hope.

ISAIAH 42:21–25

[21] The LORD was pleased, for the sake of his righteousness,
  to magnify his teaching and make it glorious.
[22] But this is a people robbed and plundered;
  all of them are trapped in holes
  and hidden in prisons;
they have become a prey with no one to rescue,
  a spoil with no one to say, "Restore!"
[23] Who among you will give heed to this;
  who will attend and listen for the time to come?
[24] Who gave up Jacob to the spoiler
  and Israel to the robbers?
Was it not the LORD, against whom they have sinned,
  in whose ways they would not walk,
  and whose law they would not obey?
[25] So he poured upon him the heat of his anger
  and the fury of war;
it set him on fire all around, but he did not understand;
  it burned him, but he did not take it to heart.

These lines continue the themes, imagery, and general tone of the previous passage's bursting out of pent-up anger. The audience encounter an anonymous voice, presumably that of the prophetic poet, who closely echoes the irritation expressed by the divine voice in the preceding poetic unit.[215] This change of speaker lessens the intensity of the encounter, yet the experience this poetic unit offers remains one of challenge and conflict. Destruction, plunder, warfare, and burning resonate with the exiles'

---

[215] I am calling this a "poetic unit" rather than a poem. It is so closely linked to the lines that precede it that it appears equally reasonable to treat them as one poem or two.

# Isaiah 42:21–25

experience and appear in this poetic unit as things that have already happened.[216] However, the closing lines sound an ominous note indicating that despite these things, the people have not recognized the cause of divine anger, implying that the activities that incited the burning continue.

The opening lines of this poetic unit contrast the LORD, glorious and majestic, with the audience, diminished, confined, and vulnerable. Sound play between the verbs presenting the LORD as "pleased" (*ḥāpēṣ*), and the audience as "trapped" (*hāpēaḥ*),[217] emphasizes the contrast. While the people are depicted passively, the LORD acts as subject and instigator of action.[218] The teaching, which the LORD expands here, is a reference to Torah, that is, law or instruction, and there is no reason to see this teaching as belonging to the servant or anyone other than the LORD in this context. There is no suffix to represent "his" in the Hebrew text and the servant has not been spoken about with reference to his teaching since 42:4. In context this is most naturally God's law, as mentioned later in this poetic unit (v. 24). The word "make glorious" (root *'dr*) appears only here and in the song celebrating God's victory over the Egyptians at the Red Sea (Exod 15:6, 11).[219] There it underscores the power by which the LORD vanquished Israel's captors in order to bring them to safety. Here it sits in ironic contrast to the people's current condition, "trapped in holes and hidden in prisons" (v. 22).[220] These people, who were liberated from bondage by the "glorious" "right hand" of the LORD (Exod 15:6), are currently imprisoned and have not obeyed the "law" of their liberator (v. 24).

The poetic depiction of the audience's current state is repetitively elaborated. The verbal pair "robbed and plundered" (*bāzûz wĕšāsûy*, v. 22), whose passive voice sits in direct contrast to the LORD's activities in the

---

[216] The verbs for these actions are completed action verbal forms.

[217] This verb occurs only here in the Hebrew Bible. The MT vocalizes it as a *hip 'il* infinitive absolute (BDB, 809), though the meaning makes best sense as passive. It seems likely that the form reflects its close similarity of sound with *ḥāpēṣ*, whether caused by auditory scribal confusion or intentional poetic allusion.

[218] The verbs "magnify" and "make ... glorious" are in the *hip 'il*, i.e., they are causative.

[219] See also J. Goldingay and D. Payne, *Isaiah 40–55* (2006) 1:263.

[220] Against C. Westermann, *Isaiah 40–66* (1969), 112, who sees a problem that "the prophet would put his description of Israel's presentation in such a remarkably concrete way if he meant it to be taken only figuratively" as supporting an argument that the images are responses to the specifics of Israel's laments; it is the nature of poetry to employ such figurative language precisely to convey the strength of its claims. Here the images sit in diametric contrast to the images for the LORD.

86                                                                                  *Commentary*

immediately preceding line, finds an echo in the noun forms employed as subjects of the proclaimed absence of actors in the next couplet.[221] There the people are "prey" (*baz*) who do not have a deliverer and "spoil" (*měšissâ*) who have no one to speak for their restoration. This repetition, which underscores the audience's subjected state, surrounds a visual image that reinforces it. The vivid phrases "trapped in holes" and "hidden in prisons" each express dark, confinement, and the absence of escape. In a possible poetic echo of earlier Isaian prophecy, the image here juxtaposes exile with hiding from the wrath of God (2:10, 19) directed at idolaters. Since idolatry is also a concern in the immediate context of this passage (42:17) and the context contains other possible allusions to the ministry of Isaiah of Jerusalem, it is possible that the "law" that the audience have not followed relates to the worship of other "gods." However, it is more likely that the concern is larger and deals with Israel's way of life, including but not limited to idolatry, as suggested by the parallel phrase about following the LORD's "ways" (42:24).[222]

Rhetorical questions shift the poetry from description to direct confrontation. Three questions urge the audience to respond and to overcome the blindness and deafness that characterize their relationship with God, especially as depicted in earlier chapters of Isaiah. In language that echoes the preceding unit's concern about hearing that does not produce obedience and sight that does not result in understanding, the prophetic poet asks who will "give heed" (*ya'ăzîn*, i.e., give ear; cf. 42:20) and who will "listen" (*wěyišma'*; cf. 42:20). Here, the prophetic poet insists that the audience should know these things through the rhetorical form of the questions and through the echoes of earlier texts, even while implicitly reminding them that the testimony of the larger book is that they do not know. Isaiah of Jerusalem was called to invoke an absence of insight-bearing sight and hearing to result in destruction and burning (6:9–13). The book opened with an unflattering depiction of the people as exhibiting less understanding than livestock (1:3), who were offered the removal of their "sins" (*hātā'ēkem*, 1:18; cf. *hātā'nû*, 42:24), and who were offered a

---

[221] See J. Goldingay, "Isaiah 42.18–25" (1995), 58.

[222] J. Goldingay and D. Payne, *Isaiah 40–55* (2006), 1:265, connect the language of spoil and plunder to Isaiah 8 and 10 commenting that "The people's experience contrasts with the promise about their plunderers and despoilers in 17.14; cf. 13.16; 33.23."

*Isaiah 42:21–25* 87

choice between being "willing" (*tō 'bû*, 1:19; cf. *'ābû*, 42:24) and rebellion, along with the results of each (see further A Closer Look: The Final Form and the Former Things and A Closer Look: Indictment, Sarcasm, and Rhetorical Questions).[223] The people's plight might be desperate, as depicted by the spoil and plunder imagery, but the rhetorical questions confront the audience with the claim that this result, emphatically repeated in the second question, is the work of the God against whom they have rebelled (i.e., "in whose ways they would not [*lō '- 'ābû*] walk," 42:24).

There is quite a lot of reference to the failings of the past in this short poetic unit, but lest the audience think it is explanatory rather than confrontational, the final rhetorical question incorporates them directly. Instead of the "we" reference "tak[ing] the edge off the prophet's confrontation";[224] it seems that the "we" speech supplies words for the audience to identify with and even speak (cf. Isa 53), thus intensifying the level of engagement. The words "we have sinned" (*ḥāṭā 'nû*; cf. NRSV[ue] "they sinned")[225] bring the difficulty out of the ancient past making the absence of an answer to "who will give heed" and "who will attend" (42:23) symptomatic of the ongoing "blindness" highlighted in the previous poetic unit. If the audience were beginning to think that the recognition the poem urges them to is a case of seeing the source of their current distress in the actions of their predecessors, that hope is dashed. In these words, the poem shares the blame and makes the difficulty explicitly an ongoing one.

The final burning image is made all the more intense by the audience's inclusion through this "we" language. It is an image with what Robert Alter has rightly called "an instructive element of shock . . . the people is burning

---

[223] J. Goldingay and D. Payne, *Isaiah 40–55* (2006), 1:268, also make the connection to vocabulary overlap with Isaiah 1:19, among other parallels, but regard this as indicating resistance to the prophetic word rather than developing it as an element of Second Isaiah's employment of Isaiah 1–39 as among the former things. They do note the clear connection to fire in this context, which they acknowledge in their comment on v. 25 (1:269). See also B. D. Sommer, *A Prophet Reads* (1998), 97–99, who makes a compelling connection between this passage and Isaiah 30:9–14, interpreting the allusion as part of Second Isaiah's explanation of Israel's "current state" (98) as well as his reassurance that his new positive prophecies are reliable.

[224] J. Goldingay and D. Payne, *Isaiah 40–55* (2006), 1:256.

[225] NRSV[ue] reads "they sinned" citing the Greek. I agree with J. Goldingay and D. Payne, *Isaiah 40–55* (2006), 1:268, who note that the Greek here is "surely tidying up the text." "We" is the preferable, i.e., more likely original, reading here.

88  Commentary

alive, suffering divine retribution, but it is so blind that it doesn't even realize it is on fire."[226] Just as the people's inability to recognize and understand continued to the point of total destruction, imaged as burning in Isaiah of Jerusalem's commission, so here "heat," "fire," and "fury" fail to produce comprehension and obedience (v. 25). The tone of this reminder is ominous, as the audience themselves are the blind servant who "does not hear" (v. 20).[227]

A CLOSER LOOK: INDICTMENT, SARCASM, AND
RHETORICAL QUESTIONS

One feature of the divine voice in these chapters is its tendency to use features that color its tone (see Glossary of Poetic Terminology) as angry or condemnatory. This tone is directed mainly at figures associated with the audience (e.g., 42:14–20; 43:22–28; 46:5–13) but also includes other figures (e.g., Babylon in 47:1–15, other "gods" 41:21–26). Indictment features, such as disputation language (e.g., 41:21; 45:9; 49:25), carry implications of prophetic invectives and convey a posture of judgment, aggravation, and wrath.[228] Rhetorical questions (e.g., 40:25–28; 44:7–8) repeatedly reinforce the divine speaker's superior knowledge, sometimes with the added emphasis of being phrased sarcastically (e.g., 45:9–10). As Sharon Moughtin-Mumby insightfully comments, "we could say that *Isaiah* 40–55 takes rhetorical questions to another level, displaying a characteristic tendency to provide the answers itself. This unusual technique allows the poetry to introduce new, perhaps startling, concepts as if they were well established; presenting a rhetorical question as if the answer were perfectly obvious, while at the same time guiding the reader towards the desired,

---

[226] R. Alter, *Hebrew Bible* (2019), 762.

[227] See J. L. McKenzie, *Second Isaiah* (1968), 48, who observes "Obviously the tone of the 'Book of Consolations' is changed in this poem. The discourse of Second Isaiah is not a simple statement that everything is going to be all right now that the worst is over."

[228] For further discussion of this motif, see Michael De Roche, "Yahweh's *RÎB* Against Israel: A Reassessment of the So-Called Prophetic Lawsuit in the Preexilic Prophets," *JBL* 102 (1983): 564, who helpfully distinguishes between the terminology and practice of ancient Israel and the assumption of modern courtroom dynamics often implicit in our use of these terms. He points to the term *rîb* meaning "confronting someone with a complaint" (571), which helpfully captures the emotional elements of this encounter.

*Isaiah 43:1–21*

89

often entirely unexpected conclusion."[229] Military and violent images (e.g. 42:25; 43:28) color the wrathful tone particularly darkly adding emotional freight and intimating danger to the object of the divine rage. These elements together work to produce a tone that in some poems offers the audience a particularly harrowing encounter with a wrathful divine speaker. The juxtaposition between this tone and the other major tones of the divine speaking voice (see A Closer Look: The Majestic Divine Speaker and A Closer Look: The Voice of Comfort)[230] produces a powerful poetic persuasive effect. By setting the consequences of the audience's resistance in sharp relief with the offered reconciliation, the poems together urge the audience to embrace renewed relationship. Additionally, the power of each of these tones reinforces the reliability of the divine voice and its ability to carry out both punishment and promise.

ISAIAH 43:1–21

> [1] But now thus says the LORD,
>> he who created you, O Jacob,
>> he who formed you, O Israel:
> Do not fear, for I have redeemed you;
>> I have called you by name; you are mine.
> [2] When you pass through the waters, I will be with you,
>> and through the rivers, they shall not overwhelm you;
> when you walk through fire you shall not be burned,
>> and the flame shall not consume you.
> [3] For I am the LORD your God,
>> the Holy One of Israel, your Savior.
> I give Egypt as your ransom,
>> Cush and Seba in exchange for you.
> [4] Because you are precious in my sight
>> and honored and I love you,

---

[229] Sharon Moughtin-Mumby, *Sexual and Marital Metaphors in Hosea, Jeremiah, Isaiah, and Ezekiel* (Oxford: Oxford University Press, 2008), 125.

[230] Further description of these three major tonalities of the divine speaking voice in Isaiah 40–55 appears in K. M. Heffelfinger, *I Am Large* (2011), 176–193.

I give people in return for you,
nations in exchange for your life.
⁵ Do not fear, for I am with you;
I will bring your offspring from the east,
and from the west I will gather you;
⁶ I will say to the north, "Give them up,"
and to the south, "Do not withhold;
bring my sons from far away
and my daughters from the end of the earth –
⁷ everyone who is called by my name,
whom I created for my glory,
whom I formed and made."

⁸ Bring forth the people who are blind yet have eyes,
who are deaf yet have ears!
⁹ Let all the nations gather together,
and let the peoples assemble.
Who among them declared this
and foretold to us the former things?
Let them bring their witnesses to justify them,
and let them hear and say, "It is true."
¹⁰ You are my witnesses, says the LORD,
and my servant whom I have chosen,
so that you may know and believe me
and understand that I am he.
Before me no god was formed,
nor shall there be any after me.
¹¹ I, I am the LORD,
and besides me there is no savior.
¹² I am the one who declared and saved and proclaimed,
not some strange god among you;
you are my witnesses, says the LORD, and I am God.
¹³ Indeed, since that day I am he;
there is no one who can deliver from my hand;
I work, and who can hinder it?

¹⁴ Thus says the LORD,
your Redeemer, the Holy One of Israel:

*Isaiah 43:1–21*  91

For your sake I will send to Babylon
    and break down all the bars,
    and the shouting of the Chaldeans will be turned to lamentation.
[15] I am the LORD, your Holy One,
    the Creator of Israel, your King.
[16] Thus says the LORD,
    who makes a way in the sea,
    a path in the mighty waters,
[17] who brings out chariot and horse,
    army and warrior;
they lie down; they cannot rise;
    they are extinguished, quenched like a wick:
[18] Do not remember the former things
    or consider the things of old.
[19] I am about to do a new thing;
    now it springs forth; do you not perceive it?
I will make a way in the wilderness
    and rivers in the desert.
[20] The wild animals will honor me,
    the jackals and the ostriches,
for I give water in the wilderness,
    rivers in the desert,
to give drink to my chosen people,
    [21] the people whom I formed for myself
    so that they might declare my praise.[231]

This intensely comforting poem moves through shifts and shades of tone in the divine speaking voice. Throughout, the speaker is Israel's God, and the divine voice focuses on the intention to restore the addressees. In offering reassurance, the divine speaker emphasizes relationship and draws upon a rich vocabulary of deliverance through allusion. The opening (vv. 1–7) and closing (vv. 14–21) sections echo one another with the closing section building upon and developing the themes of the

---

[231] My lineation departs from that of the NRSV[ue] here. It is unnecessary to treat the final line as a monocolon. It is better understood as the final line of a triplet.

92                                                                    *Commentary*

opening section.[232] Those who are "formed" and called by God (v. 7), are "formed" to "declare" God's "praise" (v. 21), thus developing the imagery in its repetition. The central verses (vv. 8–13) of this poem, by contrast, pick up motifs of divine power, rhetorical questions, the LORD's uniqueness, and charges against those who "have eyes" but cannot see (v. 8). These elements of a more indicting tone, firmly embedded within an immediate context of consolation and deliverance, do not progress to outright indictment but do magnify both the potency of the militaristic metaphors used to express deliverance and the urgency of the audience's role in expressing the divine glory (v. 21).

The poem's opening unit lays considerable emphasis on the relationship between the divine speaker and the audience.[233] The opening lines characterize the one speaking as the one "who created you" and "who formed you" (43:1). These characterizations give way to a short threefold recital – "I have redeemed you," "I have called you by name," "you are mine" (43:1) – and quickly progress to promises of what the divine speaker will do.[234] This intention to act on the audience's behalf dominates the remainder of this unit, which is punctuated by periodic reminders that the audience belongs to God (43:3, 7). Within the structure of opening and closing emphasis upon the fact that the audience have been created and formed by and for God, the unit moves through imagistic depictions of restoration.

The first of these images, fire and flood, juxtaposes opposing dangers from the natural world. It is not necessary to see each of these as referring to some specific condition of the exiles' situation or some aspect of Israel's

---

[232]  This may be considered a faint inclusio (see Glossary of Poetic Terminology) structure. The echo moves the thought along developing it (see "parallelism," in Glossary of Poetic Terminology]. A number of commentators, e.g., C. Westermann, *Isaiah 40–66* (1969), 115; and J. Goldingay and D. Payne, *Isaiah 40–55* (2006) 1:270, treat vv. 1–7 as a separate unit and comment on its internal parallel between opening and closing sections. The return to the opening motifs in vv. 14–21 offer support for considering them together, as is done here, regardless of their possible original independence.

[233]  J. Goldingay and D. Payne, *Isaiah 40–55* (2006), 1:273, also note the relational quality of these lines.

[234]  K. Baltzer, *Deutero-Isaiah* (2001), 156–157, discusses the claim "I have called you by name" with reference to "the installation accounts of prophets" (156). While I am not convinced by this entire argument, not least because of the non-fit of "redeemed" into this paradigm as discussed by Baltzer (158), the idea that Israel is called in an important sense to act as proclaimers (the text uses the term "witnesses") fits well with the aims of this passage, as does Baltzer's comment that "To give a name is also to give a charge and an authorization . . .. It is true for every single individual among God's people" (157).

*Isaiah 43:1–21*

history. Rather, water and fire vividly portray potential danger.[235] Each is powerful and potentially destructive (see, e.g., fire in Judg 1:8; 9:15; 14:15; 15:5; Isa 1:7; Amos 1:4, 7, 10, 12, 14; and water in Ps 69:2 [Heb. 69:3]; 88:17 [Heb. 88:18]; 124:4–5; Isa 28:7; Job 27:20; Lam 3:54). Each has a connection with judgment in biblical passages (see, e.g., fire in Gen 19:24; Lev 10:1–2; Num 11:1–3; Deut 32:22; Ps 11:6; Isa 47:14; 50:11; 66:15–16, 24; and water in Gen 6:17; Hos 5:10). Each has the ability to evoke fear. Yet, precisely in this context, the divine voice forbids fear (43:1, 5) and promises God's own presence (v. 1) and commitment (v. 3) (see Bridging the Horizons: Fear Not).

The second depiction of restoration surrounds a threefold repetition of verbs conveying the LORD's special relationship of care and concern for the audience ("you are precious . . . and honored," "I love you," v. 4a) with specific (Egypt, Ethiopia, and Sheba, v. 3b) and then general (people, nations, v. 4b) expressions of a divine "exchange" (*taḥtêkā*). While numerous commentators helpfully observe the invasion of these north African nations by the Persians, which takes place under Cambyses,[236] in context the nations must be seen to convey distance[237] and the costliness (i.e., value) of Israel. As Muilenburg notes, "Here Yahweh is to give the wealthy peoples in exchange for his beloved people, and it is a heavy price he is to pay. This measures how precious a treasure Israel is to him. Literalistic interpretations do violence to the meaning."[238]

In the third image of restoration, the divine voice promises to bring people from each of the points of the compass. Again, the poetry does not point to the need to identify exiles in each of these directions and the nations from which they might be returning.[239] As Westermann writes, "Deutero-Isaiah's language is often sweeping and extravagant, and we would do him an injustice if we attempted to specify the four quarters geographically or politically."[240] Like fire and flood, which together as opposites convey the whole of what might be feared in the natural world

---

[235] See J. Muilenburg, "Isaiah 40–66" (1956), 5:481–482.

[236] See, e.g., J. Muilenburg, "Isaiah 40–66" (1956), 483; J. D. W. Watts, *Isaiah 34–66* (2005), 133.

[237] See J. Goldingay and D. Payne, *Isaiah 40–55* (2006), 1:276.

[238] J. Muilenburg, "Isaiah 40–66" (1956), 5:483. See also B. S. Childs, *Isaiah* (2001), 334–335.

[239] R. Alter, *Hebrew Bible* (2019), 763, makes this point, calling "the point of invoking the four points of the compass . . . the sweep of poetic hyperbole."

[240] C. Westermann, *Isaiah 40–66* (1969), 119.

94                                                    *Commentary*

(see "merism," in Glossary of Poetic Terminology], north, south, east, and west, together cast a wide vision of God's intentions to restore.[241] All of those who belong to the LORD are to be restored.[242]

Following such an expansive and intensely reassuring encounter with the divine speaker, the command to "Bring forth" the blind and deaf creates a jarring juxtaposition. It calls to mind the immediately preceding poem with its claims that the LORD's servant is blind (42:19) and its indictment against the audience for their failure to "observe" (42:20) and "understand" (42:25) what they see and hear.[243] In this context, the poetry suggests through juxtaposition that the "blind" who "have eyes" and the "deaf" who "have ears" (43:8) are the audience themselves. The poem imagistically places the audience among a throng of nations whom the divine voice rhetorically interrogates appealing for witnesses (43:9b).

The repetitive and emphatic "you are my witnesses, says the LORD" (43:10 and 12) places the audience in direct contrast in two directions. They contrast with the nations, whose witnesses are implicitly nonexistent and for whom no answer is supplied to the query "who among them declared this" (43:9), and the LORD who "declared and saved and proclaimed" (43:12).[244] The final line of v. 12 neatly encapsulates the emphases of this unit: "you are my witnesses, says the LORD, and I am God." Here the people's commission to be witnesses, paired with the echoes of previous indictments of their failure to do so, appear in significant tension with the emphatic self-reference of the divine voice.

While the people do not appear to have fully embraced and understood their commission to testify to the power and singularity of the LORD, the divine voice insists upon God's own uniqueness. Expansive self-references dominate 43:10b–13. "I am he" (*'anî hû'*) is the first (43:10)

---

[241]  J. Goldingay and D. Payne, *Isaiah 40–55* (2006), 1:278, likewise call this a "merism." They further observe that the male and female (sons and daughters) reference "generates a further merism" (279).

[242]  C. Westermann, *Isaiah 40–66* (1969), 119.

[243]  J. Goldingay and D. Payne, *Isaiah 40–55* (2006), 1:283, similarly read the image in line with its appearance in Isaiah 42.

[244]  See J. Goldingay and D. Payne, *Isaiah 40–55* (2006), 1:282. While I agree with Goldingay and Payne that the other side's witnesses "have never really appeared," I see this as precisely a part of the poetry's appeal to the audience.

# Isaiah 43:1–21 95

and last (43:13) of the nominal phrases conveying God's uniqueness in these verses.[245] A neatly parallel couplet presents the LORD's uniqueness in time, insisting there is nothing either "before" or "after," and drawing upon the language previously deployed for God's creation of the audience, "no god was formed." A longer form of the personal pronoun (*'ānōkî*) appears, repetitively adding emphasis to successive couplets. The doubled self-reference in the announcement "I, I am the LORD" stands in contrastive parallel to the denial of the existence of any other savior (43:11). The word translated "besides me" is relatively rare. Of seventeen references in the Hebrew Bible, five appear in Isaiah 43–45, all of which indicate that there is no other god. This heavy concentration in Isaiah 43–45 reveals the emphasis upon the LORD's uniqueness in these chapters. The following couplet (43:12) opens by repeating the emphasis on the divine speaking subject, again deploying "I" (*'ānōkî*) emphatically, this time using it to govern three active verbs expressing the LORD's past activities.[246] This abundance of action stands in stark contrast to the parallel line, which lacks any verbal form and which denies the existence of that which it does not fully name.[247] Following the direct contrast between the audience as witnesses and the LORD as God, an intense and powerful triplet draws this portion of the poem to a close. The difficult phrase "Indeed, since that day" (*gam-mîyôm*), forms a repetitive sound play with "from my hand" (*mîyādî*) and "who" (*mî*).[248] The final rhetorical question, along with the reference to the divine hand, conveys power and the certain accomplishment of the LORD's aims. There is no other, and the speaking voice has insisted on its own presence, vitality, and effectiveness.

---

[245] J. Goldingay and D. Payne, *Isaiah 40–55* (2006), 1:281, comment on vv. 8–13, "The prominence of the divine 'I' is noteworthy."

[246] The pronoun is emphatic because Hebrew verbs are marked for the person and number of their subject. In this case, all three active verbs are marked as having first person singular subjects. The personal pronoun "I" here is not needed to convey "I" as subject but adds significant emphasis, particularly following the repetitive use of the same form in the preceding line. J. Goldingay and D. Payne, *Isaiah 40–55* (2006), 1:288, also note that this pronoun is emphatic.

[247] The NRSV[ue] translates "strange god" here for *zār* which simply means "strange" or "foreign."

[248] For discussion of the possibilities for reading this phrase, see further J. Goldingay and D. Payne, *Isaiah 40–55* (2006), 1:289–290.

96                                                                Commentary

The poem returns to its opening motifs but with significant differences. In poetically recasting Israel's testimony to who the LORD is, this poem offers a new Isaianic vision of God's work. The majestic and powerful divine speaker's self-references have colored the tone. They underscore the power of the speaker placing the promises of deliverance in an explicit context of divine might. Now, the historical enemies fade, and the exiles' own context is in view. Both Babylon and Chaldea refer to those who held the exiles away from their homes. Now the powerful redeemer (43:1), who has expressed to the audience that they are precious and loved (43:4), is turning those enemies' triumph to misery (43:14). The LORD, who commands that the exiles look only to what God is now doing, does so ironically.[249] The voice that commands "Do not remember the former things" (43:18) is precisely the one who introduces that speech by referring to the events of the Exodus, particularly through the language of the triumphant Song of the Sea (Exodus 15:1–18) (see A Closer Look: Conflicted Commands and Competing Contentions in the Memory Motif).[250] The wilderness is again transformed with images of water and rivers echoing the promise of protection from earlier in the poem (43:2). Divine might, emphasized in the center of the poem, here offers assurance that the LORD can accomplish the promised deliverance. The echoes of the mighty divine deliverance from Egypt underscore this idea. At the same time, the poem concludes with the insistence, again drawing upon the central section, that the people whom the LORD has "formed" are delivered and sustained so that they might "declare" God's praise.[251]

---

[249] Contra C. Westermann, *Isaiah 40–66* (1969), 128, it is not satisfactory to read "Do not remember" as a prohibition specifically of remembering in the course of lament. The precisely opposed phrasings of "Do not remember the former things" (43:18) and "remember the former things" (46:9) demand a reading that accounts for both (see A Closer Look: Conflicted Commands and Competing Contentions in the Memory Motif). As B. S. Childs, *Isaiah* (2001), 336–337, comments, "That this prophetic rhetoric is dialogical and not absolute is made clear in the succeeding verses with the exactly opposite admonition."

[250] Resonances with the language of Exodus 15 include: "sea" (*yām*, Isa 43:16, Exod 15:1, 4, 8, 10, 11), "chariot and horse" (*rekeb-wāsûs*, Isa 43:17; cf. "horse and rider" *sûs wĕrōkĕbô*; Exod 15:1, "chariots" *markĕbōt*, Exod 15:4), "army" (*ḥayil*, Isa 43:17; *ḥêlô*, Exod 15:4), and "the people whom" (*'am-zû*, Isa 43:21; Exod 15:13, 16). See C. Westermann, *Isaiah 40–66* (1969), 127; J. Goldingay and D. Payne, *Isaiah 40–55* (2006), 1:297; J. Blenkinsopp, *Isaiah 40–55* (2002), 227; and J. Muilenburg, "Isaiah 40–66" (1956), 5:495.

[251] C. Westermann, *Isaiah 40–66* (1969), 119, commenting on v. 7, makes a similar claim.

# ISAIAH 43:22–28

[22] Yet you did not call upon me, O Jacob;
   but you have been weary of me, O Israel!
[23] You have not brought me your sheep for burnt offerings
   or honored me with your sacrifices.
I have not burdened you with offerings
   or wearied you with frankincense.
[24] You have not bought me sweet cane with money
   or satisfied me with the fat of your sacrifices.
Rather, you have burdened me with your sins;
   you have wearied me with your iniquities.

[25] I alone am the one
   who blots out your transgressions for my own sake,
   and I will not remember your sins.
[26] Accuse me; let us go to trial;
   set forth your case, so that you may be proved right.
[27] Your first ancestor sinned,
   and your mediators rebelled against me.
[28] Therefore I profaned the princes of the sanctuary;
   I delivered Jacob to utter destruction
   and Israel to reviling.

Juxtaposition with two comforting poems (43:1–21 and 44:1–5) intensifies the stinging indictment of this short poem.[252] Confrontational repetition, irony, legal imagery, and vivid images of punishment combine to create for the exilic audience a fearsome encounter with the divine voice (see A Closer Look: Indictment, Sarcasm, and Rhetorical Questions and "tone," in Glossary of Poetic Terminology). In light of the juxtaposition with comfort passages, this fearsome encounter seems designed to motivate the audience's positive response to the proclaimed coming divine comfort. However, despite a likely comforting ultimate rhetorical aim, this passage's fearsomeness should not be overlooked. It stands as a testimony to the

---

[252] See John Goldingay, "Isaiah 43, 22–28," *ZAW* 110 (1998): 173; J. L. McKenzie, *Second Isaiah* (1968), 60; and J. Blenkinsopp, *Isaiah 40–55* (2002), 230.

98 Commentary

poetic tension of these poems and their use of intense encounters to facilitate ultimate reconciliation.

The poem divides into two units. The first focuses almost exclusively on what the audience has not done, while the second focuses heavily on what the LORD does and will do. This contrast between the LORD and the audience pervades the poem and conveys its confrontational tone. The word "no" begins each of the four couplets in verses 22–24a. This repetition emphasizes the tone of indictment. Commentators debate the meaning of these charges with many pointing out that sacrifice would not have been possible during the exile as the Temple was destroyed.[253] McKenzie seems to be right in concluding "We know in fact very little about the cultic practices followed by Jews resident in Babylon; the passage suggests that the prophet did not regard them as fulfilling the duty of the cult."[254] Given the emphasis on the LORD as the object of their inactivity (v. 22), worship of idols also seems a plausible implication in these charges.[255] That the LORD is the offended party is also made emphatically clear by the poetry's form. The first words of the poem, $w\check{e}l\bar{o}$ '- '$\bar{o}t\hat{i}$ (i.e., "not with me," NRSV[ue] translates "you did not," 43:22), place the object of the verbal (in)action first, violating the more common word order and resoundingly calling attention to the LORD as both speaker and as the one who has not been attended to appropriately by the audience.[256] The second half of this opening couplet introduces a motif that will run through these opening charges of inaction. That motif, weariness, will appear in the second half of alternate couplets throughout the rest of this first unit of the poem.

---

[253]  See, e.g., J. Muilenburg, "Isaiah 40–66" (1956), 5:498–499; J. McKenzie, *Second Isaiah* (1968), 60.

[254]  J. McKenzie, *Second Isaiah* (1968), 60–61.

[255]  J. Goldingay and D. Payne, *Isaiah 40–55* (2006), 1:308–309, raise, but dismiss this possibility. J. Blenkinsopp, *Isaiah 40–55* (2002), 231, likewise rejects idolatry as the meaning of the charges because, while plausible in the historical context, it is not specifically named as non-Yahwistic here as it is "In every instance" (231). However, it seems likely that the word order of 43:22 implies a problem with the neglect of the LORD and given the allusive nature of this poet's style, this seems a reasonable objection to Blenkinsopp's observation.

[256]  See J. Goldingay, "Isaiah 43, 22–28" (1998), 176; and J. Goldingay and D. Payne, *Isaiah 40–55* (2006), 1:307, who point out this "suggests that Israel's problem lies not in a failure to call but in the direction of its calling." See also K. Baltzer, *Deutero-Isaiah* (2001), 177; and J. D. W. Watts, *Isaiah 34–66* (2005), 144.

*Isaiah 43:22–28*  99

The patterned interjection of the verb meaning "to be weary" (*yg*ʿ) presents a challenging irony. The audience "have been weary of me" (43:22), but the divine voice has not "wearied" them (43:23). Finally, the audience has "wearied" the divine speaker (43:24), not with sacrifices, which have been in view up to this point, but with their "iniquities." The parallel claim, "I have not burdened you" (43:23) and "you have burdened me" (43:24) highlights the contrast between the audience and the divine speaker here. The verb for "to burden" here is a causative form of the verb "to serve," the verb whose noun form has conveyed the audience's special calling by and relationship to God, my servant.[257] They, the servant, have not been made to serve with offerings but have instead made the LORD serve through their transgression (43:24). They have reversed the divine and human roles, an irony that points to the precarious situation in which they will find themselves, should they take up the challenge in the following line's, "Accuse me" (43:26).[258]

The tone of indictment, thick with irony, intensifies as the divine voice turns from focusing on what the audience has not done to what the LORD does. In the first stanza, the audience were the subjects of all verbs except "I have not burdened" and "[I have not] wearied" (43:23). In vv. 25–28, the LORD is the subject of all the verbs except the imperatives "Accuse me," and "set forth" and the references to past sins v. 27. As the LORD moves from primarily the object of inaction to subject of the lines, the emphatic double self-reference reappears, taking the same form as it did in 43:11 (ʾ*ānōkî*, ʾ*ānōkî*). The repetition calls to mind the earlier proclamations of divine power and exclusivity, not least "there is no one who can deliver from my hand" (43:13). In the context of the current indictment, such an insistence is portentous. While the notion that the LORD is the one who blots out transgressions belongs to a comforting and restorative trajectory, such a sense is immediately undermined by the divine voice's insistence that such obliteration is "for my own sake."[259] Similarly, "I will not

---

[257] See further C. Westermann, *Isaiah 40–66* (1969), 131. On the relationship of the Servant and Israel, see further A Closer Look: The Servant and His "Songs."

[258] See C. Westermann, *Isaiah 40–66* (1969), 131, who calls this a "reversal of the natural relationship between God and man, in which God is lord and man is God's servant"; and K. Baltzer, *Deutero-Isaiah* (2001), 179.

[259] See J. Goldingay, "Isaiah 43, 22–28" (1998), 175, who indicates that verse 25 might be more "confrontational" than it is typically considered to be.

100                                                                   *Commentary*

remember your sins" (*lō ʾ ʾezkōr*, 43:25) stands juxtaposed to an invitation (*hazkîrēnî*, i.e., "remind me," 43:26; cf. NRSV[ue], which translates "Accuse me" 43:26). Far from an open invitation to reach a mutually agreeable settlement, it is clear that in this context the verdict is certain and will not be in the audience's favor.[260] The couplet employs legal imagery but does so in a way that continues the comparison of vv. 22–24. "Accuse," "trial," and "case" are each translations that reflect a legal interpretation of 43:26. While I would not dispute that there is a courtroom motif being employed in this context, the text's reference to memory (43:26) and an apparent invitation to judgment (*niššāpĕṭâ yāḥad*, i.e, woodenly, "let us be judged together"; cf. NRSV[ue]'s "let us go to trial"), point to the comparison already at hand between what the LORD has done and what the audience have failed to do. This is a judgment between the LORD and the exiles, and the comparison does not reflect well on the audience. They can "set forth" (*sappēr*) for themselves, but the very words used here indict them once again as they were to "declare" (*yĕsapērû*, i.e., "set forth") the LORD's praise (43:21), something they apparently have not done in a context that censures them for their lack of sacrifices (vv. 22–24). Such a conclusion is confirmed by the divine voice tracing the trouble back to the audience's ancestral history, likely alluding to the tradition that Hosea 12:2–4 knows (see further A Closer Look: Jacob-Israel and the Exiles).[261]

This poem's closing triplet presents a terrifying image of judgment. The verbs indicate incomplete action and offer the possibility of being read as an expression of impending judgment for the audience.[262] The image of the

---

[260]  Against J. Muilenburg, "Isaiah 40–66" (1956), 5:500, who says "Israel will have the opportunity to state its case," I agree with J. Goldingay, "Isaiah 43, 22–28" (1998), 187, who points to the "ironic tone" of this invitation to "remind" the LORD and the likelihood that such a reminder will result in self-incrimination.

[261]  Against J. Blenkinsopp, *Isaiah 40–55* (2002), 232, it does seem that Hos 12 knows of some traditional association of transgression with Jacob as C. Westermann, *Isaiah 40–66* (1969), 133; and J. L. McKenzie, *Second Isaiah* (1968), 59, indicate. K. Baltzer, *Deutero-Isaiah* (2001), 180–182, considers a number of parallels with the Jacob story.

[262]  NRSV[ue], along with several commentators (e.g., J. L. McKenzie, *Second Isaiah* [1968], 58; and K. Baltzer, *Deutero-Isaiah* [2001], 176, who indicates his reading is in agreement with the Septuagint) appears to be following an emendation that takes the verbs as narrative past. While this is a reasonable emendation of the Masoretic text and requires only the change of vowels, it is not necessary and undermines the impact of the lines. Jacob and Israel have not been utterly annihilated as a completed action reading of *ḥērem* would indicate, as they are the audience of the poem itself. For an overview of the Septuagint and Masoretic Text arguments here, see Philip D. Stern, *The Biblical Ḥerem:*

*Isaiah 43:22–28*

LORD "profan[ing] the princes of the sanctuary" (employing the noun form of the adjective for "holy" used for "your Holy One" in v. 15) contains both a potential double entendre and significant irony. The idea that the "Holy One" could and would "profane" something is challenging. In addition, the verb "profane" can mean both this sense of defiling and to pierce.[263] The image blurs the lines between violence and removal of sacredness and it seems likely that both are implied as expressions of divine wrath.[264]

Such a suspicion is supported by a similar overlap of meanings in the second element of this triplet. The idea of "utter destruction" to which the LORD will give Jacob employs the concept of "the ban" (Hebrew *ḥērem*). This image of total destruction in the context of holy war carries both the ideas of sacrifice, an element that cannot be overlooked in the context of vv. 22–24, and extreme violence.[265] Opening and closing references to the audience by the names Jacob and Israel in parallel lend a sense of totality to the poem.[266] What opened with an indictment of Jacob-Israel for failure to serve with "sacrifices" (43:23, 24), concludes with a punishment that is violent and alludes to sacrifice.

These lines (43:22–28) are among those that complicate the notion that the exilic chapters of Isaiah proclaim, "nothing but salvation."[267] While their location between comforting poems appears to function to intensify the invitation to accept the LORD's promised reconciliation and restoration, they also disclose a significant tension within the book. They stand as indicting and violent lines in their own right and their juxtaposition with other tones in the divine speaking voice serves to intensify their potency.

---

*A Window on Israel's Religious Experience* (Atlanta: Scholars Press, 1991), https://doi-org.elib.tcd.ie/10.26300/81mj-et71, location 379.

[263] BDB, 319–320.

[264] On the literary features of this line, see further P. D. Stern, *The Biblical Ḥerem* (1991), location 380; and K. M. Heffelfinger, *I Am Large* (2009), 213–215.

[265] See J. Goldingay and D. Payne, *Isaiah 40–55* (2006), 1:318; and P. D. Stern, *Biblical Ḥerem* (1991), location 382.

[266] As J. Goldingay and D. Payne, *Isaiah 40–55* (2006), 1:308, note of the Jacob-Israel references in v. 22: "There are no friendly epithets such as 'my servant'/'my chosen' here."

[267] C. Westermann, *Isaiah 40–66* (1969), 9.

102                                                                   *Commentary*

ISAIAH 44:1–5

¹ But now hear, O Jacob my servant,
       Israel whom I have chosen!
² Thus says the LORD who made you,
       who formed you in the womb and will help you:
Do not fear, O Jacob my servant,
       Jeshurun whom I have chosen.
³ For I will pour water on the thirsty land
       and streams on the dry ground;
I will pour my spirit upon your descendants
       and my blessing on your offspring.
⁴ They shall spring up like a green tamarisk,
       like willows by flowing streams.
⁵ This one will say, "I am the LORD's";
       another will be called by the name of Jacob;
yet another will write on the hand, "The LORD's";
       and adopt the name of Israel.

In this short poem, the divine voice picks up motifs that have appeared already in passages about the servant and progresses them through parallelism.[268] The audience are offered a vision of themselves as servant that moves from the divine claim that they belong to the LORD to the point of casting a vision of a future in which they will embrace that belonging for themselves.

Repetition of titles for Jacob call attention to this poem's focus on the audience and their relationship with the LORD. Very closely paralleled couplets employ identical phrasing of some elements ("my servant" *'abdî*, and "whom I have chosen" *bāḥartî bô*, 44:1, 2). These identical phrasings call attention to the close resemblance of these couplets, separated by just one intervening couplet. This parallelism highlights the distinctions between these occurrences through contrast.[269] Those distinctions include a progression from the call to "hear" (v. 1), to an injunction against "fear"

---

[268] Parallelism is more than repetition (see further "parallelism," in Glossary of Poetic Terminology).
[269] J. Goldingay and D. Payne, *Isaiah 40–55* (2006), 1:322, similarly highlight both the "parallelism" and the "different imperative."

*Isaiah 44:1–5*　103

(v. 2), a reversal of the ordering of the elements *ya ʿăqōb ʿabdî* ("Jacob, my servant," v. 1,) and *ʿabdî ya ʿăqōb* (i.e., "my servant, Jacob"; cf. NRSV[ue] "O Jacob, my servant," v. 2), and, perhaps most significantly, a change of the second name for the audience from Israel (v. 1) to Jeshurun (v. 2).

The transition from Israel to Jeshurun appears to continue a play on Jacob's name begun in Isaiah 40. There, the anonymous calling voice cast a vision of transformation of "the rough places" (*he ʿāqōb*) being leveled (*lĕmîšôr*, i.e., "to a plain," NRSV[ue] "and the rough places a plain"). Given the allusive nature of the opening poem, it is not hard to suspect that the choice of the word otherwise unattested with the meaning "rough places," which is derived from the same verb as Jacob and is employed in the etymology of Jacob's name in Genesis, is lurking in this usage. The adjective *ʿāqōb* appears in Jer 17:9 where the NRSV[ue] translates "devious" and in Hosea 6:8 where it relates to the noun meaning heel. The story of Jacob draws on both of these meanings as he is born grasping his brother's heel (Gen 25:26) and Esau responds to Jacob tricking their father into giving him the blessing with the words "Is he not rightly named Jacob? For he has supplanted me these two times" (Gen 27:36). Similarly, the word *lĕmîšôr* (i.e., "to a plain") conveys both "a level place" and "uprightness" and derives from the same root as Jeshurun.[270] This name for Israel is unusual and appears designed to convey a meaning close to "upright one." This name appears only in this passage and in Deuteronomy 32 and 33. It is not possible to determine to what extent the meaning here relates to that other usage. It seems most probable that the prophetic poet here is playing both with the tradition that Jacob's name was changed by God (Gen 32:28) and the use already made of this term in connection to a transformation of that which is "rough" or "devious" to that which is "smooth" and "upright." Thus, the parallelism moves the audience from being addressed as "Jacob my servant, Israel whom I have chosen" (44:1) to "my servant" and "Jeshurun whom I have chosen" (44:2). Transformed again from the one who "has striven with God" (Gen 32:28), they are invited to see themselves as embracing the titles "servant" and "chosen" and thus to be appropriately called "upright."

That motif of embrace of the attributions spoken by the divine voice progresses further in the final two couplets of this short poem. Here, the

---

[270]　BDB, 449.

104            *Commentary*

idea of being called by name and belonging to the LORD reappears. This idea had been expressed by the LORD in Isa 43:1 "I have called you by name; you are mine" a verse that finds a number of other verbal echoes in this poem. "Do not fear" (43:1, 44:2), "Thus says the LORD" (43:1, 44:2), "formed you" (43:1, 44:2), and "called" (43:1)/ "be called" (44:5), while common enough Second Isaian vocabulary, express a strong link between these two passages. Here, in an a pattern that alternates between self-attribution of belonging to the LORD (*layhvāh 'ānî*, "I am the LORD's," and *layhvāh*, "The LORD's," 44:5) and references to the "name of" Jacob and "name of" Israel, the poem offers a vision of the future in which "I have called you by name, you are mine" (43:1) becomes the people's own testimony about themselves, likely on the lips of their descendants (vv. 3–4).

There is progression within the parallelism of these two couplets as well. They do not simply repeat the belonging and name motifs. Instead, the second couplet employs a visual image for belonging that moves beyond speaking to marking oneself. The image of writing on the hand, though employing different words, will find an echo in the LORD's words to Zion in Isa 49:16 "I have inscribed you on the palms of my hands." Likewise, the language "adopt" the name of Israel employs a rare term that conveys a laudable title.[271] In each of these images, the poetry progresses the motif from the LORD's attribution (44:1, 2), to the audience's own embrace of that attribution (44:5a), to an intensification of that embrace (44:5b). In this way, the poetry presents to the audience's imagination a vision of their own acceptance of the LORD's vision for them.[272]

The center of the poem is loosely chiastically structured (see "chiasm," in Glossary of Poetic Terminology), placing the audience's "descendants" in focus. Heavy alliteration of ṣ and ʾ sounds bind these lines together and

---

[271]   The verb is used for the LORD's naming of Cyrus in 45:4 (NRSV[ue] "give you a title") and in Job 32:21–22 where the NRSV[ue] translates "flattery" and "flatter." BDB, 487, supplies the meaning "betitle, title, give an epithet or cognomen."

[272]   This approach contrasts with readings that focus on converts to the religion of the LORD's people. See J. Blenkinsopp, *Isaiah 40–55* (2002), 233; and C. Westermann, *Isaiah 40–66* (1969), 136. Given the reference to "your descendants" and the clearly metaphorical nature of the passage, it seems plausible to read these references to taking on an identity as one who belongs to the LORD in the manner indicated above. Scholars who point to the importance of context here for an Israel-focused reading include J. D. W. Watts, *Isaiah 34–66* (2005), 145; and J. Goldingay and D. Payne, *Isaiah 40–55* (2006), 1:327.

*Isaiah 44:6–22*

give them further cohesion. Water (*mayim*, v. 3, *māyim*, v. 4) and the similar sounding "thirsty" (*ṣāmē*ʾ, v. 3) and "spring up" (*ṣāmĕḥû*, v. 4) form the frame. The promise to "pour water" (ʾ*eṣṣāq-mayim*, v. 3) is repeated in the promise to "pour my spirit" (ʾ*eṣṣōq rûḥî*, v. 3). The "descendants" are figured using imagery that also conveys transformation through parallelism. They are "offspring" (*ṣeʾĕṣāʾêkā*), which in a previous servant passage seems to convey what grows out of the earth (cf. 42:5), and they will "spring up" like herbage.[273] The word that appears here is a term for grass (*ḥāṣîr*)[274] that is already familiar to the audience of Isaiah 40–55 as the element of the landscape to which they were compared in Isaiah 40:6, 7, and 8. There, the sense of the impermanence of grasses was conveyed. Here, the reference to grass is parallel to "willows" and places this image within both the watering of the landscape and tree motifs, each of which convey restoration and the overturning of judgment (see further A Closer Look: The Reforestation Imagery of Isaiah 40–66 in the Context of the Book of Isaiah).[275]

This poem draws together multiple elements of the divine voice's vision of restoration spoken thus far and presents to the audience a glimpse of what it would look like to embrace it for themselves. The encounter this poem produces is not confrontational but rather visionary.[276] It projects a future in which the comfort promised by Isaiah 40's opening lines is a reality, and the people are formed into the servant into which the poems aim to shape them.

ISAIAH 44:6–22

⁶ Thus says the LORD, the King of Israel,
    and his Redeemer, the LORD of hosts:

---

[273] See also J. Goldingay and D. Payne, *Isaiah 40–55* (2006), 1:325.

[274] NRSV^ue's "tamarisk" here is a reading of a Qumran manuscript as indicated by NRSV^ue's footnote. On "grass" here, see also J. Goldingay and D. Payne, *Isaiah 40–55* (2006), 1:325.

[275] J. Goldingay and D. Payne, *Isaiah 40–55* (2006), 1:326, helpfully highlight "the connotation of transitoriness" to offer the idea "the prophet is again starting from the fact of the people's dried up, withered state. They will spring up in the midst of the evidence of witheredness and transience."

[276] Cf. J. Goldingay and D. Payne, *Isaiah 40–55* (2006), 1:320, who comment "Isaiah 44.1–5 need not refer to a more distant future than earlier oracles ... though it does use more imaginative speech."

I am the first, and I am the last;
> besides me there is no god.
⁷ Who is like me? Let them proclaim it;
> let them declare and set it forth before me.
Who has announced from of old the things to come?
> Let them tell us what is yet to be.
⁸ Do not fear, or be afraid;
>> have I not told you from of old and declared it?
>> You are my witnesses!
Is there any god besides me?
> There is no other rock; I know not one.
⁹ All who make idols are nothing,[277]
> and the things they delight in do not profit;
their witnesses neither see
> nor know,[278] and so they will be put to shame.
¹⁰ Who would fashion a god or cast an image
> that can do no good?
¹¹ All its devotees shall be put to shame;
> the artisans, too, are merely human.

---

[277] The NRSV^ue does not lineate vv. 9–20. However, these lines exhibit the same sorts of parallelism and other poetic features as does the majority of Second Isaiah. For that reason, I have lineated them here. B. S. Childs, *Isaiah* (2001), 343, notes "*BHS* has printed the text as poetry, a stylistic evaluation with increasing support (Muilenburg, Clifford, Beuken)." C. Westermann, *Isaiah 40–66* (1969), 148, also treats vv. 9–20 as poetry and describes them as exhibiting "deliberate parallelism." The relationship between scholars' opinions on whether the passage is poetry or prose and their consideration of the likelihood of its authenticity and original placement in this location is an interesting matter. J. Goldingay and D. Payne, *Isaiah 40–55* (2006), 1:333, helpfully observe that the connection between style and consideration of the passage as an addition is reflective of scholars' preference for "lyrical, imaginative poetry," which "encourages them to come to a negative aesthetic judgment on vv. 9–20." It is worth observing that discontinuities and shifts are a significant element of Second Isaiah's poetic style and should serve as grounds for considering these passages both poetic and participants in their larger Isaian context.

[278] The constructions *bal-yir'û* (i.e., "they do not see"; cf. NRSV^ue "neither see") and *bal-yēdĕ'û* (i.e., "they do not know"; cf. NRSV^ue "nor know") are neatly parallel and belong in paired lines. These constructions mirror "I know not one" (v. 8) and "do not profit" (v. 9). These are the only four negatives constructed this way in the poem. The MT's lineation appears to assess the situation in the same way. The translation given by the NRSV^ue obscures the parallelism.

*Isaiah 44:6–22*

Let them all assemble; let them stand up;
>they shall be terrified; they shall all be put to shame.
[12] The blacksmith works it
>with a tool over the coals,
shaping it with hammers
>and forging it with his strong arm;
he becomes hungry, and his strength fails;
>he drinks no water and is faint.
[13] The carpenter stretches a line,
>marks it out with a stylus,
fashions it with planes,
>and marks it with a compass;
he makes it in human form,
>with human beauty, to be set up in a shrine.
[14] He cuts down cedars
>or chooses a holm tree or an oak
and lets it grow strong among the trees of the forest.
>He plants a cedar and the rain nourishes it.
[15] Then it can be used as fuel.
>Part of it he takes and warms himself;
>he kindles a fire and bakes bread.
Then he makes a god and worships it,
>makes it a carved image and bows down before it.
[16] Half of it he burns in the fire;
>over this half he roasts meat, eats it, and is satisfied.
He also warms himself and says,
>"Ah, I am warm by the fire!"
[17] The rest of it he makes into a god, his idol,
>bows down to it and worships it;
he prays to it and says,
>"Save me, for you are my god!"
[18] They do not know, nor do they comprehend,
>for their eyes are shut, so that they cannot see,
>and their minds as well, so that they cannot understand.
[19] No one considers,
>nor is there knowledge or discernment to say,

108                                                              *Commentary*

"Half of it I burned in the fire;
> I also baked bread on its coals;
> I roasted meat and have eaten.
Now shall I make the rest of it an abomination?
> Shall I fall down before a block of wood?"
[20] He feeds on ashes; a deluded mind has led him astray,
> and he cannot save himself
> or say, "Is not this thing in my right hand a fraud?"[279]
[21] Remember these things, O Jacob,
> and Israel, for you are my servant;
I formed you, you are my servant;
> O Israel, do not forget me.
[22] I have swept away your transgressions like a cloud,
> and your sins like mist;
return to me, for I have redeemed you.

In this poem the divine voice addresses the audience applying God's own incomparability to the task of obliterating their fears. Opening and closing sections emphasize the LORD's role as redeemer and the audience's special relationship to God. The central section provides a parody of those whom the exiles apparently fear. By repetitively highlighting the utter ridiculousness of their behavior, the divine voice undermines their ability to instill fear.

An opening announcement from the divine voice employs familiar imagery and techniques to reiterate the incomparability of Israel's God. As has been the case frequently, the announcement of the divine voice's speaking "Thus says the LORD" (v. 6) is modified by descriptors glorifying the deity. While these descriptors often express the audience's special relationship with God (e.g. "who created you," 43:1, "who formed you," 43:1; "your Redeemer, the Holy One of Israel," 43:14; "who made you," 44:2), here the audience is referred to in the third person as the LORD is extolled as "King of Israel" and "his Redeemer." The pairing of these terms with "LORD of hosts" implies a militaristic set of images and underscores God's might. In the realm of world powers, this is Israel's king, the one

---

[279]  The clauses negating the verbs "save" and "say" are constructed in parallel fashion and it seems best to regard them as belonging in parallel lines.

*Isaiah 44:6–22*                                                                                       109

who leads Israel out of bondage and the one who commands armies. The LORD expresses God's own incomparability repeatedly and emphatically in this unit, drawing on the absence of witnesses to other gods as developed in 41:21–24 and 43:8–13, twice employing the term for uniqueness that appeared in 43:11 "besides me" (*mibbal'āday*, vv. 6 and 8) and deploying rhetorical questions ("Who" 44:7; "have I not," 44:8; and "Is there any," 44:8).

The turn toward the audience in this opening unit's only triplet flags up their fear as a central concern of the poem. Reversal of the expected order of terms, from the less familiar to the more familiar,[280] draws attention to this prohibition against fear[281] (see Bridging the Horizons: Fear Not). The LORD's incomparability, and reliability conveyed through the metaphor of a rock, provide an initial response to the audience's fear. However, the parody of the idol makers constitutes an extended response, a response designed to undermine the fearsomeness of their enemies both rhetorically and emotionally through humor.

Repetition, vivid depiction, and a heavily sarcastic tone combine to entirely undercut the idol makers' fearsomeness. Here the parody appears to be deployed against the audience's enemies. The depiction is not addressed to the audience as "you." Rather, the poem invites them to look

---

[280] I am reading *'al-tîr'û* (i.e., "do not fear") with 1QIsaᵃ. J. D. W. Watts, *Isaiah 34–66* (2005), 141; and J. Muilenburg, "Isaiah 40–66" (1956), 5:507, note their agreement with this ancient evidence. The MT's *'al-tirhû* is likely a textual error, perhaps caused by the following *hălo'*, which could supply both the extra *he* through dittography and the missing aleph by haplography. If MT is taken as correct it is the occurrence of an otherwise unattested verb in a context in which the common word for "fear" makes good sense and is commonly used in such situations within Second Isaiah. J. Goldingay and D. Payne, *Isaiah 40–55* (2006), 1:342, read this term as the otherwise unattested verb noting the intensification created by the pairing of rare words and the expectation of *tîr'û*. While the intensification is clear, textual error appears a more likely explanation here and the reversal of terms provides the intensification.

[281] It is a common claim in the study of biblical Hebrew poetry that parallelism moves from the more familiar to the less familiar. See, e.g., Robert Alter, *Art of Biblical Poetry* (New York: Basic Books, 1985), 13. Here, the relatively rare word *tiphădû* (i.e., "be in dread"; cf. NRSVᵘᵉ "fear"), appears prior to the common term *tîr'û* (i.e., "fear," NRSVᵘᵉ "be afraid"). Such a reversal conveys emphasis on the less common term and sets up the direct contrast between the audience who are commanded against fear here (*tiphădû*, 44:8) and the idol makers who will "be terrified" (*yiphădû*, 44:11). J. Goldingay and D. Payne, *Isaiah 40–55* (2006), 1:341, note that *phd* is the less common and thus potentially more intense. They treat it as preceding *yr'* in all cited examples, except one (p. 342). Notably, the one exception is the only Isian occurrence in their list (51:12–13).

at those who worship idols from the LORD's perspective. If there are temptations toward worship of other nations' gods, this polemic would be effective against those temptations. However, in this context it seems designed primarily to undermine the exiles' fear of other nations by highlighting their lack of understanding and the apparent senselessness of their actions.

Shame and lack of knowledge are repeated motifs in this parody. Three times in the opening three verses, the audience hear that those who worship idols will be "put to shame" (44:9, 11a, 11b). Two of the verbs used for the idol makers' activities (fashion and work) participate in possible ironic word play. They are repeatedly engaged in the activity of "fashioning" (NRSV[ue]: "make" *yōṣērê*, 44:9; "fashion" *yāṣar*, 44:10; and "shaping it" *yiṣṣĕrēhû*, 44:12). This is precisely the activity that the LORD regularly claims to have done for Israel and that appears with that meaning near the end of this poem (NRSV[ue]: "I formed you," *yĕṣartîkā*, 44:21).[282] While the idols have these human beings, whose comprehension will be explicitly and vividly questioned in what follows, as the ones who formed them; for the audience, that role is filled by the incomparable LORD.[283]

Further undermining the credibility of both parties on the idols/idol maker side of the comparison, the roles are reversed. The "gods" have humans as their makers, while Israel has God as its maker.[284] This reversal is one that the poem will further play with as it insists "the artisans, too, are merely human" (44:11) and as it vividly describes the work of these craftspeople as they create a thing to worship.[285] Similarly, the divine voice repeatedly refers to the artisans' activities as "work" (root *p 'l*, NRSV[ue]: "works," 44:12; "forging," 44:12; and "makes," 44:15), a verb that sounds similar to the word meaning "idol" (*pesel*) used repeatedly in this passage (e.g., 44:9, 10, 15, 17), conveying with heavy irony that the idols are "made."

---

[282] Interestingly, K. Baltzer, *Deutero-Isaiah* (2001), 194, points to the resonance between *tohû* here and the creation narrative.

[283] K. Baltzer, *Deutero-Isaiah* (2001), 205, is similar.

[284] J. Goldingay and D. Payne, *Isaiah 40–55* (2006), 1:334, make a similar connection drawing on additional parallels between imagery for the idol makers and for the LORD in broader Second Isaian context.

[285] See K. Baltzer, *Deutero-Isaiah* (2001), 199.

*Isaiah 44:6–22*

The vivid depictions of the "artisans" employ repetition with expansion to develop and intensify the ironic tone of the passage.[286] The "artisans" (*ḥārāšîm*) are introduced as "merely human" (44:11). The depiction of the "blacksmith" (*ḥāraš barzel*, i.e., "artisan of iron") expands the vision of the "terrified" (v. 11) craftspeople by depicting him as forgetting to eat and drink. The descriptions of his weakened state draw heavily on the language of Second Isaiah's opening poem. There the LORD is extolled as one who does not "faint" (*yî'āp*, 40:28), as one who provides might "to the faint" (*layyā'ēp*, 40:29), and who will make those who wait upon the LORD "not faint" (*yî'āpû*, 40:31). Strength (*kōaḥ*) is what the LORD gives to "the powerless" (40:29) and renews for those waiting upon the LORD (40:31). Here, the one working to create a God fails in "strength" (*kōaḥ*, 44:12) and "is faint" (*yî'āp*, 44:12).[287] The powerlessness of both the idol maker and the idol are underscored by this implicit contrast with what the LORD does for those who wait.

A much more elaborate expansion pertains to the "carpenter" (*ḥāraš 'ēṣîm*, i.e., "artisan of trees," 44:13). Repetition and doubling back on actions already described underscore the sense that this is not a narrative describing the process of making a wooden idol. Rather, the repetition of references to wood, fire, and eating underscore the irony of the woodworker's inability to perceive the reality of his actions. Detail in the opening lines of this section set the expansive tone. Lists of tools and tree species signal that the divine voice is intensifying the depiction. The introduction of the trees motif into this poem further underscores the sense that this is not a depiction of a process, as the references to the trees do not form a reasonable sequence. This scrambling of the order of chopping down, choosing, allowing to "grow" and "plant[ing]" (44:14) illustrates both that the poem is not moving narratively and that its assessment of the worker's

---

[286] While K. Baltzer, *Deutero-Isaiah* (2001), 200, helpfully identifies these repetitions, his proposal that the repetitions are to be read as different dramatic "actors" assigns the repetitions to different voices rather than treating them as poetic repetitions. The analysis that follows will pursue the alternative suggestion that the repetitions convey poetic emphasis and meaning. J. Goldingay and D. Payne, *Isaiah 40–55* (2006), 1:336, observe the repetitions noting their "increasing length."

[287] K. Baltzer, *Deutero-Isaiah* (2001), 198, observes the "ironical contrast between 'his strong arm'... and 'no strength.'" However, the more pointed contrast is the broader one in context between these idol maker's lack of strength and the strength that the LORD gives. See also J. Goldingay and D. Payne, *Isaiah 40–55* (2006), 1:334.

112                                                                    *Commentary*

approach is that it is not coherent. While Westermann proposes that the answer to the problem of ordering here results from viewing it "in reverse: in light of the end result" and the poet's "verdict" on it,[288] the nonnarrative ordering instead points to the confused nature of the idol makers' actions as judged by the poem. That is, they are doing that which makes no sense, and the way it is described likewise is nonsensical.

Three times in this passage the combination of fire/warmth, cooking, and worship appear. Their repetition underscores the divine voice's parody of these activities. The first two occurrences appear in immediate succession (44:15b, 44:16–17). The second occurrence expands upon the first, making clear the implicit claim in the first iteration that the fuel for the fire and the source of the idol are the same piece of wood (44:16) and expanding each element of the combination. The cooking motif expands from "bakes bread" (44:15) to "he roasts meat, eats it, and is satisfied" (44:16). The heat motif expands from "warms himself" to include a citation of what he says: "Ah, I am warm by the fire" (44:16). The worship motif expands to include both prayer and the content of that prayer, again through citation "Save me, for you are my god!" (44:17). In each of these expansions, the idol maker's awareness is highlighted, further underscoring the irony when the divine voice observes that "They do not know," "they cannot see," and "they cannot understand" (44:18).[289] The citation of what the woodworker says is also significant in that the divine voice will chastise him directly for what he does not say, which constitutes the third repetition of the combination of fire, food (both bread and meat), and worship (44:19). The sarcasm of this verse is intensified by the very nearly identical phrasing of "Half of it he burns in the fire" (44:16) and "Half of it I burned in the fire" (44:19), which opens the third recital.[290] As further evidence of his lack of perception and comprehension (44:18), the woodworker is unable to say even that which has already been said in the poem itself. Nor can he say what the poem invites the audience to recognize, that the idol is "a fraud" (44:20).

---

[288]  C. Westermann, *Isaiah 40–66* (1969), 150.
[289]  B. S. Childs, *Isaiah* (2001), 344, observes the emphasis on the idol makers' "lacking in understanding or knowledge."
[290]  The only difference in otherwise identical lines is the person of the verb.

*Isaiah 44:6–22*

The irony in this passage is thick. The depiction of the idol maker cooking over and worshipping "a block of wood" (44:19) combined with the repeated and expanding images of his inability to recognize his own folly constitutes a comedic[291] undermining of the audience's enemies. They are not to be imitated. They are not to be feared. They are not to be the focus of the audience's attention. Instead, the divine voice brings the poem to a close by drawing their attention back to the twin themes of their redemption and their role as servant (44:21–22). Their role as "my servant" receives emphasis appearing twice in a construction that embeds their place as servant within a context of memory. Memory language appears both before and after the pair of reminders that they are "my servant." They are to remember (44:21) and "not forget me" (44:21).[292] In contrast to the firm "rock" (44:8) that is the LORD, their "sins" are depicted in terms of ephemerality (44:22).[293] In contrast to those who "form" idols, they are "formed" by the LORD (44:21). They can trust in the one who is their "Redeemer" (44:6) and who now claims, "I have redeemed you" (44:22). The idols have been parodied as ones who can do nothing, who cannot save, and who exhaust those who make them (44:12).[294] By contrast, Israel's redeemer confirms having already accomplished much on Israel's behalf.

---

[291] See K. Baltzer, *Deutero-Isaiah* (2001), 199; J. D. W. Watts, *Isaiah 34–66* (2005), 145; and J. Muilenburg, "Isaiah 40–66" (1956), 5:514, each of whom treat the passage as either laughing at or inviting its audience to laugh at the idol makers. J. Goldingay and D. Payne, *Isaiah 40–66* (2006), 1:333, accurately reflect the purposes of this tone, writing, "Biblical humour is serious humour – not a light-hearted joking but dark subversive disparagement releasing social aggression and undermining convention and authority."

[292] The translation here is the subject of some debate. The verb itself appears as a mixture of forms. It is a passive verb with an object ending that is more appropriate for an active verb. J. Goldingay and D. Payne, *Isaiah 40–55* (2006), 1:364, consider that the current form of the text reflects a "composite reading" and translates with an intentional "ambiguity" rendering the phrase "there is to be no forgetting" (363).

[293] J. Blenkinsopp, *Isaiah 40–55* (2002), 237, helpfully observes that "rock" as divine attribute "appears often in psalms in which trust in God is called for in unpromising circumstances."

[294] Contra J. Blenkinsopp, *Isaiah 40–55* (2002), 242, who considers that the idol maker's plea "save me" contains "a note of possibly unconscious pathos," the tone of the poem conveys more comedic/satirical rebuttal than sympathy. C. Westermann, *Isaiah 40–66* (1969), 149, calls "the section . . . a masterpiece of satirical writing." As C. Westermann, *Isaiah 40–66* (1969), 151; J. L. McKenzie, *Second Isaiah* (1968), 68; and J. Muilenburg, "Isaiah 40–66" (1956), 5:515, note, the satire does not accurately represent the worship it depicts. However, as Westermann recognizes, the point is not an accurate

114                                                       *Commentary*

ISAIAH 44:23

Sing, O heavens, for the LORD has done it;
    shout, O depths of the earth;
break forth into singing, O mountains,
    O forest and every tree in it!
For the LORD has redeemed Jacob
    and will be glorified in Israel.

In this very short poem, an unspecified voice, presumably that of the prophetic poet, interjects a note of praise offering what Muilenburg calls "an ecstatic cry of joy."[295] The command to praise is all encompassing. Three plural imperatives command heavens, earth, and mountains to join in the worship. After a poem parodying the futility of human beings worshipping idols that are nothing, made by people, and made from materials of the created world (44:6–22), these three crisp couplets express the rightful orientation of God's world. Here heavens and earth express the totality of the imaginable reaches of the world and mountains and forest embrace features of the landscape. As Westermann notes, "This gives God's saving activity a far wider horizon than the human race ... the whole cosmos shares in it."[296] Since the parody dwelt heavily on the ridiculousness of bowing down to pieces of trees, it seems no accident that here "every tree" is commanded to praise the LORD.[297] The prophetic poet commands glory to be given in the appropriate direction. Ironically, the artisans of the previous poem aimed to give "human beauty" (44:13) to their idols. Here that glory is rightfully redirected. The LORD "will be glorified" by Israel. As Goldingay and Payne observe in light of the connection between v. 13 and v. 23, "The artisans' ... attempt to create a thing of beauty is outclassed by Yhwh's achievement with Israel."[298] The

representation of idolatry. Instead "it has no intention of understanding; its desire is to 'take off'" (C. Westermann, *Isaiah 40–66* [1969], 151).

[295] J. Muilenburg, "Isaiah 40–66" (1956), 5:510.
[296] C. Westermann, *Isaiah 40–66* (1969), 144. J. Goldingay and D. Payne, *Isaiah 40–55* (2006), 1:365, similarly comment "the bicolon invites the whole created reality to join in praise."
[297] K. Baltzer, *Deutero-Isaiah* (2001), 207, considers this reference to "forge a link" with the parody of the idols noting that "they need no longer fear that their wood will be misused for idols."
[298] J. Goldingay and D. Payne, *Isaiah 40–55* (2006), 1:335.

*Isaiah 44:24–28*

prophetic poet underscores the insight that glory is not best given by humans making gods in their own image but rather when they embrace their ability to give glory to the LORD.

ISAIAH 44:24–28

<sup>24</sup> Thus says the LORD, your Redeemer,
    who formed you in the womb:
I am the LORD, who made all things,
    who alone stretched out the heavens,
    who by myself spread out the earth;
<sup>25</sup> who frustrates the omens of soothsayers
    and makes fools of diviners;
who turns back the wise
    and makes their knowledge foolish;
<sup>26</sup> who confirms the word of his servant
    and fulfills the prediction of his messengers;
who says of Jerusalem, "It shall be inhabited,"
    and of the cities of Judah, "They shall be rebuilt,
    and I will raise up their ruins";
<sup>27</sup> who says to the deep, "Be dry –
    I will dry up your rivers";
<sup>28</sup> who says of Cyrus, "He is my shepherd,
    and he shall carry out all my purpose";
and who says of Jerusalem, "It shall be rebuilt,"
    and of the temple, "Your foundation shall be laid."

This short poem includes the first reference in Isaiah 40–55 to a figure whose presence has commanded a great deal of attention from interpreters, Cyrus the Persian (see A Closer Look: Cyrus the Persian). However, Cyrus is not the focus of this poem. Instead, the poem presents reliable expect-ation of coming good things as something in which the exiles can place their trust, precisely because of the nature of the one who brings all things, including these good things, into being. Throughout, the divine voice speaks, exuding and expounding its own magnificence. The poem offers an encounter with the divine speaker that reassures through the

116                                                                   *Commentary*

magnificence and confidence of the divine speaking voice and that proclaims concrete expectations into which the exiles are invited to place their trust.

The opening couplet announces divine speech in a characteristic way.[299] Following a format that the audience has come to expect in these chapters, the messenger formula ("Thus says the LORD") is followed by participles that glorify the divine speaker (see A Closer Look: The Majestic Divine Speaker). "Your Redeemer" and "who formed you" each pick up on motifs from earlier poems. There the audience found themselves contrasted, as those formed by the LORD (44:21), with the idols, which are formed by human beings (44:9, 10, 12).[300] Immediately preceding this poem they have heard emphatic announcements that the LORD has redeemed Jacob (44:23), an invitation to return to the LORD because the LORD has redeemed them (44:22), and the claim that the LORD is Israel's redeemer (44:6). The short pair of attributions expands the reference to the divine speaker and draws the preceding assurances of divine care to mind.

What the divine voice says following this introduction is almost entirely composed of further self-description.[301] The message itself, which has been introduced as coming from the audience's redeemer and fashioner, is "I am the LORD."[302] This claim, then, is expanded through a long chain of participial attributions, which appear in patterned groups. Throughout, the emphasis is on the speaker and the reliability of the divine speaker's speech.

The first set of participles relate to the LORD's cosmic uniqueness. The first attribution "who made all things" gains its apparent creation

---

[299] J. Goldingay and D. Payne, *Isaiah 40–55* (2006), 2:4, similarly refer to the LORD's name here "being characteristically glossed."

[300] J. Blenkinsopp, *Isaiah 40–55* (2002), 246, points out the repetition of this claim about the LORD "forming" the addressee in 43:1, 7, 21; 44:21; 45:11, seeing it as an "indication of an integrative concept behind chs. 40–48."

[301] J. Goldingay and D. Payne, *Isaiah 40–55* (2006), 2:4, refer to vv. 24–28 as containing "the densest cluster of . . . participial attributions in Isaiah 40–55."

[302] Contra J. Goldingay and D. Payne, *Isaiah 40–55* (2006), 2:4, who see the absence of a "main verb" as an argument against treating vv. 24–28 as "a self-contained oracle" and contend that "in substance its actual message appears in vv. 26b–28" (J. Goldingay and D. Payne, *Isaiah 40–55* [2006], 2:8), I understand this verb-less statement to be the core of the message expanded and enhanced by the descriptors that surround it. My position is in agreement with J. Muilenburg, "Isaiah 40–66" (1956), 5:517, who calls the statement "The word of revelation which the rest of the poem develops."

*Isaiah 44:24–28*

orientation from the lines that stand in parallel to it. However, it also echoes back to the command to the heavens to "Sing" in 44:23. There they were commanded precisely because of the Lord's activity. There "the LORD" is the subject of the verb "has done" ( *'āśāh*; NRSV[ue] adds the implied object "it"). Here the divine voice proclaims that the LORD who is speaking is the one who does all ( *'ōśeh kōl*, i.e., "does all"; cf. NRSV[ue] "who made all things"). This claim about uniqueness certainly includes creation, as will become explicit in the two parallel lines that follow. However, it continues to convey divine uniqueness and the universality of divine activity as well, as illustrated in the comment alongside the references to expanding each of the heavens and the earth that these were done "alone" and "by myself" (44:24). The choice of "stretched out" and "spread out" also convey the sense of divine magnificence and reinforce the claim to have made "all things." The "heavens" and "earth" stand as opposites that convey the whole (i.e., "merism"; see Glossary of Poetic Terminology) and each employs an image of being pulled into its massive size by one who greatly exceeds it.[303]

A different set of participles contrasts with the expansiveness of these creation images and sets up the poem's focus on the reliability of messages spoken on the LORD's behalf. A series of participles that are grammatically marked as belonging together (i.e., they are all *hipʿil* participles and are marked out with *mē* initial sounds)[304] present a central contrast between what the LORD brings to fulfilment (i.e., the word of the LORD's own "messengers," 44:26) and what the LORD makes unreliable (44:25). Drawing upon imagery of the wise and the foolish, the divine voice contrasts the announcements of the "soothsayers" with words spoken on the LORD's behalf. The word "soothsayers" (*baddîm*)[305] plays with the word meaning "alone" (*lĕbaddî*) in 44:24, further reinforcing the contrast between these figures and the one who brings about everything that

---

[303] J. Goldingay and D. Payne, *Isaiah 40–55* (2006), 2:9, also describe this parallel as "merism."

[304] K. Baltzer, *Deutero-Isaiah* (2001), 211, also observes this repetition including it among his stylistic comments on patterns of threes in the passage.

[305] NRSV had translated the term "liars," which is in harmony with the understanding of the word as represented in the meaning "empty, idle talk" (BDB, 95). This element seems relevant to the nuance of "soothsayers" (NRSV[ue]) in this context.

118                                                                        *Commentary*

happens.[306] The two participles conveying the LORD's undermining of these figures ("frustrates" and "turns back") give way to one that opposes them "who confirms." A neat chiasm structures the couplet that presents the servant and messengers in contrast with these unreliable figures, conveying a poetic emphasis on the divine voice's insistence upon the reliability of the "word" (*děbar*) of "his servant" and "his messengers."

In the final set of participial attributions, repetition of the verb "to say" conveys specific expectations in which the exiles are invited to place their trust. They can do so precisely because the LORD, who is the one who speaks them, is the one who "made all" (44:24) and who "confirms the word of his servant" (44:26). Three times in vv. 26–28 the divine voice further modifies "I am the LORD" (44:24) with "who says" (*hā 'ōmēr*, vv. 26, 27, 28). These sayings include rebuilding of cities of the exiles' homeland (44:26), cosmic parching (44:27) as has appeared in 42:15–16, and the announcement that Cyrus is bringing about the LORD's intentions (44:28). The construction "who says to" (44:27) and "who says of" (44:26, 28) is precisely the same in each of these three instances, placing "Jerusalem," "the deep," and "Cyrus" in direct parallel, potentially conveying that they are of relatively equal levels of importance to the poem. However, the final couplet, whose form differs slightly and which draws the poem to a close,[307] returns to Jerusalem, this time placing it in parallel to the temple (44:28), rather than other Judean cities (44:26).[308] That Jerusalem frames the chain of attributions focused on what the LORD says likely indicates that the restoration of Jerusalem, its people, and its worship are of greater importance to the poem's overall message than is the reference to Cyrus.[309] However, the specificity of each of these references,

---

[306] J. Goldingay and D. Payne, *Isaiah 40–55* (2006), 2:10, refer to this sound play in terms of "alliteration" and observe its emphasizing of "contrast" citing Fokkelman.

[307] On change and poetic closure, see Barbara Herrnstein Smith, *Poetic Closure: A Study of How Poems End* (Chicago: University of Chicago Press, 1968), 33–34. An example of application of these ideas to a biblical text appears in the work of F. W. Dobbs-Allsopp, *Lamentations* (2002), 140.

[308] K. Baltzer, *Deutero-Isaiah* (2001), 220, helpfully notes of Isaiah 40–55 that "temple and cult play a minor role. His mention of the founding of the Temple here is the only time it is mentioned at all."

[309] J. Goldingay and D. Payne, *Isaiah 40–55* (2006), 2:16, note that "v 28b has the effect of bringing us back to the event to which Yhwh's intent is ultimately directed, the restoration of city and temple." Compare J. D. W. Watts, *Isaiah 34–66* (2005), 156; and J. Muilenburg, "Isaiah 40–66" (1956), 5:516, whose comments focus heavily on

*Bridging the Horizons: On Loving Poetry and Poetry's Loves* 119

the cities, the temple, and the Persian ruler, call attention to themselves by appearing in a larger context that is generally less specific.[310] They gain the audience's attention, directing them to that which the LORD is doing and characteristically does.

The encounter that this poem offers is explicitly one with the divine speaker, whose message is "I am the LORD." This claim of divine existence, speaking presence and uniqueness, is developed in terms of the origin of all things being in the divine will (44:24) and the reliability of that which the LORD commands and conveys (44:25–26). On this basis, specific expectations appear, grounded in the speaking of the one who addresses the audience with the LORD's own reliability. This is a poem that invites trust, not solely through promises of provision but primarily because of the magnificence and uniqueness of the divine speaker, the one who addresses the exiles and invites their trust.

## BRIDGING THE HORIZONS: ON LOVING POETRY AND POETRY'S LOVES

Matthew Mullins observes, "It seems just about everyone hates poetry, even those who write it and study it for a living."[311] The sense that poetry is confusing, perplexing, difficult, and perhaps just plain odd might well be shared broadly in our culture. As Mullins helpfully demonstrates, a large portion of our frustration with poetry comes from our demands to it to be what it is not. We want explanations and information, things poetry is not designed to offer.[312] However, we desperately need what poetry does offer, particularly in this cultural moment, because learning to love poetry and to embrace the way that it operates allows it to do more vital and formational work than the informative.

Poetry shapes its readers. It acts on us by orienting our inmost selves. By acting so differently from our expectations, poetry can play a role in

---

Cyrus. The poetic form with its return to and repetition of reference to Jerusalem, points to the city rather than the Persian ruler the primary focus of the divine voice's promised restorative activity.

[310] J. Muilenburg, "Isaiah 40–66" (1956), 5:518, commenting on v. 26 calls "The whole context . . . general and spacious."

[311] Matthew Mullins, *Enjoying the Bible: Literary Approaches to Loving the Scriptures* (Grand Rapids: Baker Academic, 2021), 2.

[312] M. Mullins, *Enjoying the Bible* (2021), 3–4.

offering what we urgently and desperately need: expansion of our "personal density"[313] and retraining of our "loves."[314] Perhaps surprisingly, it seems increasingly clear that we ultimately act not out of what we think but out of how our selves are shaped, by our habits, by what we long for, by what we "love."[315] So it is vital that we allow what is "true," "honorable," "just," and "pleasing" (Phil 4:8) to shape our inmost selves. Spiritual formation vitally needs to attend to the training of our "desires."[316] Reading Scripture not solely for information but for "formational encounters" is one way that people of faith can embrace this essential part of their journey.[317] Formation of our loves, a reshaping of our desires to align with God's vision for the world and for our flourishing through encounters with poetry does not dispense with reason, indeed it draws upon reason and intense intellectual engagement to accomplish its work, but it does instill tolerance for complexity, ambiguity, and opaqueness, making generous engagement possible.[318]

Prophetic poetry, like that of Isaiah 40–66, is a vital resource for faithful living in our time. It has the capacity to remold vision, imagination, and desires and in so doing to transform attitudes, opinions, and behaviors more effectively than through discursive argumentation. The way to invite these texts to speak to us is to allow them to act on us through the appeal and disgust, rage and peace, fear and joy they evoke and thereby shape us through. Rather than seeking to explain or comprehend this poetry, what it

---

[313] The phrase is drawn from Alan Jacobs, *Breaking Bread with the Dead: A Reader's Guide to a More Tranquil Mind* (New York: Penguin, 2020), 19. While Jacobs uses it to describe the impact of "deeper . . . understanding of the past" (18–19) in the course of his more general defense of reading, application to the impact of the more specific category of ancient poetry seems appropriate and Jacobs' argument for the needfulness of this trait in the contemporary context is compelling (19–23).

[314] See James K. A. Smith, *You Are What You Love: The Spiritual Power of Habit* (Grand Rapids: Brazos, 2016), 19, who describes discipleship as "rehabituation of your loves." Smith will go on to describe the relevance of habit and therefore worship and ritual to this kind of formation.

[315] See extended development of this idea in James K. A. Smith, *Desiring the Kingdom: Worship, Worldview, and Cultural Formation* (Grand Rapids: Baker Academic, 2009), 46–63. See also the discussion about how the human brain works and the centrality of our "way of being in the world" to the "intuitive assessment" that takes the primary role in decision making in I. McGilchrist, *The Master and His Emissary* (2019), 184.

[316] See J. K. A. Smith, *Desiring the Kingdom* (2009), 25.

[317] I have discussed further what I mean by "formational encounters" in K. M. Heffelfinger, "Truth and Hidden Things" (2023), 172–173.

[318] See further K. M. Heffelfinger, "Truth and Hidden Things" (2023), 159–160.

*Isaiah 45:1–8*                                                                              121

most invites is an encounter that reorients its readers, that invites them into its world. Sympathetic, empathy-enhancing engagements with a world not ours are opportunities to be expanded as people, to grow in our capacity to love both God and neighbor through growth of our horizons, and to allow these ancient texts to re-form us. In short, it is to allow them to function as Scripture.[319]

## ISAIAH 45:1–8

[1] Thus says the LORD to his anointed, to Cyrus,
      whose right hand I have grasped
to subdue nations before him
      and strip kings of their robes,
to open doors before him –
      and the gates shall not be closed:
[2] I will go before you
      and level the mountains;
I will break in pieces the doors of bronze
      and cut through the bars of iron;
[3] I will give you the treasures of darkness
      and riches hidden in secret places,
so that you may know that it is I, the LORD,
      the God of Israel, who call you by your name.
[4] For the sake of my servant Jacob
      and Israel my chosen,
I call you by your name;
      I give you a title, though you do not know me.
[5] I am the LORD, and there is no other;
      besides me there is no god.
      I arm you, though you do not know me,
[6] so that they may know, from the rising of the sun and from the west,
      that there is no one besides me;[320]

---

[319]  See K. M. Heffelfinger, "Truth and Hidden Things" (2023), 172–173.
[320]  I am departing from NRSV[ue]'s lineation here and in the following two couplets. I am following, instead, the lineation printed in the MT, which appears to account for the parallelism and the chiastic arrangement of the couplets in vv. 6–7.

122                                                                    *Commentary*

> I am the LORD, and there is no other.
>     [7] I form light and create darkness,
> I make weal and create woe;
>     I the LORD do all these things.
> [8] Shower, O heavens, from above,[321]
>     and let the skies rain down righteousness;
> let the earth open, that salvation may spring up,
>     and let it cause righteousness to sprout up also;
>     I the LORD have created it.

Cyrus the Persian, the named addressee of this poem, commands attention as he would have for the exiles listening in (see further A Closer Look: Cyrus the Persian). He appears twice in successive verses (44:28 and 45:1) and this repetition, combined with his specificity in a series of prophetic texts that does not tend toward political detail, and the likely apparent relevance of this name to the audience's immediate context, make him stand out as an object of attention. But the poem is not oriented toward emphasizing Cyrus' importance. Rather, it positions him as yet another indicator of the power, presence, and centrality of Israel's God, who is speaking to them through the poem. While the poem addresses Cyrus, it is a poem that appears designed for "overhearing" as the exiles themselves are the true audience whose attention the poem attempts to shift by addressing them indirectly.[322] Throughout, the attention is on the LORD, who speaks, who acts, and who brings all things into being for the LORD's own purposes.[323] Those purposes, the spread of knowledge of God (45:3, 6), undermine the characterization of Cyrus, who is explicitly and repeatedly one who does not know the LORD (45:4, 5).

The imagery used for Cyrus, both here and in the preceding poem, is kingly. The divine voice calls him "his anointed"[324] (*měšîḥô*, 45:1) and has

---

[321]  NRSV[ue] breaks v. 8 into a new unit. This is not necessary given the parallelism between the conclusion of this verse and the preceding verse.

[322]  Similarly, J. Goldingay and D. Payne, *Isaiah 40–55* (2006), 2:17, indicate that they read the "oracle itself" as "for Jacob-Israel's sake" despite its being "addressed" to Cyrus.

[323]  J. Goldingay and D. Payne, *Isaiah 40–55* (2006), 2:19, point to repetition and a chiastic structure of vv. 1–8 in support of the claim "the verses' ultimate concern is not Cyrus's victories but Yhwh's recognition."

[324]  J. Blenkinsopp, *Isaiah 40–55* (2002), 248–249, helpfully articulates the primary meaning of this term as "above all a royal ritual." See also the discussion of this term in Lisbeth S. Fried, "Cyrus the Messiah? The Historical Background to Isaiah 45:1," *HTR* 95 (2002):

*Isaiah 45:1–8*

already called him "my shepherd" (44:28), a term heavily associated with kingship in the ancient Near East and within Israel's traditions concerning its shepherd King, David.[325] So, it is not surprising that the lines that develop the depiction of Cyrus point to triumph over "nations" and "kings" (45:1). However, as victorious as he may appear, the poem undermines the glorifying description by employing the same term for divine support as was used for the fearful Jacob-Israel in Isa 41:13. There the LORD claimed to "hold your right hand" (*mahăzîq yĕmînekā*). Here the LORD "grasped" his "right hand" (*hehĕzaqtî bîmînô*).[326] Cyrus may be the object of special divine attention, but the audience may be expected to recognize the terms used for their own receipt of special divine attention here.[327] Cyrus' victories sit alongside the promised victories of the people as the LORD's instruments (see, e.g., 41:15–16) and, as will become clear later in this poem, his use by the LORD is explicitly for the sake of the exiles themselves (45:4).

The imagery that illustrates Cyrus' victories alternates between likely allusions to political events and cosmic motifs that resonate with other passages in these chapters. Doors and gates appear as protective features of besieged cities.[328] Bars appeared in connection with Babylon in Isaiah 43:14 where the LORD promised to "break down all the bars."[329] Together, these features, which likely connote the exiles' captors' defenses, are presented as no trouble to the conqueror that the LORD equips. In one couplet these

---

379. Fried's discussion of terms as "a mechanism of divine selection for a specific task" (379) is helpful.

[325] J. Blenkinsopp, *Isaiah 40–55* (2002), 248; J. D. W. Watts, *Isaiah 34–66* (2005), 156; K. Baltzer, *Deutero-Isaiah* (2001), 219; and J. Goldingay and D. Payne, *Isaiah 40–55* (2006), 2:15, all discuss shepherd language as kingly.

[326] C. Westermann, *Isaiah 40–66* (1969), 158, points out that connection of the language of this passage with the Cyrus Cylinder is common. However, it is perhaps more pertinent for the interpretation of the whole that Israel is also addressed in parallel fashion in these chapters. J. Muilenburg, "Isaiah 40–66" (1956) 5:522, suggests comparison with other Isaian passages two of which are among those that refer to the LORD taking the audience by the hand (41:13 and 42:6).

[327] Contra L. S. Fried, "Cyrus the Messiah?" (2002), 391–392, who picks up on the Davidic overtones and reads these verses as endorsing Cyrus as taking on the role of the Davidides. While Davidic elements are present, the poem as a whole subjects Cyrus to Yhwh, and as I will argue, contrasts his shortcomings with what the audience are invited to embrace.

[328] See further J. Goldingay and D. Payne, *Isaiah 40–55* (2006), 2:21.

[329] Cf. J. Goldingay and D. Payne, *Isaiah 40–55* (2006), 2:22, who indicate the necessity of reading the vowels differently in 43:14 to arrive at this interpretation.

124                                                                 *Commentary*

stand open and unobstructive (45:1), in another they are destroyed (45:2).[330]
These depictions stand together as alternative depictions of the power of
divine might. They do not need to be harmonized into a sequence of
events. Rather, they combine to present a tensive picture through
juxtaposition. What matters in this depiction is not the means by which
city defenses pose no opposition but the fact that it is the LORD who
makes it so. Similarly, it is emphatically the LORD who "will go before
you" in a couplet that draws upon the transformation of the landscape
imagery employed elsewhere in these chapters (see, e.g., 40:4; 41:15, 18;
42:15–16). It is also LORD who gives mysterious treasures (*'ôṣĕrôt*), perhaps
alluding to the treasures (NRSV[ue] "his storehouses" *ōṣĕrōtāyw*, 39:2) that
Hezekiah showed to the Babylonians.

The emphasis here falls not on Cyrus who benefits from all of these
actions but on the LORD who does them. The active verbs point repeatedly
to the LORD. In addition to the repeated "I will" statements translated by the
NRSV[ue] in 45:2 and 3, the verbs "level" and "cut through" are marked in the
first person, as are "I have grasped" (45:1) and "strip kings" (45:1). In the two
couplets of verse 2, each line concludes with a first-person verb, creating a
repetitive pattern of sounds (*'ēlēk, 'ăwaššēr, 'ăšabbēr, 'ăgaddēa'*) at the end
of each line.[331] This pattern reinforces the emphasis already created by the
first line's additional and therefore emphatic "I" (*'ănî*, 45:2). It is the LORD,
the speaker of this poem, who does these things, not Cyrus.[332]

In what will become a poetic refrain, the divine voice announces the
purpose of these divine actions from which Cyrus benefits. It is in order
that "you may know" that "I am the LORD."[333] Ironically, this is precisely
what Cyrus emphatically does not know (45:4, 5). The intensification of this
refrain strongly suggests that the poem is further undermining the

---

[330] The phrase "to open" (*liptoaḥ*, 45:1) could convey forcible opening. However, the
contrast between such opening here and "break in pieces" 45:2 remains.

[331] K. Baltzer, *Deutero-Isaiah* (2001), 222, picks up on the sound patterning noting that
"The triple repetition of the vowel sequence ... can hardly be fortuitous" and noting
that the style corresponds to the "content" stating "Yahweh is the ruler, not Cyrus."

[332] J. Goldingay and D. Payne, *Isaiah 40–55* (2006), 2:22, comment similarly on the
emphasis of v. 2a.

[333] NRSV[ue] translates this way in 45:5 and 6. The refrain "I am the LORD" (*'ănî yĕhwâ*)
appears in v. 3 with "for" attached and again in 45:5, 6, 7, and 8. J. Muilenburg, "Isaiah
40–66" (1956), 5:524, highlights the importance of repetition in v. 5 calling the move to
"reorder .... a mistaken procedure, for Second Isaiah is making here one of his
strongest emphases."

*Isaiah 45:1–8*

apparent interest in Cyrus as addressee and moving to shift the exiles' attention away from Cyrus toward the LORD.[334] Three occurrences of the preposition pointing to purpose (*lĕma'an*, NRSV[ue] translates: "so that" 45:3; "for the sake of" 45:4; and "so that" 45:6) emphasize the centrality of the LORD's purposes to this poem's meaning. The claim that these things happen so that Cyrus may know that the LORD is behind it all, may well be ironic and stands immediately juxtaposed to the claim that it is for the sake of Jacob-Israel (45:4). The audience, who have been critiqued for their lack of knowledge (40:28), may be here invited to see themselves, who are also "called ... by name" (43:1) in contrast to this victor with whom they have been implicitly compared. Emphatically, repeatedly, the divine voice will say to Cyrus "you do not know me" (45:4, 5) even though "I call you by your name" (45:4). Thus, the audience are invited to see and to understand what they are seeing as the work of the LORD.

Repetitions of "I am the LORD" intensify the speaking presence of the deity and punctuate claims of exclusivity, creative power, and the ability to bring about God's own purposes. In a chiastic structure, "you do not know me" (45:4, 5) frames statements of the nonexistence of anything else ("there is no other," "there is no god" 45:5), further underscoring the irony of Cyrus' lack of knowledge of the only one. Cyrus ceases to be of interest following the second notice "you do not know me" as the divine voice further expounds the idea of the LORD's uniqueness by illustrating that everything comes from the LORD. A second chiastic structure drives the point home as "I am the LORD," that is, the thing that Cyrus should have known, occupies the same framing places in this second chiasm as "you do not know me" had, while the central lines attribute all things that are to God's creative action. In this structure "light" and "darkness," "weal" and "woe" stand as surprising and all-encompassing opposites.[335] The impact

---

[334] Cf. C. Westermann, *Isaiah 40–66* (1969), 160, who recognizes that the "repetition of the words ... underlines their importance" and that the idea emphasized is that these things happen "for Israel's sake" but does not indicate that the poem directs the audience's attention toward the LORD in connection with these observations.

[335] See commentators' emphases on "transend[ence]," C. Westermann, *Isaiah 40–66* (1969), 162; and "sovereignty," J. Goldingay and D. Payne, *Isaiah 40–55* (2006), 2:27, in these verses. Against J. D. W. Watts, *Isaiah 34–66* (2005), 157, who thinks the pairs implicitly refute "Persian ... religion," while the poetic merisms do "overcome inherent dualism [s]" that is not the point here. Rather, all-encompassing majesty appears to be emphasized in a manner already familiar in Isaian poetry. J. Muilenburg, "Isaiah

of the image is to wrap the entirety of that which is imaginable in the envelope of divine causation.

As if to demonstrate the power of the divine speaker to cause everything that is and everything that is imaginable, the divine voice commands some difficult to imagine things. Again employing opposites in a way that conveys completeness, the LORD commands "heavens" and "the earth" to produce "righteousness" and "salvation." The image develops a complex metaphor in which the skies as the source of rain and the earth as the location of crop growth are together commanded to produce an atypical harvest. Together the command issued to inanimate aspects of creation and the image of the LORD making deliverance emerge from an unlikely source, further undermine the sense that Cyrus himself is particularly noteworthy. He stands alongside these features of the created world as things that the LORD can turn to unlikely outcomes and to the LORD's own purposes.

The poem as a whole moves the audience away from attention to its addressee and shifts that focus onto the divine speaker. The refrain "I am the LORD" is instrumental in this shift, as are the various modes of undermining Cyrus that the poem employs. Repeated emphasis on Cyrus' lack of knowledge and his depiction using terms that have already been used for the audience diminish his importance while the poem directs the exiles' attention to the one who brings everything about. The poem offers Cyrus' name with its ability to draw the audience's attention but works throughout to point the exiles to the one to whom they should be looking, the divine speaker.

ISAIAH 45:9–25[336]

9 Woe to those who strive with their Maker,
    earthen vessels with the potter!

---

40–66" (1956), 5:524, similarly rejects the suggestion that this imagery combats "Zoroastrian dualism" noting "The primary thought is the oneness of God."

[336] My unit division here is distinctive and merits some defense. The opening of the unit is clearly marked by the shift in addressee and sharp shift in tone. A number of scholars agree a unit break here. See, e.g., J. Goldingay and D. Payne, *Isaiah 40–55* (2006), 2:31; J. Blenkinsopp, *Isaiah 40–55* (2002), 250; and K. Baltzer, *Deutero-Isaiah* (2001), 232. The continuation of the unit is disputed with C. Westermann, *Isaiah 40–66* (1969), 169–176,

# Isaiah 45:9–25

Does the clay say to the one who fashions it, "What are you making"?
  or "Your work has no handles"?
¹⁰ Woe to anyone who says to a father, "What are you fathering?"
  or to a woman, "With what are you in labor?"
¹¹ Thus says the LORD,
  the Holy One of Israel and its Maker:
Will you question me about my children
  or command me concerning the work of my hands?
¹² I made the earth
  and created humankind upon it;
it was my hands that stretched out the heavens,
  and I commanded all their host.
¹³ I have aroused Cyrus in righteousness,[337]
  and I will make all his paths straight;
he shall build my city
  and set my exiles free,
not for price or reward,
  says the LORD of hosts.

¹⁴ Thus says the LORD:
The wealth of Egypt and the merchandise of Cush
  and the Sabeans, tall of stature,
shall come over to you and be yours;
  they shall follow you;
  they shall come over in chains and bow down to you.
They will make supplication to you, saying,
  "God is with you alone, and there is no other;
  there is no god besides him."
¹⁵ Truly, you are a God who hides himself,
  O God of Israel, the Savior.

---

for example, breaking the poem into numerous small units and many scholars starting a new unit at verse 14. See, e.g., J. Blenkinsopp, *Isaiah 40–55* (2002), 256; and K. Baltzer, *Deutero-Isaiah* (2001), 238. However, aside from the interjections and embedded citations of others' speech, the poem remains in the divine voice, and the imagery is heavily interwoven throughout these lines. For these reasons, I treat these verses together, despite poetic subunits within.

[337] Cyrus does not appear in the Hebrew text. NRSV$^{ue}$ is translating the ambiguous "him" as a reference to this figure. See further the comment below.

$^{16}$ All of them are put to shame and confounded;
    the makers of idols go in disgrace together.
$^{17}$ But Israel is saved by the LORD
    with everlasting salvation;
    you shall not be put to shame or confounded ever again.

$^{18}$ For thus says the LORD,
who created the heavens
    (he is God!),
who formed the earth and made it
    (he established it;
he did not create it a chaos;
    he formed it to be inhabited!):
I am the LORD, and there is no other.
$^{19}$ I did not speak in secret
    in a land of darkness;
I did not say to the offspring of Jacob,
    "Seek me in chaos."
I the LORD speak the truth;
    I declare what is right.

$^{20}$ Assemble yourselves and come together;
    draw near, you survivors of the nations!
They have no knowledge –
    those who carry about their wooden idols
and keep on praying to a god
    that cannot save.
$^{21}$ Declare and present your case;
    let them take counsel together!
Who told this long ago?
    Who declared it of old?
Was it not I, the LORD?
    There is no other god besides me,
a righteous God and a Savior;
    there is no one besides me.

$^{22}$ Turn to me and be saved,
    all the ends of the earth!
    For I am God, and there is no other.

*Isaiah 45:9–25*

[23] By myself I have sworn;
  from my mouth has gone forth in righteousness
  a word that shall not return:
"To me every knee shall bow,
  every tongue shall swear."

[24] Only in the LORD, it shall be said of me,
  are righteousness and strength;
all who were incensed against him
  shall come to him and be ashamed.
[25] In the LORD all the offspring of Israel
  shall triumph and glory.

This poem evokes an attitude shift. It juxtaposes intense refutation with images of restoration creating emotional tension and a profoundly arresting, humbling encounter. Each of these tones in the divine speaker reinforce one another and work to overcome an apparent objection by the audience to what the prophetic poet has been claiming that the LORD is doing.[338] The divine voice speaks both strident refutation and magnificent imagery of restoration and it insists throughout on the reliability of its own speech. The poem consistently contrasts the dependability of the LORD's own speech with the potential speech of others, presenting an encounter with the LORD whose speech relativizes the speech of all competitors. It thus places the audience within its vision of renewed dependence, homage, and humility.

An intensely ominous tone opens this poem. Even before it is clear who is speaking or to whom, "Woe" has been declared twice. The particle translated "Woe" here (*hôy*, 45:9, 10) appears only a handful of times in the exilic portions of Isaiah (45:9, 10 and 55:1) but frequently introduces an indictment in Isaiah's earlier chapters (see especially 1:4, 24; 5:8, 11, 20, 21, 22).[339] For hearers familiar with the preceding chapters of the book of Isaiah, or indeed with Israelite prophecy generally (see, e.g., Amos 5:18; 6:1;

---

[338] Scholars who think overcoming objection is a factor in this passage's tone include C. Westermann, *Isaiah 40–66* (1969), 165–166; J. Goldingay and D. Payne, *Isaiah 40–55* (2006), 2:33; and J. Blenkinsopp, *Isaiah 40–55* (2002), 252.

[339] It is worth noting that the other occurrence in this portion of Isaiah is quite different in tone from these. See further the discussion of Isaiah 55:1.

130                                                                 *Commentary*

Zeph 2:5; 3:1), these interjections create an expectation that someone is about to be judged harshly.[340]

That expectation is not disappointed by the poetic lines that follow. Interspersed with rhetorical questions and riddled with ironic reiterations and sound plays with earlier terms, this opening set of lines constitutes an emphatic reorientation of someone's attempt to contend with the LORD. It seems most probable that the addressee is the audience. However, the poetry leaves the addressee ambiguous, which has the impact of drawing the audience into the rhetoric of their own indictment. The "Woe" lines are impersonal. However, the idea that the one who contends does so with their own maker (*yōṣěrô*, 45:9) ought to suggest to the audience that they are the people being described, since one of the prophetic poet's frequent claims is that the LORD is Israel's maker, employing forms of this same verb (see, e.g., 43:1, 7; 44:2, 21, 24).[341] This attribution appears to confirm such a suspicion when the divine speaker is finally properly introduced (45:11) with the attributions "the Holy One of Israel and its Maker" (*yōṣěrô*, 45:11), where "its" most probably refers to "Israel" in context.[342] The poetic imagery hints and alludes, drawing the audience in and involving them emotionally in its act of indicting them. As they increasingly recognize themselves in the description, they increasingly perceive themselves as the indictee.

A pair of images develops the implausibility of one contending with one's own creator. Both the potter, who works with an inanimate substance, and the parents, who conceive and deliver one who is far from ready to speak, are deployed as references to the LORD as is made explicit in the rhetorical questions of v. 11 that draw on both "children" and the "work of my hands."[343] Ironically, potential speech for rebuttal is supplied, with the "clay" (*ḥōmer*, 45:9) resonating through sound play with the one

---

[340] See C. Westermann, *Isaiah 40–66* (1969), 166; and especially J. Goldingay and D. Payne, *Isaiah 40–55* (2006), 2:31, on the range of uses and the "worrying note" that this term conveys.

[341] See also J. Blenkinsopp, *Isaiah 40–55* (2002), 254, who makes these connections.

[342] See also J. Goldingay and D. Payne, *Isaiah 40–55* (2006), 2:34, who also treat v. 11 as making this idea "explicit."

[343] Interestingly, both male (father) and female (woman) depictions are deployed to convey the parental image which is applied by the divine voice to itself (v. 11). See further J. Goldingay and D. Payne, *Isaiah 40–55* (2006), 2:36. See further A Closer Look: Birth and Breastfeeding Imagery in Isaiah 40–66.

# Isaiah 45:9–25

who speaks (*'ōmēr*, 45:10) as well as with the divine speaker whose speaking and whose word are heavily marked out for attention in the poem (45:11, 13, 14, and especially 19). The complaint from the dirt "What are you making" and particularly "Your work has no handles"[344] comes from one who does not, presumably, in addition to the apparent absence of hands, have a mouth either and sets up a contrast between the work (*pā'ălĕkā*) with no hands (*'ên-yādayim*) and the one who asks "Will you … command me concerning the work (*pō'al*) of my hands (*yāday*)?" (45:11). Given the ironic redeployment of this term in the rhetorical questions, it seems most likely that the word is chosen not primarily for its ability to indicate a part of the potter's creation but to stand in tension with the audience's description as the work of God's own hand.[345] Such word play intensifies the rhetorical questions' pointed indictment of those who would question the LORD. Their speech, the very image of speech that is misplaced and untenable, will stand in stark contrast to that of the divine voice, which the poem will laud as righteous and reliable (45:23).

The "you" who are not directly addressed in the impersonal ironic depiction of the complaining "earthen vessels" become directly and emphatically the addressee when the divine voice embraces the parental and potter images in v. 11. The contrast between the emphatic line-opening "Will you" (45:11) and the series of emphatic first person line-opening pronouns that follow (45:12, 13)[346] continues the ironic redeployment of the caricature of the speaking pot. In a stinging pair of rhetorical questions, the divine voice reveals the import of the opening ironic set of images. The addressee is to be associated with the pot and the child and the divine voice presents the addressees' complaint as comparable to the questions that have been rejected already. A possible allusion to Genesis 2 makes sense of the juxtaposition of parental imagery and the potter forming (*yōṣĕrô*) the dust (*'ădāmâ*, 45:9).[347] In Genesis 2:7, the LORD forms (root *yṣr*) the man

---

[344] The NRSV[ue] translates "handles" here for the dual form of "hands." J. Goldingay and D. Payne, *Isaiah 40–55* (2006), 2:35, note that "there is no biblical parallel" for this meaning. J. Blenkinsopp, *Isaiah 40–55* (2002), 251, comments similarly.

[345] See also K. Baltzer, *Deutero-Isaiah* (2001), 234.

[346] J. Goldingay and D. Payne, *Isaiah 40–55* (2006), 2:32, treat these features among those that "provide formal patterning."

[347] See also J. Muilenburg, "Isaiah 40–66" (1956), 5:526; K. Baltzer, *Deutero-Isaiah* (2001), 234; R. Alter, *Hebrew Bible* (2019), 773; and Blenkinsopp, *Isaiah 40–55* (2002), 253–254,

(*hā 'ādām*) from the dust (*min-hā 'ădamâ*). Here, the divine voice claims "I . . . created humankind (*'ādām*)," insists on having made the earth, and emphasizes that the LORD's own hands (*yāday*, v. 12, note also v. 11) "stretched out the heavens" and "commanded" (v. 12, note also v. 11) "their host." By underscoring the LORD's power as creator, the divine voice relativizes objections to God's activities.[348]

The emphatic "I" statements about what God has done initially relate to developing the depiction of the powerful divine creator.[349] However, the third of these statements places the raising up of an unspecified figure into the context of divine activities that belong beyond the questioning of the audience. While it seems most likely, as the NRSV[ue]'s translation assumes, that the figure is Cyrus, not least because the claim that the LORD has stirred up (each of these are forms of the verb *'wr*) a figure alluded to Cyrus in 41:2 and 25, his commission is juxtaposed with a reference to the rebuilding of Jerusalem (44:26), and the "victor" is referred to using the language of "righteousness" (41:2), that connection is not made explicit. There is overlap as well with "you" here as this figure is to "set my exiles free" (45:13) and is called "in righteousness" (45:13) while "you" were called "in righteousness" (42:6) and were to liberate "prisoners" (42:7). It is worth noting that the poem could have used the name of this figure and does not. Indeed, there is no clear referent for the pronoun at all in the immediate context, complicating the task of determining the point of reference. The potential ambiguity, or at the very least, the lack of a clear referent for the pronoun, underscores the sense that the emphasis is not primarily on the figure but on the LORD who raises him up and on the sovereign right of the LORD to do so, even if the addressees do not understand.

Immediately juxtaposed to the intense rebuttal of the audience's apparent questioning of the LORD's purposes stands a largely comforting portion of the poem. No explanation is given for this shift. Instead, lavish honors and a pointed contrast between the audience and other nations surrounds a mysterious allusion to the audience's complaint. It is as if the poem works at the problem of the audience's apparent complaint from

---

who pick up on this resonance with Genesis 2. Interestingly, J. Goldingay and D. Payne, *Isaiah 40–55* (2006), 2:39, connect v. 12 with Genesis 1.

[348] See J. Blenkinsopp, *Isaiah 40–55* (2002), 252, who summarizes, "The creature cannot question the Creator of heaven and earth about Cyrus or anything else."

[349] See also J. Muilenburg, "Isaiah 40–66" (1956), 5:527.

# Isaiah 45:9–25

precisely the opposite emotional angle and juxtaposes the two responses (45:9–13 and 45:14–17), intensifying their paired emotional impact.[350]

An unidentified voice interjects "Truly, you are a God who hides himself, O God of Israel, the Savior" (45:15) into the divine voice's promises of impending homage and wealth coming from the same places that the LORD referred to in conveying the audience's preciousness (43:3).[351] The poetic voice is blurred in the following verses (45:16–17) but it seems most likely that this line stands alone and that its implied speaker does not speak any of the surrounding lines.[352] Verses 16 and 17, if they do not return to the divine voice, are spoken by a voice that shares the LORD's perspective, possibly that of the prophetic poet. It is also possible that these lines continue the cited direct speech of the nations bringing homage (45:14). However, this seems unlikely as well since those lines address the audience, and these lines addresses the deity.

The intriguing idea that God "hides himself" (*mistattēr*) (see further A Closer Look: A God Who Hides Himself) seems to allude to the audience's cited complaint in Isa 40:27. There they charged that their "way" was "hidden" (*nistĕrâ*) from God.[353] If 45:15 does in fact allude to

---

[350] Contra J. Muilenburg, "Isaiah 40–66" (1956), 5:527, there is "real judgment" and emotional intensity in the opening verses of this poem. It is more than "only condemnation of Israel's caviling" and the contrast between the opening and the more comforting section produce poetic rhetorical power.

[351] On these nations' appearance in chapter 43, see also J. L. McKenzie, *Second Isaiah* (1968), 82; and J. Goldingay and D. Payne, *Isaiah 40–55* (2006), 2:43. I agree with J. Muilenburg, "Isaiah 40–66" (1956), 5:529; and J. Goldingay and D. Payne, *Isaiah 40–55* (2006), 2:44, each of whom see the exiles as the envisioned recipients of this homage. This position is opposed to that of K. Baltzer, *Deutero-Isaiah* (2001), 240–241, who takes the passage as describing payment offered to Cyrus as a "ransom" for Israel. This reading sits awkwardly with the context, which cites the lack of reward (45:13) and which points heavily toward universal worship of Israel's God.

[352] Regarding various proposals for the speaker here, see further Christine Pilkington, "The Hidden God in Isaiah 45:15 – A Reflection from Holocaust Theology," *SJT* 48 (1995): 287–289; and Samuel Balentine, "Isaiah 45: God's 'I Am,' Israel's 'You Are,'" *HBT* 16 (1994): 107–108.

[353] Interestingly, C. Westermann, *Isaiah 40–66* (1969), 173, sees v. 19 as a verse "that deals with almost the same subject as the conclusion of the great disputation which comes at the beginning of the book, 40.27–31" but does not mention the verbal overlaps in that connection. See also J. Goldingay and D. Payne, *Isaiah 40–55* (2006), 2:33. Contra J. L. McKenzie, *Second Isaiah* (1968), 83, who treats the hidden imagery as a reference to Yhwh being "attached" to such a politically insignificant group as Israel. Instead, the interweaving of this imagery with the other references to divine hiddenness in Isaiah 40–55 argues against such a reading here.

134  Commentary

Isa. 40:27, it further undermines certainty about Cyrus being the referent in 45:13. There the figure's ways (NRSV[ue] "paths") were to be made "straight." It is precisely Jacob's "way" ("My way" *darkî*) that he complains is "hidden" from God in Isa. 40:27. Rather than an immediate rebuttal of this apparent charge of hiddenness in 45:15, the poem contrasts the "shame" and "confound[ing]" of idolators with Israel's "salvation" (45:16–17). That is, the poem surrounds the complaint with images of restoration.

The divine voice returns to the imagery of hiddenness as the tone of the poem returns to its opening intensity. Deploying the creation verbs that expressed the refutation of those who would contend with their own creator ("created" *bôrē'* 45:18; cf. 45:12; "formed" *yōṣēr* and *yĕṣārāh* 45:18; cf. 45:9, 11; "made" *'ōśāh* 45:18; cf. 45:9, 12), the divine voice reasserts the LORD's own uniqueness (45:18) before explicitly engaging with the claim: "I did not speak in secret (*lō' bassēter dibbartî*, 45:19)." Perhaps ironically developing the earlier refutation of the speaking pot, the divine voice proclaims the virtue of its own speaking, deploying the same pairing of righteousness (*ṣedeq*) and straightness (*mêšārîm*; cf. the use of the verb from which this noun is derived in v.13) as described the one the LORD raised up (v. 13).[354] The poetic imagery sets this depiction within the context of creation imagery (v. 18) and deliverance images (v. 20). The claim itself has expansive implications not limited to factuality as might be inferred from a translation like the NRSV[ue]'s "truth" but embracing the world-making speech of the creator God and the deliverance-producing speech of Israel's savior (45:21).[355] This is speech that is reliable, steadfast, world constituting, and world altering. Thus, the poem ties the earlier indictment, with its insistence upon the divine prerogative to raise up an unspecified figure, with this response to the idea that God is hidden.

Interestingly, here the divine voice specifically treats divine speech as unhidden, employing expansive and ambiguous language to do so, while the interjection had been less specific, "you are a God who hides himself"

---

[354]  R. Alter, *Hebrew Bible* (2019), 775, translates the final lines of v. 19 "I am the LORD speaking justice, telling uprightness."

[355]  On the "salvation" connotations of *ṣedeq* in Second Isaiah, see R. Rendtorff, "Isaiah 56:1"(1993), 183. For further discussion of potential meanings of *ṣedeq*, see also Matthijis J. de Jong, "A Note on the Meaning of *bᵉṣædæq* in Isaiah 42,6 and 45,13," *ZAW* 123 (2011): 259.

*Isaiah 45:9–25*

(45:15). In a poem that thematizes divine speech, it is divine speech that counters this charge of hiddenness, but there are aspects of divine hiddenness left uncontested in this response (see 54:8). Divine hiddenness, raised in the opening poem, will remain at issue in the complex relationship between the people and their God. The statement "you are a God who hides himself" is left in the poem as a potential expression of the poem's reality. In a poem that enacts a humbling of its audience's apparent overconfidence in their perspective on events, the hiddenness of God stands as an expression of humble human living. God is proclaimed as both hidden and savior, inviting unpretentious, uncontentious trust.

The ironic tone and interest in the reliability of divine speech continues when the rhetorical questions reappear (45:21). The invitation to "Declare and present" leaves the object of these verbs gapped in the Hebrew text,[356] while the query "Who told this long ago?" and its parallel "Who declared it of old?" with their explicit connection to the LORD each supply their object ("this" *zō 't* and "it" as the suffix *āh*). It is as if those who speak do so in such obvious incompleteness when compared to the divine voice that even what they are invited to say does not merit direct reference.

As the poem's concluding lines invite "all the ends of the earth" to turn to the LORD for salvation, the insistence on the reliability of divine speech continues,[357] and a transformation appears in the speech of others. The parallelism between the divine voice's claim "By myself I have sworn" (*bî nišba 'tî*, 45:23), and the image of "every tongue" that will "swear" (*tiššāba '*, 45:23) to the LORD illustrates this transition. The future transformed speech claims that "only in the LORD" do "righteousness and strength" (*ṣĕdāqôt wā 'ōz*) belong (45:24). It is not said explicitly that this will result for those who "Turn to me," but the poetic juxtaposition suggests the possibility. The security of the divine word is again characterized by "righteousness" (*ṣĕdāqâ*, 45:23), which is language applied to the "triumph" of Israel (*yiṣdĕqû*, 45:25) who stands in direct contrast to those who contend (45:24). The poem that began by refuting the contenders through a strident caricature concludes by offering a vision of the transformation of

---

[356] The verbs simply read "Declare and present." The NRSV[ue] supplies "your case" which is not indicated in the Hebrew as the object of these verbs.

[357] See J. L. McKenzie, *Second Isaiah* (1968), 84, on the effectiveness of the divine word.

136                                                                          *Commentary*

those who would complain into those who proclaim the uniqueness and righteousness of the LORD.

Throughout, the poem retains its interest in overcoming the audience's apparent objections to what the LORD is doing through utter transformation of their perspective. It insists on the divine voice's freedom to leave itself unexplained, all the while glorifying its speech in contrast to that of its questioners. It is a poem that humbles the audience yet assures them of their preciousness. It accomplishes these effects through a juxtaposition of tones in the divine speaking voice, through meaningful ambiguity and through allusion and word play. Ironic indictment and gentle reassurance combine with the same apparent goal: to invite the audience out of the objections they have raised to inhabit the LORD's vision of the future. It is a vision that is sketched in imagery of honor among the nations but that remains, at least in part, hidden and unrevealed. The audience are invited into a relationship of trust in the one whose word is trustworthy, but their complaint about divine "hiddenness" remains part of the tensive fabric of the poems.

A CLOSER LOOK: A GOD WHO HIDES HIMSELF

The statement "Truly, you are a God who hides himself, O God of Israel, the Savior" (45:15) expresses one of the central tensions of Isaiah 40–55. That is, it further articulates one of the two complaints expressed in one of the voices to be closely identified with the audience. In Isaiah 40:27, Jacob-Israel's cited complaint includes "My way is hidden from the LORD." As with Zion's complaint that the LORD had "forsaken" and "forgotten" her (49:14), the divine voice refutes the charge of hiddenness in Isa 45:19 (see also 49:15).[358] Ultimately, however, the rebuttals of each of these charges stand juxtaposed within the book as a whole with the divine voice's statement in Isa 54:7–8 "For a brief moment I abandoned you .... In overflowing wrath for a moment I hid my face from you." This apparent

---

[358]  The divine voice makes a less clear claim in Isaiah 48:16. See further commentary on that passage. There the claim *lō ' mērō 'š bassēter dibbartî* (i.e., woodenly, "not from the first have I spoken in secret"; NRSV[ue]: "From the beginning I have not spoken in secret") stands slightly in tension with this more categorical claim "I did not speak in secret" (45:19) but is less contradictory than the statement of Isaiah 54:8. On the ambiguity of the voice speaking in 40:27, see further the commentary on that passage.

# A Closer Look: A God Who Hides Himself

contradiction is part of the poetic meaning-making mode of the Isaian poetry. It juxtaposes both claim and counterclaim and allows their resonances and dissonances to work emotionally upon the audience.

These are poems about the relationship between the LORD and the people. That relationship is one in which the people express their sense of alienation and are charged with sin and rebellion (42:24; 43:22–24; 43:27; 48:8–11) and in which the LORD both extends comfort (e.g., 40:1; 43:1–7; 44:1–4; 49:19–23; 51:12) and burns with indignation (e.g., 42:18–25; 43:22–28; 48:1–11; 50:1–3). Reconciliation of such an emotionally charged breach is not achieved through straightforward proclamation of comfort but through a juxtaposition of compassion and wrath that allows the audience to imagine the results of each. The divine voice's movement between compassion and wrath throughout the series of poems addressed to the exiles in Babylon achieves a resolution in Isaiah 54:7–8 where the breach of relationship of which the audience complained is admitted but marked as entirely past.[359] The tension produced by the rebuttals of these complaints earlier in the series of poems contributes heavily to the emotional impact and sense of resolution produced by these lines.

The reappearance of this imagery in chapters 56–66 appears to reopen the issue in a new situation (see further Historical Context and Isaiah 56–66 in the Introduction). In Isaiah 57:17, the divine voice indicts and indicates that God hides in anger but immediately expresses an intention to "heal" and "comfort" (57:18). In Isaiah 59:2, sin is again the cause of hiding, this time not indicating that God hides but making "your sins" the thing that has hidden God. The final chapters of the book as a whole return to this idea, juxtaposing the complaint "you have hidden your face from us" (64:7) with images of contrast between restoration for the "servants" (see further A Closer Look: From Servant to Servants) and judgment on those who rebel (see, e.g., 65:24).

While divine hiddenness might achieve resolution in these chapters, it is not an idea that is rejected as unrelated to the faith of God's people.

---

[359] See further K. M. Heffelfinger, *I Am Large* (2011), 265–269. Samuel E. Balentine, *The Hidden God: The Hiding of the Face of God in the Old Testament* (Oxford: Oxford University Press, 1983), 148, treats Isaiah 54:7–8's use of "two of the prominent themes of the hiddenness of God – the hiding of God's face and forsaking" as a usage distinct from both "lament" and "judgement" indicating that "here both these contexts are superseded by placing the themes within the context of the affirmation of God's love."

138 Commentary

Balentine helpfully observes about the faith portrayed in the biblical texts that in them God is "both hidden and present, both near and far away. This is precisely the dilemma which faith in God presents. It is not, however, a dilemma that undermines Israel's faith, though it does stretch it to its farthest dimensions."[360] As a book ultimately about relationship, Isaiah resolves tensions but allows them to stand as testimony to the nature of divine-human interaction and the ongoing journey into which it invites its audience.

ISAIAH 46:1–13

[1] Bel bows down; Nebo stoops;
  their idols are on beasts and cattle;
these things you carry are loaded
  as burdens on weary animals.
[2] They stoop; they bow down together;
  they cannot save the burden
  but themselves go into captivity.
[3] Listen to me, O house of Jacob,
  all the remnant of the house of Israel,
who have been borne by me from your birth,
  carried from the womb;
[4] even to your old age I am he;
  even when you turn gray I will carry you.
I have made, and I will bear;
  I will carry and will save.

[5] To whom will you liken me and make me equal
  and compare me, as though we were alike?
[6] Those who lavish gold from the purse
  and weigh out silver in the scales –
they hire a goldsmith, who makes it into a god;
  then they fall down and worship!

---

[360] S. E. Balentine, *The Hidden God* (1983), 172.

*Isaiah 46:1–13*

139

⁷ They lift it to their shoulders; they carry it;
 they set it in its place, and it stands there;
 it cannot move from its place.
If one cries out to it, it does not answer
 or save anyone from trouble.

⁸ Remember this and consider;
 recall it to mind, you transgressors;
⁹ remember the former things of old,[361]
 for I am God, and there is no other;
 I am God, and there is no one like me,
¹⁰ declaring the outcome from the beginning
 and from ancient times things not yet done,
saying, "My purpose shall stand,
 and I will fulfill my intention,"
¹¹ calling a bird of prey from the east,
 the man for my purpose from a far country.
I have spoken, and I will bring it to pass;
 I have planned, and I will do it.

¹² Listen to me, you stubborn of heart,
 you who are far from deliverance:
¹³ I bring near my deliverance; it is not far off,
 and my salvation will not tarry;
I will put salvation in Zion,
 for Israel my glory.

Again in this poem the divine voice speaks in a confrontational tone.[362] The heart of the problem appears to be an inability or unwillingness of the addressees to recognize they have been cared for by the LORD and to trust in God's promises of coming deliverance. The poem does not state this problem directly. Instead, it engages the audience with a comparison

---

[361] I am departing from NRSVᵘᵉ's lineation here. The two commands to remember stand in clear parallelism to one another, which seems best represented by arranging them in line-initial positions.

[362] K. Baltzer, *Deutero-Isaiah* (2001), 254, observes the repeated "sharp *s* sound" in vv. 1–4, commenting that "it may also have to do with content. The hiss is a gesture of repulsion and defense."

140                                                                    *Commentary*

between the idols and the LORD alongside reminders of past deliverance. It emphasizes the supreme sovereignty and superiority of the LORD over any and all others.[363] Imperatives, rhetorical questions, and such forms of address as "transgressors" (46:8) and "stubborn of heart" (46:12) give the poem its argumentative tone.

The opening lines of the poem employ a vivid image of the weakness and ineffectiveness of idols. These lines employ specific names of Babylonian deities and possibly recall a scene that the exiles might have witnessed as Babylonian idols were brought from their sanctuaries into the city of Babylon for safekeeping prior to the impending attack by Cyrus. Briant points to the Nabonidus Chronicle's indications that Nabonidus moved "cult statues" of several Babylonian sanctuaries to Babylon as evidence that "direct hostilities . . . had perhaps (or probably) begun before 540."[364] Indeed, the Nabonidus Chronicle lists the names of gods who "entered" Babylon, just before it recounts an attack by Cyrus "at Opis on [the bank(?)] of the Tigris against the army of the land of Akkad."[365] Notably, the gods mentioned by the Chronicle are not those named in Isa 46:1, but the imagery and its associations with impending battle would have resonated.[366] Here the poetic imagery paints an ironic picture of the gods to whom the Babylonians prayed for deliverance as themselves requiring deliverance in the face of impending battle.[367]

In diametric contrast to the idols that must be carried (*nĕśu 'ōtêkem*, 46:1 and '*ămûsôt*, 46:1) and which cannot "save" (*mallēṭ*, 46:2), the audience are addressed by the LORD who has "carried" them (*ha 'ămusîm*, 46:3 and *hannĕśu 'îm*, 46:3), and "will save" ('*amallēṭ*, 46:4).[368] The contrast offered has the potential to be reassuring. However, in the broader context, it

---

[363]  J. Muilenburg, "Isaiah 40–66" (1956), 5:535, says this idea "emerges out of the first two strophes."

[364]  P. Briant, *From Cyrus* (2002), 41.

[365]  B. T. Arnold, "Chronicle 7" (2006), 420.

[366]  Interestingly, K. Baltzer, *Deutero-Isaiah* (2001), 256, observes that the two deities named here are the ones who appear as "Cyrus' tutelary gods" in the Cyrus Cylinder text.

[367]  The imagery may be doubly ominous if, as Hanspeter Schaudig, "'Bēl Bows, Nabû Stoops!' The Prophecy of Isaiah xlvi 1–2 as a Reflection of Babylonian 'Processional Omens,'" *VT* 58 (2008): 357–571, esp. 567, argues, it reflects Babylonian omens derived from the statues' positioning during ceremonial procession, in which case the apparent implication is impending destruction of the city. See also C. Westermann, *Isaiah 40–55* (1969), 178–179; and B. S. Childs, *Isaiah* (2001), 359.

[368]  See also M. A. Sweeney, *Isaiah 40–66* (2016), 130.

*Isaiah 46:1–13* 141

becomes clear that the exiles, though they should be reassured, are not being primarily addressed in a comforting and consoling tone.

The addressees are "house of Jacob" and "remnant of the house of Israel" (46:3) and are offered a broadly encompassing vision that casts their whole existence, from the "womb" to "old age," as being "carried" by the divine speaker. While the audience are quite commonly addressed as Jacob (see A Closer Look: Jacob-Israel and the Exiles), this is the first occurrence of the phrase "house of Jacob" in the chapters addressed to the exiles where it is comparatively rare. In light of the pairing "house of Jacob" and "remnant ... of Israel," it seems likely that the prophetic poet is casting the audience's mind back to the work of Isaiah of Jerusalem, who described a day when the "remnant of Israel and the survivors of the house of Jacob will no longer lean on the one who struck them but will lean on the LORD" (10:20).[369] Such an allusion subtly suggests that though the divine voice claims to have been carrying them all along, the audience have incorrectly identified the source of their support. The stanza's closing insistence that the LORD is the one who has done and will do these things reinforces the sense that the exiles have misidentified their deliverer.

Following on from language that elsewhere underscores the LORD's uniqueness, "I am he" (*'ănî hû'*, 46:4), the divine voice deploys a chain of emphatic self-references "I will carry," "I have made," "I will bear," "I will carry."[370] Each of these underscores the first-person speaker by adding a first-person pronoun to a construction that already marks the verb as first person.[371] Combined with the doubling up of active verbs, two per line in the final couplet of the stanza (46:4), the emphatic self-reference produces

---

[369] Isaiah 10:20 is among those in chapters 1–39 whose association with an eighth-century date is disputed by scholars, see, e.g., the discussion in H. G. M. Williamson, *Book Called Isaiah* (1994), 44; and Hans Wildberger, *Isaiah 1–12* (CC; trans. Thomas H. Trapp; Minneapolis: Fortress, 1991), 435. On treating the resonances of the text in its final form, see A Closer Look: The Final Form and the Former Things. Scholars who pick up resonances between this text and Isaiah's preceding chapters include J. D. W. Watts, *Isaiah 34–66* (2005), 166; and J. Blenkinsopp, *Isaiah 40–55* (2002), 268.

[370] Given the tone of the passage, I am inclined to agree with J. Blenkinsopp, *Isaiah 40–55* (2002), 269, who, noting the positive connotations of the image of YHWH bearing, as in carrying, the audience, also observes "the author's penchant for *double entendre*: Yahveh bears Israel, but Israel continues to be a burden." See further K. Baltzer, *Deutero-Isaiah* (2001), 254–255, on the potential resonances and thematic importance of "burden" in vv. 1–4.

[371] See J. Goldingay and D. Payne, *Isaiah 40–55* (2006), 2:75, on the recurrence of the letter *'ālep* here.

142                                                                      *Commentary*

an intensity of insistence not just upon the activities but upon the one who brings them about.

A brief reiteration of polemic against the idol makers reinforces the intensely challenging tone of the poem by opening with a rhetorical question inviting the audience to suggest a comparison partner for the LORD. The question itself is ironic as the divine voice has already offered a comparison, directly contrasting the LORD with the idols. They clearly cannot produce an adequate comparison partner. The LORD has already shown the comparison to be unsatisfactory. This depiction of the idol makers reinforces the immobility and inability of these figures to help, giving more attention than the previous depiction did to their worshippers who "fall down and worship" (46:6) and who "cr[y] out to it" (46:7). The stanza sits as a parallel to the image of the idols being carried on cattle. Here their origin in someone's "purse" (46:6) and their inability to "move," to "answer," or to "save" (46:7) underscores their uselessness, in direct contrast to the one who is answering by speaking this very poem.

Imperatives paired with negative attributions for the addresses intensify the indicting tone of the poem in the final two stanzas.[372] They are commanded to "Remember this" (46:8) and "remember the former things" (46:9) as well as to "Listen to me" (46:12). The command "remember the former things" in particular suggests a strident tone, for only a few poems ago, in a context of describing comfort so overwhelming it would make memory of past deliverances unnecessary, the audience were commanded "Do not remember the former things" (43:18) (see further A Closer Look: Conflicted Commands and Competing Contentions in the Memory Motif). They are "transgressors" (46:8) and "stubborn of heart" (46:12). Alter translates the second of these as "bull-hearted," noting that "the sense is 'stubborn,' but the strong image of "bull" implicit in the Hebrew *'abirim* is worth retaining."[373] The pairing of these imperatives and attributions implies that the problem for which the audience are being indicted is their failure to remember and to perceive. They have not recognized the work of the LORD in carrying them and in carrying out the LORD's own plans.[374]

---

[372] In his comments on 46:8–13, J. Blenkinsopp, *Isaiah 40–55* (2002), 272, observes "a stronger note of asseveration" and "a growing sense of exasperation."

[373] R. Alter, *Hebrew Bible* (2019), 779.

[374] K. Baltzer, *Deutero-Isaiah* (2001), 262, observes that the term here is not the divine name (Yhwh) but the word God, specifically El in the first iteration in v. 9. Baltzer observes the

# A Closer Look: Jacob-Israel and the Exiles

Continuing the ironic comparison between the idols and the LORD, the idols cannot "save" (*yôšî'ennû*, 46:7), but the LORD provides "salvation" (*tĕšû'â*, 46:13). The audience may be "far"(*hārĕḥôqîm*, 46:12) from rescue but the LORD, who is bringing a deliverer from "far" (*merḥāq*, 46:11), offers deliverance that "is not far off" (*lō' tirḥāq*, 46:13).

This poem presents promises of coming deliverance[375] and salvation (*tĕšû'ātî*, 46:13) but does so in a tone that strongly conveys aggravation from the divine voice. The passing mention of "the man for my purpose from a far country" (46:11) might suggest that the exiles have resisted the proclamation that the LORD was using Cyrus to accomplish God's own purposes for Israel, but if so, this resistance is not cited.[376] While the intention to deliver remains (46:13), the exiles stand indicted as an audience who cannot correctly perceive the strength and power of the LORD as overwhelmingly and incomparably greater than the idols who can do nothing.[377]

## A CLOSER LOOK: JACOB-ISRAEL AND THE EXILES

Second Isaiah's preferred term of address for its audience is the parallel pair Jacob and Israel. This is especially the case in chapters 40–48.[378] This particular patriarch perhaps appeals to an exilic audience since Jacob is associated with living outside the land both during his service to Laban

---

sound resonances of this word in context and comments that "The God of the whole world is Israel's God too."

[375] It is noteworthy that both v. 12 and 13 employ forms of the root *ṣdq*, a word that the prophetic poet often associates with the LORD, and particularly divine deliverance, in these chapters. See R. Rendtorff, "Isaiah 56:1" (1993), 183. See also the way this term is used in the preceding poem in the comment on Isa 45:9–25, and in the comment of J. L. McKenzie, *Second Isaiah* (1968), 87.

[376] See Michael Jay Chan, "Cyrus, Yhwh's Bird of Prey (Isa. 46.11): Echoes of an Ancient Near Eastern Metaphor," *JSOT* 35.1 (2010): 113–127, who argues that an Ancient Near Eastern "convention . . . associates royal monarchs and their military activities with the behavior of birds of prey" (116). J. Goldingay and D. Payne, *Isaiah 40–55* (2006), 2:84, observe that "the one called is not named" (83) and illustrate the range of suggestions that have been made, concluding that "one can hardly fail to infer that Cyrus is the primary referent of v. 11" (84). As K. Baltzer, *Deutero-Isaiah* (2001), 263, observes, "more important than this particular person is his place in God's 'plan.'"

[377] As B. S. Childs, *Isaiah* (2001), 359, comments, "the real focus of the chapter" is "the radical contrast between the Gods of Babylon and the only true God of Israel."

[378] See T. Linafelt, *Surviving Lamentations* (2000), 66.

(Gen 28–33)[379] and when he joined his son Joseph in Egypt at the end of his life (Gen 46–50). This last episode may convey some motivation for exilic attachment to him as he expresses his fidelity to the land by making Joseph promise to bury him there (Gen 50:29–33). In addition, they may well have welcomed association with a patriarch to whom God said of his coming departure from the land "do not be afraid . . . for I will make of you a great nation there. I myself will go down with you . . . and I will also bring you up again" (Gen 46:3–4). These promises resonate closely with Second Isaiah's message to the exiles in their own day. They were to reject fear (see Bridging the Horizons: Fear Not) and to trust that God was restoring them.

The poetry also appears to put the patriarchal attribution to work for its own purposes. The blessing Isaac gives to Jacob envisions him receiving honor and service from the peoples of other lands, an idea that resonates with Second Isaiah's vision of restoration (Gen 27:29; cf. 49:22–23; 55:5). On the other hand, Jacob is a "trickster" figure, whose exile is the result of angering his brother Esau (Gen 27:42–45).[380] While it is fair to say that Genesis does not evaluate Jacob negatively, it does appear that Second Isaiah relies on some tradition that treats his deception negatively, possibly the same tradition that Hosea 12 knows.[381]

Second Isaiah may work with the negative elements of a tradition about Jacob, but the poet also seems to work to transform the audience by means of this motif. The pairing Jacob-Israel alludes to the patriarch's name change.[382] The second term of the pair is one given to him with the words

---

[379] As J. Blenkinsopp, *Isaiah 40–55* (2002), 194, comments, "It is noteworthy how often those addressed in chs. 40–48 are named after the ancestor who spent twenty years in exile in Mesopotamia, raised a family there, and returned to the ancestral land." See K. Baltzer, *Deutero-Isaiah* (2001), 180–181, who draws out numerous parallels between Isa 43 and the Jacob story in Genesis.

[380] See the discussion of trickster figures in Susan Niditch, "Genesis," in *Women's Bible Commentary* (20th Anniversary ed.; eds. Carol A. Newsom, Sharon H. Ringe, and Jacqueline E. Lapsley; Louisville: Westminster John Knox, 2012), 33, and her discussion of Jacob as trickster (38).

[381] See, e.g., J. L. McKenzie, *Second Isaiah* (1968), 59; and J. Goldingay and D. Payne, *Isaiah 40–55* (2006), 1:315, who also point to Isa 58:14's reference to Jacob as ancestor.

[382] See also H. G. M. Williamson, *Book Called Isaiah* (1994), 145, who notes the choice of Jacob as "one of Deutero-Isaiah's favourite names for the exiled Israelites" and who also observes that "he generally uses Jacob for the empirical Israel of his day – that is to say, for the people in their dispirited and depressed condition rather than as the Israel full of faith which the prophet holds out before them and towards which he encourages them

*Isaiah 47:1–15*  145

"you have striven with God and with humans and have prevailed" (Gen 32:28). In a prophetic book that addresses the exiles' complaint and that discloses numerous indications of "striving," such an allusion is two-edged. The exiles may hear both that they are "strivers" and that they have prevailed.[383]

Second Isaiah seems, at times, engaged in the project of changing Jacob's name again. Poetic word play associates Jacob with "rough places" and juxtaposes that idea with "uprightness" (see further the commentary on Isa 44:1–5). Jacob is to be transformed into that which is upright, most fully characterized by the Servant of the LORD, with whom Jacob is regularly associated (see further A Closer Look: The Servant and His Songs).

ISAIAH 47:1–15

[1] Come down and sit in the dust,
    virgin daughter Babylon!
Sit on the ground without a throne,
    daughter Chaldea!
For you shall no more be called
    tender and delicate.
[2] Take the millstones and grind meal;
    remove your veil;
strip off your robe; uncover your legs;
    pass through the rivers.
[3] Your nakedness shall be uncovered,
    and your shame shall be seen.

---

to move." Contra J. T. Walsh, "Summons to Judgement" (1993): 363, who thinks the names Jacob and Israel "function more or less synonymously" most of the time in Second Isaiah. However, he notes that in Isaiah 41:8, where the typical order is reversed, "there is a progression from 'Israel', the more political name for the nation, to 'Jacob', the name more deeply rooted in patriarchal traditions, to 'Abraham', a strictly individual patriarchal name."

[383] Despite the appropriate caution of William P. Brown, *A Handbook to Old Testament Exegesis* (Louisville: Westminster John Knox, 2017), 81, that the "folk etymology ... is only phonetically related to the name Israel," it is noteworthy, as Brown's comment recognizes, that the idea also appears in Hos 12:4. It could, then, reasonably be part of the traditions about Jacob's name that the poet-prophet responsible for Second Isaiah knows, whether either of these texts in their final form are known or not.

I will take vengeance,
>> and I will spare no one.
4 Our Redeemer – the LORD of hosts is his name –
>> is the Holy One of Israel.

5 Sit in silence, and go into darkness,
>> daughter Chaldea!
For you shall no more be called
>> the mistress of kingdoms.
6 I was angry with my people;
>> I profaned my heritage;
I gave them into your hand;
>> you showed them no mercy;
on the aged you made your yoke
>> exceedingly heavy.
7 You said, "I shall be mistress forever,"
>> so that you did not lay these things to heart
>> or remember their end.

8 Now therefore hear this, you lover of pleasures,
>> who sit securely,
who say in your heart,
>> "I am, and there is no one besides me;
I shall not sit as a widow
>> or know the loss of children" –
9 both these things shall come upon you
>> in a moment, in one day:
the loss of children and widowhood
>> shall come upon you in full measure,
in spite of your many sorceries
>> and the great power of your enchantments.

10 You felt secure in your wickedness;
>> you said, "No one sees me."
Your wisdom and your knowledge
>> led you astray,
and you said in your heart,
>> "I am, and there is no one besides me."

*Isaiah 47:1–15*

11 But evil shall come upon you,
  which you cannot charm away;
disaster shall fall upon you,
  which you will not be able to ward off,
and ruin shall come on you suddenly,
  of which you know nothing.

12 Stand fast in your enchantments
  and your many sorceries,
  with which you have labored from your youth;
perhaps you may be able to succeed;
  perhaps you may inspire terror.
13 You are wearied with your many consultations;
  let those who study the heavens
stand up and save you,
  those who gaze at the stars
and at each new moon predict
  what shall befall you.

14 See, they are like stubble;
  the fire consumes them;
they cannot deliver themselves
  from the power of the flame.
No coal for warming oneself is this,
  no fire to sit before!
15 Such to you are those with whom you have labored,
  who have trafficked with you from your youth;
they all wander about in their own paths;
  there is no one to save you.

For the exiles, listening to this intense poem of judgment that announces the destruction of their oppressor must have been an encouraging experience.[384] Even more intensely than the ridiculing of the idol makers

---

[384] J. Blenkinsopp, *Isaiah 40–55* (2002), 278, calls the passage "Ritualized verbal humiliation of a defeated enemy ... one of several forms adopted in oracles against a political enemy." It is certainly consumed with pronouncing Babylon's judgment by Israel's God and it does so with an overwhelming sense of "poetic justice." C. Westermann, *Isaiah 40–66* (1969), 190, observes its poeticism. These features presumably have an intended

148  *Commentary*

in preceding poems, this set of images unmasks their enemy and systematically strips away its power over the exiles. Babylon, the capital city of
their captors, personified as a woman, stands in vivid contrast to their
home (see A Closer Look: City as Woman in the Ancient Near East). This
appearance of the city personified as a woman, coming as it does before the
poems that employ the Lady Zion image, sets an expectation that the
vengeance (47:3) announced will take the form of reversal. Babylon the
haughty conqueror will find herself overthrown at the hand of the God of
the people she had taken prisoner. Images from this poem reappear in the
poems that illustrate Zion's restoration underscoring this reversal (see
A Closer Look: Daughter Zion and Daughter Babylon). The poem's effectiveness in offering comfort through the judgment of the enemy and the
reversal of that enemy's apparent triumph is carried by an angry and
sarcastic tone. The divine voice conveys that tone through the address to
the personified city, sound play, repetition, and ironic commands that
stand in contrast to the divine voice's insistence about its own
impending activities.

The poem begins by stripping away the illusion of a glorious capital city.
Imperatives demand that the city, figured as a woman, "sit" (47:1, 5) "in the
dust" (47:1), "on the ground" (47:1), and "in silence" (47:5). Heavily alliterated lines call attention to the addressee of the opening imperatives: "virgin
daughter Babylon" (*bĕtûlat bat-bābel*, v. 1).[385] While "daughter Babylon"
would ensure recognition of the trope of the city as woman, and daughter
(*bat*) is the language employed in both of the references to "daughter
Chaldea" (47:1, 5), the addition of "virgin" (*bĕtûlat*) here seems designed
to increase the attention-drawing alliteration of the line.[386] A much less
intense echoing appears between "throne" (*kissēʾ*) and "Chaldea" (*kaśdîm*),

---

rhetorical impact on the exilic audience. See J. Goldingay and D. Payne, *Isaiah 40–55*
(2006), 2:87, who note that the "our" of v. 4 implies the exilic audience's presence as "the
audience in the house."

[385] J. Goldingay and D. Payne, *Isaiah 40–55* (2006), 2:93, also note the "striking"
alliteration here.

[386] J. Goldingay and D. Payne, *Isaiah 40–55* (2006), 2:93, also treat the choice of terms and
their grammatical structure as possibly motivated by the alliteration produced. Contra
J. Muilenburg, "Isaiah 40–66" (1956), 5:544, who interprets the term "virgin" here as
based in the idea that Babylon is "unconquered." On rejecting the idea that it connotes
"inviolate," see John Goldingay, "What Happens to Ms Babylon in Isaiah 47, Why, and
Who Says So?," *TynBul* 47.2 (1996): 221.

*Isaiah 47:1–15*                                                              149

perhaps underscoring the loss of royal stature for the city and the contrast between where she is expected to sit, "a throne," and where she must now sit, "in the dust" (47:1). Lamentations began by crying out "How lonely sits the city," that is, Jerusalem (Lam 1:1). Here, the destruction that is coming for Babylon results in the same posture.[387] For exiles familiar with Lamentations, the image of Babylon sitting as a woman hints at the idea of vengeance before it is announced (47:3).

The poem undermines both Babylon's luxury and her power. Twice the divine voice says "For you shall no more be called" (47:1, 5), and each time a distinct title is removed. First, she will no longer be called "tender and delicate," terms that seem to imply having been sheltered and afforded luxury.[388] These attributes appear within a poetic unit that juxtaposes various images of humiliation.[389] Repetitive guttural sounds convey the harshness of commanded manual labor ("Take the millstones and grind meal" *qĕḥî rēḥayim wĕṭaḥănî qāmaḥ*, 47:1),[390] and repeated references to disrobing ("remove," "strip off," "uncover" all forms of *glh*) convey "shame" (47:3).[391] Exposure of "nakedness" and commanded physical labor together overturn any sense of a protected and privileged life. In much the same way as Lamentations voices the demotion of the "princess among the provinces" (Lam 1:1), here Babylon has been brought down from apparent royal stature to a humiliated and hard existence.

The second occurrence of "For you shall no more be called" (47:5) overturns the military preeminence of Babylon. The phrase "mistress of kingdoms" conveys military might. However, the divine voice insists that the might Babylon had apparently shown was actually the LORD's own

---

[387] See also J. Goldingay, "What Happens" (1996), 219.

[388] See, e.g., Deut 28:54, 56, where the nouns there translated "refined and gentle" (NRSV[ue]) are used to describe people who will begrudge others shared food as an image of the extremity of siege. The import of this word pair is to underscore extremity by indicating even those who these words describe will be reticent. In the case of the female (v. 56), the pairing is modified by the phrase "does not venture to set the sole of her foot on the ground." See also J. Goldingay and D. Payne, *Isaiah 40–55* (2006), 2:94; and J. Goldingay, "What Happens" (1996), 222.

[389] See J. Blenkinsopp, *Isaiah 40–55* (2002), 280.

[390] K. Baltzer, *Deutero-Isaiah* (2001), 271, calls it "Onomatopoeia" for "the grating sound" of ancient milling by hand. J. Muilenburg, "Isaiah 40–66" (1956), 5:544, also uses the term.

[391] K. Baltzer, *Deutero-Isaiah* (2001), 270, points to "sexual connotation" here. See also B. S. Childs, *Isaiah* (2001), 366, on the "humiliation" depicted; J. Blenkinsopp, *Isaiah 40–55* (2002), 280; and S. Moughtin-Mumby, *Sexual and Marital* (2008), 137.

150                                                                    *Commentary*

judgment upon the people. The repetition of sounds reinforces the intensity of the divine voice's insistence upon its own activity. "I" and "my" are conveyed by the long i-vowels that repeatedly conclude words in the couplet (*qāṣaptî ʿal-ʿammî ḥillaltî naḥălātî*, 47:6) with the second line of the couplet (*ḥillaltî naḥălātî*) intensifying the alliteration with "I profaned by heritage" dominated by the combination of the guttural *ḥ* with *l* and *t* sounds.[392] The heavy repetition of "I" language gives way to an invective directed at "you," which challenges Babylon's lack of mercy and lack of perception.

That daughter Babylon did not "lay these things to heart" (47:7) begins a movement in the poem from emphasizing what Babylon will no longer be called by others (47:1, 5) to an undermining of what she says of herself. Twice the divine voice chastises Babylon for saying "in your heart" (47:8, 10) words that sound very much like the LORD's own self-attribution: "I am, and there is no one besides me" (47:8, 10; cf. 43:11; 44:6–8; 45:5–6, 21–22; 46:9). Babylon's misplaced pride, as she is personified here, goes beyond a haughtiness about her role among the nations and her military prowess and instead extends to an attempt to take up that status that the poems up to this point have been insisting, quite emphatically, belongs to God alone. For the audience who have heard the preceding poems and their insistence upon the LORD's singularity, these words attributed to daughter Babylon must certainly convey a heavy irony and a serious threat.[393] They cannot expect that the divine voice, which has been insisting on God's own uniqueness, will tolerate such a statement by the exiles' oppressor.

The poem figures retribution in swift and intensely patterned imagery. Precisely what Babylon says she will not experience, being widowed and bereaved of children (47:8), the divine voice promises to turn back upon her. The turning back is perhaps conveyed by the reversal of the order of

---

[392] The single exception is the preposition *ʿal*, which is attached by a *maqqēp* to "my people."

[393] See, e.g., K. Baltzer, *Deutero-Isaiah* (2001), 276, who highlights these words' resonances with these chapters' insistence on the idea that "uniqueness is a predicate that belongs to God alone." B. S. Childs, *Isaiah* (2001), 366, also recognizes this resonance. J. Muilenburg, "Isaiah 40–66" (1956), 5:548, calls it "theocentric self-asseveration." J. L. McKenzie, *Second Isaiah* (1968), 92, also notes the self-divinizing elements here. See also Chris A. Franke, "The Function of the Satiric Lament over Babylon in Second Isaiah (XLVII)," *VT* 41.4 (1991): 413; and S. Moughtin-Mumby, *Sexual and Martial* (2008), 137–138.

*Isaiah 47:1–15*                                                                 151

these terms (47:9). The recompense will be total ("both these things"
and "in full measure" 47:9) as well as swift ("in a moment, in one day"
47:9). Heavy sarcasm attributes Babylon's delusion to her "knowledge"
(47:10), culminating in three intensely patterned couplets that convey
both the certainty of coming destruction and the ineffectiveness of
Babylon's knowledge (47:11). The first line of each couplet follows the
pattern of a verb of approach ("come," "fall," "come"), "upon you"
(*'ālayik*), and a series of words for destruction ("evil," "disaster,"
"ruin").[394] The second line of each couplet conveys Babylon's inability
to avert disaster, beginning in each instance with the negative particle
(*lō'*). The first and last of these employ the verb "you know" (*tēdĕ'î*) to
convey that inability. Emphatically, repeatedly, and in a form whose
orderliness conveys control and precision, the divine voice underscores
the futility of Babylon's "knowledge" alongside the certainty of the
destruction that approaches.

In such a context the command "Stand fast in your enchantments" can
only be read as heavily sarcastic.[395] Babylon is not here being invited to
stand when she had been ordered to "sit" (47:1, 5). Instead, the poem
ironically juxtaposes an upright and resisting posture with the humbling
that has already been spoken. Repetition of "perhaps" underscores the
ironic tone as do the images of having "labored" (v. 12, 15) and "youth"
(v. 12, 15), which recall the promise of strength for those who wait on the
LORD (40:30–31) but here convey the uselessness of those upon whom
Babylon depends. These probable references to Babylonian religious
practitioners ("those who study the heavens" and "those who gaze at
the stars," 47:13) are rejected as unable to "deliver themselves" (47:14) or
"to save you" (47:15). Instead, an image of a dangerous and powerful fire
adds to the indicting and threatening tone of the poem as it draws to
a conclusion.

---

[394] The last of these expands the pattern slightly with the addition of the word "suddenly."
See further J. Goldingay, "What Happens" (1996), 240, who also comments on
the patterning.

[395] B. S. Childs, *Isaiah* (2001), 366, calls "The tone of vv. 12–13 . . . highly ironical." See also
J. Goldingay and D. Payne, *Isaiah 40–55* (2006), 2:91; and J. Goldingay, "What Happens"
(1996), 240. See C. A. Franke, "Function" (1991), 414, 417, who notes the ironic tone of
the passage. R. Alter, *Hebrew Bible* (2019), 781, notes the additional sarcasm conveyed by
the inclusion of "the polite particle" here.

In this poem the divine voice speaks threateningly to the audience's enemy in a poem aimed at and designed for the exiles' "overhearing."[396] The personified city that has held them captive has her "knowledge" dramatically undermined, her self-presentation rejected, and her international stature taken away both in terms of luxury and might. For the exiles, this is a triumphant proclamation but one that stands in a productive tension with depictions of Zion. This daughter Babylon poem sets up motifs upon which the poetry will build in its depictions of daughter Zion's restoration even as it adds its voice to the tensive grouping of images and tones that undermine the exiles' fears and invite embrace of the divine voice's vision.

A CLOSER LOOK: DAUGHTER ZION AND DAUGHTER BABYLON

The female personification of the city of Babylon stands as a direct counterpart to the figure of Zion.[397] She directly picks up imagery used to describe Zion and depicts the overturning of Zion's punishment and its redirection onto her enemy. In Lamentations, Zion had pleaded, "Bring on the day that you have announced, and let them be as I am" (Lam 1:21). The fulsome depiction of Zion in Lamentations portrays her "thrown down . . . to earth" (2:1), as once a "princess among the provinces" (1:1), and now "like a widow" (1:1) with "fire" in her "bones" (1:13). She is "humiliated" (2:1), "weep[s]" (1:16). and seeks comfort from her "lovers" but finds none (1:17–19). She is called both "daughter" (e.g., 1:6, 2:1, 8, 10, 13, 15) and "virgin daughter" (e.g., 2:13).

The appearance of Daughter Babylon, which comes in Isaiah 47, enacts precisely the overturning called for in Lam 1:21. She is depicted in ways that echo Zion's distress in Lamentations. She, too, is "daughter" and "virgin daughter" (47:1). She is commanded to "sit in the dust" (47:1). She is no longer to be "mistress of kingdoms" (47:5). She, too, seeks aid, but "there is no one to save you" (47:15) and the threat of "fire" depicts the treacherousness of those to whom she looks for help (47:14).[398] Zion was "like a

---

[396] See further L. Stulman and H. C. P. Kim, *You Are My People* (2012), 66, who read this passage in light of trauma and exile.

[397] See J. Blenkinsopp, *Isaiah 40–55* (2002), 279; and K. Baltzer, *Deutero-Isaiah* (2001), 267.

[398] J. Goldingay and D. Payne, *Isaiah 40–55* (2006), 2:112, note the connection here.

# A Closer Look: Daughter Zion and Daughter Babylon

widow" (Lam 1:1) and there was extensive concern over the death of her children (see e.g., Lam 2:12, 19), where, as Linafelt notes, "The rhetorical move imagined by the poet is for Zion to affront YHWH with the intolerable suffering of children."[399] Babylon will become widowed and bereaved of children "in a moment, in one day" (47:9).[400] The loss of her "veil" and "robe," the stripping off of her clothing and the references to "nakedness" add clothing imagery to the depiction (47:2–3).

When the Zion personification returns in Isaiah 49 and following it picks up on these imageries directly. The overturning is brought full circle. Not only is Babylon made as Zion is, but "the cup of staggering" is "taken from" Zion and placed "into the hand" of her enemy (51:22–23). Zion is overwhelmingly restored and undergoes a role-reversal with Babylon. She hears instructions to "Stand up" (51:17) and "Shake yourself from the dust" (52:2).[401] Zion is now one to whom kings, queens, and peoples pay homage (49:22–23), even to the point of overturning the "dust" imagery with these royal figures said to "lick the dust of your feet" (49:23). The threat of fire is turned away, and the search for one who will deliver is ended, with the LORD who "created" the one "who blows the fire of coals" taking on the role and promising that "No weapon that is fashioned against you will prosper" (54:16–17).[402] The "disgrace" of "widowhood" will be forgotten (54:4), her experience of being "bereaved and barren" (49:21) is treated as a past event, and Zion is "Married" (62:4–5) to the "Lord of Hosts" (54:5). The imagery of Zion's children emphasizes the large number of them (49:18–21; 54:1, 13), their miraculous arrival (54:1; 66:8), and the honor shown to Zion by the kings and queens who serve as "foster fathers" and "nursing mothers" (49:23). While Babylon had had to "strip off" her "robe" and "veil" (47:3), Zion is invited to put on "beautiful garments" (52:1) and is to be decked in jewels (54:11–12).

---

[399] T. Linafelt, "Surviving Lamentations" (1995), 50.

[400] J. Goldingay and D. Payne, *Isaiah 40–55* (2006), 2:104, note that the term *rega* ("in a moment") "reappears in Isa 54.7–8 and takes up from Lamentations." While for Babylon the term points to how quickly two images for destruction come upon her, for Zion the term is redeployed in Isa 54 as imagery of the brevity of the LORD's wrath that is now ended.

[401] See P. Tull Willey, *Remember the Former Things* (1997), 171, who describes the thick resonances with Lamentations in this command to Zion to rise from the dust and develops the connection of "role-reversal" with Babylon.

[402] See K. Baltzer, *Deutero-Isaiah* (2001), 280.

154                                                            *Commentary*

By placing these depictions of the two cities as feminine personifications alongside each other, the poetry enacts its response to Zion's plea. It is not, as Goldingay argues, a critique of Babylon for "lack of womanly feelings"[403] nor is it an indication that "a woman's besetting sin may well be the enjoyment of apparent security rather than striving to make a mark and write her name in heaven."[404] These approaches to understanding the metaphor neglect the primary context that the poem offers. Babylon is not primarily being contrasted with masculine figures in the poems, whether Servant, Cyrus, or the King of Babylon.[405] Instead, she is being contrasted with Zion and this depiction is an enactment of a reversal of divine judgment and a direct response to Zion's plea. This imagery of judgment employing female personifications is not without its problems, particularly in terms its impact on contemporary readers. The female personifications create a context in which depiction of punishment takes on overtones of sexual violence.[406] Understood within its context, it is a reversal of Zion's own complaint, but such imagery should rightly trouble contemporary readers.

The "poetic justice" of the divine response is heavily underscored by the intensely parallel ways that Zion's restoration and Babylon's destruction are depicted, but perhaps even more importantly for Second Isaiah's message, the precision of this overturning and its correspondence to Zion's plea to let her enemies be as she is in Lamentations offers proof of the divine attention and care that Zion has complained about the lack of. The LORD has paid attention to Zion's plea and has responded through direct overturning of the very things that she lamented. Babylon is made as

---

[403] J. Goldingay, "What Happens" (1996), 231–232.

[404] J. Goldingay, "What Happens" (1996), 235.

[405] J. Goldingay, "What Happens" (1996), 235, contrasts Babylon with this last male figure noting that she is "not guilty of the assertiveness of the king of Babylon, who fancies himself as a god (14:13–14)." However, Goldingay's own comments undermine this claim as he admits "Her use of the word 'I' does risk divinising herself." On Babylon's pretensions to divinity in this passage, see further the comment on Isaiah 47.

[406] As J. Blenkinsopp, *Isaiah 40–55* (2002), 280, notes, the use of this imagery, has the "unfortunate corollary ... [of] unleashing ... violent and at times pornographic imagery focusing on the female body." S. Moughtin-Mumby, *Sexual and Marital* (2008), 139, comments that "Even if YHWH's aggression is directed at an enemy, the passage reinforces negative stereotypes of female sexuality, condoning sexual violence against women. While this prophetic poetry redeems one female, it punishes another in the same brutal way."

*A Closer Look: City as Woman in the Ancient Near East*  155

the Zion of Lamentations was, while the restoration of Zion goes further, not only transferring the punishment onto Babylon but depicting an overwhelming restoration of Zion. The two function as direct contrasts to one another, a pair of images that showcases the starkness of the reversal that the divine voice is announcing.[407]

## A CLOSER LOOK: CITY AS WOMAN IN THE ANCIENT NEAR EAST

Lady Zion and Lady Babylon stand out as female personifications in Isaiah's exilic and postexilic chapters. This figure of "city as woman" has been widely commented upon. Many commentaries refer to the city as woman as "traditional" or as part of a wider phenomenon.[408] Baltzer, for example, notes that "the personification of cities as women was connected with the development of city goddesses. The city goddess was associated with the tutelary god of the city or kingdom, the two being wife and husband."[409] Baltzer's comment depends upon the work of Aloysius Fitzgerald who argued that the female portrayal of a city developed out of a "Canaanite pattern"[410] that understood "capital cities . . . as goddesses, who were married to the patron god of the city."[411] However, as Day's analysis highlights, a narrative background such as what Fitzgerald proposes goes beyond the evidence of the biblical texts.[412] This move has

---

[407] See S. Moughtin-Mumby, *Sexual and Marital* (2008), 139, who refers to a "role reversal."

[408] J. Blenkinsopp, *Isaiah 40–55* (2002), 280, uses the language of "traditional" and points to the problematic implications of this metaphor when it is applied to "hostile cities."

[409] K. Baltzer, *Deutero-Isaiah* (2001), 270.

[410] Aloysius Fitzgerald, "*BTWLT* and *BT* as Titles for Capital Cities," *CBQ* 37 (1975): 176.

[411] Aloysius Fitzgerald, "The Mythological Background for the Presentation of Jerusalem as a Queen and False Worship as Adultery in the OT," *CBQ* 34 (1972): 405. This is what Fitzgerald names as the "thesis" of his paper. Its connection to an estimation of Canaanite religion as portrayed primarily in Israelite texts about Canaanite religion is present as a significant influence in the paper as highlighted in the analysis of Fitzgerald's work by Peggy L. Day, "The Personification of Cities as Female in the Hebrew Bible: The Thesis of Aloysius Fitzgerald, F.S.C.," in *Reading From This Place: Social Location and Biblical Interpretation in Global Perspective* (Vol. 2; eds. Fernando F. Segovia and Mary Ann Tolbert; Minneapolis: Fortress Press, 1995), 288.

[412] See especially Day's conclusions in which she articulates her rejection of Fitzgerald's findings: P. L. Day, "Personification of Cities" (1995), 301–302.

156 Commentary

important implications, most notably the potential flattening of the significance of this figure into a divine consort.[413]

The personification of Lady Zion plays an important role in the poetic meaning that exilic and postexilic Isaiah projects. Her role is not limited to the question of her status in relation to the male deity, though the imagery of marriage is directly applied in Isaiah 54. Instead, this is but one element that the female personification allows the poet to draw upon. She stands as an outworking of the personification of the city in Lamentations, which Second Isaiah clearly knows. There she develops the resonances of women as mourners in the ancient world and is figured as mother of her inhabitants.[414] It seems most likely, as Dobbs-Allsopp proposes, that the poet is drawing upon a known trope of a "weeping goddess" in Mesopotamian city laments, not least in the use of this trope in works such as Lamentations. However, as Dobbs-Allsopp stresses, this is the literary use of a known motif, not the importation of a wholesale narrative structure. And, importantly, as Day's work stresses, there is little evidence to support the construction of a narrative such as that of Fitzgerald, which treats such ancient Near Eastern goddess figures as "fertility goddesses."[415]

Jerusalem and her voice are not minimized or discounted by the Isaian poetry. She is not sidelined as a dubious figure imported from echoes of "fertility cults." Instead, she is treated as one of the primary voices that

[413] P. L. Day, "Personification of Cities" (1995) 302, notes the way Fitzgerald's analysis treats the feminine as "secondary." Tellingly, Fitzgerald describes cultures that "resist" feminization. See A. Fitzgerald, "Mythological Background" (1972), 177, 178.

[414] F. W. Dobbs-Allsopp, "The Syntagma of *bat* Followed by a Geographical Name in the Hebrew Bible: A Reconsideration of Its Meaning and Grammar," *CBQ* 57 (1995): 451–470, traces the relationship between the title "daughter" applied in the Hebrew Bible to cities and Mesopotamian city laments, noting these features of the figure among others.

[415] See especially Jo Ann Hackett, "Can a Sexist Model Liberate Us? Ancient Near Eastern 'Fertility' Goddesses," *Journal of Feminist Studies in Religion* 5 (1989): 74, who critiques the conception of "fertility goddesses" as commonly reconstructed for Canaanite religion. She helpfully notes that "the deity in Canaan who is most obviously concerned with fertility of crops is a male god, Baal, and the one most obviously concerned with human fertility is El, another male god. Yet . . . the 'fertility' epithet as a one word explanation is often reserved for the female deities of Canaan. Baal is a storm God and Asherah is a fertility goddess." P. L. Day, "Personification of Cities" (1995), 302, highlights the ways in which Fitzgerald's concerns grow out of assumptions about Canaanite religion and reflect a sharp dichotomy between his understanding of Israelite and Canaanite religion. A. Fitzgerald, "Mythological Background" (1972), 404, refers to the "promiscuous character of Canaanite fertility cults."

*Isaiah 48:1–11* 157

articulates the audience's concerns, fears, and pain. Her struggle is embraced and is addressed by the poetry's primary voice, that of the LORD. She stands alongside the personified Servant as a vision of the people's potential future (see A Closer Look: Lady Zion and the Suffering Servant, the Rhetorical Power of Juxtaposition) and she merits her own direct point of contrast in Lady Babylon (see A Closer Look: Daughter Zion and Daughter Babylon).

ISAIAH 48:1–11

[1] Hear this, O house of Jacob,
  who are called by the name of Israel
  and who came forth from the loins of Judah,
who swear by the name of the LORD
  and invoke the God of Israel
  but not in truth or right.
[2] For they call themselves after the holy city
  and lean on the God of Israel;
  the LORD of hosts is his name.

[3] The former things I declared long ago;
  they went out from my mouth, and I made them known;
  then suddenly I did them, and they came to pass.
[4] Because I know that you are obstinate,
  and your neck is an iron sinew
  and your forehead brass,
[5] I declared them to you from long ago,
  before they came to pass I announced them to you,
so that you would not say, "My idol did them;
  my carved image and my cast image commanded them."

[6] You have heard; now see all this;
  and will you not declare it?
From this time forward I tell you new things,
  hidden things that you have not known.
[7] They are created now, not long ago;
  before today you have never heard of them,
  so that you could not say, "I already knew them."

158                                                              *Commentary*

⁸ You have never heard; you have never known;
     from of old your ear has not been opened.
For I knew that you would act very treacherously
     and that from birth you were called a rebel.

⁹ For my name's sake I defer my anger;
     for the sake of my praise I restrain it for you,
     so that I may not cut you off.
¹⁰ See, I have refined you but not like silver;
     I have tested you in the furnace of adversity.
¹¹ For my own sake, for my own sake, I do it,
     for why should my name be profaned?
     My glory I will not give to another.

An ominous tone characterizes the experience this poem offers in an extended indictment of the audience that employs vivid imagery, both for their stubbornness and for the LORD's anger. Failures correctly to name themselves and their deliverer stand juxtaposed to declarations about what the LORD knows and makes known.[416]

As the poem opens, the reference to the addressee is expanded through participles. This pattern often magnifies the divine speaker (e.g., 42:5; 43:1, 16–17; 44:2, 24–26) in these chapters.[417] However, this expansion begins a poem that does not glorify the audience but chastises them. Through repeated references to "name" (48:1, 2, 9)[418] and what one is "called" (48:1, "call" 48:2, 8), the poem undermines the audience's claims about who they are while insisting upon who God is. Throughout these chapters, the divine voice has frequently called the audience by the pair of names Jacob and Israel (see A Closer Look: Jacob-Israel and the Exiles). While

---

[416] See the discussion of B. S. Childs, *Isaiah* (2001), 370–371, regarding the history of interpretation of this text and the various proposals for considering it a product of editorial work. See also the helpful comments of J. Goldingay and D. Payne, *Isaiah 40–55* (2006), 2:120–121, in this regard. The final form and poetic orientation of this commentary focus on the meaning of the passage as it finally and now stands (see A Closer Look: The Final Form and the Former Things).

[417] See, e.g., J. Goldingay and D. Payne, *Isaiah 40–55* (2006), 2:122–123.

[418] NRSV[ue]'s translation of v. 11 includes the word "name," though it does not appear in the Hebrew text. J. Muilenburg, "Isaiah 40–66" (1956), 5:558, thinks the word for name "has fallen from the Hebrew text, but is essential here." He notes its presence in the Septuagint. J. Blenkinsopp, *Isaiah 40–55* (2002), 286, comments "the Masoretes omitted *šĕmî* to avoid juxtaposing the Name of God with the verb *ḥll*, 'profane.'"

*Isaiah 48:1–11*                                                                                    159

they are "called by the name Israel" (48:1), the divine voice knows that "that from birth you were called a rebel" (48:8). Israel's birth name, Jacob, emerges not from his success in wrestling "with God and with humans" (Gen. 32:28), but from his wrestling with his brother Esau in the womb (Gen. 25:22). The poem's movement from being called by the name Israel, to being called a "rebel" since birth perhaps follows a movement reversing the renaming from Israel: "you have striven with God and with humans and have prevailed" (Gen 32:28) to Jacob, the supplanter, who strove with his brother, and found himself an exile.[419] By juxtaposing an echo of this early strife-filled depiction of Jacob with images of divine anger and the glory of God's own name, the poem hints that this moment is focused not on restoration but wrath. The audience, whose speech about the name of the LORD (48:1) is "not ... truth" and not "right"[420] hear their own name recast as "rebel" even as the LORD's name is celebrated (48:2, 9).

"Hear this" echoes the same injunction made to Babylon in the immediately preceding poem (47:8). Additionally, the command to the "house of Jacob" to "Hear this" (*šimʿû-zōʾt*, 48:1) opens a series of overlaps with Isaiah 46:1–13. The only other place in Isaiah that reference to the "house of Jacob" appears is Isa 46:3, where they are also commanded to "Listen" (*šimʿû*). There they are called "stubborn" (46:12; cf. 48:4), they have been "borne" by the LORD "from ... birth" (*minnî-beṭen*, 46:3), and are addressed as "transgressors" (*pōšeʿîm*, 46:8),[421] ideas that will come together in the divine voice's announcement in 48:8 that they have been called "rebel" (*pōšēaʿ*), since their "birth" (*mibbeṭen*).[422] The two poems share a concern over idolatry and in this poem the audience stand accused of having attributed the work of the LORD to idols.

The speech of these false speakers may initially appear problematic because of how they refer to themselves (48:2), but the main point of

---

[419]  In addition to intensity of recurrent reference to naming in this passage (see J. Goldingay and D. Payne, *Isaiah 40–55* [2006], 2:115), one might also point to the appearance of the rare word "sinew" in both the Genesis account "thigh muscle (*gîd* ) that is on the hip socket" (Gen. 32:32 NRSV[ue], Heb. v. 33) and this passage (Isa 48:4). On that connection, see further K. Baltzer, *Deutero-Isaiah* (2001), 285.

[420]  The negative particle *lōʾ* appears twice in the line giving it more emphasis than appears in translation.

[421]  See J. Blenkinsopp, *Isaiah 40–55* (2002), 286.

[422]  K. Baltzer, *Deutero-Isaiah* (2001), 283, observes that in Hosea "Jacob's guilt begins already in the womb."

160                                                           *Commentary*

contention seems to be what they fail to say about the LORD and what they say about idols. Twice the divine voice will claim that the LORD's activity has been "so that you could not say" (*pen-tō 'mar*, 48:5, 7; cf. v. 5 NRSV[ue] "would not say"). These two scenarios stand in tensive juxtaposition with one another. First, the divine voice insists on having announced what will happen and making it happen so that the exiles cannot attribute events to an "idol" (48:3–5). Second, a new event, one not announced, one that the audience knows nothing of, is to be enacted in order that the exiles could not claim foreknowledge (48:6–8). By framing the contrast of announcing and not announcing events in parallel fashion, the poem forces them to be heard together. Together they produce an image of the speaker's frustration. Whether the exiles are told or not told, they fail to know and they fail to give glory to its rightful recipient (48:6, 11).

Potent poetic imagery conveys divine aggravation with the exilic audience. A vivid picture of resistance associates the rigidity of metal (iron, brass) with parts of the body. Muscles of movement are here displaced by metals known precisely for their immovability. These metals had roles in ancient weaponry (see, e.g., 2 Sam 22:35; Ps 18:34; and Job 20:24) and together seem to convey strength (see, e.g., Job 40:18; Micah 4:13; Isa 45:2). This image expands the idiom "stiff-necked" (*qĕšēh 'ōrep*, e.g., Exod 32:9; 33:3).[423] Stiff appears as an independent attribute ("obstinate" *qāšeh*, 48:4) that stands in parallel to a "neck" (*'āreppekā*, "your neck") of "iron sinew" and a "forehead" of "brass." Neck and forehead, each of which carry associations with stubbornness, appear together only here. "Stiff-necked" is an idiom familiar in the Hebrew Bible, particularly in association with the wilderness wanderings. Prophetic texts deploy the forehead in this way (see, e.g., Jer 3:3 and Ezek 3:7).[424] The rare term "sinew" (*gîd*) echoes the sound of "declare" and may express a sound play between their resistance and both what they have received (*wā'aggîd*, "I declared," 48:5) and what they should have done in response (*hălô' taggîdû*, "will you not declare it?" 48:6). The word "sinew" (*gîd*) appears only seven times in the Hebrew Bible. Given this passage's associations with the story of the ancestor Jacob, it is interesting that two of these occurrences are in Gen

---

[423]  See K. Baltzer, *Deutero-Isaiah* (2001), 285, who says the poem "splits up the formula." See also J. Goldingay and D. Payne, *Isaiah 40–55* (2006), 2:126.

[424]  See K. Baltzer, *Deutero-Isaiah* (2001), 285.

*Isaiah 48:12–22*

32:33 (Hebrew versification, NRSV[ue] 32:32), referring to the result of Jacob's wrestling and its implications for ongoing Israelite practice.[425] These metallic images for the audience's resistance resonate sharply with the heat and burning images for the LORD's anger. The phrase "restrain it" uses a word otherwise unknown in the Hebrew Bible, which seems likely to derive from the idea of "muzzling."[426] When combined with the word for "anger," which is also the word for "nose," the image is of a burning divine anger that has to be held back.[427] The immediately following claims about smelting reinforce the associations of rage and heat and fearsomely resonate with the previous depiction of the audience's resistance with brass and iron images.

The poem offers an encounter with the LORD who is justifiably angry with the exiles. They have associated themselves with the LORD (48:1) in ways that do not bring glory (48:11) but seem instead to have "profaned" (48:11) the LORD's name through falseness (48:1) by having a tendency toward attributing divine activity to idols (48:5) and by failing to announce what they have witnessed (48:6). The LORD's rage with these treacherous rebels (48:8) is held in check (48:9), but this may not be an entirely reassuring notion as it conveys an aggravation so intense that it needs to be restrained.

## ISAIAH 48:12–22

$^{12}$ Listen to me, O Jacob,
    and Israel, whom I called:
I am he; I am the first,
    and I am the last.
$^{13}$ My hand laid the foundation of the earth,
    and my right hand spread out the heavens;
when I summon them,
    they stand at attention.

---

[425]  See K. Baltzer, *Deutero-Isaiah* (2001), 285. On the sound echoed in the verb of v. 5, see J. Goldingay and D. Payne, *Isaiah 40–55* (2006), 2:127.

[426]  See J. Goldingay and D. Payne, *Isaiah 40–55* (2006), 2:133; and *HALOT*, 1:307.

[427]  Anger is commonly associated with heart in the Hebrew Bible. See especially the common use of forms of the verb *ḥrh* ("to burn" BDB, 354) with *'ap* ("anger, nose," BDB, 60), e.g., Gen 30:2; 44:18; Exod 4:14; 22:23; 32:10; 32:11; 19; 32:22; and Num 11:1 (which makes the fire idiom explicit).

162 *Commentary*

[14] Assemble, all of you, and hear!
> Who among them has declared these things?
The one the LORD loves shall perform his purpose against Babylon,
> and his arm shall be against the Chaldeans.
[15] I, even I, have spoken and called him;
> I have brought him, and he will prosper in his way.
[16] Draw near to me; hear this!
> From the beginning I have not spoken in secret;
> from the time it came to be I have been there.
And now the Lord GOD
> has sent me and his spirit.[428]

[17] Thus says the LORD,
> your Redeemer, the Holy One of Israel:
I am the LORD your God,
> who teaches you how to succeed,
> who leads you in the way you should go.
[18] O that you had paid attention to my commandments!
> Then your prosperity would have been like a river
> and your success like the waves of the sea;
[19] your offspring would have been like the sand
> and your descendants like its grains;
their name would never be cut off
> or destroyed from before me.

[20] Go out from Babylon; flee from Chaldea;
> declare this with a shout of joy; proclaim it;
send it forth to the end of the earth;
> say, "The LORD has redeemed his servant Jacob!"
[21] They did not thirst when he led them through the deserts;
> he made water flow for them from the rock;
> he split open the rock, and the water gushed out.

[22] "There is no peace," says the LORD, "for the wicked."

---

[428] I am departing from the NRSV[ue]'s lineation here. I am following MT, which presents this line as a couplet.

*Isaiah 48:12–22* 163

In this poem, the exiles are offered a disorienting encounter with the divine speaker. The poem's startling juxtapositions seem to function as a dominant element of the poem's meaning-making. This poem shifts and changes direction with little indication of how ideas relate to their surroundings. The effect is a disorienting array of claims each of which must be weighed and considered on its own.[429] In this way, the poem seems to enact earlier poems' claim that the audience do not know what they think they know (e.g., 45:9–11; 48:8). While ambiguity and uncertainty function on one level to point the audience toward the need to follow the LORD's leading, images from Israel's ancestral past and a sharp contrast with the consequences of resistance reinforce the poem's urged response of following the LORD on another level. Together these poetic pressures point toward the urged response (48:20) with its clarity of statement in an otherwise disorienting context.

The opening couplet of the poem employs familiar imagery and conveys the majesty of the divine speaker in terms that are frequent in these chapters. The couplet invites the exilic audience, under the names Jacob-Israel, to pay attention to what the voice is speaking. However, this familiarity quickly becomes clouded by ambiguity. The audience, who are "called" (*mĕqōrā 'î*, v.12), stand juxtaposed to the apparent reference to the LORD having "called" the heavens and the earth.[430] At least, that is who appears to be being characterized as the ones who "stand" when they are called (NRSV[ue] "summon" 48:13, Heb. *qōrē '*). "Them," in the fourth couplet, has no clear antecedent, and the best point of reference in the immediate context is the "heavens" and the "earth," despite the fact that it requires some metaphorical imagination to picture these cosmic entities "stand[ing] at attention." If this is the case, the commandability of the broad expanses of creation stands in contrast to the audience,[431] who, though they have been repeatedly referred to as "called" are also those

---

[429] As F. W. Dobbs-Allsopp, *Lamentations* (2002), 25, observes of the impact of parataxis in Lamentations, "Ideas and images are routinely juxtaposed to each other without being explicitly linked. This forces the reader to consider each idea on its own and then in relation to those that are most contiguous to it. Individual truths are allowed to surface and be experienced on their own, but are also ultimately required to be considered as part of a larger whole, which acts as a strong deterrent to the domination of any single perspective."

[430] J. Muilenburg, "Isaiah 40–66" (1956), 5:558.

[431] J. D. W. Watts, *Isaiah 34–66* (2005), 178, observes this contrast.

164 Commentary

who are "obstinate" (48:4) and who need to be commanded to "Listen" (48:12).[432]

Ambiguity and juxtaposition intensify in the lines that follow. A pair of commands to "you" stand alongside a rhetorical question about "them" in a couplet that either shifts referent dramatically, contains a textual error, or continues an implied comparison between the audience and the heavens and earth (48:14). While it is possible for biblical poets to imagine the "heavens" functioning as messengers (e.g., "The heavens are telling the glory of God," Ps 19:1a), this shift is part of a movement from "you," to "them," to "one," to "I," making it most likely an element of the poem's swiftly shifting point of reference. The movement is disorienting and leaves the hearer puzzling over the significance of the varying points of reference.

Perhaps most perplexing is the sudden, unintroduced, and repeated reference to a figure (vv. 14, 15) who is to carry something out against the exiles' enemies. Who "he" is, and whether "his purpose" refers to that figure's own purpose or to the LORD's purpose, is impossible to determine simply from the immediate context and the phrasing of the lines themselves. It does seem most likely, as numerous commentators have suggested, that the "he" is an allusion to Cyrus,[433] and that the purposes to be carried out are the LORD's.[434] However, the most recent allusion to that figure in the flow of the poems as a whole was in Isaiah 46:11, where "the man for my purpose from a far country" functioned as an elaboration of the description of the glorified divine speaker.[435] In that context, though it was allusive, the reference fitted into the poem's flow and it was possible to see how reference to Cyrus supported the claim the divine voice was making. Here, the familiar question about who could have made something known is immediately juxtaposed with a series of statements about the LORD's commitment to and enabling of this "him." It is not altogether

---

[432] J. Goldingay and D. Payne, *Isaiah 40–55* (2006), 2:137, point out that "Since chapter 40, most references to people being called have suggested summoning, often summons to service." They also observe the recurrence in v. 3 (138).

[433] Scholars who take the referent to be Cyrus include J. Muilenburg, "Isaiah 40–66" (1956), 5:559–560; J. L. McKenzie, *Second Isaiah* (1968), 98; C. Westermann, *Isaiah 40–66* (1969), 200–201; J. D. W. Watts, *Isaiah 34–66* (2005), 178; J. Blenkinsopp, *Isaiah 40–55* (2002), 293–294; and K. Baltzer, *Deutero-Isaiah* (2001), 291.

[434] See the discussion of whose purpose in J. Goldingay and D. Payne, *Isaiah 40–55* (2006), 2:140.

[435] Though note that "my purpose" in 46:11 was *'ăṣātiw*, and here "his purpose" is *ḥepṣô*.

*Isaiah 48:12–22* 165

clear how the description of the "one the LORD loves" relates to the question "Who among them has declared these things?" (48:14). What is emphatically the case is that the LORD is the one who has brought these things about (48:15).[436]

Renewed commands to listen draw attention back to the speaker (48:16) and in this context the claim "I have not spoken in secret" stands in tension with its own surroundings. The line itself carries a certain amount of ambiguity.[437] The NRSV[ue] translates "From the beginning I have not spoken in secret," conveying the idea that an absence of hiddenness characterizes the LORD's speech right back into history. However, the claim itself seems less transparent than that. The phrasing allows for the negation to be of the word "from the beginning" (*lō' mērō'š*, i.e., "not from beginning"), leaving open the possibility that this an affirmation that the divine voice did speak in secret but not at first.[438] If so, it stands in obvious tension with Isa 45:19, but it would not be the only such tension in Isaiah 40–55.[439] The matter is not clarified by its immediate context. The parallel line that follows appears to emphasize the LORD's existence and presence and the next couplet is spoken by an unspecified and unintroduced speaker who appears to voice only this couplet in the poem. If it is the voice of either the "servant" or the prophetic poet, its appearance here without introduction or development further exacerbates the hearer's sense of

---

[436] See J. Goldingay and D. Payne, *Isaiah 40–55* (2006), 2:141, on the reappearance of the verb "to call" in this regard.

[437] J. L. McKenzie, *Second Isaiah* (1968), 99, writes, "The ambiguity of the speaker becomes acute in vs. 16."

[438] While the form of negation here (*lō'*) is typically used "to negate verbal clauses," Bill T. Arnold and John H. Choi, *A Guide to Biblical Hebrew Syntax* (Cambridge: Cambridge University Press, 2003), 137, it can be used to negate a single word "typically a nominal form" (137). Compare also *HALOT*, 1:511. While not conclusive, such a meaning is certainly possible here, especially considering the atypical location of the verb. K. Baltzer, *Deutero-Isaiah* (2001), 295, appears to be taking the syntax similarly – i.e., that "from the beginning" is what is being negated. However, in light of his interest in Sinai in this passage, he reads it as "spatial" as well, indicating a contrast between speech from the top of the mountain and that being proclaimed here. While I see the emphasis on the negation of beginning rather than secret as a possibility here, I do not share Baltzer's view of a spatial image, which depends heavily on his claim about Moses being in view in this context.

[439] Compare, for example, Isa 43:18 with 46:9 and see further A Closer Look: Conflicted Commands and Competing Contentions in the Memory Motif.

166                                                                                    *Commentary*

being disoriented by the movement of this poem.[440] Such disorientation enacts the broader context's claim that the exiles do not know how to evaluate their circumstances (see, e.g., 45:9–11) and that they should entrust themselves to the LORD (see, e.g., 45:22). Despite what the audience might think they know, they are surrounded by various uncertainties, and the one thing that comes through clearly in the opening stanzas of the poem is that the LORD, now speaking to them, is able to command and to bring events about.

As if offering an alternative to the experience of disorientation that has dominated the poem thus far, the poem next offers expansive images of the results of following the LORD. The ambiguity surrounding the speaker at the end of v. 16 is doubly overturned by the statements "Thus says the LORD" and "I am the LORD" (48:17). Repetitive sounds underscore the importance of following the one "who leads you in the way you should go" (*madrîkăkā bĕderek tēlēk*) and the poem reinforces this idea by drawing upon imagery from the stories of the patriarchs and the wilderness wanderings. These stories resonate with the idea of following God into something previously unknown.[441] Here the exiles are offered a vision of "prosperity" (*šĕlômekā*, i.e., "your peace") and "success" (*ṣidqātĕkā*, i.e., "your righteousness"). Water images, "river," "sea," and water from a rock allude to God's provision following the Exodus (48:18, 21),[442] while the description of offspring as numerous as the sands recalls the promise to the patriarchs (Isa 48:19; Gen 22:17).[443]

---

[440] J. Muilenburg, "Isaiah 40–66" (1956), 5:561, highlights the problems here calling the "line . . . a *crux interpretum*" and suggesting it "is probably a gloss." B. S. Childs, *Isaiah* (2001), 377, argues in favor of reading this voice as introducing the one who will become more clearly the Servant in the following chapter. C. Westermann, *Isaiah 40–66* (1969), 203, sees these words as a "fragment" that does not belong originally to this context. While textual disturbance is a possibility, the impact in the current, final poetic form is disorientation.

[441] Note the expression of a desire to "know" in Gen 15:8.

[442] See J. Muilenburg, "Isaiah 40–66" (1956), 5:562–563; See B. D. Sommer, *A Prophet Reads Scripture* (1998), 273–274 n. 8 and 276 n. 19. J. Blenkinsopp, *Isaiah 40–55* (2002), 295–296, points to a number of connections with Exodus and wilderness narratives.

[443] It is worth noting that "sand" is often used to convey the numerousness of something in the Hebrew Bible. See Gen 22:17, 32:12; Josh 11:4; Judg 7:12; 1 Sam 13:5; 2 Sam 17:11; 1 Kgs 4:20; Ps 139:18; Jer 33:22. See J. Muilenburg, "Isaiah 40–66" (1956), 5:562, and J. D. W. Watts, *Isaiah 34–66* (2005), 178–179, who also see it as recalling Abraham. J. L. McKenzie, *Second Isaiah* (1968), 99, points to texts in Gen 22 and 32 relating this promise to the people's ancestors (Abraham and Jacob respectively).

*Isaiah 49:1–13*

The imperatives "Go out from Babylon; flee from Chaldea" (48:20) stand out for their clarity and specificity in the largely disorienting poem. These statements belong to the portion of the poem that reinforces the idea that the audience would benefit from following in the way that the LORD leads by offering images of their ancestors so benefiting. This is the action they are being invited to take. Rather than attempting to know, they are urged to simply follow, to trust and to do what is commanded in the face of their uncertainty. As if to underscore the point, the poem ends with a return to striking and disorienting juxtaposition.[444] The abrupt single line "'There is no peace (*šālôm*),' says the LORD, 'for the wicked'" (48:22) emerges unintroduced and picks up the wording that characterized the offer of "prosperity" for those who obey, reversing it.[445]

The poem confronts the exiles with the reality of their limited understanding and enacts disorientation. By exposing the audience to the limitations of their own understanding, the poem urges them through poetic imagery and juxtaposition to embrace the commands of the divine speaker. They are urged to trust in the LORD's purposes and God's ability to bring them about.

## ISAIAH 49:1–13

¹ Listen to me, O coastlands:
>  pay attention, you peoples from far away!
The LORD called me before I was born;
>  while I was in my mother's womb he named me.

---

[444] John W. Olley, "'No Peace' in a Book of Consolation," *VT* 49 (1999): 365, sees the tone of this abrupt line as something that "reinforces the seriousness of the command to 'go out.'"

[445] Notably, the word "wicked" here often functions as an opposite of *ṣdqh* (righteous), the word that appeared in v. 18 paired with *šelômekā* (i.e., "your peace"). Uses of forms of the root *ṣdq* and *rš'* as opposites include, e.g., Gen 18:23, Exod 9:27, Deut 25:1, 1 Kgs 8:32, Isa 5:23; 26:10, Mal 3:18, Ps 1:6; 7:10 (9 Heb.); 37:17. J. W. Olley, "No Peace" (1999), 361–362, treats them as opposites. C. Westermann, *Isaiah 40–66* (1969), 205, is among those who see this verse as "an addition." As with 48:16's voicing by one sent, any decision about the original form of the text does not preclude an analysis of the impact of its presence in the final form. Olley is among scholars who view this verse and its parallel as playing a structural role in the final form of Isaiah. J. W. Olley, "No Peace" (1999), 353, treats the repetition in relation to the book's "intentional" stark conclusion (66:24), which he views as "an intensification" of this "refrain."

168                                                 *Commentary*

[2] He made my mouth like a sharp sword;
> in the shadow of his hand he hid me;
he made me a polished arrow;
> in his quiver he hid me away.
[3] And he said to me, "You are my servant,
> Israel, in whom I will be glorified."
[4] But I said, "I have labored in vain;
> I have spent my strength for nothing and vanity;
yet surely my cause is with the LORD
> and my reward with my God."

[5] And now the LORD says,
> who formed me in the womb to be his servant,
to bring Jacob back to him,
> and that Israel might be gathered to him,
for I am honored in the sight of the LORD,
> and my God has become my strength –
[6] he says,
"It is too light a thing that you should be my servant
> to raise up the tribes of Jacob
> and to restore the survivors of Israel;
I will give you as a light to the nations,
> that my salvation may reach to the end of the earth."

[7] Thus says the LORD,
> the Redeemer of Israel and his Holy One,
to one deeply despised, abhorred by the nations,
> the slave of rulers,
"Kings shall see and stand up;
> princes, and they shall prostrate themselves,
because of the LORD, who is faithful,
> the Holy One of Israel, who has chosen you."

[8] Thus says the LORD:
In a time of favor I have answered you;
> on a day of salvation I have helped you;
I have kept you and given you
> as a covenant to the people,

*Isaiah 49:1–13* 169

to establish the land,
    to apportion the desolate heritages,
[9] saying to the prisoners, "Come out,"
    to those who are in darkness, "Show yourselves."
They shall feed along the ways;
    on all the bare heights shall be their pasture;
[10] they shall not hunger or thirst,
    neither scorching wind nor sun shall strike them down,
for he who has pity on them will lead them
    and by springs of water will guide them.
[11] And I will turn all my mountains into a road,
    and my highways shall be raised up.
[12] Look, some shall come from far away,
    Some from the north and from the west,
    and some from the land of Syene.

[13] Sing for joy, O heavens, and exult, O earth;
    break forth, O mountains, into singing!
For the LORD has comforted his people
    and will have compassion on his suffering ones.

This poem offers the audience their first encounter with the personified Servant as speaker. The Servant's voice works persuasively on the audience through two primary identifications. First, by imitating and blending with the divine voice, the Servant's speech exudes confidence and trustworthiness, encouraging the audience to accept this voice's vision of their situation and future. Second, by merging his description of his role with their own, the Servant enacts the poetry's aim of offering the Servant personification to the audience as a vision of what it aims to make them.

The poem employs poetic means to present the Servant as a speaker who closely identifies with the divine voice. The voice exudes confidence and majesty. Its mode of speaking imitates the divine voice in its address to geographic features, its participial elaboration of the announcement of the LORD's speech, and in its blending of the LORD's speech and the Servant's speech.

First, as the LORD's voice has regularly done, this voice addresses inanimate figures, which convey magnitude (e.g., 41:1; 43:6; 45:8 and see

170                                                                Commentary

A Closer Look: The Coastlands and the Creator of the Cosmos).[446] This poem opens with an address to the islands, presenting this speaker as one whose voice is authoritative enough to command attention from "far away." Similarly, the poem closes by commanding the "heavens" and "earth," employing opposites of height and depth to convey totality (see "merism," in Glossary of Poetic Terminology). That this is a speaker whose voice merits attention is further underscored by the vivid weapon imagery used to describe it. This speaker is one whose mouth has been made "like a sharp sword" by the LORD, with the alliteration of that phrase (*cĕhereb haddâ*) emphasizing its importance.[447] It is not the case that the Servant's confidence rests in any attainments of his own, however. Rather, each of the verbs ("called," "named," "made," "hid," 49:1, 2) point to the LORD's activity as that which gives the Servant his confidence and enables his activity. The LORD is the one who "called" the Servant, and the parallel images of this happening before the Servant's birth (49:1) highlight the inability of the Servant himself to impact the outcome. Similarly, the weapon imagery places the Servant as both a "sword" in the LORD's "hand" and as an "arrow" in the LORD's "quiver" (49:2). Each image associates the Servant with an object whose action is as an implement of the LORD's activity, and which requires the LORD's action to bring it about.

Second, as the LORD's voice often does, the Servant's voice interrupts the announcement that the LORD is speaking (49:5, 7) with participles describing the LORD's activity (49:5) and with participles glorifying the LORD (49:7).[448] The Servant's speech so fully imitates the LORD's speech that it becomes particularly difficult to differentiate between these speakers.[449] The blending of these voices within this poem appears most

[446] See B. S. Childs, *Isaiah* (2001), 382–383.

[447] J. Blenkinsopp, *Isaiah 40–55* (2002), 300, considers the resonance of the "Hebrew idiom of the edge of the sword … literally, the 'mouth of the sword'" noting that "the expression connotes the power of incisive speech, the power to persuade and incite to action, to make a decisive difference in the political sphere." K. Baltzer, *Deutero-Isaiah* (2001), 307, also refers to this phrase and develops the military resonances of the imagery used here.

[448] See also J. Muilenburg, "Isaiah 40–66" (1956), 5:568, on this reflection of "the prophet's characteristic literary style and manner." See also J. Goldingay and D. Payne, *Isaiah 40–55* (2006), 2:163, and C. Westermann, *Isaiah 40–66* (1969), 211.

[449] See, e.g., the comments of J. Goldingay and D. Payne, *Isaiah 40–55* (2006), 2:175, 177, on shifts in voicing.

*Isaiah 49:1–13* 171

starkly in Isa 49:10–11 where the LORD is "he" (49:10) and "I" (49:11) in successive lines with no indication of a change of speaker, tone, theme, or point of view.[450] By mirroring the divine voice so closely that it becomes difficult to differentiate between them, the poetry enacts its depiction of the Servant's embrace of confident trust in the divine voice and his role of speaking on the LORD's behalf.[451]

Yet the Servant is a figure who is not indifferent to the audience's struggles, fears, and doubts, and the divine voice is not the only one with which this poem forges connections. Just as their lowliness is directly contrasted with divine majesty (49:7) and intense awareness of human fragility and ephemerality are not unfamiliar in these poems (e.g., 40:6–8), so the Servant's own expression embraces these themes. A single couplet, whose repetitive use of long "i" sounds lends it emphasis, expresses intense futility, calling the Servant's work (*yāga ʿtî*) "vain" and his "strength" (*kōḥî*) used "for nothing" (*lětōhû*) and "vanity" (49:4).[452] These words echo Isaiah 40, where "strength" (*kōaḥ*, 40:31) was to be provided and those who wait on the LORD would "not be weary" (*yîgā ʿû*, 40:31), and nations are rulers were like "nothing" (*kattōhû*, 40:23) compared to the LORD.[453] If the exilic

---

[450] While the pronouncements "Thus says the LORD" (vv. 7, 8), do argue in favor of treating vv. 7–13 as spoken by the divine voice (e.g., J. Goldingay and D. Payne, *Isaiah 40–55* [2006], 2:154), the Servant, who had been speaking, remains clearly in view. The poem moves from the Servant's speech about himself, to his recounting of what the LORD said to him about himself, to further announcements of divine speech that continue to be relayed by an intermediary who speaks of the LORD in the third person (vv. 7, 10), and which directly echoes previous speech of the Servant more obviously recounting divine speech. The voices blend, and while there is transition of speaker, there is also heavy overlap and continuity. Since I view the Servant as a personification of what Israel is called to be (see A Closer Look: The Servant and His Songs), I would not draw a stark distinction between the references to the Servant or to Jacob-Israel as "you" in v. 8; cf. J. Goldingay and D. Payne, *Isaiah 40–55* (2006), 2:172–177. See further Katie M. Heffelfinger, "The Servant in Poetic Juxtaposition in Isaiah 49:1–13," in *Biblical Poetry and the Art of Close Reading* (eds. J. Blake Couey and Elaine T. James; Cambridge: Cambridge University Press, 2018), 192.

[451] See further, K. M. Heffelfinger, "The Servant" (2018), 190–192.

[452] See K. Baltzer, *Deutero-Isaiah* (2001), 306, who observes "There is a striking frequency of *i* sounds in the text."

[453] Contra J. L. McKenzie, *Second Isaiah* (1968), 105, the appearance of "toil" here does not detract from the idea that the Servant should be understood as a personification of Israel. Rather, its appearance in the words that respond to Jacob's complaint (40:27) support the idea that here the poetry responds to the audience's own self-perception. Contrast also the position of B. S. Childs, *Isaiah* (2001), 384, who locates the futile toil in the difficulties the prophetic figure faces in convincing the exilic audience. Note, however, that Childs does not entirely separate the Servant from corporate Israel.

audience identify with these feelings of futility, as seems likely, they find in the Servant a figure who is not unfamiliar with their plight.[454] Such imagery builds the potential for audience identification with this figure.

However, the Servant's voice does not allow these expressions of futility to dominate the poem. Rather, they stand in tension with his opening confidence and are immediately juxtaposed with reassertions of confidence grounded in the LORD (49:4). The first-person suffixes on the words "my cause" (*mišpāṭî*) and "my reward" (*pĕʿullātî*) echo the long "î" sound whose repetition had lent emphasis to the preceding couplet's uselessness imagery.[455] By repeating this sound in an expression of confidence, the sound play further reorients the image. This complaint does not receive a rebuttal as will Zion's complaint in the following poem. Nor is it cited speech, as are both Zion's (Isa 49:14) and Jacob's (Isa 40:27) complaints. Instead, the Servant voices this sense of futility himself and overcomes it in his own voice by reorienting the imagery and expressing trust in the LORD. In this way, the personified Servant enacts for the exilic audience what the trust in the LORD, which the poems have been urging them to embrace, might accomplish for them.

Further identification between the Servant and the exilic audience develops through the overlapping of what they are called to do. This connection appears most clearly in the parallelism between "my servant" and "Israel, in whom I will be glorified" (49:3). Further, the activities to which the Servant is called overlap with a call to the audience (see especially the comments on 41:8–20 and 42:1–4 and A Closer Look: The Servant and His "Songs"). While it is certainly plausible, and not uncommon, to read 49:8–12 as elements of what the Servant is called to do for and to the audience, such an attribution is not evident and a reading (i.e., "covenant people"; cf. NRSV[ue] "as a covenant to the people") that holds together the Servant and the audience is to be preferred (see A Closer Look:

> He writes, "the extension of the servant's role in chapter 49 is not an attempt to replace an earlier corporate understanding of the servant Israel with that of an individual prophetic figure. Rather, the servant always remains Israel, but an individual Israel is now understood within the dynamic movement of the prophetic history as embodied in the suffering, individual figure who has been divinely commissioned to the selfsame task of the deliverance of the chosen people and the nations at large." (387)

[454] See further K. M. Heffelfinger, "The Servant" (2018), 189–190.
[455] On the relevance of poetic patterning here see further K. M. Heffelfinger, "The Servant" (2018), 189.

# Isaiah 49:1–13

A Covenant People).[456] Further, the claim "I have kept you" ('*ĕṣṣārĕkā*),[457] which introduces the idea of a covenant people, is a form of the same verb used for the "survivors of Israel" (*nĕṣûrê yiśrāēl*, 49:6),[458] tightening the connection between the one who is "kept" and "given" as a "covenant" and the exilic audience. Reading verse 8 as addressed to the exiles fits well with the larger context of the poem. Verse 7 described their addressee as "one deeply despised, abhorred by the nations, the slave of rulers." Such a description well fits the exiles' situation as does the idea that the LORD has "answered" the addressee (49:8) as the exiles have registered a complaint (40:27).

It is clear that there is both overlap and distinction between the exilic audience and the Servant figure here. The impulses toward identification between the two are strong but do not entirely overcome the dissonance created by the Servant being called to act for Jacob-Israel's benefit (see, e.g., 49:5). This blending with distinction fits the idea of a personification that embodies that which the poetry urges the audience to become (see A Closer Look: The Servant and His "Songs"). It is not a complete description of who they are, it is a poetic image that conveys both what they are not and what they might become.

The concluding exultation calling upon the heavens and earth to join in celebration rejoins the imagery of the Servant's opening command to the coastlands. The poem underscores the confidence it aims to form in the audience by turning to command cosmic celebration of the divine triumph.

This poem confronts the audience with a personified figure and in so doing enacts the change it aims to make in them. It demonstrates dependence upon God and offers a vision of engagement with Israel's divinely given mission. By imitating the divine voice, the Servant personification in

---

[456] It is not self-contradictory to consider the Servant a personification for Israel in light of this passage. Contra C. Westermann, *Isaiah 40–66* (1969), 209, this apparent impossibility of the Servant being as well as having a commission on behalf of the people is solved by the proposed translation "a covenant people." Similarly, Westermann's objection that the Servant must be an individual because his pre-natal life is referenced (209) misses the importance of metaphor in poetic personification. On the relevance of "metaphor" for this issue, see further M. A. Sweeney, *Isaiah 40–66* (2016), 164.

[457] On the discussion of the verbal root as *nṣr* here, see J. Blenkinsopp, *Isaiah 40–55* (2002), 303.

[458] I am reading the MT's Qere here.

174    Commentary

this poem offers a vision of transformation through dependence. By intersecting with the addressees' fears as well as their commission, it invites them to step into the role that the Servant personification plays.

A CLOSER LOOK: A COVENANT PEOPLE

The poetry of Isaiah 40–55 connects the mission of the Servant with its intended transformation of the audience (see A Closer Look: The Servant and His "Songs"), employing the phrase a "covenant people" (librît 'ām, 42:6; 49:8) to express their embodiment of the Servant's mission and to underscore the permanence of the divine commitment (see Bridging the Horizons: God's Sovereign Choice). The phrase, which the NRSV[ue] translates "as a covenant to the people," is both unique to these two verses and resistant to clear translation as the note "Meaning of Heb uncertain" in NRSV[ue] indicates.[459] The common translation "as a covenant to the people" separates the Servant figure from the audience themselves, implying that the Servant is the one who is offered as "a covenant" for them. However, this translation neglects the atypical syntax of this phrase, which appears only in Isa. 42:6 and 49:8.[460] The rarity of this phrase suggests that the two occurrences must necessarily be read together. Hebrew is capable of constructing a phrase that more clearly means "a covenant to the people" as it does in Josh 24:25 (bĕrît lā'ām, there NRSV[ue] translates "covenant with the people"). Here, it seems best to read the phrase as a Second Isaian coinage that conveys "a covenant people," a distinctive form, whose unusual word order is likely an intentional allusion to the

---

[459]  NRSV[ue] is not alone in drawing this conclusion. JPS Tanakh contains an identical note. Scholars have heavily discussed the translation of this phrase. Mark S. Smith, "BĔRÎT 'AM / BĔRÎT 'ÔLAM: A New Proposal for the Crux of Isa 42:6," JBL 100.2 (1981): 241, summarizes some of the scholarly discussion. See also J. Goldingay and D. Payne, Isaiah 40–55 (2006), 1:227–28. Notably, among modern translations the JPS Tanakkh Translation translates "a covenant people" in both Isa 42:6 and 49:8. See also the translation in M. A. Sweeney, Isaiah 40–66 (2016), 163.

[460]  The word bĕrît (i.e., "covenant") only occurs with a lamed preposition on it in Isaiah 42:6, 49:8 where it is part of the construction under discussion, in Genesis 17:7, 13, and 19, where each time it is part of the construction "an everlasting covenant" (librît 'ôlām), and in Psalm 74:20 where the preposition performs an entirely different function. This Genesis usage related to the "everlasting covenant" reinforces the sense that the poet in Isaiah 42 and 49 is creating an allusion to the permanence of the divine commitment to Israel as the covenant people.

*Isaiah 49:14–50:3* 175

"everlasting covenant" of Isaiah 55:3.[461] In Isaiah 42, a close connection between the Servant personification and the people carries forward the connection between servant language and Israel, as well as the permanence of divine commitment to Israel as expressed in Isaiah 41:8's servant imagery. In Isaiah 49, the poetry merges its vision of the audience's calling with the Servant's own testimony about that calling, drawing the two together and creating identification between the audience and the personification that embodies their response. Thus, the term becomes an attribution of who the audience are called to be and one that echoes God's promise to make an "everlasting covenant" (*librît 'ôlām*, Gen 17:7, 13, 19) with them.

ISAIAH 49:14–50:3

[14] But Zion said, "The LORD has forsaken me;
    my Lord has forgotten me."
[15] Can a woman forget her nursing child
    or show no compassion for the child of her womb?
Even these might forget,
    yet I will not forget you.
[16] See, I have inscribed you on the palms of my hands;
    your walls are continually before me.
[17] Your builders outdo your destroyers,
    and those who laid you waste go away from you.
[18] Lift up your eyes all around and see;
    they all gather; they come to you.
As I live, says the LORD,
    you shall put all of them on like an ornament,
    and like a bride you shall bind them on.

[19] For your wastelands, your desolate places,
    and your devastated land –

---

[461] See M. S. Smith, "*BĔRÎT 'AM*" (1981), 242, who highlights the "obvious phonetic resemblance" between the phrases *librît 'ām* (42:6 and 49:8) and *bĕrît 'ôlām* (55:3). While Smith draws different conclusions than this commentary about the import of this resonance, his observation is a helpful one.

now you will be too crowded for your inhabitants,
and those who swallowed you up will be far away.
20 The children born in the time of your bereavement
will yet say in your hearing:
"The place is too crowded for me;
make room for me to settle."
21 Then you will say in your heart,
"Who has borne me these?
I was bereaved and barren,
exiled and put away –
so who has reared these?
I was left all alone –
where, then, have these come from?"

22 Thus says the Lord GOD:
I will soon lift up my hand to the nations
and raise my signal to the peoples,
and they shall bring your sons in their bosom,
and your daughters shall be carried on their shoulders.
23 Kings shall be your foster fathers
and their queens your nursing mothers.
With their faces to the ground they shall bow down to you
and lick the dust of your feet.
Then you will know that I am the LORD;
those who wait for me shall not be put to shame.

24 Can the prey be taken from the mighty
or the captives of a tyrant be rescued?
25 But thus says the LORD:
Even the captives of the mighty will be taken,
and the prey of the tyrant will be rescued,
for I will contend with those who contend with you,
and I will save your children.
26 I will make your oppressors eat their own flesh,
and they shall be drunk with their own blood as with wine.
Then all flesh shall know
that I am the LORD your Savior
and your Redeemer, the Mighty One of Jacob.

*Isaiah 49:14–50:3* 177

50:1 Thus says the LORD:
Where is your mother's bill of divorce
    with which I dismissed her?
Or which of my creditors is it
    to whom I have sold you?
No, because of your sins you were sold,
    and for your transgressions your mother was dismissed.
[2] Why was no one there when I came?
    Why did no one answer when I called?
Is my arm powerless to redeem?
    Or have I no strength to deliver?
By my rebuke I dry up the sea;
    I make the rivers a desert,
so that their fish stink for lack of water
    and die of thirst.
[3] I clothe the heavens with blackness
    and make sackcloth their covering.

As this poem begins, the reader encounters another vivid personification, Lady Zion. She stands in stark contrast to the personified Servant of the previous poem. The juxtaposition between these two figures will continue through chapter 54 and forms one of these poems' modes of poetic persuasion, offering the audience contrasting depictions of embodied resistance to and acceptance of God's work in their midst (see further A Closer Look: Lady Zion and the Suffering Servant, the Rhetorical Power of Juxtaposition).[462] The poem minimizes Lady Zion's voice by embedding it within divine speech and calls her perspective into question through rebuttal and reversal of her charges against the LORD. Contrasting and compelling images of maternal forgetfulness and divine memory combine to portray the divine voice as the one who remembers rightly. As the poem progresses, the intensity of the LORD's rebuttal increases and the audience find themselves directly addressed.

---

[462] See U. Schmidt, "Servant and Zion" (2011), 85, who argues "in Isa 49–55 two kinds of future are envisioned and presented, and that these two figures, the Servant and Zion are representing them."

178                                                                                    *Commentary*

The Lady Zion that the reader encounters in this poem is a blend of city, woman, and mother imagery.[463] It develops both a metaphor (see further A Closer Look: City as Woman in the Ancient Near East) and allusions to Lamentations. In Lamentations, the speaking voice of Lady Zion echoed the lamenting poetic voice and added pathos to its cries by presenting the city as lamenting her own destruction and that of the people, her children (e.g., Lam 1:11b–22).[464] Here, in diametric opposition to the previous poem's concluding injunction to the heavens to sing because "the LORD has comforted his people," the personified city complains of having been forgotten (49:14).[465]

In Isaiah 49, it is not Zion who speaks but the LORD quoting her complaint that the LORD has "forsaken" (*ʿăzābanî*) and "forgotten" (*šĕkēḥānî*) her (49:14).[466] The complaint quoted appears in Lamentations 5:20 "Why have you forgotten (*tiškāḥēnû*) us completely? Why have you forsaken (*taʿazbēnû*) us these many days?" where the words are not Zion's but the people's.[467] By placing the people's very words of lament on the lips of personified Zion and embedding that quotation in divine speech, the divine voice gives clear evidence of the LORD's accurate memory of their distress, makes the connection between the complaining people and the personification explicit, and hints at an upcoming resolution of their

---

[463]  See U. Schmidt, "Servant and Zion" (2011), 87, on the combination of metaphors here as "personification."

[464]  See, e.g., Barbara Bakke Kaiser, "Poet as 'Female Impersonator': The Image of Daughter Zion as Speaker in Biblical Poems of Suffering," *The Journal of Religion* 67.2 (1987): 166; and T. Linafelt, "Surviving Lamentations" (1995), on the transition to the female speaker.

[465]  P. Tull Willey, *Remember the Former Things* (1997), 188, notes connections between Isa 49:13 and Lamentations pointing out, significantly, that "This is the first of four repetitions in Second Isaiah of the claim that YHWH has comforted" Kathryn R. Roberts, "Isaiah 49:14–18," *Interpretation* (2003): 58–59, reads this contrast as an objection to "painful realities of exilic life" having been apparently "glossed over" in v. 13's injunction to praise. On the juxtaposition between this complaint and the preceding call to praise, see further K. M. Heffelfinger, "The Servant" (2018), 194. See also J. Muilenburg, "Isaiah 40–66" (1956), 5:573.

[466]  K. Baltzer, *Deutero-Isaiah* (2001), 322, takes the speaker to be the LORD. Cf. J. Goldingay and D. Payne, *Isaiah 40–55* (2006), 2:184. I find the fact that the poem continues in the divine voice, which Goldingay and Payne note, convincing evidence that this is the divine voice citing Zion. While Goldingay and Payne highlight potential "ambiguity," this verse begins a new poem in which the divine speaker will clearly be present in the following verse and where no other speaker is yet apparent.

[467]  T. Linafelt, *Surviving Lamentations* (2000), 74. See also P. Tull Willey, *Remember the Former Things* (1997), 189; C. Westermann, *Isaiah 40–66* (1969), 219; and J. Goldingay and D. Payne, *Isaiah 40–55* (2006), 2:184.

*Isaiah 49:14–50:3* 179

distress. As Tull Willey observes, "the lines in their new form and context reinterpret the issue: it is not YHWH, but Zion, who is inattentive."[468] Certainly, as already noted, the presence of the LORD's speaking voice is a response to Lamentations' complaint of comforterlessness. Here, by taking up the words of that complaint, the poem links the LORD's response to the complaint itself.

The response mingles subtle indictment with overwhelming tenderness. The LORD's own commitment to Zion is greater than that of a mother to her nursing child (49:15). By employing comparison with a nursing mother, the LORD conveys tenderness, vulnerability, and care.[469] The poetry highlights the importance of this imagery through parallelism as the question is echoed by an alliterated one querying a mother's ability to fail to show "compassion" (*mēraḥēm*) for the "child of her womb" (*ben-biṭnāh*).[470]

While Zion's critique of the LORD's memory is refuted, her own memory comes into question. The query "Can a woman forget her nursing child?" implies an answer of "no," yet the LORD says, "even these (*gam-'ēlleh*) might forget" (49:15). When the divine voice supplies future words for Zion's speech "Then you will say in your heart, 'Who has borne me these ('*ēlleh*) . . . who has reared these ('*ēlleh*)? . . . Where, then, have these ('*ēlleh*) come from?'" (49:21) the repetition of "these"[471] connects Zion's failure to recognize and remember the returning offspring with the LORD's claim that mothers may indeed forget their children (49:14).[472]

---

[468] P. Tull Willey, *Remember the Former Things* (1997), 190.

[469] See further K. M. Heffelfinger, *I Am Large* (2011), 234. See also J. Goldingay and D. Payne, *Isaiah 40–55* (2006), 2:185. The choice of nursing child may also allude to Lamentations' depictions of the particular vulnerability of the very young in the siege of Jerusalem (e.g., Lam 4:4). See further K. M. Heffelfinger, "I am He" (2021); and P. Tull Willey, *Remember the Former Things* (1997), 191.

[470] Phyllis Trible, *God and the Rhetoric of Sexuality* (OBT; Philadelphia: Fortress Press, 1978), 33, draws a connection between the sound of "compassion" and "womb."

[471] The repetition of "these" also creates contrast with the immediately preceding Servant poem. See further K. M. Heffelfinger, "The Servant" (2018), 193, 195.

[472] See further K. M. Heffelfinger, *I Am Large* (2011), 236–237. Contra J. Blenkinsopp, *Isaiah 40–55* (2002), 312, the direct contrast between divine memory and that of mothers conveyed through the repetition of "these" argues against the idea that "She is not presumably wondering whether she could have had them all and herself and no longer recalled with whom." Instead, the poetry does appear to indict Zion's memory through contrast. K. R. Roberts, "Isaiah 49:14–18" (2003), 59, points to Lam 4:2–4 here and I agree

180 *Commentary*

Divine memory is affirmed. It is strong and specific. The couplet "Even these might forget, yet I will not forget you" highlights the contrast. The poem powerfully and poetically depicts a divine memory of both complaint and complainant. In contrast, while the divine voice remembers her well enough to quote her, Zion appears as one who has forgotten.[473]

Zion as woman reappears intermittently throughout the poem. She is compared to a bride adorning herself with restored people (49:18)[474] and as a bereaved mother incredulous at children she was unaware of (49:20–21). She stands as the maternal figure behind the regal procession of "sons" and "daughters" (49:22) as well as the mother of the addressees whose "divorce" from the LORD is disputed (50:1). Her restoration conveys hope and comfort while her incredulity and complaint resonate with the more strident imagery that concludes the poem.

Just as in Lamentations, city and woman images intertwine (see, e.g., Lam 1:1–3, 1:4), here too, city images appear interspersed with the appearances of personified Lady Zion.[475] The images mingle, overlap with, and develop one another. The "you" who will not be forgotten is one with "walls" and "builders" (49:16–17). Immediately juxtaposed to the woman and child imagery, and carrying a similar level of emotional intensity, the divine voice proclaims "See, I have inscribed you on the palms of my hands," as if offering the metaphorical divine "palms" for inspection (49:16).[476] Engraving on the "palms" combines a permanent mode of

---

that maternal forgetfulness of a most horrific kind as in Lamentations' complaint is alluded to here. While Roberts highlights the restorative orientation of Isa 49:15, this verse is more a strong refutation of Zion's credibility as accuser than her comments highlight.

[473] K. M. Heffelfinger, *I Am Large* (2011), 237.

[474] P. Tull Willey, *Remember the Former Things* (1997), 198–200, presents a convincing argument that the bridal ornaments imagery develops an intertextual link with Jeremiah. Such a relationship further underscores the reversal of Zion's accusation of divine forgetfulness. See P. Tull Willey, *Remember the Former Things* (1997), 200. See also B. D. Sommer, *A Prophet Reads* (1998), 37.

[475] See K. Baltzer, *Deutero-Isaiah* (2001), 323, on "interweaving" of images in Isaiah 49:17–19.

[476] See K. M. Heffelfinger, *I Am Large* (2011), 239.

# Isaiah 49:14–50:3

writing employed for hard, inanimate objects, with a soft bodily surface and willing embrace of such costly memory.[477] The dramatic picture evoked by these lines conveys permanence as well as pain.[478]

Destruction is overturned, introducing the image of an overwhelming growth of population. While Lamentations depicted the "city that once was full of people" as "lonely" (Lam 1:1), here the city is "too crowded" (49:19, 20). Again, city and woman intermingle with "children" (49:20) conveying the "inhabitants" (49:19). The exuberance of restoration appears in Zion's rhetorical question (49:21) as well as the imagery of royal figures humbling themselves before Zion and serving as substitute caregivers for her children. This image perhaps reinforces the superabundance of the children, that is, she could not nurse and mother them all and so needs "foster fathers" and "nursing mothers." It almost certainly also conveys the humbling of the rulers of the nations as it stands in parallel to the imagery of them bowing (49:23) and employs likely feminizing imagery for foreign kings.[479] However, the imagery of substitute "nursing mothers" cannot fail to resonate with the divine voice's rhetorical question about whether a woman could "forget her nursing child" (49:15). The presence of substitutes for this role continues the subtle implication that Zion herself has managed to forget.

At least as powerful as the nursing mother and inscribed palms imagery but with distinctly less tender emotional freight are the depictions of the LORD's opposition to Zion's "oppressors" (49:24–26). Repetition and

---

[477] The verb "I have inscribed" (*ḥaqqōtîk*) is used with hard surfaces (see e.g., Isa 22:16 and Ezek 4:1). It appears in parallel to "write ... on a tablet" where it is the mode of writing "on a scroll" (Isa 30:8). The emphasis on permanence as well as the reference to walls in this context argue in favor of a translation that conveys etching, as does NRSV[ue]'s "inscribed." The use of "palms" (*kappayim*) as opposed to "hand" (*yād*) is specific and likely avoids the common "hand" of the LORD imagery, which, as J. Goldingay and D. Payne, *Isaiah 40–55* (2006), 2:187, indicate, carries the "connotation of power and violence," which *kap* does not.

[478] See further K. M. Heffelfinger, *I Am Large* (2011), 239–240.

[479] While the word here translated by the NRSV[ue] "your foster fathers" ( *'ōmĕnayik*), can convey a fairly masculine "guardian" role, e.g., 2 Kings 10:1, 5, it appears in parallel with the needs of suckling children both here (NRSV[ue] "your nursing mothers," *mêniqōtayik*) and in Moses' complaint, "Did I conceive all this people? Did I give birth to them, that you should say to me, 'Carry them in your bosom as a wet nurse (*hā 'ōmēn*, i.e., "the nurse") carries a nursing child (*hayyōnēq*, i.e., "the suckling")'" (Num 11:12). A similar use of the term is apparently in use in Ruth 4:16, where Naomi lays Obed "in her bosom and became his nurse ( *'ōmenet*)." So, while feminization of the kings is not explicit, it may well be hinted at in the imagery employed here.

182                                                                    *Commentary*

emphatic first-person pronouns mark out these verses as intense and of
central importance to the meaning of the poem. The rhetorical questions
about whether "prey" can be "taken from the mighty"[480] and "captives of a
tyrant be rescued" echo the earlier query about whether it was possible for
a mother to forget her nursling (49:15) and again it seems that the poem
creates a context where the expected answer is "no." As the earlier pattern
leads the reader to expect, the divine voice overturns that idea. The
response again begins with "Even" (*gam*),[481] but instead of the simple
contrast between "these" and "I" as appeared in 49:15, here the contrast is
expanded. A couplet reorients the parallelism of the questions with "captives" now belonging with "the mighty" and "prey" with "tyrant."[482]
Alongside this double reversal of the implied "no" is a double, emphatic,
and alliterated insistence upon the LORD's active involvement in deliverance: "I will contend" (*'ānōkî 'ārîb*) and "I will save" (*'ānōkî 'ôšîa'*).[483]

   The disturbing image of self-cannibalism for the oppressors underscores
the reversal of Zion's complaint. While warfare cannibalism appears in
Lamentations as an indication of the desperation of the suffering population (Lam 2:20; 4:10) and carries particular associations with the very
young, here the oppressors (*mônayik*), the sound of which echoes the
sound of the word for nursing child (*yônēq*, as in Lam 4:4),[484] are forced
to visit upon themselves the suffering that has been experienced by the
inhabitants of Zion.[485] The LORD is emphatically the architect of this

---

[480]   There is considerable discussion of the translation of this word, which most naturally
means "righteous." See, e.g., K. Balzter, *Deutero-Isaiah* (2001), 331; and J. Goldingay and
D. Payne, *Isaiah 40–55* (2006), 2:196–97. Note, however, the use of this same term in,
e.g., Isa 41:2, where the NRSV[ue] translates it "victor." See BDB, 842 and discussion of
*ṣdqh* in Isaiah 1–39 and 40–55 respectively in R. Rendtorff, "Isaiah 56:1" (1993), 183.

[481]   See also J. Goldingay and D. Payne, *Isaiah 40–55* (2006), 2:197.

[482]   See J. Goldingay and D. Payne, *Isaiah 40–55* (2006), 2:197, who comment that this
"unexpected reversal . . . mirrors the unexpected reversal the line speaks of."

[483]   See J. Goldingay and D. Payne, *Isaiah 40–55* (2006), 2:198; and R. Alter, *Hebrew Bible*
(2019), 790.

[484]   A related term (*mêniqōtayik*) is used for the "nursing mothers" of Isa 49:23. However,
the "nursing child" of Isa 49:15 differs.

[485]   P. Tull Willey, *Remember the Former Things* (1997), 192, treats the imagery as recalling
Lamentations and visiting its horrors upon Zion's enemies. See further K. M.
Heffelfinger, "I am He" (2021), 95–96; and K. M. Heffelfinger, *I Am Large* (2011),
242–243. Many scholarly treatments of this imagery make limited comment. See, e.g.,
J. D. W. Watts, *Isaiah 34–66* (2005), 193. C. Westermann, *Isaiah 40–66* (1969), 222,
specifically distances the imagery of destruction of enemies from the prophet, noting
that "the things just mentioned do not represent what interested him personally."

*Isaiah 49:14–50:3* 183

reversal of fortunes and its violence is a reminder of the passion of the God who speaks, delivers, and who will make "all flesh … know" that deliverance.[486]

The ominous insistence upon the might of the LORD continues as the final section of the poem shifts the Lady Zion metaphor to address her "children." While, as we have seen, the image already includes and incorporates them, not least by making the audience's complaint Zion's own; this shift to address the audience directly as Zion's metaphorical children intensifies the encounter with the divine speaking voice and adds a layer of indictment. Legal language had already appeared in the claim that the LORD would "contend ( *'ārîb*) with those who contend ( *yĕrîbēk*) with you" (49:25).[487] Now, rhetorical questions reject "divorce" and "creditors" as possibilities for the breach, insisting instead that the audience's own "sins" and "transgressions" are the direct cause (50:1). A strident chain of rhetorical questions peppers the audience with indictments for their failure to respond to the LORD and progresses to apparently sarcastic questions that imply the audience thinks that the God who has just proclaimed violent divine might is powerless to bring about their rescue (50:2).[488]

Rather than answer its own rhetorical questions, as it has done up to this point in the poem, the divine voice depicts its might with cosmic battle imagery. Drying up "sea" and "rivers" picks up the imagery of Isaiah 42:14–15, as well as Exodus imagery and the triumph of the creator over watery chaos.[489] These are not past occurrences of deliverance only, though

---

J. Blenkinsopp, *Isaiah 40–55* (2002), 315, disallows self-cannibalism relating the imagery to "internecine strife."

[486] The issue of divine violence in prophetic texts is a thorny one and should not be straightforwardly equated with human violence. A fascinating engagement with the subject is offered by Corrine Carvalho, "The Beauty of the Bloody God: The Divine Warrior in Prophetic Literature," in *The Aesthetics of Violence in the Prophets* (eds. Julia M. O'Brien and Chris Franke; London: T&T Clark, 2010).

[487] See J. Goldingay and D. Payne, *Isaiah 40–55* (2006), 2:198.

[488] See further C. Westermann, *Isaiah 40–66* (1969), 225.

[489] B. S. Childs, *Isaiah* (2001), 394, recognizes Exodus imagery here. J. Goldingay and D. Payne, *Isaiah 40–55* (2006), 2:202, note potential resonance but comment that "the way the language develops in v. 2b moves away from suggesting any specific link with the exodus. It refers more generally to Yhwh's power over forces of disorder." I agree and think that faint echoes of both Exodus and Creation motifs here are unspecified but add to the resonance of the poetry with these themes. B. D. Sommer, *A Prophet Reads* (1998), 267, also identifies Exodus and Creation "themes" here noting their commonality as opposed to specific textual allusion.

184　　　　　　　　　　　　　　　　　　　　　　　　　　*Commentary*

the echoes of past and known liberations ought to reassure the audience of their truth. Rather, the verbs that convey the divine might in these lines indicate incomplete action.[490] The LORD still acts with power, and while these refutations of doubt in the LORD's ability to deliver are essentially claims of impending deliverance, they are conveyed with indictment and accusation from the mighty one.

In direct contrast to the conclusion to the previous poem, the LORD will make the same celestial bodies that were commanded to sing out about the people's deliverance wear mourning garb.[491] The difference between the result of an encounter with the personified Servant and personified Zion could not be starker. One leads to a cosmic rejoicing through acceptance of the divine commission. The other leads to celestial mourning through resistance and resulting rebuke. Through this juxtaposition and its stark contrast, the audience are invited to identify a Servant-like embrace of proclaimed divine deliverance as the overwhelmingly more positive stance.[492] The two personifications offer visions of the audience's stance toward the LORD and their starkly contrasting reliability, appeal, and outcome poetically urge the audience toward embrace of their potential "Servant" response.

A CLOSER LOOK: LADY ZION AND THE SUFFERING SERVANT, THE RHETORICAL POWER OF JUXTAPOSITION

Two compelling personifications stand out from the text of Isaiah 40–55. The personified, destroyed city of Jerusalem embodies the people's complaint (see A Closer Look: Zion and the Audience). This figure who spoke vividly in Lamentations is now largely silent but is frequently spoken to and about. She is offered comfort and her grounds for resistance are undermined as unreliable (see comment on 49:14–50:3). In contrast, the

---

[490] "I dry up," and "I make" are imperfect forms.

[491] J. Muilenburg, "Isaiah 40–66" (1956), 5:582, takes this as "mourning" imagery. See also J. Goldingay and D. Payne, *Isaiah 40–55* (2006), 2:203.

[492] See K. M. Heffelfinger, "The Servant" (2018). See also U. Schmidt, "Servant and Zion" (2011), 91, who sees the personifications as presenting "two options." While I would argue in contrast to Schmidt that there is "differentiation of better and worse" in these personifications, that the text does depict the Servant more favorably and attempt to persuade the audience into embracing it rather than Zion, Schmidt's observation of the "juxtaposition" of the two is a central insight.

# A Closer Look: Lady Zion and the Suffering Servant

man of Lamentations 3, who spoke little in that book, seems to stand behind the personified voice of the Servant in these chapters.[493] This figure presents the audience with an embodiment of that into which the poems aim to transform them and appears closely aligned to, strengthened and vindicated by the LORD (see A Closer Look: The Servant and His "Songs"). The allusion to Lamentations that develops through these two voices appearing in the same text but not together does powerful poetic work in its response to the audience's complaint.[494] They are placed between vivid depictions of what they are and the complaint they voice (Zion) and what they can be if they step into the promised comfort (Servant). The series of poems does not offer this as a logical either/or choice. Rather, it juxtaposes the pair of evocative, emotional, metaphorical figures and allows the tension and harmony between them to do its poetic, rhetorical work.[495]

In Isaiah 54 these juxtaposed personifications begin to come together. There the language of "servants," which will become more prominent in chapters 56–66 appears and stands alongside Zion herself for the first time.[496] In this moment of transition, reconciliation embraces both Zion's and Jacob-Israel's complaints (see A Closer Look: Conflicted Commands and Competing Contentions in the Memory Motif) and the imagery of restoration includes both a rebuilt and glorified Zion (54:11–12) and protection for the "servants" (54:17). The drawing together of the two juxtaposed personifications and their associated imageries poetically enacts the embrace of reconciliation that the pair of personifications aims to urge the reader toward (see further comment on Isa 54:1–17). In the chapters that follow, Zion imagery will increasingly convey divine comfort and

---

[493] See P. Tull Willey, *Remember the Former Things* (1997), 209–228, who presents a convincing argument for taking Lamentations 3 as a significant source of the Servant imagery and considers the relationship between the Servant imagery and Zion imagery in Second Isaiah.

[494] See P. Tull Willey, *Remember the Former Things* (1997), 105, who shows how the text "alternates" between attention to Zion and the Servant.

[495] K. M. Heffelfinger, "The Servant" (2018). On the juxtaposition see also U. Schmidt, "Servant and Zion" (2011).

[496] See W. A. M. Beuken, "The Main Theme of Trito-Isaiah 'The Servants of YHWH,'" *JSOT* 47 (1990): 67, who highlights the shift to the plural "precisely *before* the end" of Isaiah 40–55 and notes that "The city addressed in ch. 54 learns that its children will live as the servants of YHWH on their own heritage." See also P. Tull Willey, *Remember the Former Things* (1997), 232–233.

186                                                                    *Commentary*

restoration (see A Closer Look: Birth and Breastfeeding Imagery in Isaiah 40–66) and the "servants" will depict recipients of restoration and contrast sharply with those the prophet condemns (see, e.g., 65:13; 66:14) as the poetry increasingly depicts distinct groupings in its vision of the beneficiaries of divine comfort (see A Closer Look: From Servant to Servants).

ISAIAH 50:4–11

4 The Lord GOD has given me
     a trained tongue,
that I may know how to sustain
     the weary with a word.
Morning by morning he wakens,
     wakens my ear
     to listen as those who are taught.
5 The Lord GOD has opened my ear,
     and I was not rebellious;
     I did not turn backward.
6 I gave my back to those who struck me
     and my cheeks to those who pulled out the beard;
I did not hide my face
     from insult and spitting.

7 The Lord GOD helps me;
     therefore I have not been disgraced;
therefore I have set my face like flint,
     and I know that I shall not be put to shame;
8 he who vindicates me is near.
Who will contend with me?
     Let us stand in court together.
Who are my adversaries?
     Let them confront me.
9 It is the Lord GOD who helps me;
     who will declare me guilty?
All of them will wear out like a garment;
     the moth will eat them up.

*Isaiah 50:4–11*

[10] Who among you fears the LORD
    and obeys the voice of his servant,
who walks in darkness
    and has no light,
yet trusts in the name of the LORD
    and relies upon his God?
[11] But all of you are kindlers of fire,
    lighters of firebrands.
Walk in the flame of your fire
    and among the brands that you have kindled!
This is what you shall have from my hand:
    you shall lie down in torment.

This second encounter with the speaking voice of the Servant continues to work persuasively on the audience, urging them to embrace the response to the LORD's deliverance that the Servant embodies. Contrast with Zion's resistance continues as this figure expresses overwhelming trust and dependence upon God (see A Closer Look: Lady Zion and the Suffering Servant, the Rhetorical Power of Juxtaposition).[497] The Servant's voice exudes trust and trustworthiness through the way he characterizes his speech, through his vivid depictions of perseverance in the face of shame, and through the passage's allusions to the "man" of Lamentations 3.

The voice speaking this passage is somewhat ambiguous. The voice does not directly state that it is the Servant.[498] However, it embodies the characteristics that are features of the Servant. As in the first poem that the Servant spoke, this voice blends with the divine voice in its mode of speaking; and by the end of this passage (50:10–11), it is unclear whether the LORD has begun speaking or whether the Servant continues.

From the first lines of this poem, the audience encounters a speaker whose trustworthiness receives particular emphasis. Perhaps faintly echoing and developing the previous Servant poem's interest in the Servant's mouth (49:2), the opening image is of the Servant having a learned tongue.

---

[497] See also J. Goldingay and D. Payne, *Isaiah 40–55* (2006), 2:205.
[498] B. S. Childs, *Isaiah* (2001), 394, comments "Although the term *servant* is not used in vv. 4–9, the larger context, before and after, removes any possible doubt that the speaker is the servant."

The NRSV[ue]'s "trained tongue" reflects the adjective that seems formed on the basis of a passive verb and would most naturally connote the student rather than the teacher (cf. NRSV "tongue of a teacher").[499] The occurrences of this rare term beyond this verse, especially those within the book of Isaiah, seem most naturally to convey the one instructed rather than the one giving instruction (see 8:16 and 54:13). The remaining occurrence referring to human beings is Jer 13:23 where it seems to refer to habituation in wickedness, more likely learned in doing evil than teachers of evil. Williamson highlights the rarity of this term as an argument in support of seeing Isa 8:16 as having influenced Isa 50:4-9, as well as the other Isaian occurrences. He comments "At 50:4, Deutero-Isaiah consciously includes himself among the group of those who witnessed the sealing of the prophetic teaching."[500] While the purpose of the Servant's being taught is to speak to others, here the emphasis is on his dependence upon instruction from the LORD.

Both his ears (50:4) and his tongue (50:4) are "taught" building an image of a receptive figure whose words are reliable because they come from the LORD.[501] The repetitive phrase "Morning by morning" conveys consistent and ongoing receptivity to the LORD's instruction. In dramatic contrast to the brief, embedded, and refuted speech offered by Lady Zion in the preceding poem (49:14), this voice speaks with the authority of having been given instruction from the LORD. The purpose of his speech also matches the LORD's commission. This voice is instructed so that he might "sustain the weary with a word" (50:4), employing the term ("weary" yā 'ēp) that appeared heavily in Isaiah 40:28-31 characterizing the LORD's unwearying nature and the strength to come to those "who wait for the LORD."[502]

---

[499] See also J. Blenkinsopp, *Isaiah 40-55* (2002), 317; K. Baltzer, *Deutero-Isaiah* (2001), 338; J. Goldingay and D. Payne, *Isaiah 40-55* (2006), 2:207; B. S. Childs, *Isaiah* (2001), 394; and C. Westermann, *Isaiah 40-66* (1969), 225.

[500] H. G. M. Williamson, *Book Called Isaiah* (1994), 108. See also B. D. Sommer, *A Prophet Reads Scripture* (1998), 291.

[501] See J. Blenkinsopp, *Isaiah 40-55* (2002), 320.

[502] J. Blenkinsopp, *Isaiah 40-55* (2002), 319, notes this connection and interprets it as supporting the idea that "the mission is to his fellow-Judeans." On "weary," see also J. D. W. Watts, *Isaiah 34-66* (2005), 201; and J. Goldingay and D. Payne, *Isaiah 40-55* (2006), 2:209.

*Isaiah 50:4–11*                                                                                              189

Throughout, the overwhelming insistence of this poem is that the speaker depends entirely upon the LORD. The refrain-like statement "The Lord GOD helps me" (50:7; cf. 50:9)[503] expresses the Servant's confidence emphatically while pointing to its source. Repeatedly in these chapters, the divine voice has announced that it will "help" the audience in contexts where they are addressed as "servant" (41:10, 13, 14; 44:2).[504] Here, the Servant's embrace of that help and dependence upon it illustrate the attitudes toward which the poems have been pointing.

Two looming threats present themselves as the things about which the Servant has placed his trust in the LORD: humiliation (vv. 6–7) and judgment (vv. 8–9). Vivid bodily imagery presents the Servant's willing submission to violent degradation. Echoing the "man" of Lamentations 3, who advised "one should wait quietly" (Lam 3:26) and "give (*yittēn*) one's cheek (*leḥî*) to the smiter (*lĕmakkēhû*) and be filled with insults" (Lam 3:30), and who proclaimed that God's "mercies" were "new every morning" (Lam 3:23),[505] the Servant's response to his morning listening (50:4) to the LORD develops through parallel claims of what he does not do, that is, rebel and "turn backward" (50:5), and what he does, that is, willingly embrace violent humiliation (50:6).[506] The imagery drawn from what the

[503] In Hebrew the two lines are identical with the exception of the additional *hēn* that opens v. 9. The same title is used for the LORD in v. 4 of this poem as well. Within Isaiah 40–55, only the divine voice and the Servant use this title reinforcing the Servant voice's imitation of the divine voice.

[504] The one occurrence of the verb as completed action is in the personified Servant's voice recounting what the LORD has said (Isa 49:8). This repeated occurrence of "help" from the LORD in contexts that link the Servant to Jacob-Israel and the personified Servant's expressions of certainty and confidence depending upon it (Isa 49:8; 50:7, 9) support the conclusion that the Servant embodies acceptance of the restoration proclaimed to Jacob-Israel.

[505] On this parallel, see P. Tull Willey, *Remember the Former Things* (1997), 217.

[506] See P. Tull Willey, *Remember the Former Things* (1997), 215–219, for fulsome articulation of her claim that the man of Lamentations provides this imagery. See also B. D. Sommer, *A Prophet Reads* (1998), 217, who comments that Gottwald's observation of parallels includes cases among which he lists Lam 3:30 and Isa 50:6 "that may indeed result from borrowing." Commentators frequently point to comparison with Jeremiah, e.g., K. Baltzer, *Deutero-Isaiah* (2001), 339; J. Blenkinsopp, *Isaiah 40–55* (2002), 320–321; J. L. McKenzie, *Second Isaiah* (1968), 117; and C. Westermann, *Isaiah 40–66* (1969), 227–228. There are relevant connections to the Servant's treatment, see e.g., J. Blenkinsopp, *Isaiah 40–55* (2002), 321, on beating, spitting, and pulling out the beard. However, the specific word parallels argue more strongly for a connection with Lamentations, even if Isa 50 also picks up on these other motifs. J. Muilenburg, "Isaiah 40–66" (1956), 5:585 and J. Goldingay and D. Payne, *Isaiah 40–55* (2006), 2:211, each

"man" of Lamentations 3 suggests is amplified in the image the Servant employs. He "gave" (*nātattî*) to the smiters (*lĕmakkîm*) his "back" and his "cheek" (*lĕḥāyay*) to those who made it bare.[507] By spreading out the reference to those who smite the cheek in the source of the allusion, the Servant's imagery develops one act of violence, a blow to the face, to two, assaults on both the back and the beard.[508] It seems that in both Lamentations and Isaiah 50, the intent of this imagery is to convey humiliation. Again, the Isaian reuse of this motif intensifies it through expansion. While Lamentations refers once to being "filled with insults" (Lam 3:30), the Servant says that he did not "hide" from "insult and spitting" (Isa 50:6).

By drawing on and intensifying the imagery from Lamentations, this poem embodies a powerful response to the conditions of the exiles. The "man" of Lamentations 3 speaks the most hope-filled lines in the whole of the largely bleak book. He stands in contrast to the personification of Zion who weeps bitterly (Lam 1:2), yet he shares in her suffering, weeping continually himself (Lam 3:49–51) and crying out to the LORD for "help" (Lam 3:56). In the Servant the exiles encounter a figure who places his trust in the LORD and who expresses confidence that he will "not be put to shame" (Isa 50:7) but who would not be unsympathetic to their plight and instead is "the one" (cf. Heb. *'ănî haggeber*, i.e., "I am the man") "who has seen affliction under the rod of God's wrath" (Lam 3:1 NRSV[ue]). This is a personification with whom they can identify and whose willing embrace of

---

point to Neh 13:25 as relevant to considering the reference to the beard. Goldingay and Payne connect "beard-pulling" to "formal symbolic shaming." I would not dispute this understanding and recognize that there is a connection to Neh 13:25, not least in the use of the verb *mrṭ* in both cases. However, the parallel to Lam 3 is the governing resonance for interpreting this imagery, even if other biblical resonances help to illuminate the meaning of cultural practices.

[507] The NRSV[ue] renders the participle plus preposition *lĕmōrĕṭîm*, a causative form of a word meaning "make bare," by including reference to what the cheek would likely be made bare from, that is, "the beard."

[508] See P. Tull Willey, *Remember the Former Things* (1997), 216, who points out the uniqueness of the phrase to Lam 3 and Isa 50:6 and the patterned reuse of it in Isa 50:6. Both of these factors contribute convincing argumentation for a relationship between the Lamentations and Isaiah texts here, particularly in light of other evidence that Second Isaiah knows Lamentations. On definitions for considering allusion, see B. D. Sommer, *A Prophet Reads* (1998), 10–11; on the relevance of style (35), and on the "split up pattern" (68–69).

*Isaiah 50:4–11*                                                                191

God's instruction, whose rejection of rebellion, and whose confidence in the LORD's help are aspects of what they can become.

The legal imagery[509] in which the Servant expresses his confidence in the LORD's help is less expansive[510] but employs rhetorical questions in a mode that echoes the divine voice in these chapters. The tone of the Servant's rebuttal of his "adversaries" (50:8) tilts the poem toward indictment as three successive couplets employ rhetorical questions insistently demanding a response with the implication that there is none to give it (50:8–9). The absent or inadequate contenders contrast with the speaking Servant and the LORD who is "near" (50:8) and who "helps" (50:7, 9). Zion has just been promised by the LORD "I will contend (*'ārîb*) with those who contend (*yĕrîbēk*) with you" (49:25) and reminded that "those who wait for me shall not be put to shame (*lō'-yēbōšû*)" (49:23).[511] The Servant in this poem stands in contrast to the one who needed to be emphatically assured of those promises, as one who is expressing them for himself. He embodies what it looks like to trust in the one who does "contend" with one's "adversaries" to the extent he can invite "Who will contend (*yārîb*) with me?" and who can confidently announce "I shall not be put to shame" (*lō' 'ēbôš*). The audience, who may well identify with Zion, are offered a vivid depiction of what confidence in the promises made to her can look like. They are offered the Servant as a personification of what they can be.

The concluding unit of this poem turns to address the audience directly and does so in a voice who indicts and accuses them. The voice refers to both "the LORD" and "his Servant" in the third person, in contrast to preceding lines' references to the latter figure as "me" (e.g., 50:4, 7, 8, 9). The stinging closing couplet's threat of "torment" coming "from my hand"

---

[509] See J. L. McKenzie, *Second Isaiah* (1968), 117; J. Blenkinsopp, *Isaiah 40–55* (2002), 321–322; C. Westermann, *Isaiah 40–66* (1969), 231; and J. Muilenburg, "Isaiah 40–66" (1956), 5:585–586.

[510] Notably, NRSV[ue]'s "stand in court" supplies the explicit reference to "court" when it translates *na'amĕdâ yāḥad*. Compare NRSV's "Let us stand up together." There is no explicit mention of a court context in these words.

[511] Cf. J. Blenkinsopp, *Isaiah 40–55* (2002), 319, who concludes that in relation to its larger context "clear thematic and linguistic interconnections between units are not easy to detect, but they are not entirely absent either." Blenkinsopp highlights connection to chapter 51.

192                                                    *Commentary*

(50:11) suggests that the LORD is the speaker, but there is no introduction of divine speech or explicit attribution in vv. 10–11 at all.[512]

This voice employs rhetorical questions, as the divine voice does frequently in these chapters (see, e.g., 40:12, 13, 14, 18, 21, 25; 27; 43:9; 44:7, 8; 45:9, 10, 11, 21; 46:5; 48:6; 50:1, 2) and as the Servant has just done (50:8–9). As the divine voice often does in these chapters, this voice interrupts its introduction with an expanded characterization, in this case of the Servant. The elaboration of reference to the Servant reiterates the insistence upon the Servant's trust in the LORD that has characterized this poem (50:10) and alludes again to Lamentations' man in its reference to walking "in darkness" without "light" (cf. Lam 3:2).[513] This expansion of reference to the Servant in imitation of the expansions of reference to the LORD as speaker elsewhere suggests that these lines should be read as spoken by the Servant's voice. It is as though the Servant's instructed tongue has blended so fully with the LORD, his teacher, that he fully and faithfully conveys the indictment on God's behalf.

At the same time, these lines build contrast between what the Servant is and what the addressees are.[514] The Servant is one who "walks in darkness and has no light" (50:10) but they are those who light their own fire and who are exhorted to "walk" in it. In light of the contrast with the exemplary Servant walking "in darkness,"[515] the injunction to "Walk in the flame of your fire" must be read as sarcastic and condemnatory. Fire frequently conveys wrath and judgment (see, e.g., Isa 1:7; 9:29; Lam 1:13; 4:11; Ps 21:9 Eng.; 89:46 Eng.) and the recurrent reference to "brands" and "firebrands" (v. 11 Hebrew both *zîqôt*) may connote those who stir up conflict (cf. the

---

[512]    J. Goldingay and D. Payne, *Isaiah 40–55* (2006), 2:205, note the references to the Servant and the LORD as well as the apparent pointer to the divine voice in v. 11 concluding that vv. 10–11 are spoken by the LORD. See further their comments on p. 216.

[513]    See P. Tull Willey, *Remember the Former Things* (1997), 218; and J. Muilenburg, "Isaiah 40–66" (1956), 5:588.

[514]    Relevant here is B. D. Sommer, *A Prophet Reads* (1998), 253–254, who observes a "typological linkage" with the imagery for the people in Isaiah 5:30 and 8:22–9:1.

[515]    J. Blenkinsopp, *Isaiah 40–55* (2002), 322, notes that the phrasing is ambiguous and could indicate the Servant is the one who walks in darkness but rejects that reading glossing darkness as "a state of spiritual disorientation," which does not fit this figure. However, as an image of trouble, difficulty, or suffering, it does. Treating darkness here as referring to the situation of the Servant agrees with the poetry's contrasting depiction of his adversaries.

*Isaiah 51:1–8* 193

only other occurrence, Prov 26:18),[516] in which case the audience may be being associated with the Servant's adversaries in verses 8 and 9.

Whether or not they are to be associated with the contenders of the earlier verses, the audience certainly find themselves confronted, indicted, and contrasted with the exemplary Servant. While the beginning of the poem offered them a vivid image of the trust they are being exhorted to through the Servant personification, these closing lines emphasize the contrast between their apparent current attitudes and that of the Servant. A stark challenge is laid before them as the closing lines underscore the poem's persuasive aims of transforming the audience toward the character of the personified Servant.[517] By illustrating their opposition, the poem offers to their imaginations what it might look like to set themselves up in opposition to the LORD's intentions.

## ISAIAH 51:1–8

[1] Listen to me, you that pursue righteousness,
  you that seek the LORD.
Look to the rock from which you were hewn
  and to the quarry from which you were dug.
[2] Look to Abraham your father
  and to Sarah, who bore you,
for he was but one when I called him,
  but I blessed him and made him many.
[3] For the LORD will comfort Zion;
  he will comfort all her waste places
and will make her wilderness like Eden,
  her desert like the garden of the LORD;

---

[516] While Isaiah's use treats the noun as feminine and the noun in Proverbs is masculine, it seems implausible to suggest that these are not occurrences of the same term. See BDB, 278.

[517] See P. Tull Willey, *Remember the Former Things* (1997), 218–219, who describes text noting that "the concentration is on the spiritual struggle of the speaker, his coming to grips with suffering in a constructive way, and his attempt to convey a model of persevering trust to listeners who are encouraged to follow his example" (218). See also H. G. M. Williamson, *Book Called Isaiah* (1994), 109, who remarks, "Deutero-Isaiah looked forward to the day when his own faithfulness would be adopted by the whole of the new community," pointing also to the reference to "servants" in Isa 54:17.

194                                                          *Commentary*

joy and gladness will be found in her,
    thanksgiving and the voice of song.

⁴ Listen to me, my people,
    and give heed to me, my nation,
for a teaching will go out from me
    and my justice for a light to the peoples.
⁵ I will bring near my deliverance swiftly;
    my salvation has gone out
    and my arms will rule the peoples;
the coastlands wait for me,
    and for my arm they hope.
⁶ Lift up your eyes to the heavens
    and look at the earth beneath,
for the heavens will vanish like smoke,
    the earth will wear out like a garment,
    and those who live on it will die like gnats,
but my salvation will be forever,
    and my deliverance will never be ended.

⁷ Listen to me, you who know righteousness,
    you people who have my teaching in your hearts;
do not fear the reproach of others,
    and do not be dismayed when they revile you.
⁸ For the moth will eat them up like a garment,
    and the worm will eat them like wool;
but my deliverance will be forever,
    and my salvation to all generations.

In three parallel invitations to "Listen to me," the LORD echoes and endorses the attitudes exemplified by the Servant in the preceding poem.[518] The audience are invited to envision the future offered by the LORD and

---

[518] While there is no "Thus says the LORD" as is common throughout these chapters to mark divine speech, it is clear that the speaker is to be identified as the LORD. The speaker claims to have "called" and "blessed" Abraham, refers to the audience as "my people" and describes the coming of "my deliverance" and "my salvation." J. Goldingay and D. Payne, *Isaiah 40–55* (2006), 2:221, also see the speaker as the divine voice here. On the structuring impact of the repeated "exhortation to listen," see M. A. Sweeney, *Isaiah 40–66* (2016), 183.

*Isaiah 51:1–8*                                                                                    195

their own participation in it if they will embody the Servant personification in their response. Each of the invitations characterizes its addressees positively, inviting identification, and throughout the imagery employed offers a vision of impending divine deliverance as dependable and expansive.

The first and third invitations to "Listen to me" are the most closely parallel to one another.[519] Each of these employs participles to describe the addressees, a feature that has frequently characterized the descriptions of the divine speaker.[520] Here they are those "who pursue (*rōdĕpê*) righteousness," "seek (*mĕbaqšê*) the LORD" (51:1), and "who know (*yōdĕʿê*) righteousness" (51:7). By characterizing them in a way that mirrors the characterization of the divine speaker, the poetry casts the audience's relationship to the LORD in a positive light. In addition, the connection to "righteousness" offers an image of themselves that the audience may well be keen to accept. The invitation that falls between these two, "Listen to me, my people" (51:4), employs a different verb and stands out as distinct from the other two such invitations. The line is structured chiastically (see "chiasm," in Glossary of Poetic Terminology), making references to the audience as "my people" and "my nation"[521] the central terms of framing exhortations to pay attention (*haqĕšîbû* and *haʾăzînû*) and parallel indications of the speaker as the object of that attention ("to me" *ʾēlay*).[522] Thus the calls to attention (51:1, 4, 7) exhibit an orderly structure that characterizes the audience positively in terms of their seeking after righteousness and their relationship to the LORD and illustrates a measured and controlled speaker.[523]

The poem's imagery overlaps heavily with the preceding poem in the voice of the Servant. While the Servant insisted that his "tongue" was

---

[519]  See also J. Blenkinsopp, *Isaiah 40–55* (2002), 325.

[520]  See, e.g., Isa 42:5; 43:1, 16; 44:2, 24; 45:18

[521]  As K. Baltzer, *Deutero-Isaiah* (2001), 350, observes, there is a potential problem here as "my people" and "my nation" are each singular forms while the verbs addressed to them are plural. Baltzer helpfully suggests, drawing on Schoors, that the peoples here should be understood as composed of the plurality of "individuals constituting" them. J. D. W. Watts, *Isaiah 34–66* (2005), 196, also refers to "the collective sense of the nouns."

[522]  See J. Goldingay and D. Payne, *Isaiah 40–55* (2006), 2:226; and J. Muilenburg, "Isaiah 40–66" (1956), 5:593.

[523]  See further J. Goldingay and D. Payne, *Isaiah 40–55* (2006), 2:221–222, on the poetic patterning and parallelism of the passage.

196                                                                  *Commentary*

taught by the LORD (50:4), here the invitation is to pay attention to the one from whom "teaching will go out" (51:4). The exhortation to "Look to" the traditions of Abraham and Sarah perhaps functions as a worked example of such teaching with the instruction happening through the interpretation being offered of those ancestral traditions. Interestingly, in light of the consistent juxtaposition of masculine (the Servant) and feminine (Zion) personifications in these chapters (see A Closer Look: Lady Zion and the Suffering Servant, the Rhetorical Power of Juxtaposition), the imagery references the Patriarch (Abraham) and Matriarch (Sarah) in parallel fashion. Each are offered as originating figures for the addressees themselves. The claim "I . . . made him many" (51:2) allows the audience to include themselves among the "many" who are the result of God's blessing.[524] If the Abraham and Sarah images are intended to resonate with the preceding rock and quarry imagery, it is notable that each of these connote solidity and strength in a larger poetic context where the stability and certainty of what God does contrast with the fleeting and ephemeral nature of those who oppose God's work (51:8).[525] Abraham and Sarah together offer an image of the certain accomplishment of that which God intends.

For an audience who knows the stories of these figures, there is an added relevance.[526] Abraham and Sarah, each in their own way, expressed doubt at the proclamation of blessing (Gen 17:17–18; 18:12–15), yet the LORD's purposes for them were fulfilled. For an audience being urged to move away

---

[524] Lena-Sofia Tiemeyer, "Abraham – A Judahite Prerogative," *ZAW* 120 (2008): 54–56, rightly illustrates the imagery's connection to "the repopulation of Jerusalem and Judah" (56) and this imagery's focus on "*the promise of descendants*" (emphasis original, 54). However, I do not read this as an indication that the audience are in Judah, as she argues. Instead, I understand the exilic audience here being invited to envision, embrace, and participate in the flourishing depicted.

[525] "Look to the rock" shares imagery with Deut 32:18, as J. Blenkinsopp, *Isaiah 40–55* (2002), 326, observes. There the reference is to God as rock. While Blenkinsopp acknowledges the divine referent in Deuteronomy and Isaiah's familiarity with rock imagery for God, he decides in favor of Abraham and Sarah as the meaning of the rock image declaring "in the context, a reference to the ancestral couple seems preferable." However, the poetry employs this rock imagery for God's work through the "ancestral couple" exclaiming "he was but one when I called him" (51:2). Here the poem lays emphasis on the certainty of divine activity, utilizing the LORD's work through Abraham and Sarah, associated with the rock by juxtaposition, as an exemplar.

[526] See B. D. Sommer, *A Prophet Reads* (1998), 133–134, on the use of a "biblical story" as opposed to "allusion to a biblical text." He comments, "Clearly the prophet depends on older Israelite material" but indicates "one must be wary of asserting that Deutero-Isaiah refers to Genesis 22 rather than to some other text or tradition."

*Isaiah 51:1–8* 197

from their expressed misgivings (Isa 40:27; 49:14), such an image offers reassurance that their doubts will not impede God's intended deliverance.

The Servant had expressed high levels of confidence in his impending vindication by the LORD (50:8–9)[527] and employs the image of moth-eaten clothing to illustrate the inability of his adversaries to instill fear in him (50:8). Here the command to the audience not to fear human beings (51:7) is immediately juxtaposed to calling them "people who have my teaching in your hearts" (51:7). The moth-eaten clothing imagery appears as support (51:8). In these ways, the divine voice in this poem directly commands the audience to take up the receptivity and resulting confidence that characterized the Servant.[528] They are being commanded to do the things that the Servant has done and to embrace the attitudes and responses that typify the Servant. Through juxtaposition of this poem in the divine voice with the preceding poem of testimony by the Servant, together the poems work upon the audience to urge their identification with the Servant personification and to begin the process of embracing the Servant's response.

The imagery that this poem employs to illustrate deliverance invites the audience to envision the LORD's deliverance as exuberant, expansive, and dependable. The statements that the NRSV[ue] translates "the LORD will comfort Zion" and "he will comfort all her waste places" (v. 3) use a form of the verb comfort (*niḥam*) that conveys completed action. This repetitive reference to comfort, using the same verb that expressed the opening announcement of the intention to comfort (40:1), offers a vision of the certainty and dependability of the divine resolve.[529] Whether designed to express certain accomplishment of future events or already active comfort,

---

[527] See J. Blenkinsopp, *Isaiah 40–55* (2002), 328.

[528] J. Blenkinsopp, *Isaiah 40–55* (2002), 328, observes that "The third stanza (vv. 6–8) appears to be related more closely than the preceding two to the statement of the prophetic servant and the command that follows it (50:4–11)."

[529] The NRSV[ue]'s translation here seems to assume that the verbs are the so-called "prophetic perfect," a use of completed action verbs to convey the certain accomplishment of the divine will. See further J. Blenkinsopp, *Isaiah 40–55* (2002), 327; J. Goldingay and D. Payne, *Isaiah 40–55* (2006), 2:225; and J. Muilenburg, "Isaiah 40–66" (1956), 5:591, who employ varying terminology for this idea. While it is not entirely certain that this is the poet's intention here, it is noteworthy that these verbs contrast with the incomplete action (imperfect) forms preceding them. What might be expected to be past and completed action, the references to blessing and multiplying Abraham are offered in forms that would imply that the blessing and multiplying are ongoing activities, underscoring the sense that these actions include the existence of the audience themselves. For discussion of the import of incomplete action verbs for

198 Commentary

the verbs explicitly remind the audience that in a double imperative the divine voice has already announced the intention to comfort Zion.

That comfort is developed in imagery that moves their memories even further back in time. The vision is of a return to the original creation. Eden illustrates that which God created and which is presented as a place of plenty (cf. Gen 2:9–16)[530] and illustrates the contrast between destruction and undestroyed or restored places (see, e.g., Ezek 36:35 and Joel 2:3). Four parallel terms for joyfulness convey the goodness of such a return (51:3). Similarly, the repeated pair "my deliverance" and "my salvation" (51:5, 6, 8) stand in parallel relationships with images that illustrate the expansiveness of this deliverance and its contrast to that which is not lasting. The first occurrence is underscored by reference to the "coastlands" (see A Closer Look: The Coastlands and the Creator of the Cosmos) as well as to the divine might.[531] It is coming "swiftly" but will not pass away as both the "heavens" and "earth" (51:6)[532] and those who oppose the addressees (51:7–8) will. Each of these are illustrated with the garment imagery and with reference to insects, each of which seem designed to underscore their fleeting nature. Each of these images is immediately juxtaposed with the insistence upon the permanence of the "salvation" and "deliverance" that the LORD provides (51:6, 8). The juxtaposition and contrast add emphasis to the divine speaker's insistence upon the reliability of the comfort that has been proclaimed (51:3) and the deliverance that is coming (51:5).[533]

In this poem, the divine voice directly urges the addressees to take up the attitudes of confidence and reliance upon God that the Servant has just exemplified. The overlapped images between the two poems allow them to reinforce one another with the Servant illustrating confident reliance and the divine voice exhorting such trust. The audience are faced with a central

activities of the Patriarch and Matriarch and for the divine blessing of Abraham, see J. Goldingay and D. Payne, *Isaiah 40–55* (2006), 2:223–224.

[530] See J. Blenkinsopp, *Isaiah 40–55* (2002), 327, who sees reference to traditions about Eden here but notes that this "does not imply that the writer had read Gen 2–3." See also C. Westermann, *Isaiah 40–66* (1969), 237. J. Goldingay and D. Payne, *Isaiah 40–55* (2006), 2:225, point to Ezekiel for this imagery.

[531] See J. Blenkinsopp, *Isaiah 40–55* (2002), 328, who notes that the LORD's arm "signifies divine power."

[532] J. Goldingay and D. Payne, *Isaiah 40–55* (2006), 2:230, note that these are "a standard pair, a merism suggesting the whole cosmos."

[533] See J. Goldingay and D. Payne, *Isaiah 40–55* (2006), 2:231; and J. Muilenburg, "Isaiah 40–66" (1956), 5:594.

*Bridging the Horizons: Fear Not* 199

contrast. They can fear that which is fleeting, or they can place their trust in the one from whom deliverance comes (see Bridging the Horizons: Fear Not).

### BRIDGING THE HORIZONS: FEAR NOT

"Do not be afraid" are familiar biblical words. They often appear in those moments when human beings encounter God. God speaks these words to Abraham (Gen 15:1) and reassures Jacob with them (Gen 46:3). Readers of the New Testament may associate this same reassurance with the angel's appearance to Mary (Luke 1:30) and with the angelic pronouncement at the empty tomb (Matt 28:5).

The commandment not to be afraid is especially pronounced in Isaiah 40–55. Repeatedly the audience are commanded not to fear (40:9; 41:10, 13–14; 43:1, 5; 44:2, 8; 51:7; 54:4). They are asked why they are afraid of the things they fear (51:12) and they listen as the almighty puts their fears into cosmic perspective (51:12–13). Clearly, fearfulness is a problem for this audience. Equally clearly, release from their fearfulness is one of the emotional postures the poetry aims to mold in its audience. Here the LORD's majesty and transcendence place the apparent fearfulness of tyrants and enemies into their rightful place. While the poems do present the divine speaker's wrath fearfully in places (e.g., 43:22–28), these seem designed to move the audience into a restored relationship with the LORD, a relationship that carries with it the blessing of the strongest possible defender, the one who can render any adversary ultimately powerless (54:14–17).

Our moment is also a fear-ridden one. The fears of the moment embrace global infectious disease, escalating military conflict, massive human displacement (see Bridging the Horizons: Isaiah 40–66 and Human Migration), and an uncertain ecological future. We are bombarded by a nearly constant stream of information, much of it about circumstances well beyond our control.[534] In our context, too, the divine voice of Second Isaiah's poems resonates. Just as the powerful might of the cosmic creator's voice speaks soothing into its original audience's ears, so too its aims

---

[534] See the description of contemporary fearfulness in Jonathan Sacks, *Morality: Restoring the Common Good in Divided Times* (London: Hodder & Stoughton, 2020), 3.

address contemporary ones. The poems do not just announce the prohibition of fear. Instead, they enact it in two ways. By placing human power and perception into cosmic perspective they set our moment, too, into its rightful relative place beside the all-pervasive grandeur and might of the LORD. They undermine the illusion of human control. In the vision of these poems, neither the apparent power of human threats nor individual responsibilities in the face of uncertainty ultimately control the future. God does. At the same time, the poems form an attitude of trust in God who speaks. By setting its hearers into the presence of the divine voice who speaks with surpassing confidence (see A Closer Look: The Majestic Divine Speaker), the poems shape attitudes of trust and of release from fear through encounter.

ISAIAH 51:9–16

<sup>9</sup> Awake, awake, put on strength,
  O arm of the LORD!
Awake, as in days of old,
  the generations of long ago!
Was it not you who cut Rahab in pieces,
  who pierced the dragon?
<sup>10</sup> Was it not you who dried up the sea,
  the waters of the great deep;
who made the depths of the sea a way
  for the redeemed to cross over?
<sup>11</sup> So the ransomed of the LORD shall return
  and come to Zion with rejoicing;
everlasting joy shall be upon their heads;
  they shall obtain joy and gladness,
  and sorrow and sighing shall flee away.

<sup>12</sup> I, I am he who comforts you;
  why then are you afraid of a mere mortal who must die,
  a human being who fades like grass?
<sup>13</sup> You have forgotten the LORD, your Maker,
  who stretched out the heavens
  and laid the foundations of the earth.

*Isaiah 51:9–16*

You fear continually all day long
>    because of the fury of the oppressor,
who is bent on destruction.
>    But where is the fury of the oppressor?
¹⁴ The oppressed shall speedily be released;
>    they shall not die and go down to the Pit,
>    nor shall they lack bread.
¹⁵ For I am the LORD your God,
>    who stirs up the sea so that its waves roar –
>    the LORD of hosts is his name.
¹⁶ I have put my words in your mouth
>    and hidden you in the shadow of my hand,
stretching out the heavens
>    and laying the foundations of the earth
>    and saying to Zion, "You are my people."

In this poem, the reader encounters two voices whose conflicting visions of restoration stand juxtaposed. The cries "Awake, awake" (51:9) seem to convey the perspective of the exiles, though the words are not attributed in the way that Zion's (49:14) and Jacob's (40:27) complaints were.[535] However, the rebuttal that follows mirrors the response to each of these figures and while there is no "Thus says the LORD" introducing the response, it is clearly spoken in the divine voice (see, e.g., 51:15).[536] This response corrects the audience's implied misapprehension of their situation and strengthens the doubled imperatives in the poems that follow.

The opening imperatives invoke the aid of the "arm of the LORD" employing a feminine personification of that figure. The "arm of the LORD" is a relatively common image of divine strength.[537] The personification employs ancient Near Eastern creation imagery that depicts the ordering of the world as coming about through the deity's victory over the forces of watery chaos, here named as "Rahab" and "the dragon" (51:9)

---

[535] While the perspective is one that the divine voice aims to correct, the speaker of the opening invocation to the arm remains ambiguous. It appears to represent the audience, though whether it does so directly or via the mediation of the prophetic voice is not made clear by the text.

[536] See C. Westermann, *Isaiah 40–66* (1969), 243, who refers to vv. 12–16 as "the divine answer." See also K. Baltzer, *Deutero-Isaiah* (2001), 361.

[537] See J. D. W. Watts, *Isaiah 34–66* (2005), 211; and J. Blenkinsopp, *Isaiah 40–55* (2002), 332.

(cf. Ps 89:11 [10 Eng.], Job 26:12, Ps 74:13).[538] The questions, which the NRSV[ue] translates "was it not you," are addressed to this feminine personified arm using the matching grammatical forms and might be rendered "Are you not she" (51:9, 10).[539] By calling up imagery of an ancient cosmic creation battle and joining this imagery with allusions to the deliverance of the Israelites from Egypt, the poem's opening unit (vv. 9–11) encompasses grand visions of divinely accomplished salvation with strong militaristic overtones.[540] This vision of deliverance is violent and the divine conqueror invoked is seen as one who has been accomplishing such deliverance from the beginning.

In dramatic contrast to this depiction of the "arm of the LORD," the vision of the exiles themselves is as recipients of deliverance. Their "joy and gladness" stand in parallelistic contrast to "sorrow and sighing" and v. 11's emphasis falls upon the images of the joyful celebration of those who are to be redeemed by the arm.[541] Vivid images of the returnees wearing joy "upon their heads" contrast with the personified "sorrow and sighing" making their escape (51:11). However, there is a lurking impermanence in this imagery. Both the "joy" of the redeemed and the "strength" of the arm are presented as worn upon the body.[542] Garments have featured in the immediately preceding poems and have been images of transience with emphasis on their becoming worn out (see 50:9, 51:6, 8).

---

[538] See, e.g., J. Muilenburg, "Isaiah 40–66" (1956), 5:596–597; J. Goldingay and D. Payne, *Isaiah 40–55* (2006), 2:236–238; J. L. McKenzie, *Second Isaiah* (1968), 123; J. Blenkinsopp, *Isaiah 40–55* (2002), 332–333; J. D. W. Watts, *Isaiah 34–66* (2005), 211; K. Baltzer, *Deutero-Isaiah* (2001), 356–357; and esp. P. Tull Willey, *Remember the Former Things* (1997), 145–151, on the resonances of lament psalms and their imagery here.

[539] This is the translation I offered in Katie M. Heffelfinger, "Embodiment in Isaiah 51–52 and Psalm 62: A Feminist Biblical Theology of Salvation," in *After Exegesis: Feminist Biblical Theology* (eds. Patricia K. Tull and Jacqueline E. Lapsley; Waco, TX: Baylor University Press, 2015), 65. On the subversion of this imagery, see Jeremy M. Hutton, "Isaiah 51:9–11 and the Rhetorical Appropriation and Subversion on Hostile Theologies," *JBL* 126.2 (2007): 271–303.

[540] See J. Muilenburg, "Isaiah 40–66" (1956), 5:596; C. Westermann, *Isaiah 40–66* (1969), 241; J. L. McKenzie, *Second Isaiah* (1968), 126; and P. Tull Willey, *Remember the Former Things* (1997), 115.

[541] J. Goldingay and D. Payne, *Isaiah 40–55* (2006), 2:240, note that the verbs used here for what joy and gladness, sorrow and sighing do are related to "military" and "battle" contexts commonly. They comment "it is as if grief and sighing are running away in a panic, in shame."

[542] See J. M. Hutton, "Isaiah 51:9–11" (2007), 295–296, on allusion to Ps 93:1 in "wear strength."

*Isaiah 51:9–16*                                                                 203

The larger poem's firm rejection of the invocation to the arm to "awake" is not apparent until the portion of the poem spoken in the divine voice (51:12–16). The unclear speaker contributes to such ambiguity. It is entirely possible to read 51:9–11 on its own as the voice of the prophet inviting the LORD's aid[543] or as an expression of the people who have accepted the proclamation of the previous poem. They have just been offered a vision of the world looking for the "arm" of the LORD and of God's power over the created world (51:5–6). It is not until the divine voice reverses the terms in which the LORD has been invoked that it becomes clear that the people's perception is flawed.[544] In this way, the poem draws its audience into its persuasive aims and increases the power of the divine rebuttal.

Here the LORD refutes the characterization that the poem has offered of the LORD, of the deliverance needed, and of the exiles themselves. The emphatic doubled "I" mirrors the doubled imperative "awake" and the line "I, I am he who comforts you" explicitly overturns the address to the personified divine arm "Are you not she"[545] (cf. NRSV[ue] "was it not you").[546] Not only does the LORD reject the feminine personification, the entire set of images of creation as victory over chaos appears rejected by the divine speaker.[547] Neither creation nor the deliverance at hand are presented as a battle requiring the agency of the divine arm.[548] In the lines spoken by the divine voice (51:12–16), creation is imaged twice, each time employing not cosmic battle imagery but building imagery: "stretched out

---

[543]  J. Muilenburg, "Isaiah 40–66" (1956), 5:595, for example, sees this as the prophet's voice, as does J. L. McKenzie, *Second Isaiah* (1968), 126.

[544]  Against J. Goldingay and D. Payne, *Isaiah 40–55* (2006), 2:234, who read v. 9 as spoken in the divine voice, the contrast with the divine voice's perspective as it appears in vv. 12–16 makes this attribution unlikely.

[545]  As translated in K. M. Heffelfinger, "Embodiment" (2015), 65; see discussion above.

[546]  See further K. M. Heffelfinger, "Embodiment" (2015), 65; and J. M. Hutton, "Isaiah 51:9–11" (2007), 279. P. Tull Willey, *Remember the Former Things* (1997), 131, comments on the rarity of the masculine participle "comforter," which she notes occurs outside of Lamentations only here and in Ecclesiastes 4:1. On the relationship of the divine claim to be comforter here and Lamentations, see also J. Goldingay and D. Payne, *Isaiah 40–55* (2006), 2:241. Note also J. D. W. Watts, *Isaiah 34–66* (2005), 212, on the contrast between the "mythical arm" and "I, I" as "God himself." K. Baltzer, *Deutero-Isaiah* (2001), 356, also observes the feminine address to the arm. See also P. Tull Willey, *Remember the Former Things* (1997), 156–157, on the rhetorical strength of the construction here.

[547]  See further J. M. Hutton, "Isaiah 51:9–11" (2007), 271–303.

[548]  However, the "arm" appears much more positively regarded in Isa 52:10. See further K. M. Heffelfinger, "Embodiment" (2015), 68–69.

204 Commentary

the heavens and laid the foundations of the earth" (51:13; cf. 51:16).[549] In addition, the opening triplet spoken in the divine voice draws a startling contrast between the audience and the LORD. Immediately following the doubly emphatic, "I, I am he who comforts you" the divine voice asks *mī- 'att* (i.e., "who are you?"; cf. NRSV[ue] "why then are you")[550] before proceeding to describe the audience not in terms of those who wear "joy and gladness" but as those who are characterized by what they fear.

Their fears are fundamentally misplaced. They fear a "human" characterized by his mortality and imaged with the same imagery of the people as grass as expressed human frailty in contrast to divine might in the opening poem (40:6–8). Repetition underscores that fear with emphasis on its persistence: "continually all day long" (51:13). These are people who have been repeatedly commanded not to fear by the divine voice in these chapters (see, e.g., 41:10, 13, 14; 43:1, 5; 44:2, 8; 51:7) (see further Bridging the Horizons: Fear Not) and have been offered the example of the personified Servant who is unafraid (50:8–9). Now, the juxtaposition of the question "Who are you?" and the statement "You fear a man, he will die"[551] (cf. NRSV[ue] "why then are you afraid of a mere mortal who must die") makes the response to a question about who these people are one that characterizes them entirely by their fearfulness.[552] It is no wonder that the next line charges them with having "forgotten" the LORD.[553] It is the LORD who is their comforter, who has commanded them not to be afraid. Yet they continue to be afraid, and the divine voice emphasizes that these fears are entirely misplaced.

---

[549] J. M. Hutton, "Isaiah 51:9–11" (2007), 296–298, points out the tension between the battle imagery in these verses and Second Isaiah's more typical imagery for creation. This contrast supports the sense that vv. 12–16 refute the perspective of vv. 9–11.

[550] The NRSV[ue]'s "why then are you" obscures the sharp contrast and strong rebuttal of the audience in this triplet as it stands in the Hebrew text. See further K. M. Heffelfinger, *I Am Large* (2011), 250 n. 222. See also J. Goldingay and D. Payne, *Isaiah 40–55* (2006), 2:240.

[551] This is the translation offered in K. M. Heffelfinger, *I Am Large* (2011), 247.

[552] My reading here contrasts with that of J. Muilenburg, "Isaiah 40–66" (1956), 5:599, whose reading underrepresents the negativity of tone implied in this juxtaposition. See C. Westermann, *Isaiah 40–66* (1969), 243, who characterizes this response as "reproof."

[553] J. Muilenburg, "Isaiah 40–66" (1956), 5:599, draws attention to the connection between fearfulness and forgetfulness here. See also J. D. W. Watts, *Isaiah 34–66* (2005), 212. See further P. Tull Willey, *Remember the Former Things* (1997), 152–155, on allusion to Jeremiah here.

*Isaiah 51:17–52:12*

The divine voice contrasts that which the audience fears with the LORD's own self in nearly alternating depictions. Their fears of the "mortal who must die" (51:12) and of the "fury of the oppressor" (51:13, 14) are each named in rhetorical questions that convey an indicting tone. Each is described in terms that make their threat limited and time-bound. The "mortal ... must die"[554] and the "fury of the oppressor" will be overcome such that his victims will "speedily be released" (51:14). The fearsomeness of this figure is named with "destruction" as well as the threat of death and starvation (51:13, 14) depicting the nature of the audience's fears.[555] The might of the LORD, by contrast, is not presented in battle imagery but as powerful creator and master of the sea (51:13, 15–16). Rather than a figure with whom the divine creator must do battle, the sea is here a feature of the created landscape, one over which the LORD has power, but not strong enough to merit a battle description. The concluding lines of this poem offer the consolation that the opening calls for deliverance invited. Ultimately, despite their failures of memory and their misplaced fears, the exiles are being addressed by "your God" (51:15), who expresses instruction, protection, and commitment in the images of "words in your mouth," being "hidden ... in the shadow of my hand," and calling Zion "my people" (Isa 51:16).

ISAIAH 51:17–52:12

> [17] Rouse yourself, rouse yourself!
> > Stand up, O Jerusalem,
> you who have drunk at the hand of the LORD
> > the cup of his wrath,
> who have drunk to the dregs
> > the cup of staggering.
> [18] There is no one to guide her
> > among all the children she has borne;

---

[554] As J. Goldingay and D. Payne, *Isaiah 40–55* (2006), 2:242, point out, human mortality likened to grass picks up on imagery already familiar from Isa 40. In that context, too, the contrast between the LORD and humanity was stressed. See also K. Baltzer, *Deutero-Isaiah* (2001), 361.

[555] See K. M. Heffelfinger, *I Am Large* (2011), 251, on the explicit topicalization of fear here.

206                                                    *Commentary*

there is no one to take her by the hand
    among all the children she has brought up.
[19] These two things have befallen you
    – who will grieve with you? –
devastation and destruction, famine and sword.
    Who will comfort you?
[20] Your children have fainted;
    they lie at the head of every street
    like an antelope in a net;
they are full of the wrath of the LORD,
    the rebuke of your God.

[21] Therefore hear this, you who are wounded,
    who are drunk but not with wine:
[22] Thus says your Sovereign, the LORD,
    your God who pleads the cause of his people:
See, I have taken from your hand
    the cup of staggering;
you shall drink no more
    from the cup of my wrath.[556]
[23] And I will put it into the hand of your tormentors,
    who have said to you,
    "Bow down, that we may walk on you,"
and you have made your back like the ground
    and like the street for them to walk on.

52:1 Awake; awake;
    put on your strength, O Zion!
Put on your beautiful garments,
    O Jerusalem, the holy city,
for the uncircumcised and the unclean
    shall enter you no more.
[2] Shake yourself from the dust; rise up,

---

[556] I am departing from the lineation of the NRSV[ue] in this verse and largely following MT's lineation. The translation inverts the ordering of the second couplet, altering the parallelism somewhat. However, that these are two parallel couplets seems most plausible.

*Isaiah 51:17–52:12*

O captive Jerusalem;
loose the bonds from your neck,
    O captive daughter Zion!

3 For thus says the LORD:
    You were sold for nothing,
    and you shall be redeemed without money.
4 For thus says the Lord GOD:
    Long ago, my people went down into Egypt to reside there as
      aliens;
    the Assyrian, too, has oppressed them without cause.
5 Now therefore what am I doing here, says the LORD,
    seeing that my people are taken away without cause?
Their rulers howl, says the LORD,
    and continually, all day long, my name is despised.
6 Therefore my people shall know my name;
    on that day they shall know
    that it is I who speak – it is I.[557]

7 How beautiful upon the mountains
    are the feet of the messenger who announces peace,
who brings good news,
    who announces salvation,
    who says to Zion, "Your God reigns."
8 Listen! Your sentinels lift up their voices;
    together they sing for joy,
for in plain sight they see
    the return of the LORD to Zion.
9 Break forth; shout together for joy,
    you ruins of Jerusalem,
for the LORD has comforted his people;
    he has redeemed Jerusalem.
10 The LORD has bared his holy arm

---

557 The NRSV[ue] treats verses 3–6 as prose. However, the parallelism continues, and I have
lineated it accordingly. B. S. Childs, *Isaiah* (2001), 405, treats these lines as poetic. J. L.
McKenzie, *Second Isaiah* (1968), 127; and J. Blenkinsopp, *Isaiah 40–55* (2002), 340, are
among scholars who treat them as prose.

208                                                      *Commentary*

> before the eyes of all the nations,
> and all the ends of the earth shall see
> the salvation of our God.
>
> [11] Depart, depart, go out from there!
> Touch no unclean thing;
> go out from the midst of it; purify yourselves,
> you who carry the vessels of the LORD.
> [12] For you shall not go out in haste,
> and you shall not go in flight,
> for the LORD will go before you,
> and the God of Israel will be your rear guard.

By interweaving its imagery with other texts, both inside and outside of Isaiah, this poem works to progress the exiles' vision of their own circumstances.[558] It offers a picture of the relationship between the exiles and the LORD in which the exiles' complaint is acknowledged and the past is being overcome. Using vivid imagery that both overturns and transfers the suffering to another, the poem invites its audience to envision their world as in the process of being transformed. By contrasting their circumstances to that of their enemy through juxtaposed personifications, the poem alters the exiles' vision of their place within the world.[559] By deploying their own invocation to the arm onto Zion, the divine voice transforms the battle cry to a celebration and offers a vision of redemption that places power and control in the hands of Israel's God.

This poem plays with sound as it transforms the battle cry into one of celebration. Three units directly echo the opening double imperative of Isaiah 51:9. "Rouse yourself, rouse yourself" (*hit'ôrĕrî, hit'ôrĕrî*, 51:17) and "Awake; awake" (*'ûrî, 'ûrî*, 52:1) each take up the same verb as the call to the arm (*'ûrî, 'ûrî*, 51:9). The invocation very closely parallels the call to the arm, as Zion is commanded to "put on your strength" (*libšî 'uzzēk*, 52:1), echoing the call to the arm to "put on strength" (*libšî-'ōz*, 51:9).[560]

---

[558]  P. Tull Willey, *Remember the Former Things* (1997), 109, calls Isaiah 51:9–52:12, "by far the most referential of all Second Isaiah's poetry."

[559]  See further K. M. Heffelfinger, "Embodiment" (2015), 66–67, on the way this poem and its relationship to Isa 51:9–16 underscores the "audience's misapprehension of the situation."

[560]  See further K. M. Heffelfinger, "Embodiment" (2015), 67–68, on the reversal of this imagery and its redeployment onto Zion. The poem commands "that Jerusalem do for herself what she was demanding of the divine forearm" (66).

*Isaiah 51:17–52:12*

The long u sound continues in the final double imperative "Depart, depart" (*sûrû sûrû*, 52:11), carrying the sound of these imperatives into a command to the exiles themselves.[561]

The sound of these double imperatives, with their long vowels, may imitate the sound of a horn, calling soldiers to battle, especially *'ûrî, 'ûrî*.[562] It is certainly deployed in a battle context in Isa 51:9. However, the sound of a horn does not always indicate impending battle. Its associations with worship (e.g., Lev 25:9; 2 Sam 6:15; Ps 98:6; Ps 150:3) as well as its connection to the anointing of a king (1 Kgs 1:34, 39; 2 Kgs 9:13) also resonate, especially as the imagery progresses through the poem. What must surely initially be perceived as a militaristic sound (51:9), seems to announce the end of the battle (51:17; cf. horn as a retreat or end of battle call, e.g., 2 Sam 2:28; 18:16) and resonates with images of royal enthronement as well as worship. It is the LORD who is announced as king (52:7) and while "sentinels" who blow the horn might be warning of invasion (e.g., Ezek 33:3–6; cf. Jer 6:17), here they celebrate the messenger's announcement of the arrival of the king (52:8) and prepare the people for worship (cf. use of horn in worship contexts, e.g., Ps 98:6; 150:3; 2 Sam 6:15). The poetic artistry is subtle in this manner. It does not describe the blowing of a horn but rather seems to enact it by echoing the sound of a horn. The repeated doubling of the opening imperatives adds emphasis while drawing the hearers' attention to the sound. Through the progressive shifting of this sound's associations, the poem gradually overcomes the natural anxiety that this sound produces (cf. Amos 3:6) and modulates its tone into one of victory, celebration, and worship.

The imperatives are not the only sounds to be employed by the poem to shift the audience's attention. Two similar sounding words "have drunk" (*šātît* 51:17, 2 times) and "two things" (*šĕttayim* 51:19) convey connection both to one another and to the overturning of a potent set of images for the exile. Drinking an intoxicating liquid is an image of judgment familiar

---

[561] This final double imperative is plural, indicating a change of addressee from the personified feminine Zion, who should be closely associated with the exiles, to a more direct address to the exilic audience themselves. K. Baltzer, *Deutero-Isaiah* (2001), 387, notes the frequency of the "long u sound" in 52:11–12.

[562] See K. M. Heffelfinger, "Embodiment" (2015), 64. Examples of texts where the horn is used to call soldiers to battle include: Jos 6:4, Judg 3:27; Judg 6:34.

210                                                                                    *Commentary*

within the Hebrew Bible (e.g., Ps 75:8, Jer 25:15–29; 48:26, Ezek 23:31–35).[563] Here the lines that convey this judgment (51:17) and its reversal (51:22) do so in a structure that reinforces their claim that the experience of drinking the LORD's "wrath" is being reversed. Each is a pair of chiastic couplets (see "chiasm," in Glossary of Poetic Terminology).[564] The ordering of these lines in Hebrew places the "cup" (*kôs*) and bowl (*qubbaʿat kôs*) imagery in the center of the pair of couplets each time. While the punishment is described as having "drunk at the hand of the LORD," the reversal is accomplished by the divine speaker claiming, "I have taken from your hand" that "cup." The associations are also reversed, adding to the sense of overturning. While the punishment is the experience of "the cup (*kôs*) of his wrath" and the bowl (*qubbaʿat kôs*) "of staggering" (cf. NRSV[ue] "cup of staggering," 51:17), when this punishment is overturned the cup (*kôs*) is "of staggering" and the bowl (*qubbaʿat kôs*) is "of my wrath" (51:22). These poetic reversals underscore the poem's claim of a reversal of the wrath of God. This intoxicating cup will no longer cause Zion suffering and is instead now being put "into the hand of your tormentors" (51:23).[565]

These reversals of the cup imagery accompany a reversal of the besieged city as "wounded" (51:21) woman imagery. Zion is depicted as facing precisely the opposite change as her counterpart, Babylon. The imagery depicting Zion's current suffering acknowledges the cries of Lamentations and stands in direct opposition to the fate of "daughter Babylon" (47:1).[566] While these poems have commanded "daughter Babylon" to "Come down

---

[563] See also J. L. McKenzie, *Second Isaiah* (1968), 123–124; and K. Baltzer, *Deutero-Isaiah* (2001), 366. P. Tull Willey, *Remember the Former Things* (1997), 162–164, points out the appearance of this imagery in Lamentations 4, a poem which bears other significant connections with this passage.

[564] See also J. Goldingay and D. Payne, *Isaiah 40–55* (2006), 2:248–249.

[565] Against J. D. W. Watts, *Isaiah 34–66* (2005), 213, who thinks the tormentors here do not refer to "the great powers" but to "Jerusalem's neighbors," the sustained contrast with Babylon as detailed below argues for understanding the "tormentors" as a reference to one specific great power of the time, namely Babylon. See J. Muilenburg, "Isaiah 40–66" (1956), 5:606, who treats the referent as the Babylonians and cites the usage of the term in Lamentations.

[566] See P. Tull Willey, *Remember the Former Things* (1997), 166–171; J. Blenkinsopp, *Isaiah 40–55* (2002), 340; J. Muilenburg, "Isaiah 40–66" (1956), 5:607; K. Baltzer, *Deutero-Isaiah* (2001), 369; and J. Goldingay and D. Payne, *Isaiah 40–55* (2006), 2:248.

*Isaiah 51:17–52:12*

and sit in the dust" (47:1), Jerusalem is invited to "Stand up" (51:17) and to "Shake" off "the dust" (52:2).[567] Babylon was told to "remove your veil" and "strip off your robe" (47:2) while Zion is invited to dress in "beautiful garments" (52:1). Jerusalem is acclaimed as "the holy city" (52:1) while Babylon is associated with "wickedness" (47:10). While two things (*šettê-'ēlleh*) that she denied being vulnerable to were to come upon Babylon (47:9), the acknowledgment of "two things" (51:19) having happened to Zion is an acceptance of Zion's own complaint. The absence of any offspring to help picks up the language of Zion's incredulous surprise at the return of offspring in Isaiah 49. The claim that she has none from all those "she has borne" (*yālādâ*, 51:18)[568] or from all those "she has brought up" (*giddēlâ*, 51:18) echo her questions "Who has borne (*yālad*, 49:21) me these?" and "who has reared these" (*giddēl*, Isa 49:21). Both what Zion has called herself ("bereaved," *šěkûlâ*, 49:21) and what Babylon has said would not happen to her (*šěkôl*, 47:8) connect to the imagery of children in this description of Zion's current state. She has none to help her (51:18) and they are depicted as lying in the "street" (51:20). Additionally, the "two things" that have "befallen" Zion are not two but four.[569] The numerical expansion of "two things" to "devastation (*haššōd*) and destruction (*wěhaššeber*), famine (*wěhārā'āb*) and sword (*wěhahereb*)" (51:19) alliterates and emphasizes what become two pairs by sound play.[570] This expansion underlines the severity of Zion's suffering and in this it accords with both Lamentations' description and the opening lines of Isa 40, which proclaim that Jerusalem has had "from the LORD's hand double for all her sins" (40:2).[571]

The image of "fainted" children in the "street" alludes to Lamentations' complaint where Zion's children are described in parallel ways (Lam 2:19 "your children who faint for hunger at the head of every street"; cf. Lam 4:1–2).[572] However, this is not merely an allusion to the distress of Zion in

---

[567] B. S. Childs, *Isaiah* (2001), 405, also observes this contrast.
[568] B. D. Sommer, *A Prophet Reads Scripture* (1998), 271 n. 51, ties this absence of children to support Zion to Lam. 1:2.
[569] See K. Baltzer, *Deutero-Isaiah* (2001), 368.
[570] Cf. Amos 1:3, 6, 9, 11, 13, 2:1, 4, and especially 2:6–8. On various possibilities for relating the "two things" to the four listed, see J. Goldingay and D. Payne, *Isaiah 40–55* (2006), 2:250–251.
[571] See J. Goldingay and D. Payne, *Isaiah 40–55* (2006), 2:251.
[572] Against J. Muilenburg, "Isaiah 40–66" (1956), 5:605, this use of Lamentations is not an insertion. Instead, its connection to Lamentations' imagery demonstrates the

Lamentations but a demonstration that the overturning and reversal of Lamentations' overturned world is characteristic of the LORD.[573] Lamentations' language is shared with that of Nahum. The only occurrences of the phrase "at the head of every street" (*bĕrō'š kol-ḥûṣôt*) in the Hebrew Bible are in Lamentations 2:19, and 4:1, Nahum 3:10, and Isa 51:20. In each case, the reference is to the children of a besieged city (though in Lam 4 this does not become evident until v. 2).[574] Isaiah's use of the imagery is certainly dependent upon Lamentations, but it appears that the author of Isaiah knows and is alluding to Nahum as well.[575] The drunken city imagery appears in Nahum (3:11) as does image of the feet of the messenger on the mountains (Nah 1:15 Eng.; 2:1 Heb.).[576]

In its reuse of Lamentations and Nahum, this Isaian text underscores its reversal imagery. Nahum deploys these images as depictions of the LORD's avenging wrath on its audience's enemies.[577] Lamentations' imagery describes the distress of the LORD's own people who have suffered the wrath of God. By redeploying this imagery, the Isaian poetry reorients the imagery again. Showing this reorientation underscores the poetry's message.[578] The LORD who speaks in this poem has avenged the people in this

overturning of Zion's heard complaint, which this poem enacts. While it is clear that Lamentations is a key source text for Second Isaiah and is relevant here, other allusions to Nahum in this section make it likely that the poet has both Lamentations and Nahum in mind.

[573] See also C. Westermann, *Isaiah 40–66* (1969), 245–256, who recognizes the relationship to Lamentations. However, Westermann's treatment of these lines as lament is not necessary. Instead, with J. Blenkinsopp, *Isaiah 40–55* (2002), 336, I see it as addressed to Zion.

[574] J. Goldingay and D. Payne, *Isaiah 40–55* (2006), 2:253, note the connection to Lamentations citing 4:1.

[575] P. Tull Willey, *Remember the Former Things* (1997), 160, notes the occurrences and comments that "From this distance it is difficult to judge whether the phrase was a typical lament formulation, or whether it passed from Nahum to one or both of the laments." B. D. Sommer, *A Prophet Reads Scripture* (1998), 129–130, reaches a similar conclusion treating Lamentations as Second Isaiah's source, pointing especially to a "large amount of shared vocabulary" and "the typical stylistic features of Deutero-Isaianic allusion." See also J. Goldingay and D. Payne, *Isaiah 40–55* (2006), 2:250, on the relationship of Isa 51:19 to Nah 3:7.

[576] See P. Tull Willey, *Remember the Former Things* (1997), 117–118, who argues convincingly that Isa 52:7 "quotes" Nahum. For further discussion, see also K. Baltzer, *Deutro-Isaiah* (2001), 378; and J. Goldingay and D. Payne, *Isaiah 40–55* (2006), 2:264.

[577] As B. D. Sommer, *A Prophet Reads Scripture* (1997), 83, points out, "historical recontextualization" is involved here as Assyria is the enemy in Nahum's prophecy.

[578] See also J. Goldingay and D. Payne, *Isaiah 40–55* (2006), 2:262, on Isaiah's use of Nahum here. See also P. Tull Willey, *Remember the Former Things* (1997), 119–120.

*Isaiah 51:17–52:12*  213

way before. They can trust the overwhelming reversal before them as it is a righting of the overturned world that they know.

It is not only other texts that this poem knows and conveys its message through. The invocation to the arm that opened the chain of double imperatives continues to resonate as salvation is announced, not as something that demands a future cosmic battle but as something that the LORD has already accomplished. That triumph is being announced by a "messenger" (52:7), by "sentinels" (52:8) and by the "ruins of Jerusalem" themselves (52:9).

The poet depicts the announcement of deliverance in rich imagery. It is not the words of the "messenger" that are heard. Instead, the "feet" that carry that messenger to the recipients merit description as "beautiful" (52:7).[579] Repetitive phrasing ties the messenger (*mĕbaśśēr*, 52:7, 2 times) and the message (*mašmîa'*, 52:7, 2 times) to "peace," "good" things, and "salvation" culminating in the announcement "Your God reigns." Joyful shouts characterize the response of the "sentinels" and the "ruins" (52:8 and 9). While the audience had attempted to stir up the LORD's mighty arm to fight a cosmic battle, these lines depict that arm as already having accomplished Zion's comfort in the sight of all the earth (52:10).[580]

The final pair of imperatives in this poem have been considered to convey the main rhetorical aim of Isaiah 40–55.[581] They urge the exilic audience to "go out from there." Yet these lines again echo and reverse the complaint of Lamentations. In Lamentations, "prophets" and "priests" were "defiled with blood" because of their sins of injustice and oppression (Lam 4:13–14). Lamentations' words: "'Away! (*sûrû*) Unclean! (*ṭāmē'*)' people shouted at them; 'Away! Away! (*sûrû sûrû*) Do not touch ('*al-tiggā'û*)!'" (Lam 4:15) are here redeployed in Second Isaiah as Isaiah 52:11 uses them to command the exilic audience to join themselves to the work

---

[579] As C. Westermann, *Isaiah 40–66* (1969), 249–250, puts it, "It can be truly said that Deutero-Isaiah is here a poet. He proclaims the hour of fulfilment by giving a picture of the moment when the messenger announcing the triumph arrives."

[580] See further K. M. Heffelfinger "Embodiment" (2015), 67, who notes "Since the divine speaker occupies an entirely different realm of power than the human oppressor, salvation is not a cosmic battle between equal powers but a cosmic mismatch, as easy for the 'stretcher of the heavens' (v. 13) as transferring a cup from one hand to another. All that remains is for Jerusalem to see, rejoice, and act."

[581] E.g., C. Westermann, *Isaiah 40–66* (1969), 252.

214                                                                        *Commentary*

of the LORD's comforting Zion.[582] They are commanded "Depart, depart (*sûrû sûrû*), go out from there! Touch no unclean thing (*ṭāmē' 'al-tiggā'û*)."[583] It is not simply that they are to return from exile but that the relationship between the people and their God is being reconciled. Zion "has received from the LORD's hand double for all her sins" (40:2) and the reversal of God's wrath is an image of reconciliation between the people and the LORD. The priests, the bearers of the holy things (52:11), are no longer so defiled that others must avoid them to keep from being contaminated. Now the impurity characterizes the place from which the LORD is delivering them.[584] The exiles' world has been overturned again and they now are those who are being offered a journey alongside the LORD (52:12). The reconciliation between the people and their God is the primary image. The journey and return to the holy city become imagery of that restoration and the turn from the wrath of the LORD to comfort.

Thus, this poem conveys its message of restoration and reversal by alluding heavily to other passages. It presents Zion's restoration as the opposite of both her plight in Lamentations and Babylon's impending destruction. It portrays the LORD's overturning work as a reversal of the reversal that Lamentations depicts by alluding to Lamentations' own allusion to Nahum and it overturns the people's injunction to the "arm of the LORD" (51:9) by presenting salvation as already accomplished by the

---

[582] See esp. P. Tull Willey, *Remember the Former Things* (1997), 126–127. See also B. D. Sommer, *A Prophet Reads Scripture* (1997), 272 n. 55. Cf. J. Goldingay and D. Payne, *Isaiah 40–55* (2006), 2:269, who note the connection to Lam 4:15 but interpret the relationship to this verse in terms of the potential for the exiles to "bring the stain of exile back to Judah." As B. S. Childs, *Isaiah* (2001), 406–407, observes, "there is no mention of Babylon" here and "the issue is hardly one of geography."

[583] Transformation of language used by Lamentations to depict the desperation of the people's plight helps to explain the use of this imagery of purity in this context which J. Blenkinsopp, *Isaiah 40–55* (2002), 343, calls "somewhat unexpected." It is not necessary to account for this "unusual" "cultic emphasis" (J. Muilenburg, "Isaiah 40–66," [1956], 5:613) with recourse to historical explanations about the necessary purification for a "holy occasion" (J. Muilenburg, "Isaiah 40–66," [1956], 5:613; cf. also K. Baltzer, *Deutero-Isaiah* [2001], 389–390, on purification and the Levites). There is certainly some allusion to the Exodus deliverance here as J. Muilenburg, "Isaiah 40–66" (1956), 5:613; P. Tull Willey, *Remember the Former Things* (1997), 132–134; and others demonstrate. However, in light of the close verbal parallels, Lamentations seems the text being invoked in the purity motif here.

[584] P. Tull Willey, *Remember the Former Things* (1997), 127.

*Isaiah 52:13–53:12*

glorious "holy arm" (52:10), which has brought salvation and comfort to the people who belong to the LORD.

## ISAIAH 52:13–53:12

<sup>13</sup> See, my servant shall prosper;
  he shall be exalted and lifted up
  and shall be very high.
<sup>14</sup> Just as there were many who were astonished at him
  – so marred was his appearance, beyond human semblance,
  and his form beyond that of mortals –
<sup>15</sup> so he shall startle many nations;
  kings shall shut their mouths because of him,
for that which had not been told them they shall see,
  and that which they had not heard they shall contemplate.

53:1 Who has believed what we have heard?[585]
  And to whom has the arm of the LORD been revealed?
<sup>2</sup> For he grew up before him like a young plant
  and like a root out of dry ground;
he had no form or majesty that we should look at him,
  nothing in his appearance that we should desire him.
<sup>3</sup> He was despised and rejected by others;
  a man of suffering and acquainted with infirmity,
and as one from whom others hide their faces
  he was despised, and we held him of no account.

<sup>4</sup> Surely he has borne our infirmities
  and carried our diseases,
yet we accounted him stricken,
  struck down by God, and afflicted.
<sup>5</sup> But he was wounded for our transgressions,
  crushed for our iniquities;
upon him was the punishment that made us whole,

---

[585] The NRSV<sup>ue</sup> does not mark a stanza break here. However, one is indicated by the shift in voicing to "we" speech.

216                                                    *Commentary*

and by his bruises we are healed.
⁶ All we like sheep have gone astray;
        we have all turned to our own way,
and the LORD has laid on him
        the iniquity of us all.

⁷ He was oppressed, and he was afflicted,
        yet he did not open his mouth;
like a lamb that is led to the slaughter
        and like a sheep that before its shearers is silent,
        so he did not open his mouth.
⁸ By a perversion of justice he was taken away.
        Who could have imagined his future?
For he was cut off from the land of the living,
        stricken for the transgression of my people.
⁹ They made his grave with the wicked
        and his tomb with the rich,
although he had done no violence,
        and there was no deceit in his mouth.

¹⁰ Yet it was the will of the LORD to crush him with affliction.
        When you make his life an offering for sin,
he shall see his offspring, and shall prolong his days;
        through him the will of the LORD shall prosper.[586]
¹¹ Out of his anguish he shall see;
        he shall find satisfaction through his knowledge.
The righteous one, my servant, shall make many righteous,
        and he shall bear their iniquities.[587]
¹² Therefore I will allot him a portion with the great,
        and he shall divide the spoil with the strong,

[586]  I have departed from the NRSV^ue's lineation of verse 10. NRSV^ue treats the first line
        separately from the couplets that follow. However, the MT's arrangement of the verse
        into two couplets is preferable. It is true that this pair of couplets has a chiastic
        arrangement, but it is best to treat them as two closely related line pairs. The
        NRSV^ue's arrangement impacts upon the lines that follow. The parallelism of the first
        line of v. 11 is clear and it is best to arrange v. 10 in a way that allows v. 11 to begin with its
        evident couplet.
[587]  As noted above, I have departed from the NRSV^ue's lineation of this verse and follow
        that of MT. It is clear that this verse comprises two parallel couplets.

*Isaiah 52:13–53:12*  217

because he poured out himself to death
    and was numbered with the transgressors,
yet he bore the sin of many
    and made intercession for the transgressors.

While the preceding poem employed a contrast between Zion's impending rising up and Babylon's fall, this return to the Servant imagery juxtaposes exaltation and humiliation images to illustrate the mystery of the Servant's apparent "humiliation" as the redemptive and glorifying work of Israel's God.[588] Between the divine voice's acclamations of the Servant's glory, the poetry supplies words for the exilic audience themselves to speak about the Servant, thus bringing its aims of offering him as a personification of their own potential acceptance of the LORD's intentions for them to an intensified point. These are confessional words, words that articulate a recognition of wrong and a rejection of past attitudes. In this way, the words the audience are given to speak enact the change that the juxtaposition between the Servant and Zion has been urging.[589] The Servant's suffering and exaltation both resonate with Zion's and contrast with it as the people are invited to voice their misunderstanding of God's work.[590]

The poem begins and ends in the divine voice.[591] The LORD's is the controlling perspective of this poem and the LORD's voice presents this servant as "exalted" and "very high" (52:13) and intends to "allot him a portion with the great" (53:12).[592] The opening height imagery recalls the upward movement of Zion out of the dust (52:2) in the preceding poem.

---

[588] See J. Goldingay and D. Payne, *Isaiah 40–55* (2006), 2:279, on "contrast" and "connection." J. Muilenburg, "Isaiah 40–66" (1956), 5:615, comments, "the whole poem is dominated by the contrast between humiliation and suffering on the one hand, and exaltation and triumph on the other."

[589] See further K. M. Heffelfinger, "The Servant" (2018), 198.

[590] See P. Tull Willey, *Remember the Former Things* (1997), 227–228, on the poems' attitudes to these masculine and feminine personifications.

[591] The boundaries of this unit are largely agreed. As B. S. Childs, *Isaiah* (2001), 411, puts it "There is wide agreement going back to the first century A.D." on this matter.

[592] See further Katie M. Heffelfinger, "The Cross and the Poetic Imagination," in *Atonement as Gift: Re-Imagining the Cross for the Church and the World* (eds. Katie M. Heffelfinger and Patrick G. McGlinchey; Milton Keynes: Paternoster, 2014), 160, who writes, "The poem tells us from the very beginning that we are to read the suffering servant as a glorified figure. In this way, the poem highlights the 'we's' misunderstanding. The readers already know that, however shocking it may seem, this 'despised and rejected' (Isa 53:3) one is honoured by God." See also B. S. Childs, *Isaiah* (2001), 412.

218                                                                  *Commentary*

She was being restored from her humiliation and it is being passed instead to her enemies (51:21–23). However, the Servant, in his trust in the LORD, has known that he would not be humiliated (50:7) and has willingly submitted himself to apparent shaming (50:6). That tension continues in this poem. The divine perspective is that the Servant is vindicated, but the audience, in words supplied for them, express their observation of his apparent rejection. What has seemed shameful and degrading has been, ironically, the way to righteousness (53:11).[593]

The main body of this poem is spoken by a voice that has not said much up to this point in Isaiah 40–55. There was a very brief interlude in which the "we" spoke (42:24). Just as in the case of that earlier "we" speech, the "we" voice in this poem takes a confessional stance. The "we" are inherently ambiguous and underdefined, much like the mysterious "he." That is part of the power of the poetry at this point. By voicing its confession of misunderstanding as "we," it inherently incorporates the audience into its viewpoint.[594]

The Servant's voice in Isaiah 40–55, as I have been arguing, is employed to express the attitudes and behaviors toward which the poems are urging the audience (see A Closer Look: The Servant and His "Songs"). Here, in the final poem dominated by the Servant, the "we" are offered words that not only laud the personified Servant but also confess their misunderstanding of him.[595] By placing such words onto the lips of the audience, the

---

[593] As B. D. Sommer, *A Prophet Reads Scripture* (1998), 251, puts it, "By creating the figure of the servant (whether he represents the people Israel or serves as the exemplar of the ideal individual) Deutero-Isaiah repeats Isaiah's idea regarding the place of humility for an individual or nation."

[594] It is not necessary to conclude with T. N. D. Mettinger, *Farewell* (1983), 38–39, that the "we" are Gentile voices. Instead, the other appearance of the "we" (Isa 42:24), where it is much more clearly Jacob-Israel, illuminates this similarly confessional "we." However, Mettinger, *Farewell* (1983), 38, is undoubtedly correct that "the Servant is to be understood as Israel in the corpus of the book. It would be a completely surprising manoeuvre of the prophet if he suddenly brought onto the scene a new Servant." Indeed, the servant here stands as a personification of who corporate Israel is being called to be. That the "we" who are among those who are to be included in corporate Israel and who are in the process of being convinced of their misunderstanding of Israel's exile are those who voice that misunderstanding is no barrier to such a reading. See D. J. A. Clines, *I, He, We, & They: A Literary Approach to Isaiah 53* (JSOTSup 1; Sheffield; University of Sheffield Press, 1976), 37, for seminal delineation of "the four personae – 'I', 'he', 'we', and 'they.'"

[595] K. Baltzer, *Deutero-Isaiah* (2001), 409, helpfully notes of the "we" voice's confession about their view of the servant that "The admission is certainly meant to serve as instruction for the present."

*Isaiah 52:13–53:12*

poetry enacts the embrace of the personification toward whose attitudes it has been moving them.[596] Juxtaposed on either side by Zion passages that reorient and overturn the world of suffering that has dominated the exiles' vision, the Servant stands here as a testimony to the paradox of their reality.[597] They are suffering. They have known the wrath of God (53:6),[598] but ironically this is an honorable state (52:13) and one that will "make many righteous" (53:11).[599]

The "many" (*rabbîm*) who both react (52:14, 15) and who benefit (53:11, 12) are not named within the speech of the "we." Ambiguity dominates the relationship between the "many" and the "we" who stand as two different images of groups within the poem's two main sections. The "many" are referred to by the voice of the frame (52:13–15; 53:10–12), while the "we" speak the poem's central portion (53:1–9). It is not clear whether the "many" are the same as the "we" or whether the "we" might be seen as a smaller grouping from among the "many."[600] The poetry steadfastly resists reduction to simple referents. Together, these two ambiguous groups stand as testimony to the broad and corporate reach of the deliverance that the poetry depicts. It may be that the fracture within the community that becomes evident in the "servants" imagery from Isa 55 onwards (see A Closer Look: From Servant to Servants) makes an initial appearance

---

[596] On the "we" and in particular the impact of "re-uttering" such "we" speech in contemporary worship contexts, see further K. M. Heffelfinger, "The Cross" (2014), 157–158.

[597] An additional paradox may be captured in what B. D. Sommer, *A Prophet Reads Scripture* (1998), 95, argues is an "inversion" of the language used in Isa 6's depiction of Isaiah of Jerusalem's call. He comments, "Insofar as the Deutero-Isaian passage contains good news for the people and ends with the servant's vindication, the passage also represents a case of reversal: the national guilt described in Isaiah 6 has been lifted." See also H. G. M. Williamson, *Book Called Isaiah* (1994), 39–40, on the relationship between this passage and Isa 6.

[598] See further Michael L. Barré, "Textual and Rhetorical-critical Observations on the Last Servant Song (Isaiah 52:13–53:12)," *CBQ* 62 (2000): 13–15.

[599] See Ananda Geyser-Fouché and Thomas M. Munengwa, "The Concept of Vicarious Suffering in the Old Testament," *HTS Teologiese Studies/ Theological Studies* 75 (2019), 4, https://doi.org/10.4102/hts.v75i4.5352.

[600] See John W. Olley, "'The Many': How Is Isa 53, 12a To Be Understood?," *Biblica* 68 (1987): 354, who treats the "we" and "the many" as distinct but not "mutually exclusive." He presents it as "probable that the 'many' is a wide term embracing the nations, but including rebellious Israel." He implies the "we" voice is the people Israel writing, "The 'many' do not benefit apart from 'us', but the benefits are not limited to 'us.'" (355). See D. J. A. Clines, *I, He, We, & They* (1976), 29–33, who observes "ambiguity" in the case of both "we" and "they."

220  Commentary

here in the tension between the "many" who benefit, the "we" who announce their misunderstanding, and the individualized personification.[601] Some of the suffering community itself are among those who benefit from the willing embrace of suffering enacted by those members of the community who conform themselves to the vision of patient endurance offered by the Servant personification.[602]

The Servant personification does not function in the way that literal referents do (see further A Closer Look: The Servant and His "Songs"). If the poetry employed a historical or literal figure to represent nonresistance to the suffering of the exile, it would, indeed, be problematic that this figure's suffering benefits those it attempts to include within it. However, this is a poetic image, much like the use of the ancestral figure Jacob-Israel to embrace a community. This is a community that has suffered and understands that suffering as punishment for its sins (Isa 40:2; 42:24; cf. Lam 1:5, 8, 14; 3:39, 42–43). However, by confessing both the sin and the suffering (Lam 3:39, 42, 49), and by expressing in personalized terms the anguish of corporate punishment (Lam 3:1–18), this figure represents one who has "no deceit in his mouth" (53:9). He is a truthful representative of a complex and perplexing reality.[603]

The Servant's standing as representative seems to be a helpful way of understanding what the text offers as a vision of his relationship both to the audience and to their sins. As Brevard Childs puts it, "The servant did not ritually obliterate sin ... rather the terminology is that he 'bore' or 'carried it' (*ns'*, *sbl*)."[604] That he stands with and alongside the people in their suffering accords well with the way the Servant is presented both in

---

[601] See Jaap Dekker, "The High and Lofty One Dwelling in the Heights and with his Servants: Intertextual Connections of Theological Significance between Isaiah 6, 53 and 57," *JSOT* 41.4 (2017): 479–480, who indicates that the "servants" group, as described in Isa 57 are intertextually linked with the Servant of 53.

[602] Interestingly, this idea runs parallel to the way Dan 11 may well be interpreting and applying the imagery to a persecuted community in its own day. As Marc Brettler and Amy-Jill Levine, "Isaiah's Suffering Servant: Before and After Christianity," *Interpretation: A Journal of Bible and Theology* 73.2 (2019): 164–165, summarize, "the author understands the servant to represent a collective and as referring to the near future. Isaiah's servant represents righteous individuals who resisted the decrees of Antiochus IV."

[603] P. Tull Willey, *Remember the Former Things* (1997), 222–223, observes that both Zion and the Servant "are depicted paradoxically."

[604] B. S. Childs, *Isaiah* (2001), 418. See, importantly, Jeremy Schipper, "Interpreting the Lamb Imagery in Isaiah 53," *JBL* 132.2 (2013): 315–325, who argues convincingly that the

*Isaiah 52:13–53:12* 221

terms that mirror the audience's own language about themselves (e.g., sheep, lamb) and in language that directly corresponds to language for the audience elsewhere in these chapters (see A Closer Look: The Servant and His "Songs"). In addition, the chapter heavily alludes to both Isa 6[605] and to Lam 3,[606] each of which present their central figure as among, and included within, the people who have sinned. So, while "vicarious" has been heavily used to describe the nature of the Servant's suffering,[607] it is not entirely clear that this is the most helpful designation in this context. The ideas of "solidarity"[608] and of "inclusive place-taking"[609] may better express the idea embodied in this poem.

The audience's own misunderstanding stands in tension with the attitude they are urged to adopt. They have "rejected" (53:3) the submissive sufferer, the one who asks, "Why should any who draw breath complain about the punishment of their sins?" (Lam 3:39). Yet, he shows them the way. He illustrates what it is to be righteous and to "make many righteous" (53:11). The one who adopts these attitudes embraces a suffering that benefits others, including, but seemingly not limited to, the audience who confess their misunderstanding.

Poetic ambiguity and overlap between the poem's figures invite the audience into the personification. Within this poem, the imagery used for the Servant and that for the audience is blended, for example, in the use of sheep imagery for both (53:6, 7).[610] The poem does not hold rigid distinctions separating the figures it offers to the audience's imagination.

---

imagery does not present the Servant as a sacrificial lamb, but precisely as "a lamb unfit for ritual sacrifice" (325).

[605] See especially B. D. Sommer, *A Prophet Reads Scripture* (1998), 93–95.

[606] See the discussion of these connections below.

[607] See the discussion in B. S. Childs, *Isaiah* (2001), 415–416.

[608] J. L. McKenzie, *Second Isaiah* (1968), 134–135, offers the idea of "solidarity," pointing, for example, to the idea of sparing Sodom for the sake of some who were righteous.

[609] A. Geyser-Fouchè and T. M. Munengwa, "Concept" (2019), 5. Their definitional discussion helpfully delineates "inclusive" and "exclusive" categories, noting that "inclusive 'place-taking' denotes partaking or sharing in the experience that the other is experiencing." See also the discussion of the apparent interpretation made in the Septuagint in Leslie Brisman, "From Metaphor to Theology: The Suffering Servant," *Religion and the Arts* 19 (2015): 314. Brisman characterizes the Septuagint's meaning in this way: "The people owe much to this servant who *represents* their suffering in order to help them see their iniquity; but this servant does not vicariously atone for others' sins."

[610] See Bo H. Lim, "The Lynching of the Suffering Servant of Isaiah: Death at the Hands of Persons Unknown," *Ex Auditu* 31 (2015): 113–114, on anonymity and blended voicing.

222                                                                          *Commentary*

Instead, it invites them into the LORD's mysterious deliverance and to the Servant's willing embrace of it. The transformed vision of their own situation offered by adopting the perspective that the servant embodies, allows the exiles to understand their punishment and exile as an element of their deliverance at the LORD's hand,[611] and their suffering as an element in the divine mystery of their impending glorification.[612]

Sound and sight contrast in this poem, underscoring the ironic contrast between the audience's perception and their understanding.[613] The contrast appears first in the divine voice's introduction where the "startle[d]" reaction of the nations is due to their seeing and considering things "they had not heard" (52:15). The "we" speech, by contrast, has "heard" (53:1) but what they tell us of their own vision underscores their confession of their own misunderstanding (53:3–4). The "we" voice their impressions of the Servant based on what they have seen, his "form" and his "appearance" (53:2).

Tellingly, "the man" (Lam 3:1, e.g., NIV, JPS, NET; Heb. *haggeber*; cf. NRSV[ue] "the one") of Lamentations 3, with whom the Servant seems repeatedly to be related by the poetry (see A Closer Look: Lady Zion and the Suffering Servant, the Rhetorical Power of Juxtaposition), is one "who has seen affliction" (Lam 3:1).[614] In this poem, the Servant is reckoned to be "afflicted" (53:4, 7) but that is not what he "sees." Instead, his vindication is expressed through what he sees: "he shall see his offspring" (53:10) and "Out of his anguish he shall see" 53:11). Similarly, the Servant has been one

---

[611]  T. N. D. Mettinger, *Farewell* (1983), 40, connects exile to the suffering of the collective Israel envisioned here. B. S. Childs, *Isaiah* (2001), 415, observes regarding 53:4, 6, "What occurred was not some unfortunate tragedy of human history but actually formed the center of the divine plan for the redemption of his people and indeed of the world."

[612]  Childs' comment is instructive: "The role of the servant resulted in Israel's forgiveness because of God's acceptance of the servant's obedient suffering. Israel not only recognized the freedom that the servant had won for it, but in the experience of encountering the hidden plan of God, was itself transformed into the new Israel, which shared in the coming redemptive age. Already the scene for Israel's restoration was set as God designated the servant as the embodiment of Israel (49:3), through whom God would be glorified and the nation gathered again to him" (B. S. Childs, *Isaiah* [2001], 418).

[613]  See further Paul R. Raabe, "Critical Notes: The Effect of Repetition in the Suffering Servant Song," *JBL* 103.1 (1984): 77–81. Regarding sight and light imagery, see also P. Stern, "Blind Servant" (1994), 228–229 and see D. J. A. Clines, *I, He, We, & They* (1976), 40–41.

[614]  See P. Tull Willey, *Remember the Former Things* (1997), 209–228; and C. Westermann, *Isaiah 40–66* (1969), 262.

*Isaiah 52:13–53:12* 223

whose resolve not to resist those who would humiliate him (50:6) echoed the man of Lamentations 3's claim that it is "good ... to sit alone in silence ... to give one's cheek to the smiter" (Lam 3:27–30).[615] Here the "we" testify twice that the Servant "did not open his mouth" (53:7). While in Lamentations the mocking of enemies was conveyed as these figures opening their mouths (Lam 1:16; 3:46), here the Servant's exaltation is so unsettling that "kings shall shut their mouths" (52:15).

Violence pervades this poem and the emphasis falls upon the Servant's lack of resistance. Just as in the Servant's own testimony that he submitted himself to those who would cause him injury (50:6), the "we" observe that he neither speaks (53:7) in response nor acts violently (53:9). Alongside explicit reference to his "bruises" (53:5), wounds (53:5), and having been "crushed" (53:5; cf. "crush" 53:10) are metaphors for the Servant that reinforce his unresisting nature.[616] He is described using "plant" (53:2) and "sheep" (53:7) imagery. The plant image illustrates his lack of notability and visibility, but plant imagery has been used in these chapters to indicate human frailty (40:6–8; 51:12). There is nothing aggressive, violent, or defensive about "a young plant" (53:2). Similarly, the "lamb" and "sheep" images offer a vision of one who does not resist, a creature that does not attack. The audience describe not only the Servant using sheep imagery but themselves as well (53:6). While they characterize themselves as wandering, the joining of the imagery for the Servant with imagery for themselves offers a way of speaking about themselves in Servant-like terms.[617]

This poem is not a "story" about a figure whose death paradoxically comes in the middle of the narrative about him.[618] Rather, the poem

---

[615] See also K. Baltzer, *Deutero-Isaiah* (2001), 414, who notes but does not develop this similarity. J. Muilenburg, "Isaiah 40–66" (1956), 5:619, observes the similarity between what he calls the servant's "life story of suffering" and "the autobiographical lament of Jerusalem in Lam. 3:1–20." See also P. Tull Willey, *Remember the Former Things* (1997), 219.

[616] The language of having been "crushed" (*dk'*) is another connection between this passage and Lamentations 3, where the word appears in v. 34. See P. Tull Willey, *Remember the Former Things* (1997), 219.

[617] See further K. M. Heffelfinger "The Cross" (2014), 163, who writes "By matching its language about the servant to its language about the 'we,' the poem creates a radical identification between the servant who accomplishes redemption, and the 'we' who acknowledge that it was for them."

[618] See K. M. Heffelfinger, *I Am Large* (2011), 46–48; and K. M. Heffelfinger, "The Cross" (2014), 154.

presents the paradox of the exiles' own experience and offers them words to confess their misunderstanding of it. The climactic moment in the series of appearances of this personification is the poem that invites the audience to speak what they have until now failed to see. By both expressing the reality of suffering, and submitting to it, the Servant offers a vision of a positive response to the God who speaks compassion and comfort.

It is indisputable that this passage has commanded a wide range of interpretations in the long history of commentary and discussion on it. No single commentary could hope to capture the richness and multiple layers of meaning that it evokes and invites.[619] This analysis has examined only some of its resonances. Its poetry invites continued encounter and openness.[620]

### BRIDGING THE HORIZONS: SEEING JESUS AND SEEING THE SERVANT TODAY

Approaches to interpreting the Servant imagery of Isaiah 40–66 by associating him with Jesus are familiar. Such readings have been important expressions of Christian spirituality and theology for centuries.[621] There is no doubt that Christian readers can and do hear resonances between their belief in Jesus and the poetic depiction of the Servant's suffering in Isaiah 52:13–53:12. However, arguably readings of the Servant that treat Isaiah solely as a predictive pointer to Jesus can have the impact of reducing rather than enhancing readers' appreciation of the Isaian text

---

[619] As M. Brettler and A. Levine, "Suffering Servant" (2019), 172, point out, "the diversity of interpretations warns us against reading the text in only one way or at the expense of someone else." On "various meanings" see also D. J. A. Clines, *I, He, We, & They* (1976), 60–61.

[620] As B. D. Sommer, *A Prophet Reads Scripture* (1998), 96, helpfully points out: "The study of Deutero-Isaiah's allusions cannot solve the interpretive crux. However, by showing that the text is based on an intermingling of many borrowed elements, such study does allow readers to understand that the passage is so multivalent precisely because it is a mosaic: it is as rich in possible meanings as it is dependent on earlier sources."

[621] John F. A. Sawyer, *The Fifth Gospel: Isaiah in the History of Christianity* (Cambridge: Cambridge University Press, 1996), esp. 83–99, traces historical readings. One outworking of his study is a demonstration of the different emphases that different historical periods place on different portions of Isaiah and the different uses that they put these passages to. Sawyer's study also demonstrates that Christian readings have at times been oriented toward justice and at other times have been damaging to and dangerous for other groups.

*Bridging the Horizons: Seeing Jesus and Seeing the Servant Today* 225

itself. In this mode, readers find correspondences with concepts and commitments they already hold and their attention shifts to these things rather than to what the passage might offer.[622] That is not to say that Christian readers should not perceive and respond to resonances between the Servant and Jesus. Instead, such resonances do "the very opposite of giving us permission to claim that the text refers to Jesus and then move on from reading it closely."[623] However, such resonances demand careful, close attention not only to the poetry of this passage but to other sufferers in human history, most especially those who read this text differently and those whose suffering has been either directly or indirectly a result of Christian readings of this text.[624]

Rabbi A. James Rudin points out that Good Friday "was a time of terrible dread for many Jews" and highlights the tragic reality that "violent language and action" against their Jewish neighbors came from those "who had just concluded worship services that commemorated the death of a single Jew in Jerusalem."[625] While Rudin's reflection is on Psalm 22, notably Isaiah 52:13–53:12 is a reading for Good Friday in all years of the Revised Common Lectionary.

Care must be taken to learn the lessons of our interpretive history. It is vital that Christian readers appreciate the breadth and richness of Isaiah's imagery, allowing other readings to inform understandings of what the text may mean and how it might invite faithful responses in our time. Not to do so is to diminish the testimonies not only of Isaiah but also of other readers to whom this text belongs. Indeed, as Brettler and Levine comment, "In looking at Isaiah's 'servant' through different lenses, readers will find a text overflowing with meaning, some of which, possibly, Christians and Jews can share."[626] Isaiah 40–66's poetry, as this commentary has aimed to

---

[622] See I. McGilchrist, *The Master and His Emissary* (2019), 180, who points out the reductive nature of "explicitness."

[623] K. M. Heffelfinger, "The Cross and the Poetic Imagination" (2014), 153. As Goldingay and Payne put it, "The developed Christian conviction that Jesus 'fulfilled' the prophecy in 52.13–53.12 risks robbing the passage of much of its power; the passage is simply a prediction of Jesus which has been fulfilled and has therefore fulfilled its function." J. Goldingay and D. Payne, *Isaiah 40–55* (2006), 2:286.

[624] See the discussion in in J. Goldingay and D. Payne, *Isaiah 40–55* (2016), 2:287.

[625] A. James Rudin, "A Rabbi Speaks at Good Friday Services," *Journal for Preachers* 18.2 (1995): 22.

[626] M. Brettler and A. Levine, "Isaiah's Suffering Servant" (2019), 159.

show, is rich and multifaceted. It continually repays close attention, and it has the capacity to enrich and expand the committed reader's experience of God. This is true of the whole and it is true of the Servant imagery as well. Attention to the rich variety of ways that the Servant imagery has been read by both Christians and Jews has the potential to expand readers' understanding of the Isaian text as well as their interaction with their own faith and the faiths of others.

This commentary has offered the idea that the Servant in Isaiah 40–55 is best encountered as a poetic personification (see A Closer Look: The Servant and His "Songs" and A Closer Look: From Servant to Servants). As a personification, this figure is both resonant and resonating. Rather than reaching in a limited way to a singular referent, it invites audience identification and imaginative engagement. The Servant embodies a way of seeing human responsiveness to God in the context of exile. The servants of Isaiah 56–66 invite application of that responsiveness in the postexilic context. In each of these instances, the poetry shapes its audience's response by offering the possibility of identifying with this figure (see A Closer Look: The Servant and His "Songs" and A Closer Look: Lady Zion and the Suffering Servant, the Rhetorical Power of Juxtaposition).

In this light, it is not surprising that readers have continued and will continue to find resonances between the Servant and themselves, their communities, and others. Clearly one of these potential outworkings in Christian theology is a recognition of the ways that Jesus embodies such responsiveness to the divine will. Believers identify themselves with the sufferings and glorification of Christ as a feature of Christian doctrine and spiritual practice (see, e.g., Phil 2:5–12; Luke 9:23–26). This claim does not deny, and might even suggest, that other resonances between the Servant and human lived experience are both relevant and possible. Indeed, it is necessary for readers of these texts to continue to see the ways in which the poetry's portrayal of profound obedience to the divine will as well as the provocative depiction of undeserved suffering call forth continued recognition both of the power of faithfulness and of the necessity of ethical response to injustice. To fail to recognize the contemporary power of these poems to depict and evoke responses to the real human other in our own moment is to deny the ultimate power of the text to transform the human experience.

*Bridging the Horizons: Seeing Jesus and Seeing the Servant Today*   227

Connection between the "Suffering Servant" and Christ's crucifixion is widespread in Christian thinking, perhaps exemplified most clearly, as noted above, in Isaiah 52:13–53:12 being assigned as the Old Testament lesson for Good Friday in all three years of the Revised Common Lectionary. This is a passage that when read confessionally in the context of worship may construct humility through its "we" language's expression of confusing glory and ignominy.[627] That is, this passage "challenge[s] our notions of what it means to be exalted."[628] When read in contexts like Good Friday, its resonances with what Christians proclaim about Jesus offer another lens for the intimacy of those claims about who Jesus is and what he has done through its close identification between the "sheep" that the "we" voice uses to describe itself and the "lamb" imagery applied to the one they have not recognized.[629] Through the emotional impact of its stark depiction of suffering, the poem has the potential to form compassion as the encounter it offers with "the vision of the 'marred' and 'wounded' suffering servant confronts any self-protective walls we may have constructed between ourselves and the cruelty of the world in which we live."[630]

Interestingly, this passage, which has provided Christians a crucial means of expressing their own understanding of Jesus, does not appear cited at any length in the New Testament. The Gospels' crucifixion narratives, for example, depend much more heavily on Psalm 22.[631] The book of Acts quotes portions of Isa 53:7–8 as the text that the Ethiopian Eunuch

---

[627] For a full description of what I mean by reading this passage confessionally in Christian worship see K. M. Heffelfinger, "The Cross and the Poetic Imagination" (2014). What I emphatically do not mean is to imply that a connection with Jesus is the only potential reading of this passage. Nor do I intend to deny the continuing significance of the meanings that attach to the passage from its original context or those that other contemporary readers express through them. Instead, as I said in that volume "belated readers find in these texts words which give voice to their beliefs, or express their experience of God" (p. 237). These resonances, then, form what we mean when we re-utter ancient words as our own in a new theological and liturgical context.

[628] K. M. Heffelfinger, "The Cross and the Poetic Imagination" (2014), 161.

[629] K. M. Heffelfinger, "The Cross and the Poetic Imagination" (2014), 163–164.

[630] K. M. Heffelfinger, "The Cross and the Poetic Imagination" (2014), 165.

[631] John R. Donahue and Daniel J. Harrington, *The Gospel of Mark* (Sacra Pagina; Collegeville, MN: The Liturgical Press, 2002), 445, observe that "The most prominent biblical text in Mark's crucifixion narrative is Psalm 22." They observe a few potential "echoes" of Isaiah 40–55 in the trial and mocking of Jesus (Mark 15:1–20), p. 439. In his commentary on the crucifixion narrative, Ben Witherington III, *John's Wisdom: A Commentary on the Fourth Gospel* (Louisville: Westminster John Knox Press, 1995),

228 Commentary

was reading that serves as a prompt for a conversation with Philip (Acts 8:30–35). The narrative says that Philip uses the text to begin a conversation about Jesus but does not tell us what was said and leaves open how exactly the passage was applied to Jesus.[632] Matthew uses a small portion of these verses "He took our infirmities and bore our diseases" in connection with Jesus' earthly ministry of healing and exorcism (Matt 8:17).[633] In what Goldingay and Payne name as "the nearest to a concerted exposition [of Isaiah 52:13–53:12] in the NT,"[634] 1 Peter 2:22–25 uses the imagery and language of the Isaiah passage to express its proclamation of the redemptive quality of Jesus' death. In doing so, the 1 Peter passage again redeploys the imagery inviting its own audience in its own time to persevere in the face of undeserved suffering (1 Peter 2:20–21) explicitly citing Isaiah in support of the claim that "Christ also suffered for you, leaving you an example, so that you should follow in his steps" (1 Peter 2:21).[635]

While Christian readings have often, especially following the Church Fathers, treated the Servant in individual terms, Jewish interpretation has frequently favored "communal interpretation."[636] Brettler and Levine highlight the importance of Rashi's commentary and its context during

---

308–309, points out that John draws on Psalms, both 22 and 69, as well as on Passover lamb imagery. George R. Beasley-Murray, *John* (WBC 36; Waco, TX: Word Books, 1987), 339, notes connection to Isa 53:7 in John's reference to Jesus' silence before Pilate. Beasley-Murray's description of the crucifixion points out parallels to Psalms and to the Passover, pp. 351–355. Luke 22:37 cites Isaiah 53:12 as part of its description of the conditions of Jesus' arrest in the garden "And he was counted among the lawless." Some ancient sources of Mark 15:28 include this same verse in connection to the two criminals on crosses on either side of Jesus at his crucifixion (see NA[27]). See also the comments of John Nolland, *The Gospel of Matthew* (NIGTC; Grand Rapids: William B. Eerdmans, 2005), 1194–1195, who sees the potential connection between Matthew 26:55 and Isa 53:12 but observes that "since there are no links in vocabulary in any of the Gospels, we cannot be sure this had been spotted." See the chart in J. F. A. Sawyer, *Fifth Gospel* (1996), 26–28. As noted, these texts do not draw heavily on Isaiah 52–53 in the shaping of their account of Jesus' suffering on the cross, though several examples apply elements of the Isaiah passage to some of the events surrounding the crucifixion including the arrest and trial.

[632] See J. Goldingay and D. Payne, *Isaiah 40–55* (2016), 2:286.

[633] As J. Nolland, *Matthew* (2005), 361, observes, "What Matthew takes up from the Isaiah text is the release from suffering brought by the mysterious figure of Is. 53."

[634] J. Goldingay and D. Payne, *Isaiah 40–55* (2016), 2:285.

[635] See Lewis R. Donelson, *I & II Peter and Jude* (NTL; Louisville: Westminster John Knox Press, 2013), 84–85, on the "theology of suffering" in 1 Peter as expressed in these verses.

[636] M. Brettler and A. Levine, "Isaiah's Suffering Servant" (2019), 169. See also Joel E. Rembaum, "The Development of a Jewish Exegetical Tradition Regarding Isaiah 53," *HTR* 75:3 (1982): 310.

*Bridging the Horizons: Seeing Jesus and Seeing the Servant Today* 229

the "devastation of the Rhineland Jewish Communities" in the First Crusade. They note that for the persecuted Jews of this period, "the servant both explained their persecution and promised them a reward for their fidelity."[637] Detailed work with the poems in this commentary has demonstrated repeatedly that the Servant imagery has communal aims. It seems most likely to offer a personification of what the whole people are called to be in Isaiah 40–55 and it becomes explicitly plural in Isaiah 56–66. This connection between community suffering and the collective interpretation of the Servant figure has the capacity to challenge Christian readers' potential limiting of the Servant to Jesus, not least because such readings have been contributors to further Jewish suffering.

If encounters with the "Suffering Servant," not least through the "confessional" posture of the "we" voice of Isaiah 53:1–6, have the capacity to form more ethical postures of humility and compassion, they must do so not least by the recognition that the Servant calls forth repentance from Christian communities who have used these words to justify atrocities against Jewish neighbors. Particularly in contexts where social and political power is unbalanced, readers should bear in mind the potential for abuses of that power in privileging their own readings.[638] Indeed, Christians must learn to listen to the voices of those who, like Brettler and Levine, rightly warn us against "reading the text in only one way or at the expense of someone else."[639]

Compassionate, humble, ethically oriented readings of the Servant in our own time invite us to hear the words of this poem as richly descriptive of many historical and contemporary experiences of profound human suffering. Robert Lassalle-Klein points to the work of the Jesuit Ignacio Ellacuría who urged recognition of the way the Suffering Servant may give expression to the experience of the "vast portion of humankind that is literally and actually crucified by ... historical, and personal oppressions."[640] Lassalle-Klein employs this theology to laud the work of

---

[637] M. Brettler and A. Levine, "Isaiah's Suffering Servant" (2019), 171. Note also J. E. Rembaum, "The Development of a Jewish Exegetical Tradition" (1982), 292–299, who traces the development of Jewish interpretation in this period.

[638] See J. F. A. Sawyer, *The Fifth Gospel* (1996), 248.

[639] M. Brettler and A. Levine, "Isaiah's Suffering Servant" (2019), 172.

[640] Cited in Robert Lassalle-Klein, "Voice of the Suffering Servant, Cry of the Crucified People: A Response to Lucía Cerna," *Explore Journal* 18 (2015), 34, https://scholarcommons.scu.edu/explore/35/. M. Brettler and A. Levine, "Isaiah's Suffering

230 *Commentary*

Lucía Cerna, a "domestic worker and a servant, a refugee from political violence and intimidation, and an immigrant mother torn from her children and her community"[641] who suffered for bearing witness to the murders of Ellacuría and his colleagues at the Universidad de Centroamericana in 1989.[642] In this reading, her voice becomes "the voice of the suffering servant of Isaiah, the persecuted prophet of God's word, the cry of the crucified people who innocently bear the burden of our sins, the historical continuation in our day of God's self-offer in Jesus Christ."[643]

Bo H. Lim employs the term "lynching" for the death of the Servant, in a reading that "triangulates"[644] a connection between "lynching and Isa 53 [both of which] are anachronistic with Jesus' crucifixion" but which each have been drawn into relationship with that crucifixion in literature and theology.[645] The "lynching" lens highlights the "representative" and "corporate" elements of Isaiah 53 and, in turn, this reading of Isaiah 53 offers insights into the impact of lynching as "public act[s] of terror," which had a corporate impact on "the entire black community."[646] Lim draws a direct connection between this reading of Isaiah 53 and contemporary racial injustice in the United States, writing "If our congregations are able to see how the legacy of lynching continues to affect law enforcement and the judicial system, particularly in police violence directed toward black communities and state sponsored executions of black men, perhaps they might make steps toward possessing hearts to feel this problem as their own."[647]

Contemporary readings like these, which invite listeners to hear resonances between sufferers in their own day and the ongoing impact on human lives in the present continue the work of reapplying the Servant personification already exhibited in Isaiah 56–66 and demonstrated in the work of New Testament writers as well as Jewish interpreters. Time and

---

Servant" (2019), 172, refer to Ellacuría's reading in support of their comment that "perhaps Jews and Christians can unite in endorsing new readings of Isaiah."

[641] R. Lassalle-Klein, "Voice of the Suffering Servant" (2015), 34.

[642] A portion of Cerna's published account can be read in Lucía Cerna and Mary Jo Ignoffo, "Truth in the Service of Justice: Excerpts from *La Verdad: Witness to the Salvadoran Martyrs*," *Explore Journal* 18 (2015), 34, https://scholarcommons.scu.edu/explore/35/.

[643] R. Lassalle-Klein, "Voice of the Suffering Servant" (2015), 32.

[644] B. H. Lim, "Lynching of the Suffering Servant" (2015), 113.

[645] B. H. Lim, "Lynching of the Suffering Servant" (2015), 112.

[646] B. H. Lim, "Lynching of the Suffering Servant" (2015), 114–115

[647] B. H. Lim, "Lynching of the Suffering Servant" (2015), 119.

*Isaiah 54:1–17*

again, the Servant figure, perhaps especially as portrayed in Isaiah 52:13–53:12 invites a re-embrace of the human struggle with suffering and invites recognition of the dignity and value of the innocent sufferer. It calls its audience to respond with compassion and honor and to strive to allow the voices and experiences of those who have suffered innocently and unjustly to draw out actions that respond directly to the structures of injustice in their own day.

## ISAIAH 54:1–17

1 Shout for joy, O barren one who has borne no children;
    burst into song and shout,
    you who have not been in labor!
For the children of the desolate woman will be more
    than the children of the one who is married, says the LORD.
2 Enlarge the site of your tent,
    and let the curtains of your habitations be stretched out;
do not hold back; lengthen your cords
    and strengthen your stakes.
3 For you will spread out to the right and to the left,
    and your descendants will possess nations
    and will settle desolate towns.

4 Do not fear, for you will not be ashamed;
    do not be discouraged, for you will not suffer disgrace,
for you will forget the shame of your youth,
    and the disgrace of your widowhood you will remember no more.
5 For your Maker is your husband;
    the LORD of hosts is his name;
the Holy One of Israel is your Redeemer;
    the God of the whole earth he is called.

6 For the LORD has called you like a wife forsaken and grieved in spirit,
    like the wife of a man's youth when she is cast off, says your God.[648]

---

[648] I have treated v. 6 as beginning a new stanza and as a single couplet. This is in contrast to NRSV[ue], which treats vv. 4–8 as one stanza and v. 6 as a pair of couplets. Parallelism supports the lineation. The description of the abandoned wife belongs with the

## 232 Commentary

$^7$ For a brief moment I abandoned you,
  but with great compassion I will gather you.
$^8$ In overflowing wrath for a moment
  I hid my face from you,
but with everlasting love I will have compassion on you,
  says the LORD, your Redeemer.

$^9$ This is like the days of Noah to me:
  Just as I swore that the waters of Noah
  would never again go over the earth,
so I have sworn that I will not be angry with you
  and will not rebuke you.
$^{10}$ For the mountains may depart
  and the hills be removed,
but my steadfast love shall not depart from you,
  and my covenant of peace shall not be removed,
  says the LORD, who has compassion on you.

$^{11}$ O afflicted one, storm-tossed and not comforted,
  I am about to set your stones in antimony
  and lay your foundations with sapphires.
$^{12}$ I will make your pinnacles of rubies,
  your gates of jewels,
  and all your wall of precious stones.
$^{13}$ All your children shall be taught by the LORD,
  and great shall be the prosperity of your children.
$^{14}$ In righteousness you shall be established;
  you shall be far from oppression; indeed, you shall not fear;
  and from terror; indeed, it shall not come near you.
$^{15}$ If anyone stirs up strife, it is not from me;
  whoever stirs up strife with you shall fall because of you.[649]
$^{16}$ See, it is I who have created the smith
  who blows the fire of coals

---

statement about abandonment in v. 7. The whole of the stanza expresses this abandonment, its conclusion, and its unrepeatability. A new image, that of the city built with jewels, follows.

[649] My lineation here differs from that presented in the NRSV$^{ue}$. Parallelism and length support treating this verse as a single couplet.

# Isaiah 54:1–17

and produces a weapon fit for its purpose;
  I have also created the ravager to destroy.[650]
[17] No weapon that is fashioned against you shall prosper,[651]
  and you shall confute every tongue that rises against you in
    judgment.
This is the heritage of the servants of the LORD
  and their vindication from me, says the LORD.

The overwhelming tenderness of the divine voice in this passage expresses the resolution of tension between the LORD and the people. Refutation of Zion's cited complaint characterizes the poem strongly parallel to this one in Isa 49:14–50:3. There, the divine voice employed intense imagery to respond to Zion's complaint about being "forsaken" and "forgotten" (49:14) with an insistence that the LORD had not forgotten her (49:15–16). Now it is Zion's memory that is in view and she will "forget" and "remember no more" her "shame" and "disgrace" in lines that underscore the importance of this claim through the repetitive patterning of word order and meaning.[652] Here, immediately following the poem that offered words for the exiles to confess their failure to understand God's purposes (e.g., 53:4–6), the divine voice responds directly to their complaint, claiming that such forsakenness has happened but is past and never to be returned to again (see further A Closer Look: A God Who Hides Himself).

The opening line's command "Shout for joy, O barren one" (*rānnî*, 54:1) invites the feminine personification to join in the celebration previously commanded of the heavens because of the LORD's comforting of the people (*rānnû*, 49:13, NRSV[ue] "Sing for joy").[653] It is precisely in that moment of the earlier poetry that Zion makes her complaint. The

---

[650] Verse 16 is a pair of couplets whose word order is chiastic. This lineation differs from NRSV[ue] and follows MT. See also J. Goldingay and D. Payne, *Isaiah 40–55* (2006), 2:359–360.

[651] The clear parallelism of the two portions of v. 17 supports their existence as a couplet rather than treating the first half as more closely related to v. 16 as does NRSV[ue].

[652] See further K. M. Heffelfinger, *I Am Large* (2011), 262–263.

[653] The verb "sing" is the same, though in Isa 49:13 it is marked for the plural "heavens" and in Isa 54:1 it is addressed to the singular "barren one" and translated "Shout for joy" by NRSV[ue]. B. S. Childs, *Isaiah* (2001), 427, citing Beuken points to the namelessness of the figure addressed. See also M. A. Sweeney, *Isaiah 40–66* (2016), 220–221, who highlights this same namelessness but argues in favor of clear association with Zion.

234 *Commentary*

invitation to exuberant rejoicing here using the same term signals the connection to that earlier Zion poem and poetically illustrates Zion's inclusion among those who recognize and express the joyful news of divine comfort.[654]

The feminine personification of Zion expands to express the fullness of restoration at work in this passage. The imagery focuses on the overturning of "shame" (54:4). It is not helpful to attempt to create a story that moves the addressee through the conditions of infertility (54:1), widowhood (54:4), and abandonment (54:1, 6).[655] The metaphors encompass a range of forms of suffering and struggle. Just as in Lamentations the imageries were mixed and employed to convey vast and uncontainable suffering, so here a mixture of images embraces multiple facets of exilic distress.[656] All of this is overcome, and the disjunction between depictions of distress enhances rather than diminishes the fulsomeness of response.[657] As Moughtin-Mumby rightly emphasizes, the imagery "in 54:1–6 is not concerned with creating a consistent portrayal of Zion, as many presume. It is seeking to acknowledge Zion's self-understanding and transform it."[658] Here the divine voice offers and reverses an encompassing set of images for Zion's distress, as the poem progresses toward its most significant overturning, the movement from rejection to reconciliation, from abandonment to gathering (54:7–8).

The poem presents a resolution of conflict between the LORD and the people through imagery of marital reconciliation.[659] The "wife forsaken"

[654] See J. Goldingay and D. Payne, *Isaiah 40–55* (2006), 2:339–340, on the pattern of commandments to praise in a number of places in Isaiah 40–55.

[655] NRSV[ue] translates "desolate woman." Despite the fact that the term typically refers to places in terms of destruction or loss of inhabitants, it seems best to understand the metaphorical use of the term in light of the contrast within the poetic line. This "desolate" woman is one who is unlike the one who has a husband. See further K. M. Heffelfinger, *I Am Large* (2011), 255.

[656] See further K. M. Heffelfinger, *I Am Large* (2011), 259–264.

[657] B. S. Childs, *Isaiah* (2001), 428, comments, "The reader is not to look for any strict consistency within the variety of the imagery." A poetic approach accepts the inconsistency and goes beyond Childs' caveat to ask what the inconsistency itself conveys.

[658] S. Moughtin-Mumby, *Sexual and Marital* (2008), 131.

[659] S. Moughtin-Mumby, *Sexual and Marital* (2008), 132–133, highlights the rarity of this marriage language and urges resistance to reading the marriage language in 54:5 as part of a broader set of assumptions about a love story between the LORD and Zion. She contends that this marriage imagery "is instead caught up in this prophetic poetry's daring reversal of Zion's self-perceptions and theme of transformation."

*Isaiah 54:1–17*

and the "cast off" one offer an image that addresses the audience's accusation directly. Figures closely associated with their viewpoint have claimed to have been abandoned (see A Closer Look: Zion and the Audience and A Closer Look: Jacob-Israel and the Exiles), and while the LORD vigorously challenged their claim, refuting both forgetfulness and divorce (49:15–16; 50:1), here the LORD claims to have "abandoned" them (54:7).[660]

The poetry underscores the difference between the brevity of the LORD's rejection and the expansiveness of reconciliation. The word "moment" (*rega'*) appears twice, accompanying both the statement of abandonment (54:7) and hiding (54:8). The poems have refuted the claims voiced by Jacob-Israel (40:27) and it has been explicitly the divine voice that has contested Zion's complaint (49:14),[661] as well as the charge of hiding (45:19). Here the LORD says that these have happened but names them as a "moment."[662] The heavily alliterated phrase "In overflowing wrath" (*běšeṣep qeṣep*) conveys and underscores the reason for this momentary abandonment.[663] Divine wrath is not inconsequential here. It is intense and significant. The breach between the people and the LORD was profound. However, the poetry lays its emphasis on "compassion," which appears twice and is modified by "great" and "everlasting love." The patterning of the poetry answers each statement of rejection "I abandoned you" and "I hid my face from you," with contrasting and expansive claims of reconciliation "with great compassion I will gather you" and "with everlasting love I will have compassion on you."[664]

That promise is supported by appropriately firm imagery. The comparison with the flood in Noah's time emphasizes unrepeatability. An echo between the flood-like imagery of divine wrath and this epic biblical flood, here called simply the "waters of Noah" (54:9), underscores the

---

[660] On the relationship of this line to the complex tensions of Isaiah 40–55, see further K. M. Heffelfinger, *I Am Large* (2011), 264–265.

[661] See P. Tull Willey, *Remember the Former Things* (1997), 233–234, who points out that Zion's statement in Isa 49:14 uses language from Lamentations 5:20 and notes that "The question of forgetting had been answered immediately in 49:15, but the second accusation was left unaddressed. In chapter 54 it is finally answered" (quotation p. 234). She convincingly demonstrates the responsiveness of the depiction of restoration in Isaiah 54:6–8 to the complaints of Lamentations 5.

[662] Cf. this analysis with that of J. Goldingay and D. Payne, *Isaiah 40–55* (2006), 2:338–339.

[663] See further K. M. Heffelfinger, *I Am Large* (2011), 267.

[664] For additional structural emphases on the restoration motif here see further J. Goldingay and D. Payne, *Isaiah 40–55* (2006), 2:348–349.

similarity.[665] Immovable elements of the landscape, mountains and hills (54:10),[666] are more movable than the divine resolve to persist and not turn away from "steadfast love" (54:10).

Zion is the silent recipient of these promises. Unlike in Isa 49 where she queried the multiplication of her children, here she is commanded to spread out to accommodate them. The repetitive and detailed instructions employing the image of an enlarging tent convey the exuberance of these claims.[667] The figure who had been childless and alone is now urged to make room (54:2–3). Her reunion with her majestic husband is appropriately illustrated in her being rebuilt in jewels. Expanding upon the imagery of the bride bedecking herself in her children as ornaments (49:18), the divine voice promises to build Zion in "precious stones" (54:11–12). Combining city and woman imagery for Zion, the sparkling city built of rubies and "sapphires" overturns Lamentations' complaint, which drew together her children and her sacred stones in the image of destruction (Lam 4:1–2).[668] The rebuilt city, so full of "precious children ... worth their weight in fine gold" (Lam 4:2) is luxuriously appointed, made of precious materials, conveying the majesty and generosity of her husband.[669]

Restored Zion benefits from the same promises that had inspired the Servant's confidence, and this poem addressing comfort to her stands immediately juxtaposed to a Servant poem creating resonances between them.[670] Zion's children, that is, the exilic audience themselves, are to be "taught (*limmûdê*) by the LORD" (54:13),[671] and the Servant's non-

---

[665] See K. M. Heffelfinger, *I Am Large* (2011), 268.

[666] J. Goldingay and D. Payne, *Isaiah 40–55* (2006), 2:352, refer to these geographic features as "a natural image for stability and security."

[667] Note the observation of C. Westermann, *Isaiah 40–66* (1969), 272–273, that the tent reference evokes the patriarchal period. Regarding "the use of the tent metaphor in an age when Israel had for long had houses as her dwelling-places – Deutero-Isaiah deliberately recalls the days of old when the promise of increase mattered so much."

[668] As J. Goldingay and D. Payne, *Isaiah 40–55* (2006), 2:337, point out, "the city is personified as a woman throughout, but the manner of the personification changes and the city itself becomes more prominent as the chapter unfolds."

[669] See C. Westermann, *Isaiah 40–66* (1969), 277, who notes "the accent falls on the city's splendour."

[670] See P. Tull Willey, *Remember the Former Things* (1997), 231.

[671] As P. Tull Willey, *Remember the Former Things* (1997), 247, helpfully points out regarding Zion's children relating to the barren woman theme of this chapter, "enough ambiguity is maintained to blur the lines between the various families of

# Isaiah 54:1-17

rebellion emanated from his being "trained" (*limmûdîm*, i.e., taught, 50:4–5). Zion need not "fear" (54:14) because all those who contend against her (54:15) or seek to judge (54:17) will not succeed[672] because of the "vindication" offered by the LORD, just as the Servant exuded confidence because he trusted in the vindication that comes from the LORD (50:8). In both 50:8 and 54:17, the words for this vindication are forms of *ṣdq* (i.e., "righteousness"), the very thing that the Servant was to cause to happen for "many" (53:11). The "many" are precisely how Zion's children in this poem are named (54:1).[673]

The Servant, whose nonresistance to suffering evoked the confession of the "we," that they had not recognized correctly what it looked like for God to be at work in their circumstances, stands juxtaposed to this poem's resolution of the tension between wrath and comfort. The audience are prompted to "confess" their sinfulness and resistance, and the divine voice expresses both the reality of rejection and its full and irrevocable overturning. In the metaphorical space between these two points of resolution, the reconciliation of the breach between the exiles and the LORD is depicted. Those who embrace the role of the Servant, that is, the "servants,"[674] and Zion's children, that is, the exiles, converge (see further A Closer Look: From Servant to Servants). By refiguring and recasting its audience in this way, the poetry enacts its persuasive aims. It presents the vision toward which it has been urging its hearers by inviting them to see themselves as the "servants" who live out the personified Servant's role.

---

Zion: Zion's children are here explicitly identified neither with descendents still living in Jerusalem nor with descendents of the Babylonian exiles though both groups, understanding themselves as children of the city, are free to read themselves into the text."

[672] K. Baltzer, *Deutero-Isaiah* (2001), 459, makes the intriguing comment that the word *kĕlî* (translated "weapon" by NRSV^ue) in v. 17 is "curiously neutral," pointing out it could "be rendered 'tools' or 'weapons'" and that if divine protection offered is in place the weapons are mere tools. In this case the term's potential ambiguity conveys the intended impact of the poetic line. See also J. Muilenburg, "Isaiah 40–66" (1956), 5:644.

[673] NRSV^ue's "more" translates both *rabbîm* (i.e., "many") and the comparative in the following line, conveying the sense of this construction in English. See J. Goldingay and D. Payne, *Isaiah 40–55* (2006), 2:340, for discussion of connections between the preceding passage and this one.

[674] See C. Westermann, *Isaiah 40–66* (1969), 279; B. S. Childs, *Isaiah* (2001), 430–431; and P. Tull Willey, *Remember the Former Things* (1997), 232–233.

238                                                                    *Commentary*

A CLOSER LOOK: ZION AND THE AUDIENCE

The figure of personified Zion appears closely aligned to the plight of the audience and their perspective on their own circumstances. Her one occasion of cited speech, Isa 49:14, overlaps heavily with the complaint of Jacob-Israel (40:27), also an embedded quotation. She is not straightforwardly to be identified with the exilic audience themselves, who sometimes appear represented as her children (e.g., 50:1). She is a poetic personification who embodies a particularly potent evocation of their distress. She conveys both the loss of the city and the loss of those who died in its capture (see, e.g., 49:21). As discussed above, the depiction of the ruined city as a bereaved and grief-stricken woman alludes to the dominant voice of Lamentations. In Second Isaiah, that voice is subsumed to the voice of the LORD, as the divine voice poetically urges the audience toward a renewed and restored divine-human relationship. This personification sits alongside another powerful poetic personification, the Servant, and the poetic juxtaposition between them works to move the audience from identification with Zion and her children, to embrace of the Servant's mission, as conveyed by Zion's inclusion in the "heritage of the servants of the LORD" (54:17) (see A Closer Look: Lady Zion and the Suffering Servant, the Rhetorical Power of Juxtaposition).

ISAIAH 55:1–13

<sup>1</sup> Hear, everyone who thirsts;
  come to the waters;
and you that have no money,
  come, buy and eat!
Come, buy wine and milk
  without money and without price.
<sup>2</sup> Why do you spend your money for that which is not bread
  and your earnings for that which does not satisfy?
Listen carefully to me, and eat what is good,
  and delight yourselves in rich food.
<sup>3</sup> Incline your ear, and come to me;
  listen, so that you may live.
I will make with you an everlasting covenant,

*Isaiah 55:1–13*

my steadfast, sure love for David.
⁴ See, I made him a witness to the peoples,
    a leader and commander for the peoples.
⁵ Now you shall call nations that you do not know,
    and nations that do not know you shall run to you,
because of the LORD your God, the Holy One of Israel,
    for he has glorified you.

⁶ Seek the LORD while he may be found;
    call upon him while he is near;
⁷ let the wicked forsake their way
    and the unrighteous their thoughts;
let them return to the LORD, that he may have mercy on them,
    and to our God, for he will abundantly pardon.
⁸ For my thoughts are not your thoughts,
    nor are your ways my ways, says the LORD.
⁹ For as the heavens are higher than the earth,
    so are my ways higher than your ways
    and my thoughts than your thoughts.

¹⁰ For as the rain and the snow come down from heaven
    and do not return there until they have watered the earth,
making it bring forth and sprout,
    giving seed to the sower and bread to the eater,
¹¹ so shall my word be that goes out from my mouth;
    it shall not return to me empty,
but it shall accomplish that which I purpose
    and succeed in the thing for which I sent it.

¹² For you shall go out in joy
    and be led back in peace;
the mountains and the hills before you
    shall burst into song,
    and all the trees of the field shall clap their hands.
¹³ Instead of the thorn shall come up the cypress;
    instead of the brier shall come up the myrtle,
and it shall be to the LORD for a memorial,
    for an everlasting sign that shall not be cut off.

240 *Commentary*

This poem addresses the exilic audience directly, inviting them into the benefits of divine comfort. Gone are all hints of indictment or confrontation.[675] Now the divine voice speaks assurances and describes blessings. The central sections of the poem take up the imagery of the LORD's magnificent superiority, an idea that has been deployed throughout the preceding chapters to rebuke and to reject doubts and support invitations to and assurances of reliability of comfort (e.g., 40:21–25; 45:9–19; 46:5–13; 48:6–13; see further A Closer Look: The Majestic Divine Speaker). Here, claims of the LORD's distinction from humanity emphasize the reliability and certain accomplishment of the LORD's promises. The opening and closing portions of the poem surround this certainty with images of lavish provision. By answering past complaints and alluding to previous prophetic warnings, the imagery itself reinforces the reliability of the LORD's work and underscores the exuberance of its promised provision.

Repeated plural imperatives, "come" (*lĕkû*), open the poem in direct address. No longer speaking to personifications, three times in the first verse the voice says "come." The invitation is open. It is to all of those who are thirsty (55:1). The ironic invitation to buy "without money," which appears twice in different forms, conveys more than the idea that the provision is freely available. It also responds to and overturns the complaints of Lamentations. Images of desperate hunger appear throughout Lamentations (e.g., Lam 1:11, 19; 2:12, 19; 4:4, 5, 9; 5:9, 10) and Lamentations 5 depicts the purchase of basic necessities of water and bread (Lam 5:4, 6).[676] Here, explicitly overturning that scarcity, payment is not required and the sustenance on offer is more than the bread and water of necessity. Here the offerings that are explicitly freely given are "wine," "milk," and "rich food" (55:1, 2).[677]

---

[675] Contra J. Goldingay and D. Payne, *Isaiah 40–55* (2006), 2:365, while there are rhetorical questions and an encouragement to change direction, the tone does not seem to qualify as "argumentative ways of speech" (365).

[676] See P. Tull Willey, *Remember the Former Things* (1997), 237; and Marjo C. A. Korpel, "Metaphors in Isaiah LV," *VT* 46 (1996): 49.

[677] Westermann's idea that the tone might imitate "the cries of the water-sellers and others who shouted their wares in the market" (C. Westermann, *Isaiah 40–66* [1969], 282; see also J. Goldingay and D. Payne, *Isaiah 40–55* [2006], 2:364), is not necessarily irrelevant to this depiction, nor is the idea of comparison with wisdom as personification (see J. Goldingay and D. Payne, *Isaiah 40–55* [2006], 2:364). Each of these suggestions offer potential imagery for the depiction of a voice, which is in this instance overturning the conditions of Lamentations' complaint.

*Isaiah 55:1–13*                                                                 241

The overturning implied in this image goes further. At the beginning of the canonical book of Isaiah, the LORD declared "If you are willing (*tō 'bû*) and obedient (*ûšĕma'tem*), you shall eat (*tō 'kēlû*) the good (*ṭôb*) of the land; but if you refuse and rebel, you shall be devoured by the sword" (1:19–20). Here, the people are invited to "Listen carefully (*šim'û šāmôa'*) ... and eat what is good (*wĕ 'iklû-ṭôb*)" (55:2).[678] By answering Lamentations' complaint about hunger and buying necessary water with an overturning that references the promise that those who listen and do not rebel will eat the good, the prophetic poet encapsulates Lamentations' suffering within the prophetic rhythm of the book of Isaiah. The LORD had warned the people of the punishment for rebellion. Now they have "received from the LORD's hand double" (40:2) and have admitted that they were not willing to walk (*wĕlō '- 'ābû bidrākāyw hālôk*) in the LORD's "ways" (42:24).[679] The punishment is complete and the opportunity to "eat what is good" is again on offer. The LORD has done precisely what the LORD promised to do. Now the people are given both the ability to see their struggle within the context of warning, punishment and restoration, and the opportunity to see this past suffering as proof of the reliability of the word of the LORD.[680]

The imagery of an "everlasting covenant" (55:3) underscores this sense that permanence and reliability are central to the concerns of this poem. The imagery picks up the covenant language of the preceding poem where Zion was promised "my covenant of peace shall not be removed" (54:10). These are the covenant people (42:6) (see further A Closer Look: A Covenant People) and here they are promised a covenant that will not come to an end.

---

[678] H. G. M. Williamson, *Book Called Isaiah* (1994), 82–83, discusses debates about how and when Isa 1:19–20 may have come into the book of Isaiah. Discussing a different relationship to Isaiah 40–55, he indicates that in his view v. 20 would have been available as "a probable source of influence on Deutero-Isaiah at 40:5" (83).

[679] NRSV[ue] "in whose ways they would not walk" obscures the presence of the verb *'ābû* (i.e., "they were willing") negated here and shared with Isa 1:19. B. D. Sommer, *A Prophet Reads Scripture* (1998), 97–98, treats Isa 42:18–25 as developing the rebelliousness imagery of Isa 30:9–14, highlighting *šm'* and *'bh* in both passages.

[680] As B. D. Sommer, *A Prophet Reads Scripture* (1998), 99, notes while discussing 42:18–25, "just as the negative prophecies of the past were fulfilled, so too the people can have confidence that the new, positive ones will come true." While it would possibly be too much to argue for a definitive allusion here, it does seem that Isa 55 picks up imagery and language of Isa 1–39 with a conclusion-drawing effect.

242                                                    Commentary

David appears as an illustration of divine commitment. Like the other figures from Israel's history who appear in these chapters, it seems best to regard the David reference here as calling up memories of David's own story through allusion. The LORD made a covenant with David, and in his final words David refers to this as an "everlasting covenant" (*běrît 'ôlām*).[681] Rather than conveying primarily a distribution of kingly privileges to the whole of the people, the reference to David seems offered as evidence of the LORD's reliability to bring about what has been promised.[682] However unlikely David's promotion from shepherd to king might have seemed (1 Sam 16), the LORD who intended it brought it about. He was "leader and commander for the peoples" (Isa 55:4). Likewise, the

---

[681]   Though it is not certain as an allusion, it seems likely that the Isaian poetry knows 2 Sam 23:1–7. It is a poem embedded within a narrative context and the poet of these chapters has shown a tendency to allude to other poetic texts, particularly Lamentations. The poem immediately preceding it in 2 Samuel shares imagery with other parts of Isaiah 40–55 and 2 Sam 22:51 also uses both the terms *'ôlām* (i.e., "everlasting"; NRSV[ue] in that context "forever") and *ḥesed* (i.e., "steadfast"). J. Muilenburg, "Isaiah 40–66" (1956), 5:645, also observes the shared vocabulary between these passages. 2 Sam 23:2 appears echoed later in the Isaian corpus, see comment on Isa 61:1 and David's query "Will he not cause to prosper (*yaṣmîaḥ*) all my help and my desire (*ḥēpeṣ*)? (2 Sam 23:5)" shares terminology with Isa 55:10–11: "sprout" (*wěhiṣmîḥāh*) and "I purpose" (*ḥāpaṣtî*), each of which are things that the LORD does in both contexts. Additionally, the shared sound of these two words, makes them appear likely an intentional pair. B. D. Sommer, *A Prophet Reads Scripture* (1998), 117–118, points to connection with 2 Sam 7 and Ps 89 as relevant to the use of the David theme here. J. Goldingay and D. Payne, *Isaiah 40–55* (2006), 2:371, note the appearance of covenant language in the preceding chapter and comment on the importance of covenant in the context of Babylonian exile. They point out that the covenant promised here "will be like the covenant with Noah, or Abraham, or David, which (unlike the Mosaic covenant) did not break down when it did not meet with appropriate response. It is thus a covenant that Yhwh makes 'for you' not 'with you.'"

[682]   The David reference here has attracted a great deal of scholarly attention. See, e.g., B. S. Childs, *Isaiah* (2001), 435–437; C. Westermann, *Isaiah 40–66* (1969), 283–285; J. Goldingay and D. Payne, *Isaiah 40–55* (2006), 2:372–373, and has often been connected to a transferring of the promises to David to the people as a whole (see, e.g., J. Goldingay and D. Payne, *Isaiah 40–55* [2006], 2:372–373). It is certainly a promise oriented toward the audience as a whole, but the emphasis seems to fall on permanence and allusions to other covenants are drawn on in support, e.g., Noah, pointing away from an entirely kingly focus. J. Muilenburg, "Isaiah 40–66" (1956), 5:646, observes that "it seems likely that our prophet is spiritualizing David's mission, although national features are by no means absent . . . .. Her [Israel] task was to be Yahweh's witness (43:10; 44:8), and she was to be exalted and established among the peoples." While "spiritualizing" might not be the term I would choose, Muilenburg's insight that it is not primarily the political elements of David that are in view here are apposite.

*Isaiah 55:1–13* 243

people who are promised that nations will see their glory, can rely on the word of the God who brought David to prominence.[683]

The prophetic poet appears to break into the poem briefly (55:6–7) to call the audience to repentance.[684] This is not an invective expressing divine anger and warning of wrath (cf. 42:21–25; 48:1–11). Instead, the invitation is to "forsake" both "way" and "thoughts" with an expectation of "mercy" and "pardon." The phrase "forsake (*ya'ăzōb*) their way (*darkô*)" has the ability to pick up the complaints of both Jacob, whose charge was "My way (*darkî*) is hidden from the LORD" (40:27), and Zion, who claimed to have been "forsaken" (*'ăzābanî*, 49:14). Here, however, after the divine voice's utterance placing hiddenness (54:8) and forsakenness (54:6) explicitly into the past, there is no rebuttal of these claims. Instead, the "way" and "thoughts" are redeployed to illustrate the vast difference between the LORD and the people. After the parallelistic introduction of these two terms (55:7), the divine voice reemerges and employs them in a chiastic comparison.[685] The central point employs a merism (see Glossary of Poetic Terminology) to illustrate immense difference through the contrast of opposites, heaven and earth. In the explicit comparisons of "my ways" and "your ways," "my thoughts" and "your thoughts," which surround the contrast between heavens and earth, the double reference to "ways" and "thoughts" within each line draws attention to the comparison through repetition.[686]

An expansion of the heavens and earth merism further illustrates the dependability of the divine promise. Heaven and earth, the ends of the spectrum of difference in v. 9, are now the place from which the rain comes and to which it goes with productive results. By gathering up images of growth and food production, the poem evokes its opening promises of provision.[687] Additionally, by offering images of rain that supports life and

---

[683] J. Blenkinsopp, *Isaiah 40–55* (2002), 370, helpfully puts it this way, "What is promised is that the hearers will experience the same tokens of God's faithful love ... that God performed in former times on behalf of David." See the helpful grammatical clarification in K. Baltzer, *Deutero-Isaiah* (2001), 470.

[684] J. L. McKenzie, *Second Isaiah* (1968), 143.

[685] See also B. S. Childs, *Isaiah* (2001), 437.

[686] The first of these (v. 8) is also chiastic within itself in terms of its ordering of references to "your" and "my."

[687] See also M. C. A. Korpel, "Metaphors" (1996), 44, who points out that "The comparison of the word of God with water in *vv.* 1–3 has an obvious parallel in *vv* 10–11 where the word of God is compared to life-giving rain."

244                                                    Commentary

does not overstep its boundaries, the poetry subtly evokes the imagery of
unrepeatability in Isaiah 54: the covenant with Noah (Gen 9:16).[688] The
purpose of the illustration is clear, to demonstrate the reliability of the
word of God. The comparison echoes Isaiah 40's claims that the "word of
our God will stand forever" (40:8), which also stood in contrast to human
frailty.[689] There the plant imagery conveyed human limitation. Here,
plants are illustrations of divine provision, but they reinforce the echo
between the two passages nonetheless. Between them, the claims of the
reliability of the LORD's word in Isa 40 and 55 frame an expanse of divine
speech.[690] Together they support and reinforce the aims of that divine
speech throughout, to urge its audience to trust in it.

The final lines of this poem offer an exuberant vision of jubilant
restoration. The features of the landscape erupt into song. Mountains
and hills have connoted stability and solidity (e.g., 54:10) and that which
the LORD will transform (40:4; 49:11). The mountains were invited to sing
in Isa 44:23. Now, the mountains and hills are leaders of worship. The
image of hills dancing puts the immovable into metaphorical motion.
A similar extravagance appears in the image of inanimate trees clapping
their hands. However, rejoicing of trees also conveys an end of judgment
(see further A Closer Look: The Reforestation Imagery of Isaiah 40–66 in
the Context of the Book of Isaiah). The replacement of prickly "scrub"[691]
with stately trees conveys both restoration and the solid dependability that
the poem has been claiming. The restoration and turn away from judgment
illustrated by these trees is permanent. They will stand as an "everlasting
sign" (55:13).

In this poem the exilic period poetic section reaches its exuberant end.[692]
Rejoicing overwhelms lamentation, overturning the realities of devastation
with renewal and grounding its inviting vision of restoration in the security

---

[688]  J. Goldingay and D. Payne, *Isaiah 40–55* (2006), 2:371, note the presence of covenant
language in 54:10 and the Noachic covenant as like the Davidic and Abrahamic ones.

[689]  On the connection between Isaiah 55:11 and 40:8, see also K. Baltzer, *Deutero-Isaiah*
(2001), 482–483. There also seems to be an echo of Isa 45:8 "let the skies rain down
righteousness; let the earth open, that salvation may spring up, and let it cause
righteousness to sprout up also."

[690]  See, e.g., C. Westermann, *Isaiah 40–66* (1969), 287.

[691]  J. Muilenburg, "Isaiah 40–66" (1956), 5:651, uses this term to describe the plants which
will give way to trees in the prophet's vision.

[692]  See, e.g., J. Muilenburg, "Isaiah 40–66" (1956), 5:642.

*A Closer Look: The Reforestation Imagery of Isaiah 40–66* 245

of the promise of the LORD, the one who promised and brought about the whole journey of the past. The audience, having been offered the image of "servants" for themselves are now explicitly urged to actively embrace the blessing and abundance that accompanies that description.[693]

## A CLOSER LOOK: THE REFORESTATION IMAGERY OF ISAIAH 40–66 IN THE CONTEXT OF THE BOOK OF ISAIAH

Lists of trees appear at key moments in Isaiah 40–66. Perhaps most notably, a list of plant exchanges offers the final image of Isaiah 40–55, where trees taking the place of thornbushes are promised as "an everlasting sign" (55:13). To the modern reader, the replacement of prickly plant life with significant trees may seem like a straightforward improvement of the landscape and yet a somewhat less compelling image than might be anticipated at such a moment. However, given the whole book of Isaiah's use of tree and plant imagery, this tree imagery evokes a strong claim that the judgment has passed and restoration has begun.

Trees and other plants appear throughout the book of Isaiah and Philip King and Lawrence Stager appropriately observe that "Isaiah uses the richest vocabulary of plant names in the Bible."[694] The early chapters develop judgment motifs with images of destruction of trees. Divine judgment against the loftiness of "the cedars of Lebanon" and "the oaks of Bashan" appears in Isaiah 2:12–13, while Isaiah's own prophetic call commands him to prophesy against the people in ways that will hold back their understanding.[695] This is to continue up to the point that the cities are destroyed and "Even if a tenth part remain in it, it will be burned again, like

---

[693] See B. S. Childs, *Isaiah* (2001), 434, on this poem's invitation and its connection to the "servants" in Isa 54:17.

[694] Philip J. King and Lawrence E. Stager, *Life in Biblical Israel* (London: Westminster John Knox, 2001), 108.

[695] K. Nielsen, *Hope for a Tree* (1989), 179, comments on a connection between the "cedars of Lebanon" and the "oaks of Bashan" in Isaiah 2 and the "holy tree" comparing this idea to the association of "high mountains" and "holy places." She presents 2:12–17 as "yet another example of how central the arrogance motif is to Isaiah's message, and how the image of the high trees was employed to refer to the political leaders, who have been guilty of arrogance and therefore deserve the punishment to come."

246                                                                              *Commentary*

a terebinth or an oak whose stump remains standing when it is felled" (6:13).[696]

The association of destruction of trees with divine judgment seems to bear some relationship to the warfare tactics employed by the nations through which Isaiah presents God as enacting such judgment. In Isa 9:10, the people describe their sycamores as being cut down and in the prophecy of the destruction of Babylon the cypresses and cedars rejoice because after Babylon's fall "no one comes to cut us down" (14:8). Similarly, briers and thorns convey the aftermath of judgment that has come through warfare.[697] In the description of a largely depopulated land following Assyrian conquest and "displacement,"[698] Isaiah 7:23–25 depicts the land as taken over by "briers and thorns" where agriculture had been.

In light of these prophecies of judgment, Isaiah 40–66's use of tree imagery appears as a strong visual image of restoration. While the destruction images draw upon one or two plant species, Isaiah 40–66 employs sequences of plant names, drawing attention to its use of the theme and also emphasizing the exuberance of this restoration.

A particularly long list of plant species appears in Isaiah 41, where the desert is to be transformed into a forest. Here, both trees that occur frequently[699] and those that are quite rare[700] appear together. Each of the trees that will replace the thorns in Isaiah 55 are among those that will appear in the desert according to Isaiah 41; and each of the species that are coming to the rebuilt Jerusalem in Isaiah 60:13 and are connected to the restored sanctuary appear in Isaiah 41:19. Thus, this image of restoration finds its fullest expression in Isaiah 41 and is picked up and applied both to

---

[696] K. Nielsen, *Hope for a Tree* (1989), 150, demonstrates how the tree image as used here "contains the tension between the negative and the positive. The tree is felled, but it still has the power to sprout."

[697] See also M. C. A. Korpel, "Metaphors" (1996): 51–52, particularly her comments on the use of this imagery in the Song of the Vineyard (52).

[698] See J. Ahn, "Exile" (2012), 198, who notes "The proper term when referring to involuntary mass-movement of people is 'displacement.'"

[699] E.g., 'erez, NRSV[ue] "cedar," which occurs in Isaiah 2:13 as well as 14:8 and 37:24 and is a commonly occurring tree species in the Bible; bĕrôš, NRSV[ue] "cypress," which appeared in connection with the cedar in Isa. 14:8 and 37:24 as well as in the lists in 55:13 and 60:13

[700] E.g., the pair *tidhār* NRSV[ue] "plane" and *tĕ'aššûr* NRSV[ue] "pine." These two occur together in Isa 41:19 and 60:13. "Plane" *tidhār* occurs nowhere else, and "pine" arguably is the correct reference of two difficult terms in Ezekiel (27:6 and 31:3), bringing the total potential biblical occurrences up to four. See *HALOT*, 2:1677.

*Isaiah 56:1–8*

the confirmation of a decisive turn away from wrath (55:13) and to the rebuilding of Jerusalem (60:13). Trees are not simply symbols of restoration and divine consolation for the audience in these chapters. Rather, they join in the rejoicing. In Isaiah 44:23, they are commanded to rejoice at the divine deliverance; and in Isaiah 55:12, they will "clap their hands" at the people's restoration.

Trees appear not only in the prophecies of judgment and restoration for the audience. Their association with idolatry functions to reinforce the distinction between the people who are being restored and those they are delivered from. A list of tree species in Isaiah 40–66 appears in the parody of the idol makers. In contrast to the trees that sprout, grow, and rejoice at divine deliverance, wood from various tree species appears listed in the idol maker's craft (44:14) and are lifeless, "a block of wood" (44:19). Similarly, 45:20 indicts "those who carry about their wooden idols." In Isaiah 57:5, the connection between oaks and idolatry appears in an indictment against the members of the audience who have turned away from the LORD.

ISAIAH 56:1–8

¹ Thus says the LORD:
      Maintain justice, and do what is right,
for soon my salvation will come
      and my deliverance be revealed.

² Happy is the mortal who does this,
      the one who holds it fast,
who keeps the Sabbath, not profaning it,
      and refrains from doing any evil.

³ Do not let the foreigner joined to the LORD say,
      "The LORD will surely separate me from his people,"
and do not let the eunuch say,
      "I am just a dry tree."
⁴ For thus says the LORD:
      To the eunuchs who keep my Sabbaths,
who choose the things that please me
      and hold fast my covenant,

248                                                              *Commentary*

⁵ I will give, in my house and within my walls,
        a monument and a name
        better than sons and daughters;
I will give them an everlasting name
        that shall not be cut off.

⁶ And the foreigners who join themselves to the LORD,
        to minister to him, to love the name of the LORD,
        and to be his servants,
all who keep the Sabbath and do not profane it
        and hold fast my covenant –
⁷ these I will bring to my holy mountain
        and make them joyful in my house of prayer;
their burnt offerings and their sacrifices will be accepted on my altar,
        for my house shall be called a house of prayer for all peoples.⁷⁰¹
⁸ Thus says the Lord GOD,
        who gathers the outcasts of Israel:
I will gather others to them
        besides those already gathered.

In this short poetic unit, the divine voice offers a vivid depiction of restoration that embraces those who might suspect that they are not to be included. Its inclusive vision places obligations on the restoration community and is more explicitly conditional upon their observance of particular requirements than has been the case in the preceding chapters.⁷⁰² This shift can be seen as part of its being the beginning of what is generally considered a separate unit in the book (see About the Audience(s) in the Introduction). However, this poem does more than merely shift audiences and locations. By uniting emphases present in different portions of the book of Isaiah, it draws together divine initiative and human response and presents an expansive vision of restoration through the synthesis of images from texts that warn and console.

---

⁷⁰¹   I am following the lineation of MT over that of NRSV[ue] here. The parallelism appears primarily between the two lines of the couplet as shown above and there seems to be no clear reason to divide these lines internally.
⁷⁰²   See also J. Blenkinsopp, *Isaiah 56–66* (2003), 143.

*Isaiah 56:1–8* 249

As Rolf Rendtorff has rightly observed, the opening verse employs a single term in two different pairings with distinctively different meanings.[703] The NRSV[ue] translates the term two different ways reflective of these different meanings: "what is right" (*ṣĕdāqâ*) and "my deliverance" (*ṣidqātî*). The first, the commandment to "do what is right," is paired with "justice" just as it is frequently in Isaiah 1–39 where the pair often points to obligations on the audience.[704] The second refers to "deliverance," which comes from the LORD and which is paired with "salvation," a way of using the word that is typical of Isaiah 40–55.[705] Here, the two visions of righteousness stand in parallel with one another. The commandments to enact "justice" and act with righteousness are responses to the "salvation" that the LORD will accomplish. Here, the juxtaposition of these two references offers a new vision.[706] It is a vision of a people who respond to God's "deliverance" by enacting "what is right."[707]

The poem continues by announcing blessing in lines that express both generality and condition. The recipient of the blessing is "the mortal" (*'ĕnôš*) and "the one" (*ben-'ādām*). This pair of terms seems to convey general humanity.[708] However, the next couplet narrows the field of blessing recipients considerably. Using forms of the same word by which justice was commanded (*šimrû*, i.e., "keep," NRSV[ue] "maintain," v. 1), the recipient of the blessing is clarified as the one "who keeps (*šōmēr*) the Sabbath" and who keeps (*šōmēr*; cf. NRSV[ue] "refrains," v. 2) from "doing any evil."

---

[703] R. Rendtorff, "Isaiah 56:1" (1993), 183. See also C. Westermann, *Isaiah 40–66* (1969), 309–310; and J. Blenkinsopp, *Isaiah 56–66* (2003), 137.

[704] R. Rendtorff, "Isaiah 56:1" (1993), 183.

[705] R. Rendtorff, "Isaiah 56:1" (1993), 183.

[706] R. Rendtorff, "Isaiah 56:1" (1993), 184, sees the author of Isa 56:1 as intentionally drawing together these different uses of the word. Rendtorff's analysis continues by considering what this might mean for the history of the composition of the book of Isaiah as a whole and his comments are constructive and insightful in this regard. This approach opens up the possibility of the author of this verse offering his vision as one that draws together both the warnings about the need to act justly and the promises of restoration to present a vision of the obligations of the restored community. See further R. Rendtorff, "Composition" (1993), 162–164.

[707] See also B. S. Childs, *Isaiah* (2001), 455–456, who highlights the "mutual obligations of just behavior" in the meaning of the term.

[708] In Isaiah 51:12, this same pair indicated those that the audience need not fear, i.e., mortal human beings.

250                                                                    *Commentary*

The pair of expanded images that follow express and embody this combination of openness to unexpected recipients and the necessity of obedience. The condition that they "keep my Sabbaths" (56:4; cf. 56:6) and "hold fast my covenant" (56:4, 6) is placed upon both the eunuch and the foreigner. These two figures appear as unlikely beneficiaries of "salvation" and "deliverance" (56:1). They are initially envisioned as despairing of their own inclusion. Their words appear as embedded potential speech. That is, they are not cited for what they have said but told not to say what they might. Unlike embedded citations of Jacob-Israel (40:27) or Zion (49:14), these potential words are not complaints to be refuted. Instead, they are expressions of potential despair overwhelmed by assurance in advance.

Each receives an expansive response. The eunuch's imagery "I am just a dry tree" is arresting and receives a response that ties the eunuch's inclusion to the lavish and everlasting restoration of Isaiah 55:13. It seems likely that the eunuch's potential self-attribution "dry tree" is an allusion to conditions of service imposed upon him by his foreign masters. While the term here translated "eunuch" seems to refer to a range of royal officials, and it is not clear that all of them have been made unable to produce offspring, that meaning does seem to apply in this instance given the promise of something better than descendants.

Royal officials who serve in a range of monarchs' courts appear referenced by this term (*sārîs*, "eunuch"). In some cases, Israelite or Judean court officials are intended (e.g., 1 Sam 8:15; 1 Kgs 22:9; 2 Kgs 8:6, 9:32; 24:12, 15; 1 Chron 28:1). In other places, it is clear that foreign court officials are intended (e.g., Gen 37:36; 39:1; 40:2, 7; Est 1:10, 15, 2:3, 14, 15, 21; 4:4, 5; 6:2, 14; 7:9; Dan 1:3, 7, 8, 9, 10, 11, 18). Offspring of such figures are not explicitly referenced, though one of them (Potiphar) is married. When referring to Israelite or Judean figures, the NRSV[ue] typically translates with some term other than "eunuch," probably indicating a notion that sterilization was a foreign palace practice rather than an Israelite one. Jezebel's attendants being referred to as "eunuchs" (2 Kgs 9:32) reinforces such an interpretation of the translation tendency (on Jezebel see, e.g., 1 Kgs 16:31; 1 Kgs 21:25–26).[709] While eunuchs are referenced in relationship to the care of the women of the palace (e.g., Est 2:3, 14, 15; 4:4), this is not universally so. The

---

[709]  Though note NRSV[ue] also avoids "eunuch" for Potiphar and other Egyptian officials in the Joseph story.

Persian king is himself attended by eunuchs and appears to use them as messengers (Est 1:10, 15; 6:14) and as guards (Est 2:21; 6:2) and Daniel is among a group of young men who are overseen by a eunuch (Dan 1:3, 7, 8, 9, 10, 11, 18).[710]

It is noteworthy that prior to exile Isaiah of Jerusalem warned Hezekiah that the Babylonians would carry off some of his sons to be "eunuchs in the palace of the king of Babylon" (2 Kgs 20:18; Isa 39:7). In the context of a poem that follows immediately on the heels of the exuberant promise "you shall go out in joy and be led back in peace" (55:13), this return of reference to eunuchs signals restoration. Babylon no longer holds these men captive, and the blessings of their inclusion in the restoration community overturn their plight with something that the text calls "better." Like the trees that were to grow up in place of the "thorn" and the "brier," the "monument" and "name" that the LORD is giving the eunuchs is "everlasting" and "shall not be cut off" (56:5 and 55:13).[711] In Isaiah 55, the announcement "it shall be for the LORD for a memorial (lĕšēm, i.e., for a name)" explicitly calls the sign "everlasting" ('ôlām) and not to be "cut off" (yikkārēt).[712]

---

[710]  See the discussion in J. D. W. Watts, *Isaiah 34–66* (2005), 249; and J. Blenkinsopp, *Isaiah 56–66* (2003), 137. Blenkinsopp in particular notes that these figures in this context are "in all probability, of non-Jewish origin," connecting them to the foreigner elsewhere in the passage, employing the language of "subcategory."

[711]  The word "monument" is *yād*, a word most commonly used in Hebrew to refer to the body part "hand." It is sometimes suggested that the term can be used as a euphemism for the "*membrum virile*" (C. Westermann, *Isaiah 40–66* [1969], 323, referring to Isa 57:8) as might be indicated by the context in Isa 57:8 where NRSV[ue] translates "nakedness." If so, "hand" for monument may employ word play to euphemistically overturn that which the eunuch has euphemistically bemoaned. See J. Blenkinsopp, *Isaiah 56–66* (2003), 139, who points to the loss of the possibility of a descendant and the phrasing related to one's name being cut off. While multiple poetic resonances seem typical of the passage's poetic style, this euphemism should probably not be allowed to dominate the reading in this context. See S. Moughtin-Mumby, *Sexual and Marital* (2008), 146–149, on the history of reading *yād* in Isa 57 and relevant cautions. Additionally, it should not be overlooked that the meaning "monument" comes through in this context as well. There may be some allusion to Absalom, David's son, who set up a "pillar" saying that it was because he had "no son to keep my name in remembrance" (2 Sam 18:18). The text notes that the pillar was called "Absalom's Monument," using *yād*. On the parallel with Absalom, see also C. Westermann, *Isaiah 40–66* (1969), 314, who seems to view the promise as referring to "a monument erected to him within the precincts of the temple." Contrast J. Muilenburg, "Isaiah 40–66" (1956), 5:657, who points to Absalom as an example of the kind of literal monument that is not meant.

[712]  See also Ulrich Berges, "Trito-Isaiah and the Reforms of Ezra/Nehemiah: Consent or Conflict?" *Biblica* (2017): 188, who sees the "broadened admission to the worship of YHWH in Isa 56, 1–8 . . . as a continuation of Isa 55, 12–13." For a contrasting view, see

252                                                                                   *Commentary*

Thus, the language of the two poems side by side creates a new vision of what the eunuch is. They may see themselves as "dry tree[s]," but trees are not things to be cast aside, the divine voice reminds the eunuchs. Instead, trees have been the image of restoration, something that stands forever. The divine voice takes up their potential derogatory self-designation and transforms it by allusion into a sign of the LORD's deliverance. The eunuch is given more than just a place within the community, the eunuch becomes a symbol of the LORD's restoration when the eunuch does "the things that please" the LORD by keeping Sabbath and covenant.[713]

Like the eunuch, the "foreigners" have their concerns over being excluded from the LORD's people overturned and they become themselves images of restoration.[714] Again, the text elaborates its reference to the foreigners with indications of their commitment to the ways of the LORD. The highly alliterated phrase "foreigners who join themselves" to the LORD (*ben-hannēkār hannilwāh*, 56:3; cf. v. 6) appears in slightly varied form both times that these people are named (56:3, 6). They serve and "love" and receive the title "servants" (see further A Closer Look: From Servant to Servants).

The conditions of Sabbath observance and covenant keeping that applied to the eunuch appear here. It is noteworthy here that these foreigners receive approval of that which the LORD has rejected from

---

J. Blenkinsopp, *Isaiah 56–66* (2003), 131, who observes the overlap of language but draws differing conclusions. On connection to Isa 55, see further J. Stromberg, *Israel After Exile* (2011), 78–79.

[713]  Notably, the response to the eunuch's concerns centers around "name" and offspring. There is no mention of inclusion or exclusion from specific worship practices. The term "eunuch" is not employed in the two Pentateuchal texts that are associated with exclusion from sanctuary service for males with damaged reproductive organs (Lev 21:20; Deut 23:1 NRSV[ue], Heb. Deut 23:2). These texts each employ terms that are used only once in the whole of the Hebrew Bible (i.e., not the same terms in each of Lev 21:20 and Deut 23:2) and whose translation poses difficulties. While the traditional interpretation of these prohibitions is probably accurate, it is not clear that this was either a concern of the eunuchs addressed in Isa 56 or that these prohibitions were intended to refer to the same condition. On the details of terminology related to temple service and the distinct issues concerning eunuchs and foreigners here, see B. D. Sommer, *A Prophet Reads Scripture* (1998), 146–147. On the difficulties of directly connecting Deut 23:2 with this passage, see further B. D. Sommer, *A Prophet Reads Scripture* (1998), 279 n. 46.

[714]  See, e.g., J. D. W. Watts, *Isaiah 34–66* (2005), 249, on potential connections to exclusion of foreigners from the returnee community, especially as highlighted in Ezra. See also U. Berges, "Trito-Isaiah" (2017), 174, 184.

# A Closer Look: From Servant to Servants

the Judeans earlier in the canonical book. In Isaiah's first chapter, "your sacrifices" (*zibḥêkem*, 1:11) and "burnt offerings" (*ʿōlôt*, 1:11) were rejected because of the people's "evil" (1:16) and they were told to "seek justice" (*mišpāṭ*, Isa 1:17). To the exiles, the divine voice charges that they have not brought "burnt offerings" or "sacrifices" (43:23) employing forms of the same words. Here, it is precisely those things that the "foreigner" will bring and will have "accepted" in the LORD's house. The vision of the LORD's expansive restoration offers an image in which the injustice and bloodshed that brought about punishment and that made the people's worship repellent (1:12–17) is now overcome, and those who might expect to be outside the bounds of this restoration are explicitly included.[715]

The poem draws together the warnings of this book that preceded the exile with the vision of restoration and deliverance that come from God's own compassion in the poems addressed to the exiles. Together, the eunuch and the foreigner point to a restoration that is expansive and generously offered by the LORD but that insists upon a response of active justice and the keeping of the LORD's covenant and Sabbath.[716]

## A CLOSER LOOK: FROM SERVANT TO SERVANTS

The Servant personification undergoes a significant shift as the poems move from the exilic context to the postexilic one. W. A. M. Beuken has made the important observation that the servant language becomes plural in Isaiah 56–66 and that the shift to this plural form comes "precisely *before* the end" of Isaiah 40–55, in Isaiah 54:17.[717] That shift from singular occurs, then, at a significant moment for the poetically persuasive aims of

---

[715] The Pentateuch prohibits foreigners from providing sacrificial animals, Lev 22:25.

[716] See U. Berges, "Trito-Isaiah" (2017), 186, who comments, "this policy does not advocate a total cancellation of boundaries. On the contrary, the admission to YHWH's <<people>> (Isa 56,3) is inextricably tied to the imperative demanding a moral conduct of life." See also B. Schramm, *Opponents* (1995), 122–123, on distinguishing between "open[ness] to proselytes and the modern theological concept of 'universalism'" (122). It is the former that is in view here. See also M. A. Sweeney, *Isaiah 40-66* (2016), 255, who says of the foreigners in this passage "such persons would constitute converts to Judaism insofar as these foreigners affirm the covenant between YHWH and the Jewish people."

[717] W. A. M. Beuken, "Main Theme" (1990), 67. See also discussion of Beuken's proposal in J. Stromberg, *Isaiah after Exile* (2011), 79–82.

Isaiah 40–55 (see further A Closer Look: Lady Zion and the Suffering Servant, the Rhetorical Power of Juxtaposition).

If one of the primary ways that Isaiah 40–55 went about moving its audience's attitudes toward reconciliation was through embrace of the compelling and appealing personification of the Servant, the "servants" imagery of Isaiah 56–66 adapts the personification to a new rhetorical context. In Isaiah 40–55, the poems seemed not to distinguish in any way between members of their exilic audience but sought to draw all of them together into a restored relationship with the LORD. A single figure as personification is appropriate for such a unified aim. Isaiah 56–66, on the other hand, exhibits a pervasive division within the community it addresses. A conflict emerges between those who are the LORD's "servants" and those who face severe judgment for their consistent pursuit of "their own ways" (e.g., 57:17).

The "servants" in these chapters are "humble" and "contrite" (57:15),[718] they do what pleases the LORD (56:4) and keep the LORD's "covenant" (56:4, 6). In contrast to covenantal loyalty and commitment to the LORD's ways that characterize the "servants," the others who stand contrasted with them appear in expansive descriptions of idolatry (65:3–5), rebellion (65:2), "violence" and injustice (59:4–8), and embrace of things that do not please the LORD (57:1–10; 65:12). The contrast becomes particularly pointed as Isaiah 56–66 reaches its final poems (see especially comment on Isa 65:1–25 and Isa 66:1–24). Here, expansive visions of glorious abundance and cosmic flourishing stand juxtaposed to violent and ongoing judgment.

Just as the juxtaposition between Zion and the Servant in Isaiah 40–55 seemed designed to work in a poetically persuasive way to urge its audience to embrace the Servant's attitude toward the LORD, so the juxtaposition between the "servants" and their adversaries in Isaiah 56–66 appears to do poetically persuasive work. In a social context that appears to have featured conflict between rival groups, the audience are invited to see the conflict

---

[718] The language of "servants" is not used in Isaiah 57:15. However, see J. Dekker, "High and Lofty" (2017), 479, who points out the connection between these terms and the Servant in Isaiah 53:10. He views the "servants" as "the Servant's spiritual offspring." W. A. M. Beuken, "Main Theme" (1990), 69, also draws a connection between the sufferers in this passage and the Servant. So, while "humble" and "contrite" might not be explicitly and directly connected to the "servants" in Isaiah 56–66, they are implicitly connected, and this language resonates with their presentation in these poems.

*Isaiah 56:9–57:21*

between groups in terms of resistance to or embrace of the LORD's ways. The intensely negative emotions conjured up by the expansive descriptions of idolatry and rebellion (see comment on Isa 56:9–57:21) have the power to shift allegiances and to realign loyalties. The audience are again invited to embrace the Servant personification, this time by joining the group of the "servants."[719] Thus, they are encouraged to embrace hope, restoration, and healing.

ISAIAH 56:9–57:21

<sup>9</sup> All you wild animals,
>     all you wild animals in the forest, come to devour!
<sup>10</sup> Israel's sentinels are blind;
>     they are all without knowledge;
they are all silent dogs
>     that cannot bark,
dreaming, lying down,
>     loving to slumber.
<sup>11</sup> The dogs have a mighty appetite;
>     they never have enough.
The shepherds also have no understanding;
>     they have all turned to their own way,
>     to their own gain, one and all.
<sup>12</sup> "Come," they say, "let us get wine;
>     let us fill ourselves with strong drink.
And tomorrow will be like today,
>     great beyond measure."

57:1 The righteous perish,
>     and no one considers why;
the devout are taken away,
>     while no one understands

---

[719] See also M. A. Sweeney, *Isaiah 40–66* (2016), 333, who presents the persuasive aims of the sharp dichotomy between the righteous and the wicked in reference to Isaiah 63–66 in this way: "to convince the people that they will want to be included among the righteous by observing YHWH's covenant and thereby avoid the fate of the wicked portrayed at the end of the book."

256            *Commentary*

that it is due to evil that the righteous are taken away.
² Those who walk uprightly enter into peace
  and rest on their couches.
³ But as for you, come here,
    you children of a sorceress,
    you offspring of an adulterer and a prostitute.
⁴ Whom are you mocking?
    Against whom do you open your mouth wide
    and stick out your tongue?
Are you not children of transgression,
    the offspring of deceit –
⁵ you who burn with lust among the oaks,
    under every green tree;
you that slaughter your children in the valleys,
    under the clefts of the rocks?
⁶ Among the smooth stones of the valley is your portion;
    it is they who are your lot;
to them you have poured out a drink offering;
    you have brought a grain offering.
    Should these acts cause me to relent?
⁷ Upon a high and lofty mountain
    you have set your bed,
    and there you went up to offer sacrifice.
⁸ Behind the door and the doorpost
    you have set up your symbol,
for in deserting me you have uncovered your bed;
    you have gone up to it;
    you have made it wide;
and you have made a bargain for yourself with them;
    you have loved their bed;
    you have gazed on their nakedness.
⁹ You journeyed to Molech with oil
    and multiplied your perfumes;
you sent your envoys far away
    and sent them down to Sheol.
¹⁰ You grew weary from your many wanderings,
    but you did not say, "It is no use!"

*Isaiah 56:9–57:21*

You found your desire rekindled,
   and so you did not weaken.

¹¹ Whom did you dread and fear
      so that you lied
and did not remember me
      or give me a thought?
Have I not kept silent and closed my eyes,
      and so you do not fear me?
¹² I will announce your verdict,
      and the objects you made will not help you.
¹³ When you cry out, let your collection of idols deliver you!
      The wind will carry them off;
      a breath will take them away.
But whoever takes refuge in me shall possess the land
      and inherit my holy mountain.

¹⁴ It shall be said, "Build up, build up, prepare the way;[720]
      remove every obstruction from my people's way."
¹⁵ For thus says the high and lofty one
      who inhabits eternity, whose name is Holy:
I dwell in the high and holy place
      and also with those who are contrite and humble in spirit,
to revive the spirit of the humble
      and to revive the heart of the contrite.
¹⁶ For I will not continually accuse,
      nor will I always be angry,
for then the spirits would grow faint before me,
      even the souls that I have made.
¹⁷ Because of their wicked covetousness I was angry;
      I struck them; I hid and was angry,
      but they kept turning back to their own ways.
¹⁸ I have seen their ways, but I will heal them;
      I will lead them and repay them with comfort,

---

[720] My lineation departs from the NRSV^ue here. "It shall be said" translates a single word in Hebrew, which makes an overly short line. I have treated it as part of the first line of the couplet.

> creating for their mourners the fruit of the lips.
> [19] Peace, peace, to the far and the near,
> says the LORD, and I will heal them.[721]
> [20] But the wicked are like the tossing sea
> that cannot keep still;
> its waters toss up mire and mud.
> [21] There is no peace, says my God, for the wicked.

Like the poem before it, this poem appears to unite concerns and imagery from Isaiah 1–39 with those familiar in Isaiah 40–55. And, once again, the intersection of human moral responsibility and divine mercy appear. It seems likely that this combination indicates both a prophetic poet who is creatively redeploying earlier Isaian traditions and an audience whose return to the land involves continued struggle with similar social and religious problems as their predecessors (see further About the Audience(s) in the Introduction].[722] By reminding the audience of the trajectory of warning, punishment and restoration, and uniting imageries from these movements of the prophetic book, this poem offers a stark choice between peace, comfort, and healing for those who will serve the LORD faithfully and punishment for those who will not.[723] It does so through appeal and repulsion generated by emotionally charged and juxtaposed images.

The poem's first two stanzas employ common themes from Israel's prophets to portray societal injustice and religious transgression. Animal imagery both conveys impending violent punishment (56:9) and a derogatory view of those who should warn and lead (56:10, 11). Sentinels who are

---

[721] While the phrase "says the LORD" seems to refer to both halves of the couplet, better balance in the lineation is created by putting it in the second line. This is in line with the MT's lineation and contrary to the lineation shown in NRSV[ue].

[722] On the phenomenon of reuse of material and connection to historical realities, see B. S. Childs, *Isaiah* (2001), 462–463. As Childs insightfully points out, "Third Isaiah faced a new problem that bore directly on the relation between the old and the new. His was not a psychological problem of overcoming disappointment with the failure of Isaiah's promises to materialize . . . . Third Isaiah confronted a theological problem that turned on the continuing presence of the old along with the very real experience of the new." See also J. Blenkinsopp, *Isaiah 56–66* (2003), 173.

[723] As C. Westermann, *Isaiah 40–66* (1969), 328, comments regarding 57:15 in its context, "if this utterance . . . shows a combination of motifs taken from the prologue of Deutero-Isaiah and motifs taken from the vision received at his call by First Isaiah, then this is certainly no accident."

*Isaiah 56:9–57:21* 259

unable to offer a warning (56:10) and shepherds primarily concerned with their own profit (56:11) are both strong depictions of a failure of leadership to do the most basic things that it is required to do, that is, to guide and to act for the welfare of the weak.[724] The image of "dogs" is unflattering in itself. Dogs were significantly less well regarded in ancient Israel than in modern Western society.[725] And, while the imagery initially indicates laziness and one that needs to be fed constantly but does not do its most basic job,[726] the reappearance of much of the language of this description in the lines about idolatry (57:8) suggests as well that the charge is more nefarious than laziness.[727] Those who are to be looking out for Israel are driven not by the needs of the citizens but by their own appetites (56:11). Similarly, the depiction of the "shepherds" not concerned about the future and focused on intoxication supports the image of a corrupt leadership that is most concerned with satisfying its own desires.[728]

---

[724] The focus here is on the imagistic depiction of the leadership not on the precise referent of that imagery. My own view is that both prophetic and political leaders are indicted by this passage. However, the poem focuses primarily on the imagery of appetite-driven and ineffective protectors rather than identification of referents. On barkless dogs and blind sentinel imagery, see further Lena-Sofia Tiemeyer, "The Watchman Metaphor in Isaiah LVI–LXVI," *VT* 53 (2005): 385. C. Westermann, *Isaiah 40–66* (1969), 317, sees both figures as references to leaders. See also J. L. McKenzie, *Second Isaiah* (1968), 154; and B. S. Childs, *Isaiah* (2001), 464. B. D. Sommer, *A Prophet Reads Scripture* (1998), 40–41, in his convincing argument that this passage alludes to Jeremiah's condemnation of false prophets, provides important evidence that prophetic figures are in view here.

[725] See J. Muilenburg, "Isaiah 40–66" (1956), 5:662, who points to 1 Sam 17:43; 24:14; 2 Kgs 8:13 and Tell el-Amarna.

[726] While R. Alter, *Hebrew Bible* (2019), 811, points out that "There is scant evidence that watchdogs were used in ancient Israel," the poem's accusation that they "cannot bark" at the very least presents an image of failing even to do what appears to come naturally to the species, that is to make its characteristic noise.

[727] The word "lying down" (*šōkĕbîm*, 56:10) is from the same root as "your bed" (*miškābēk*; cf. also "their bed"), which appears in the description of idolatry as adultery (57:8). While the dogs love ('*ōhăbê*, 56:10) to rest, the idolatry is described as having "loved (root '*hb*, 57:8) their bed" (57:8). In light of these verbal overlaps, it seems plausible to read a sound play between "dreaming" (*hōzîm*, 56:10) and "gazed" (*ḥāzît*, 57:8). See also L. Tiemeyer, "Watchman" (2005), 388–389, who connects watchman imagery with the charge of idolatry against the leadership in Isa 57.

[728] Shepherds are a common image for political leadership in the Hebrew Bible. That seems to be an implication here, though note the comment above. See L. Tiemeyer, "Watchman" (2005), 385. Contra J. Muilenburg, "Isaiah 40–66" (1956), 5:660, who indicates his agreement with a position that sees the critiqued leaders as "religious, not political." See further K. M. Heffelfinger, "Persuasion" (2020), 45–46.

260                                                                    *Commentary*

The poem develops this image through an expansive invective against those who practice idolatry and uses adultery imagery to produce revulsion for idolatry in its audience. The image of the adulterous spouse as a means of condemning the worship of other gods is not unknown in the Hebrew Bible. The prophet Hosea uses this image in an extended metaphor.[729] This imagery appeared in the book of Isaiah's opening chapter (1:21). However, it was absent in the poems addressed to the exiles.[730] There Zion is imagined as the bride of the LORD, but there is no accusation of adultery. Idolatry is ridiculed (e.g., 44:9–20) and the people are accused of having a tendency to wrongly attribute the LORD's work to idols (48:5), but these images are not dominant, and the metaphor of marital infidelity is not applied.

Here, worship practices are explicitly linked to adultery (57:3).[731] Practices of sacrifice are juxtaposed with sexual imagery. The names of worship practices are explicit in the poem. The people "have poured out a drink offering" (57:6) and "a grain offering" (57:6).[732] They "offer sacrifice" (57:7). These are juxtaposed with sexual imagery: "set your bed" (57:7), "uncovered your bed" (57:8), "loved their bed" (57:8), "gazed on their nakedness" (57:8), "found your desire rekindled" (57:10).[733] The imagery is of embrace of the worship of foreign gods. This is most explicit in the

---

[729]   See especially Hos 2. C. Westermann, *Isaiah 40–66* (1969), 324, notes similarity with Hosea and Ezekiel. Contra S. Moughtin-Mumby, *Sexual and Marital* (2008), 145–148, the language of adultery (57:3) in this passage puts sexual imagery firmly in view in this passage. That is, it does more than "lurk in the background" (146). However, with S. Moughtin-Mumby, *Sexual and Marital* (2008), 149, it is important not to allow attention to the imagery by which idolatry is depicted here to overwhelm attention to the text's primary concern, which includes rejection of child sacrifice in idolatrous rituals.

[730]   Note the characterization of Isaiah 40–55 in S. Moughtin-Mumby, *Sexual and Marital* (2008), 152–153.

[731]   S. Moughtin-Mumby, *Sexual and Marital* (2008), 144, points out the connection between adultery imagery and child sacrifice here and in Ezek. 23:36–49.

[732]   The "drink offering" and "grain offering" appear as specific worship practices in the book of Leviticus. The two appear together in Lev 23:13, 18. The grain offering is mentioned additionally in Lev 2 and 6.

[733]   These last two each employ the euphemism "hand" as discussed in the commentary on Isa 56:5. The NRSV^ue's translation here points to such a euphemistic understanding of the term. Cf. the discussion in S. Moughtin-Mumby, *Sexual and Martial* (2008), 146–147. As noted above, I do not think sexual imagery is entirely absent here, but it is not the main interest of the poem. It is a device the poem employs to produce disgust in its audience over its depiction of child sacrifice and idolatrous worship.

*Isaiah 56:9–57:21*                                                                  261

reference to "Molech" (57:9) and the charge that "you . . . slaughter your
children in the valleys" (57:5). The practice of sacrificing children to this
god of the Ammonites (1 Kgs 11:7) is specifically forbidden (Lev 20:2–5; see
also Jer 32:35 and the removal of the places for this practice in Josiah's
reform in 2 Kgs 23:10). The locations that the poem applies to the practices
are also indicators of the worship of foreign gods. They are accused of
burning "among the oaks" and "under every green tree" (57:5). Isaiah 1:29
proclaims that when redemption comes "you shall be ashamed of the oaks"
and the phrase "every green tree" is used to indicate the places that
idolatrous worship was practiced (see, e.g., 2 Kgs 16:4; 17:10; Jer 2:20; 3:6,
13). The sexual imagery is not the poem's primary focus. It is, instead, a way
in which the poem produces some of the emotional freight of its rejection
of idolatry and child-sacrifice.[734]

This vision of a corrupt leadership and idolatrous practices resonates with
the vision of Judean society offered in Isaiah 1–39.[735] There "princes" were
"companions of thieves," and anyone could be persuaded with "a bribe"
1:23). The leaders "made a covenant with death, and with Sheol . . . an
agreement" (28:15; cf. 57:9) and trusted in "lies" (28:15; cf. 57:11). Idols are a
part of society that the prophet proclaims will one day be discarded (2:18, 20;
30:22; 31:7).[736] There these images are deployed in the context of warning and
invitation to repentance (2:5; 31:6), and the warning is sealed up for a later
time when people will be willing to listen to it (30:8; cf. 8:16).[737]

Yet this poem's images of restoration also draw together that depiction
and the imagery of comfort and reconciliation that has appeared already in
Isaiah. Restoration involves the preparation of a way (57:14; cf. 40:3)[738] and
emphasizes the majestic glory of the LORD through height imagery (e.g.,
57:15; cf. 40:22; and 2:11, 17; 6:1).[739] Those who are to be restored are the

---

[734] See S. Moughtin-Mumby, *Sexual and Marital* (2008), 149. See further K. M. Heffelfinger,
"Persuasion" (2020), 47–49.
[735] See B .D. Sommer, *A Prophet Reads Scripture* (1998), 89–92.
[736] See B. D. Sommer, *A Prophet Reads Scripture* (1998), 89–91, on connection to Isa 2.
[737] See H. G. M. Williamson, *Book Called Isaiah* (1994), 94–107.
[738] See also B. S. Childs, *Isaiah* (2001), 469.
[739] See B. S. Childs, *Isaiah* (2001), 467 and 471, on height imagery. See also H. G.
M. Williamson, *Book Called Isaiah* (1994), 39; and B. D. Sommer, *A Prophet Reads
Scripture* (1998), 88 –91, who points to Isa 57 as a case of "negative reprediction" (88) of
Isa 2:6–21, which also offers "a response to the theological problem of Isa 6.9–10" (91) in
57:16–18. See also J. Dekker, "High and Lofty One" (2017): 480–481.

"contrite (*dakkā'*) and humble" (57:15), employing the term for the Servant's condition (*dakkĕ'ô* "to crush him," 53:10)[740] as well as in the accusation that the LORD makes against Judah's leaders ("crushing my people" *tĕdakkĕ'û*, 3:15). The idea that the LORD would contend appears both in those charges (3:13) and in the promise to "contend with those who contend with you" (49:25). The LORD promises both to "heal" (57:18; see Isa 6:10; 30:26) and to "comfort" (57:18; see, e.g., 40:1; 51:3). By drawing together imagery from throughout the book of Isaiah, this vision of both indictment for those who persist in wickedness and idolatry and restoration of the "contrite" re-places its audience within the trajectory of the book in which it is set. By underscoring its indictment with allusions to earlier warnings, it emphasizes the realistic possibility of punishment for their misdeeds. By alluding to the restoration imagery of the exilic portions of the book, the poem highlights the mercy of the LORD who offers restoration.

While the dominant focus of the poem is on those whose behavior is rejected, there are indications that this is not the whole of the audience. The poem differentiates between "the righteous" (57:1) and "the wicked" (57:21). The lack of concern over the fate of "the righteous ones" is a further indication of the corruption of society (57:1)[741] but it stands juxtaposed to a promise of their deliverance and security (57:1b–2). Periodic contrasts between the fate of those who persevere in idolatry (e.g., 57:13a) and those who depend upon the LORD (e.g., 57:13b) underscore the message of indictment.[742] The wrath of God is not for all in this passage. Instead,

---

[740] Interestingly, J. Dekker, "High and Lofty" (2017), 476, connects the exaltation imagery of this passage to the "exaltation of the Servant" in Isaiah 52:13 and observes the use of the same term for "contrite" and "crush" in both Isa 53 and 57:15. See B. S. Childs, *Isaiah* (2001), 465, on not "introduc[ing] the figure of the suffering servant into v.11" and giving attention instead to the way "elements of textual resonance" create "semantic texture."

[741] NRSV[ue]'s "no one considers why" translates a phrase that might be less idiomatically rendered "there is no one who puts it upon the heart" or as the NRSV had it "no one takes it to heart." Heart here is not about emotional response but does imply taking something seriously. See, e.g., HALOT, 513–515, which includes alongside "the organ" a range of meanings that include "one's inner self," "will," "consideration," and "conscience."

[742] See further K. M. Heffelfinger, "Persuasion" (2020), 47, "The poem develops a contrast between two groups. This contrast will persist to the end of the poem and embodies one of the poem's poetic persuasive strategies. By juxtaposing two opposing possibilities for its audience's position, it invites emotional resonance with one group and rejection of the other. That is, it forms its audience's desires into conformity with the group into which it aims to move them." C. Westermannn, *Isaiah 40–66* (1969), 325, observes the contrast in the groups within the postexilic community in relation to this passage,

# Isaiah 56:9–57:21

"the contrite and humble in spirit" (57:15) can expect that the LORD will "heal" and "comfort" them (57:18).

The motif of the "way" functions powerfully in the poem. It implies that those who will reject the tendency to go "their own ways" (57:17) are those who will be offered "peace" (57:19). The shepherds "turned to their own way (*lĕdarkām*)" (56:11). The people engaged in idolatrous practices are accused of being tired from "your many wanderings (*darkēk*, i.e., your way)" (57:10). The people "kept turning back to their own ways (*bĕderek*)" (57:17), and despite seeing "their ways" (*dĕrākāyw*, 57:18),[743] the LORD resolves to restore (57:18). However, the divine voice commanded preparation of "the way" (*dārek*, 57:14) and "my people's way" (*derek*, 57:14). This is the voice that in the larger context of the book of Isaiah has contrasted "your ways (*darkêkem*)" with "my ways (*dĕrākay*)" (55:9; see also 55:8) and called upon the "wicked" to "forsake" his "way (*darkô*)" (55:7).[744] The ominous closing single line closely echoes an earlier warning (48:22), which also stood in a place of choice about the way.[745] There the divine voice had expressed that things would have gone better for the exiles had they "paid attention to my commandments" (48:18) before exhorting them to "Go out" (48:20).

Thus, the poem invites repentance but not directly. There is no imperative commanding: "repent!" Instead, the poem invites a turn through warning and contrast. It offers a vision that has the power to produce both

> though his interpretation describes the re-application of "pre-exilic prophets' oracles." See also B. S. Childs, *Isaiah* (2001), 469, on this contrast in Isa 57:14–21. See B. Schramm, *Opponents* (1995), 133, on the distinction between "my people" and "the wicked" in vv. 14–21.
>
> [743] As the transliteration shows, the pronoun here is "his" rather than "their." I have followed the NRSV[ue] which renders it "their ways." As J. Blenkinsopp, *Isaiah 56–66* (2003), 167, explains regarding his own translation of another word in this context, the plural points to the "reference to Israelites."
>
> [744] See also C. Westermann, *Isaiah 40–66* (1969), 328, who points out the resonance between Isa 40:3 and 57:14, noting that in the latter text it is used metaphorically (citing Volz). See also J. L. McKenzie, *Second Isaiah* (1968), 161. B. D. Sommer, *A Prophet Reads Scripture* (1998), 56, connects the way imagery to Jeremiah. See further J. Dekker, "High and Lofty" (2017), 482.
>
> [745] While some commentators argue that the duplication indicates one occurrence is "out of place" (J. L. McKenzie, *Second Isaiah* [1968], 162), such an argument is not necessary in a final form reading of the text where meaningful sense can be made in both occurrences. Repetition of materials from elsewhere in Isaiah is typical of this portion of the book and this passage in particular. The repetition can be understood to have meaningful poetic function however it came to be in the text as it now stands.

264                                                      *Commentary*

desire for justice and faithfulness to the LORD and an emotionally infused
rejection of idolatry and injustice. That is, it produces attitudes of repentance poetically.[746] The choice is still stark for the returnees addressed by
this poem. They can reject idolatry and injustice, be "humble" and "contrite" (57:15), and find healing and comfort, or they can persist in the way of
the "wicked" and find "no peace" (57:21).

A CLOSER LOOK: "THIRD ISAIAH" AS "UNDER-RATED" POET

It is not at all surprising to read glowing accounts of the poetic qualities of
Isaiah 40–55.[747] Isaiah 56–66's literary qualities, on the other hand, have
received a more muted reception.[748] However, Isaiah 56–66 repays careful
attention to the meaningfulness of its poetic features, and the poetic hand
(or hands) responsible for Isaiah 56–66 masterfully unites diverse materials
in new poetic synthesis.

Benjamin Sommer has helpfully outlined a number of ways that Isaiah
56–66 takes up some of Isaiah 40–55's favorite techniques. He cites "a
unique penchant to repeat imperatives" a fondness for "put[ting] similar-
sounding words next to each other," a "predilection for punning and
affection for alliteration."[749] While there are certainly shifts of focus and
changes in some characteristic literary features, much is to be gained by
considering the ways in which Isaiah 56–66 takes up, continues, and
redeploys the Isaian tradition poetically in its own time and place.[750]

Juxtaposition continues to be an important feature of Isaian poetics as
the poems progress into Isaiah 56–66. Notably, the poetry draws together
contrasts between those it includes in its vision of restoration and those it

---

[746]  See further K. M. Heffelfinger, "Persuasion" (2020), 44–45.

[747]  J. Muilenburg, "Isaiah 40–66" (1956), 5:382, goes so far as to say that "The poetic
sequence in Isa. 40–55 represents the noblest literary monument bequeathed to us
from Semitic antiquity."

[748]  See, e.g., J. Muilenburg, "Isaiah 40–66" (1956), 5:384, who says of Isaiah 56–66, "Their
literary quality is high, but uneven; at least it is not always on the same level as
chs. 40–55."

[749]  B. D. Sommer, *A Prophet Reads Scripture* (1998), 188–189.

[750]  Scholarly positions on the unity of Isaiah 56–66 and its relationship to Isaiah 40–55
demonstrate a wide range. Sommer's argument about related literary features supports
his careful articulation of the non-necessity of assigning 56–66 to a different hand or
hands (B. D. Sommer, *A Prophet Reads Scripture* [1998], 191–192). Such a position seems
well justified. See further K. M. Heffelfinger, "Isaiah 40–55" (2020), 121.

A Closer Look: "Third Isaiah" as "Under-Rated" Poet    265

condemns. These contrasts appear within poems and the juxtaposition between them is, at times, sharp and marked (e.g., 57:18–21). While Isaiah 40–55 had repeatedly featured juxtapositions in the divine voice's speaking tone (e.g., 41:8–20; 41:21–29; 45:1–8; 45:9–25) and addressed the exiles as a whole, here the voice shifts between consolation and comfort promised to those who choose the divine voice's commands (e.g., 66:1–2, 8–14) and wrath toward those who rebel (e.g., 66:3–6, 15–17, 24). Juxtaposition becomes direct and alternates, even at line level (e.g., 65:13–15) contrasting the attitude toward and future of each group. In this way, Isaiah 56–66 intensifies and makes more immediate the juxtapositions already familiar as a feature of Isaiah 40–55's poetic style.

Intensification also characterizes the trajectory of Isaiah 56–66's imagery. Images already familiar from Isaiah 40–55 are taken further as they appear redeployed in these chapters. Lavish depictions of rebuilt city features (54:11–12) progress to the employment of personified characteristics to name them with "walls" being called "Salvation" and "gates" named "Praise" (60:18). The rebuilt city will be lit with the divine presence (60:19–20). Birthing and maternal imagery progresses from astonishment at the unlikely (49:21; 54:1) to the announcement of the impossible (66:7–8) and shifts from honorific substitutes to direct intervention by God (cf. 49:22–23; 60:16; 66:10–11; 12–13) (see further A Closer Look: Birth and Breastfeeding Imagery in Isaiah 40–66). The memory motif progresses from commands about memory of the "former things"(43:18; 46:9) to divine action that eliminates memory of the "former things" (65:17) (see further A Closer Look: Conflicted Commands and Competing Contentions in the Memory Motif) and the garment imagery progresses from Zion putting on restored ones "like an ornament" (49:18) and being commanded to wear "beautiful garments" (52:1) to the LORD wearing "righteousness" and "fury" (59:17) and those delivered wearing "garments of salvation" (61:10). The people themselves appear to become a divine garment in the image of the restored people as a "crown" in the LORD's hand (62:3).

Isaiah 56–66 demonstrates a particular tendency to synthesize. The feature of uniting distinctive language use from Isaiah 1–39 with that of Isaiah 40–55, which Rendtorff observed in Isaiah 56,[751] bears a similarity to

---

[751]    R. Rendtorff, "Isaiah 56:1" (1993).

266  Commentary

the interweaving of images and language throughout Isaiah 56–66.[752] An important part of the work of these final chapters of the whole book of Isaiah is to draw together the trajectory from warning, to judgment, to restoration (see further A Closer Look: The Final Form and the Former Things). Regularly and repeatedly the poetic prophet draws together motifs from Isaiah 1–39 and Isaiah 40–55 to create a new synthesis (see comments on 56:1–8; 56:9–57:21; 58:1–14; 59:1–21; 65:1–25; 66:1–24).

However, not all of these syntheses produce a "conclusion" that places judgment and warning into a chronological frame. Isaiah 63:7–64:12, for example, complicates Isaiah 40–55's resolution by reopening the complaint through allusion to Lamentations (see further the comment on Isa 63:7–64:12). In the new context of Isaiah 56–66, where deliverance is particularized to those characterized by obedience, warnings and blessings are not simply redistributed into time periods. Ancient promises are reissued and transformed in the process by taking up Isaiah 40–55's vision of restoration and incorporating the division of the community into the restored and the judged.[753] In so doing, the poems of Isaiah 56–66 recast the tension between divine justice and mercy.

This feature is perhaps most apparent in Isaiah 65's reuse of Isaiah 11's vision of God's mountain feast of restoration. While the promises are reissued, it is a selective and transformative reissuing. Feeding imagery overwhelms the earlier passage's interest in both feeding and dwelling together, apparently taking up the concerns over food scarcity in Lamentations and their overturning in the resolution offered in Isaiah 55. However, the selection of creatures included in the vision and the explicit omission of the "serpent" (65:25) from the abundance illustrates the incorporation of differentiation. Precisely in the imagery of a figure associated with resistance to the divine will and the induction of evil into human experience, the poem draws a line between those who receive blessing and those judged (see further commentary on Isaiah 65:1–25).

---

[752] See further J. Stromberg, *Isaiah after Exile* (2011), 75.

[753] See also J. Stromberg, *Isaiah after Exile* (2011), 69–141, for detailed discussion of many allusions in Isaiah 56 and 65–66 to other parts of Isaiah. Stromberg describes the relationship as "continuity and development. Above all else he [i.e., the author of these chapters] affirmed the promises (sometimes amplifying them), while reading with a hermeneutic that withholds those promises from the wicked but opens them to the righteous" (141).

*Isaiah 58:1–14*

This taking up of earlier imagery from Isaiah 1–39, from Isaiah 40–55, and from other biblical texts is a feature of Isaiah 56–66's poetic style. These poems draw the book of Isaiah together and achieve a synthesis of their materials that illustrates how the book may be read as a whole. These poems offer an approach to the book of Isaiah that sees the culmination of warning, punishment, and restoration in a reenvisioning of promises of blessing and punishment together with a focus on differentiation between those who will commit to the ways of the LORD, to justice and righteousness, and those who persist in their own way, ways of deceit, injustice, and oppression. Juxtaposing elements of its vision in these ways, the final poems of the book of Isaiah reoffer an encounter with divine justice and divine mercy in which judgment and justice, mercy and wrath become expressions of the same moment of future divine restoration. In so doing, these final chapters explore the mystery of divinely initiated restoration and the necessity of human ethical response  (see further comment on Isaiah 56:9–57:21).

ISAIAH 58:1–14

> [1] Shout out; do not hold back!
> > Lift up your voice like a trumpet!
> Announce to my people their rebellion,
> > to the house of Jacob their sins.
> [2] Yet day after day they seek me
> > and delight to know my ways,
> as if they were a nation that practiced righteousness
> > and did not forsake the ordinance of their God;
> they ask of me righteous judgments;
> > they want God on their side.
> [3] "Why do we fast, but you do not see?
> > Why humble ourselves, but you do not notice?"
> Look, you serve your own interest on your fast day
> > and oppress all your workers.
> [4] You fast only to quarrel and to fight
> > and to strike with a wicked fist.

Such fasting as you do today
　　　　will not make your voice heard on high.
⁵ Is such the fast that I choose,
　　　　a day to humble oneself?
Is it to bow down the head like a bulrush
　　　　and to lie in sackcloth and ashes?
Will you call this a fast,
　　　　a day acceptable to the LORD?

⁶ Is not this the fast that I choose:
　　　　to loose the bonds of injustice,
　　　　to undo the straps of the yoke,
to let the oppressed go free,
　　　　and to break every yoke?
⁷ Is it not to share your bread with the hungry
　　　　and bring the homeless poor into your house;
when you see the naked, to cover them,
　　　　and not to hide yourself from your own kin?
⁸ Then your light shall break forth like the dawn,
　　　　and your healing shall spring up quickly;
your vindicator shall go before you;
　　　　the glory of the LORD shall be your rear guard.
⁹ Then you shall call, and the LORD will answer;
　　　　you shall cry for help, and he will say, "Here I am."

If you remove the yoke from among you,
　　　　the pointing of the finger, the speaking of evil,
¹⁰ if you offer your food to the hungry
　　　　and satisfy the needs of the afflicted,
then your light shall rise in the darkness
　　　　and your gloom be like the noonday.
¹¹ The LORD will guide you continually
　　　　and satisfy your needs in parched places
　　　　and make your bones strong,
and you shall be like a watered garden,
　　　　like a spring of water
　　　　whose waters never fail.
¹² Your ancient ruins shall be rebuilt;

*Isaiah 58:1–14*                                                                   269

> you shall raise up the foundations of many generations;
> you shall be called the repairer of the breach,
>> the restorer of streets to live in.
>
> <sup>13</sup> If you refrain from trampling the Sabbath,
>> from pursuing your own interests on my holy day;
> if you call the Sabbath a delight
>> and the holy day of the LORD honorable;
> if you honor it, not going your own ways,
>> serving your own interests or pursuing your own affairs;
> <sup>14</sup> then you shall take delight in the LORD,
>> and I will make you ride upon the heights of the earth;
> I will feed you with the heritage of your ancestor Jacob,
>> for the mouth of the LORD has spoken.

This poem commands the audience's attention. It insists that while they persist in pursuing actions that they see as laudable, their perception of what is praise-worthy is not only inaccurate but inverted. Through recurrent word play and sound play the poem enacts an inversion of the people's misunderstanding. They present themselves as worthy recipients of divine attention, but in actuality they are acting unjustly and cloaking their injustice in outward acts of religious devotion. Like those to whom the opening poem of Isaiah is addressed, their religious actions provoke not the favor but the wrath of God. These acts of worship are not accompanied by righteousness but by injustice (see 1:10–20). They are seeking not what God wants, but what they want (58:3, 13).

The poem begins by commanding full attention. The opening imperative invites an unspecified addressee to call out. Such a command to proclaim something recalls earlier poems' injunctions to rejoice at the deliverance the LORD has accomplished (e.g., 42:10–13; 44:23; 49:13). The opening couplet conveys urgency with its pair of commands to "Shout out" and "not hold back."[754] Parallelism intensifies the opening by placing the rarer term "throat" in the first line before the much more common "voice."[755] Similarly, the second line of the couplet announces its

---

[754] J. Muilenburg, "Isaiah 40–66" (1956), 5:678, also perceives "urgency" in this verse.

[755] What the NRSV<sup>ue</sup> translates "Shout out" is composed of the imperative "call" and "with throat." Parallelism typically moves from a more familiar term to a less familiar one as a

270                                                                                    *Commentary*

comparison partner first, emphasizing it through word ordering.[756] The "trumpet" (*šôpār*) appears within the Hebrew Bible both as a warning (see, e.g., Jer 4:19; Ezek 33:3–6) and in connection to worship (see, e.g., Lev 25:9; Ps 81:3 Eng.; 2 Sam 6:15).[757] The opening couplet's intention stands open. Something must be proclaimed with urgency, but much turns on whether the comparison with the horn sounds worship or warning, a particularly open and potent question in the context of this poem's concern with the people's expectations of their fasting.

The second couplet immediately clarifies. Whatever the people might have thought, this is surely a warning. The preceding couplet's word order inversion ceases, and the two lines echo one another in their ordering.[758] The pair "rebellion" and "sin" disambiguate the matter at hand. The "house of Jacob" stands charged with wrongdoing. The opening ambiguity is not incidental, however. It signals the poem's chief message. The "house of Jacob" has inverted the order of the LORD's intention. As the following lines make clear, they have mislabeled their reality, and what they call (opening imperative verb *qĕrā*ʾ, i.e., "call"; NRSV[ue] "Shout") things is not merely a problem of semantics. They have replaced faithfulness with false piety.

The verb "call," which issues the poem's opening imperative, reappears throughout the poem. Its relative frequency in this short poem demonstrates the centrality of the issues it names to the poem's message.[759] The rhetorical question "Will you call this a fast" (58:5) is ironic. They have indeed called it a fast, asking "Why do we fast, but you do not see?" (58:3).

---

     means of moving the reader from the line to its parallel partner with development. On this pattern, see Robert Alter, *The Art of Biblical Poetry* (New York: Basic Books, 1985), 13. By starting with a term that appears only 8 times in the Hebrew Bible, this line reverses the expected pattern of parallelism.

[756]  Typically, Hebrew would put the verb first in a sentence. While this does not necessarily hold as true for poetry, it is fair to say that the second line exhibits an unusual word order. The ordering of this second line creates a chiastic structure with its parallel in the couplet where the verb does appear first. Such a structure places emphasis on "like a trumpet," which now stands both unusually at the start of its line and at the center of the chiasm (see Glossary of Poetic Terminology).

[757]  See also J. L. McKenzie, *Second Isaiah* (1968), 165.

[758]  The verb appears only in the first line and is gapped (see Glossary of Poetic Terminology) in the second. However, the remaining elements (addressee, item to be announced) occur in the same order in both cases.

[759]  This word is among the terms B. S. Childs, *Isaiah* (2001), 476, observes as "repetition of key words." He also includes "delight," see further on this term below.

*Isaiah 58:1–14*                                                                271

However, what they call a "fast" (*ṣôm*, 58:5), is actually a "fight" (*maṣṣâ*, 58:4) and the finding (*timṣĕ ʾû*, 58:3) of their own desires.[760] By juxtaposing their self-named "fast" with terms that invert the order of the main sounds (*ṣm/mṣ*) of the word, the poem has already hinted through sound play that their fast is, in fact, the opposite of a fast. It seems that rather than critiquing religious formalism here, the prophet is indicting self-serving and self-interest.[761] It is not that the people lack desires and purposes but that their desires are their own and for their own gain, rather than those of the LORD.[762]

The poem continues its movement to invert the audience's perspective by declaring what the "fast" the LORD desires looks like. The depiction does not employ either imagery of avoidance of food or self-denial, as might be expected from the standard associations of the word. Instead, food appears as an item not to be avoided but to be shared with those who need it (58:7, 10). The phrase most commonly used for self-denial (*ʿinnînû napšēnû*, 58:3; here NRSV[ue] has "humble ourselves"), as associated especially with the Day of Atonement (see, e.g., Lev 16:29, 31; 23:27, 29, 32), appears in parallel with the sharing of food as a reference to meeting the needs of the "poor" (*ʿăniyyîm*, 58:7) and "afflicted" (*nepeš naʿănah*, 58:10). Rather than "afflicting" them "selves," they should share with others who are "afflicted."

Further developing the imagery of the fast that the LORD wants are recurrent references to the "yoke" (58:6 [twice], 9). Justice and the overturning of oppression are the activities that please the LORD. Further sound play reinforces this point. While the audience are accused of calling their outward shows of piety ("bow down," "lie in sackcloth and ashes,"

---

[760] J. Muilenburg, "Isaiah 40–66" (1956), 5:679–680, helpfully points to "fight" here as "strife" (679) connected to "personal gain and profit" (680) as opposed to irritability related to lack of food.

[761] Contra J. Muilenburg, "Isaiah 40–66" (1956), 5:680; cf. also 677, who indicates the problem of the fast was a focus on "external" rituals without sufficient connection to "expression of the heart and the deepest thought of the mind." For an example of scholarship that sees the problem as "cultic observances," see J. L. McKenzie, *Second Isaiah* (1968), 166.

[762] See B. S. Childs, *Isaiah* (2001), 476–478, who helpfully summarizes positions on the nature of the problem being addressed here, whether external piety or lack of social justice, and convincingly articulates the problem as "self-serving" (478).

58:5) "acceptable" (*rāṣôn*, 58:5), they apparently have control over the things that keep the "oppressed" (*rĕṣûṣîm*, 58:6) bound.[763]

A reorientation of their behavior will result in a change in how the audience are "called" (*qōrā᾽*, 58:12). The promises offered to those who embrace the LORD's preferred fast, that is, those who enact justice and mercy, employ images of "light" (58:8, 10), bountiful provision (58:11), restoration (58:12), and honor (58:12). Most centrally, they are promised that the need they voiced will be resolved. The audience's sense that they have been ignored despite their fasting (58:3) is explicitly resolved in the context of reoriented behavior.[764] If they will embrace justice and generosity, if they will fast from the unrighteousness that they have called piety, then they will "call" (*tiqrā᾽*, 58:9) and God will "answer" (*ya῾ăneh*, 58:9). Ironically, they have been afflicting (verb *῾nh*, 58:3) themselves to receive an "answer" (verb *῾nh*, 58:9), but the thing needed was to care for the afflicted (*῾āniyyîm*, 58:7).[765]

The final appearance of the verb "to call" points to a theme that has underlain the poem as a whole. The people have not chosen injustice over mercy by accident. Rather, their inversion of the LORD's expectations is directly related to their tendency to go after their own intentions rather than the LORD's. Verse 2 presents "delight" (*yeḥpāṣûn*, 58:2 [twice])[766] as an activity of the people in seeking the LORD. Yet the poem makes clear that this "delight" is not an activity of faithfulness. Rather, it stands

---

[763] See Ndikhokele Mtshiselwa, "Reading Isaiah 58 in Conversation with I. J. Mosala: An African Liberationist Approach," *Acta Theologica* (2016): 146, on "self-enriching tendencies."

[764] J. Muilenburg, "Isaiah 40–66" (1956), 5:676, treats this element as an indicator that "It is clear that the prophet was consulted concerning a purely cultic question: 'Why does God take no notice of our fasts?'" Given the Isaian poetry's tendency to use a sense of the audience's perspective rhetorically (e.g., 40:27; 49:14), it does not seem necessary to propose any historical consultation with the prophet on this matter. Instead, the poem represents, while transforming, its audience's perspective. See, interestingly, H. G. M. Williamson, "Promises, Promises! Some Exegetical Reflections on Isaiah 58," *Word & World* (1999): 158, who argues that those who respond to the text "are effectively being told that they will truly make a difference."

[765] See BDB, 772, 776. See also Ndikhokele Mtshiselwa, "An African Philosophical Analysis of Isaiah 58: A Hermeneutic Enthused by Ubuntu," *Scriptura* 116 (2017): 8, https://dx.doi.org/10.7833/116-1-970, on "equitable sharing of resources in order to alleviate poverty" in relation to this passage's concern to counteract self-interest.

[766] NRSV[ue]'s translation "they want God on their side" obscures the second occurrence of "delight" *yeḥpāṣûn* in v. 2. Its footnote suggestion "Or *they delight to draw near to God*" preserves it.

# Isaiah 58:1–14

ironically juxtaposed to their failures in justice and righteousness (58:2). The people's delight has clearly not been in the LORD's justice. Instead, they have pursued their "own interests" (*ḥăpāṣêkā* and *ḥepṣêkā*, both 58:13; cf. also *ḥēpeṣ*, 58:3 where NRSV[ue] reads "own interest"), conveyed using a noun from the same root as "delight."[767] They have followed their own purposes rather than the LORD's purposes. The word used here has appeared frequently in Isaiah 40–55, where it often refers to the plan or purpose of the LORD (see, e.g., 44:28; 46:10; 48:14; 53:10; 55:11). Now they are invited to turn away from their "own interests" and call (*qārā'tā*, 58:13) the things the LORD intends (here specifically the Sabbath)[768] by a new name, a delight (*'ōneg*, 58:13).[769] As the poem draws to a close, it demonstrates the people's misconception of their religious behavior. They have thought that they were pleasing the LORD, but they were pursuing their own way. Like the poem that precedes it with its emphasis on the "way," this poem demands a change of direction.

The chain of conditions indicating what the audience must not do "going your own ways," "serving your own interests," "pursuing your own affairs" (58:13), conveys this poem's charges' connection to the poems that both precede and follow. The emphasis on "way" in the preceding poem is clear, as is this poem's concern over the people's "own interests." In Isaiah 59, they are charged with "talking (*dabber*) oppression and revolt" and speaking "lying words (*dibrê-šāqer*)" (59:13). The final phrase of 58:13 (*wĕdabbēr dābār*, woodenly translated "speaking speech," NRSV[ue]: "pursuing your own affairs") may resonate with these images. When juxtaposed with a poem that expresses its dismay over the misuse of speech and its deployment in a chain of references that moves through the charges of the previous poem, the current poem, and the poem following, a pattern

---

[767] See also J. Muilenburg, "Isaiah 40–66" (1956), 5:677, J. D. W. Watts, *Isaiah 34–66* (2005), 272, and H. G. M. Williamson, "Promises" (1999), 156.

[768] See J. D. W. Watts, *Isaiah 34–66* (2005), 276, on the Sabbath as connected to divine intention. Contra J. L. McKenzie, *Second Isaiah* (1968), 167, the Sabbath is not "a secondary expansion" but is shown as part of the main emphasis of the poem through the continuation of the "call" motif.

[769] Here, see the insightful comments of B. S. Childs, *Isaiah* (2001), 481. He helpfully notes the issue of "contrast to pursuing one's own business." See, interestingly, N. Mtshiselwa, "African Philosophical" (2017), 7, on the concept of "immorality" as "that which is in opposition to the divine will."

274 *Commentary*

emerges that conveys the problem of the Sabbath as directly tied to the problems of the social evils in this series of poems.

Returning to the opening line's commanding tone, the final words of the poem place a declarative mark of intensity on the poem. The concluding statement "for the mouth of the LORD has spoken" (58:14) occurs only three times in the Hebrew Bible and always in Isaiah.[770] Perhaps tellingly, it appears within the indictment of the worship practices of the people in Isaiah 1:20 alongside the warning "If you are willing and obedient you shall eat the good of the land, but if you refuse and rebel, you shall be devoured by the sword" (1:19–20). The other occurrence is in Isaiah 40:5 in response to the announcement of the "glory of the LORD." Here, in contrast to their fasting, which is a form of rebellion, they are promised if they will turn away from their behavior and honor what the LORD commands, the LORD will "feed" them (58:14). It appears that this concluding phrase links a claim conveying certain accomplishment of what the LORD announces[771] with allusions to passages elsewhere in Isaiah that convey what the audience have missed. Readers of the canonical book of Isaiah will already know that this kind of rebellion both misses the glory of the LORD and has merited punishment. It is an ominous underscoring of the poem's message.

ISAIAH 59:1–21

¹ See, the LORD's arm is not too short to save,
    nor his ear too dull to hear.
² Rather, your iniquities have been barriers
    between you and your God,
and your sins have hidden his face from you
    so that he does not hear.
³ For your hands are defiled with blood
    and your fingers with iniquity;

---

[770] There is one very close parallel in Micah 4:4, where the phrase is the same except for the inclusion of "of hosts" following LORD.

[771] See also the reference to the "mouth" of the LORD (55:11) in the elaborate image of the certainty of the divine word in Isaiah 55:10–11.

*Isaiah 59:1–21* 275

your lips have spoken lies;
     your tongue mutters wickedness.[772]

4 No one brings suit justly;
     no one goes to law honestly;
they rely on empty pleas; they speak lies,
     conceiving mischief and begetting iniquity.
5 They hatch adders' eggs
     and weave the spider's web;
whoever eats their eggs dies,
     and the crushed egg hatches out a viper.
6 Their webs cannot serve as clothing;
     they cannot cover themselves with what they make.
Their works are works of iniquity,
     and deeds of violence are in their hands.
7 Their feet run to evil,
     and they rush to shed innocent blood;
their thoughts are thoughts of iniquity;
     desolation and destruction are in their highways.
8 The way of peace they do not know,
     and there is no justice in their ways.
Their roads they have made crooked;
     no one who walks in them knows peace.

9 Therefore justice is far from us,
     and deliverance does not reach us;
we wait for light, but there is only darkness;
     and for brightness, but we walk in gloom.
10 We grope like the blind along a wall,
     groping like those who have no eyes;
we stumble at noon as in the twilight,
     among the vigorous as though we were dead.
11 We all growl like bears;
     like doves we moan mournfully.

---

[772] I have deviated from the formatting of the NRSV[ue] here. A new poetic unit begins at v. 4 as indicated by the shift from address to "you" to characterization of "they." C. Westermann, *Isaiah 40–66* (1969), 342, also indicates a break here.

We wait for justice, but there is none;
for salvation, but it is far from us.
[12] For our transgressions before you are many,
and our sins testify against us.
Our transgressions indeed are with us,
and we know our iniquities:
[13] transgressing, and denying the LORD
and turning away from following our God,
talking oppression and revolt,
conceiving lying words and uttering them from the heart.
[14] Justice is turned back,
and deliverance stands at a distance,
for truth stumbles in the public square,
and uprightness cannot enter.
[15] Truth is lacking,
and whoever turns from evil is despoiled.

The LORD saw it, and it displeased him
that there was no justice.
[16] He saw that there was no one
and was appalled that there was no one to intervene,
so his own arm brought him victory,
and his righteousness upheld him.
[17] He put on righteousness like a breastplate
and a helmet of salvation on his head;
he put on garments of vengeance for clothing
and wrapped himself in fury as in a mantle.
[18] According to their deeds, so will he repay
wrath to his adversaries, requital to his enemies;
to the coastlands he will render requital.
[19] So those in the west shall fear the name of the LORD,
and those in the east, his glory,
for he will come like a pent-up stream
that the wind of the LORD drives on.

[20] And he will come to Zion as Redeemer,
to those in Jacob who turn from transgression, says the LORD.

# Isaiah 59:1–21

[21] And as for me, this is my covenant with them, says the LORD: my spirit that is upon you and my words that I have put in your mouth shall not depart out of your mouth or out of the mouths of your children or out of the mouths of your children's children, says the LORD, from now on and forever.

This poem, primarily in the prophetic poet's voice, continues the interest of the preceding poems in overturning unjust and sinful structures in society. The middle of the poem is "we" speech placing confession on the lips of the audience. Vivid imagery offers a compelling vision both of the audience's potential acceptance of the charges against them and of the LORD taking up the righting of these wrongs directly.

Through parallel and opposite deployments of body imagery, the opening stanza contrasts the people's apparent perception that the LORD is unable to help them with the cause of the LORD's inactivity on their behalf, their own sin. Verse 2, standing between the body imagery for the LORD and for the people, makes the cause of the apparent inaction of God clear.

Specific language for parts of the body appears frequently throughout these lines. The LORD's hand (*yad*, i.e., "hand"; NRSV[ue]: "arm"), "ear" (59:1) and "face" (59:2)[773] are juxtaposed with the people's "hands," "fingers," "lips," and "tongue" (59:3). While the metaphors for the LORD's agency are general and common uses such as "hand,"[774] and the power (hand) and perception ("ear") images stand paralleled in a single couplet, the imagery for the people's transgression is both more expansive and more particular, conveying the focus of the poem's interest. Standing in paralleled response to the refuted charge of divine inability, the people's own activity is characterized by reference to your palms (*kappêkem*, i.e., "your palms"; NRSV[ue]: "hands") and "fingers."

The charge "your hands (*kappêkem*) are defiled with blood (*něgō'ălû baddām*, 59:3)" echoes the charge in Isaiah 1:15, "your hands are full of blood (*yědêkem dāmîm mālē'û*)."[775] There, the LORD explicitly proclaims

---

[773] J. Muilenburg, "Isaiah 40–66" (1956), 5:687, highlights this imagery.

[774] See further J. Blenkinsopp, *Isaiah 56–66* (2003), 187.

[775] Scholars who mention Isaiah 1:15 in commenting on this verse include J. Muilenburg, "Isaiah 40–66" (1956), 5:688; J. D. W. Watts, *Isaiah 34–66* (2005), 282, C. Westermann, *Isaiah 40–66* (1969), 346; B. S. Childs, *Isaiah* (2001), 487; and B. Schramm, *Opponents* (1995), 138. C. Westermann, *Isaiah 40–66* (1969), 346, calls them "almost word for word identical."

278                                                                                          *Commentary*

that "I will not listen" and rejects the offering of sacrifices (1:11–15). However, the charge alludes even more closely to Lamentations 4:13–14 where the "sins" of the "prophets" and the "iniquities" of the "priests" result in the depiction of them as "defiled with blood" (*něgō 'ălû baddām*). The verb *g'l* with the meaning "defile" is relatively rare in the Hebrew Bible. It appears in this form only here and in Lam 4:14, where the text is a precise match for the phrase here. Nowhere else is it connected directly with blood[776] and while blood is common enough in the Hebrew Bible, the exact match seems to indicate some relationship between the texts, particularly in light of the likelihood that the prophetic poet knows Lamentations.[777] Together, the pair of allusions depict a people whose leaders have brought them, through violence and corruption, into a situation in which their social fabric is profoundly disrupted implicating all (59:4), their prayers are not heard, and their sacrifices are not accepted. While McKenzie comments, "The prophet does not distinguish between the leading men of the community and others, but there is no doubt that his accusations are primarily directed against those whose power and responsibility are the greatest,"[778] it does not appear that the prophet limits the scope of the accusation. The repeated references to "no one" (vv. 4, 16) aim the charges at the community as a whole. The leaders surely play a role in this matter, but they are not explicitly in view here and the remainder of the community is not left unreferenced.[779]

This poem focuses primarily on the social injustices and acts of corruption and violence that have created this situation as well as its impact upon the people. Unlike either the preceding poem or Isaiah 1, there is no

---

[776] Though note the implied connection present in Isa 63:3, a context that also appears connected to the imagery of Lam 4.

[777] C. Westermann, *Isaiah 40–66* (1969), 348, connects another phrase from Lam 4:14 to Isa 59:10. Taken together the two connections support one another. B. D. Sommer, *A Prophet Reads Scripture* (1998), 272, observes that Lau "argues that Isa 59:3 quotes Lam 4:14 . . . but this suggestion is not fully convincing, since only one phrase is parallel." Interestingly, while the verb "defile" here is nowhere else explicitly connected with blood other than Lam 4:14, it appears in connection with the implicit blood imagery in the winepress of Isaiah 63, a passage that bears other connections to Isaiah 59, on which see the commentary on that passage.

[778] J. L. McKenzie, *Second Isaiah* (1968), 172.

[779] B. S. Childs, *Isaiah* (2001), 487, points out that the accusations "focus on the universal dimension of evil that pervades the entire society." See also B. Schramm, *Opponents* (1995), 138–139.

# Isaiah 59:1–21

specific attention to particular practices of worship. However, the connection between social justice and worship continues to relate to this poem through the juxtaposition of this poem with Isaiah 58 and the allusion to Isaiah 1. This poem highlights the cause and effect of transgression in public life, while the preceding poem emphasized the response to their mistaken complaint that their religious activities were not evoking a response. The two ideas belong together, but this poem more heavily emphasizes guilt and the suffering it brings about.

Verses 4–8 dramatically elaborate the charges that "your iniquities have been barriers" and that "your sins have hidden his face from you" (59:2) (see further A Closer Look: A God Who Hides Himself). No longer directly addressing "you," the prophetic poet employs a series of images to depict the corrupt society that provokes this distance. Depiction of the total absence of public integrity[780] develops into a metaphor presenting sinful behavior as the biological offspring of deceit and dependence upon emptiness.[781]

Spiders and snakes vividly illustrate both the danger and the uselessness of such leadership. Both the "adder" (*ṣip'ônî*) and the "viper" (*'ep'eh*) represent poisonous species, as is made clear both by their other uses (see, e.g., Job 20:16; Isa 11:8; Jer 8:17) and by the reference to death in this context.[782] The "eggs" imagery continues and develops the metaphor of "mischief" and "iniquity" being the offspring of deceptive and unjust structures. The outcome of such a union proves fatal. The transparent and clingy webs of spiders appear as an apt image for the uselessness of such outworkings of corrupt societal structures. In contrast to the garment

---

[780] The NRSV[ue]'s translation of v. 4 interprets the references as being to a judicial process. However, the imagery is a bit more open than that. A wooden translation might render the opening couplet: there is none who calls in righteousness and none governs in faithfulness. Cf. J. Muilenburg, "Isaiah 40–66" (1956), 5:688, who supports reading the lines "forensically." C. Westermann, *Isaiah 40–66* (1969), 346–347, gives relevant parallels for legal resonances for these terms. Legal imagery is a possible meaning, but the lines' meaning is not entirely constrained by such reference. The broader immediate context is of societal corruption that might reasonably include judicial corruption.

[781] The NRSV[ue] here reads "they rely on empty pleas." The word translated "empty pleas" is *tōhû*, which commonly means "formlessness" and is the word used in Gen 1:2 to describe primordial chaos. See further BDB, 1062.

[782] Interestingly, neither the "adder" (*ṣip 'ônî*) nor "viper" (*'ep'eh*) employ the same word for snake as is used for the deceptive figure in Gen 3 NRSV[ue] "serpent" (Heb. *nāḥāš*). While "viper" (3 occurrences) and "adder" (4 occurrences) are both quite rare words, "serpent" (54 occurrences) is significantly more common in the Hebrew Bible.

280                                                                Commentary

imagery deployed for the LORD later in the poem (59:17), the image of spiders' webs as clothing is of something entirely ineffective as a garment, characterized by what Alter calls "flimsy, useless insubstantiality."[783] The attempt to use them in such a way is ridiculous, underscoring the poem's point.

Body imagery reappears with the reference to "feet," "hands," and "blood" returning the imagery to the concern, not simply over ineptitude in societal leadership but over the impact of deception and social corruption (59:6–7). Similarly, the "way" imagery of the final verse of this stanza highlights the absence of peace and presents an image of people persisting in going their own ways in contrast to the ways of the LORD. Neither their "thoughts" (59:7) nor their "ways" are aligned with the desires and purposes of the LORD, an image that evokes the invitation to "return to the LORD" and the promise that "he will abundantly pardon" that accompanied the expansive contrast between the LORD's ways and thoughts and those of the audience in Isaiah 55:7–9. These are people who have clearly not heeded that invitation and whose words and actions have been far from the desires of the LORD. This is the response their concern over the LORD's apparent unresponsiveness to them receives.

Echoing the charges and making them their own, the voice of the "we" offers the audience words to accept their own role in the absence of both "justice" and righteousness ($\d{s}\breve{e}d\bar{a}q\hat{a}$; cf. NRSV[ue] "deliverance," 59:9). By depicting the audience's own struggle in ways that echo earlier prophetic passages, this "confession" carries an element of admission that the audience should have known that their behavior was transgressive and that their suffering was its result.

Darkness and light are common contrasts that appear regularly to illustrate divine deliverance, not least in Isaiah.[784] Here the imagery is deployed to present the desperation of the people's state. They cannot escape the darkness (vv. 9–10). This kind of imagery conveys inescapability in the depiction of the Day of the LORD in Amos 5 where the image of resting against a wall and being "bitten by a snake" (Amos 5:19; cf. Isa

---

[783] R. Alter, *Hebrew Bible* (2019), 819; see also J. Muilenburg, "Isaiah 40–66" (1956), 5:689, who sees the image as conveying "utter futility."
[784] See also J. Muilenburg, "Isaiah 40–66" (1956), 5:690.

*Isaiah 59:1–21* 281

59:10)[785] is parallel to the imagery for the futility of flight imaged as running from a lion and encountering a bear (Amos 5:18–19).[786] In Isaiah 59, the bear's growling portrays the sounds the people themselves make (59:11). Sound imagery conveys the suffering of the people in this image and its paired comparison to the moaning of doves. The sound of u-vowels carries the growl of the bear (*kaddubbîm kullānû*) while plaintive o-vowels convey the sound of doves' cries (*wĕkayyônîm hāgōh*). The plight of the people receives vivid expression in the sound of these lines.

By setting its expression of desperation as a confession (v. 12), the poem offers the audience words to admit their "transgressions" and "sins" and to lament the absence of "justice" and righteousness (the pair appears in 59:9 and 14, in both verses NRSV[ue] renders *ṣĕdāqâ* "deliverance"; see above).[787] The absence of "justice" and "righteousness" is portrayed in compelling personifications joining the "way" imagery (59:8) with the struggle to be near, to enter, and to walk (59:14).

The final stanza of the poem offers the LORD's response to the injustice that the previous stanzas have depicted. In the total absence of a human who will respond (59:16), the LORD will directly enact retribution.[788] The lines that convey the response allude to the earlier depiction of the situation through the repeated use of the same word for absence.[789] Both

---

[785] J. Blenkinsopp, *Isaiah 56–66* (2003), 193, connects Isaiah 59:10's wall imagery to Lam 4:14, "in which people wander blindly, stained with blood through the streets." That passage seems evoked earlier in Isa 59 as noted above and Blenkinsopp's observation adds additional resonances of desperation and destruction to the imagery here.

[786] I am not claiming that there is a literary allusion here. That is, I do not think the evidence is strong enough to support a claim that the prophetic poet in Isaiah 59 is intentionally drawing upon Amos 5. However, the echoes of that prophetic text portray something of the desperation that the prophetic poet conveys when called up in the attentive reader's mind. There is, at the very least, some overlapping imagery for danger, desperation, and inescapability here.

[787] See M. A. Sweeney, *Isaiah 40–66* (2016), 295, who treats the "presentation of the people's confession" here as "persuasive."

[788] The past reference to divine action in vv. 15b–17 (English past tense in the NRSV[ue], waw consecutive imperfect in Hebrew) receives helpful exposition by B. S. Childs, *Isaiah* (2001), 489, drawing on Lau. Childs' comments are worth quoting here: "To describe the intervention of God in establishing righteousness by his own might in the past tense serves to address the present situation in Israel by affirming that God has not been inactive up to this point. The assigning to the past of God's reaction of judgment serves to describe, not one specific moment in history, but the state of the divine will."

[789] Isa 59:4 uses "no one" (*'ên*). The claim in this stanza that there was "no one" employs the same word three times (*'ên*, 59:15–16).

282                                                                                    *Commentary*

garment and body imagery return, but their use is transformed. While earlier they conveyed the ineffectiveness and corruption of the humans and their leaders, here they illustrate the effective and rightful response that the LORD makes to the people's behavior. Instead of the filmy, useless garments of spiders' webs that the corrupt ones were unable to dress themselves in, the LORD puts on solid, protective military garb ("breastplate," "helmet") composed of "righteousness," "salvation," and "fury" (59:17). Combined with the body imagery (eyes, "arm," "head")[790] and the references to "vengeance" and "fury," the depiction of the divine warrior appropriately evokes a response of "fear" (59:19).

The emphasis of this response is on retribution. It is not fury and wrath for their own sake but a visiting of a just punishment upon those who have been unjust.[791] The pairing of the activity of recompense (*yĕšallēm*, v. 18 twice; NRSV[ue]: "will he repay" and "he will render") and "requital" (*gĕmulôt* v. 18 / *gĕmûl*, v. 18 twice) frames the triplet emphasizing the appropriateness of divine response both through repetition of these terms related to the returning of specific deeds upon the perpetrator and also through the patterning of their appearance. The first line of the couplet places the two terms in precise and equal parallel. The entire line is an iteration of the direct correlation between the LORD's response and the deeds to which the LORD responds (*kĕ ʿal gĕmulôt kĕ ʿal yĕšallēm*) and the two terms appear juxtaposed in the final line resulting in the NRSV[ue]'s translation "he will render requital." The verb "recompense" is from the same root as the noun "peace," which earlier conveyed what the violent transgressors "do not know" (v. 8). While the verb can convey completion or wholeness, here it is clear that such things are not the recompense that the transgressors are about to receive. The LORD's restitution for the wrongs that the poem has so vividly presented comes with the violent intensity of a rushing river.

What was absent in the lines about the divine warrior appears in the final lines of the poem. While recompense did not refer to those who repented, but only those for whom wrath was imminent (59:18), the poem concludes with the promise of a more positive future for those who will

---

[790] The line NRSV[ue] translates "it displeased him" (59:15) includes a reference to eyes in the idiom that could be more woodenly rendered "it was evil in his eyes."

[791] See further J. Blenkinsopp, *Isaiah 56–66* (2003), 198–199.

*Isaiah 60:1–22* 283

"turn from transgression."[792] Such a move has been prepared for by the "we" lines of the poem, which offered the opportunity for the audience to recognize and confess their own "iniquities" (59:12). Whether poetic, or highly stylized prose, the final verse conveys the permanence of the LORD's commitment, referring to those who will "turn."[793]

The poem follows closely the preceding depictions of a people who have turned away from following the LORD's intentions and have practiced injustice and deceit. In this poem, there is little indication of a worship setting as the problem, except through allusion to other texts. Instead, the focus is upon the results in society when the people turn away from the "justice" and "righteousness" that the LORD demands. The poem depicts the LORD enacting justice directly through retribution for those who perpetrate these problems and the hope of deliverance for those who will repent. The poem offers a vision of God who is on the side of justice and who will punish those who reject the demand for justice. At the same time, it enacts the response it aims to evoke. It offers confessional words in "we" form, making it apparent that the vivid imagery of societal ruin and just recompense are designed to poetically and emotionally invite a repentant response.

## ISAIAH 60:1–22

¹ Arise, shine, for your light has come,
    and the glory of the LORD has risen upon you.
² For darkness shall cover the earth

---

[792] J. Blenkinsopp, *Isaiah 56–66* (2003), 200, offers those who repent as a possible reference of v. 21, nothing "The covenant promised would in that case be restricted to one section of the people – the group that emerges with increasing clarity as we read on through these chapters."

[793] Verse 21 has been viewed as a prose addition to the poem (e.g., J. McKenzie, *Second Isaiah* [1968], 171; J. Muilenburg, "Isaiah 40–66," [1956], 5:696; See the helpful discussion of the history of this issue in J. Blenkinsopp, *Isaiah 56–66* [2003], 200). While it does seem that the movement is away from a clearly discernible poetics here (though cf. J. D. W. Watts, *Isaiah 34–66* [2005], 285 and C. Westermann, *Isaiah 40–66* [1969], 344, who present the text in poetic lines), the conclusion belongs to the rhetorical aims of the final version of the poem, drawing together divine commitment and the reference to repentance in v. 20. B. S. Childs, *Isaiah* (2001), 486, calls it "an interpretive epilogue." See also his comments on page 490.

284                                    *Commentary*

and thick darkness the peoples,
  but the LORD will arise upon you,
    and his glory will appear over you.
³ Nations shall come to your light
    and kings to the brightness of your dawn.
⁴ Lift up your eyes and look around;
    they all gather together; they come to you;
your sons shall come from far away,
    and your daughters shall be carried in their nurses' arms.
⁵ Then you shall see and be radiant;
    your heart shall thrill and rejoice,
because the abundance of the sea shall be brought to you;
    the wealth of the nations shall come to you.
⁶ A multitude of camels shall cover you,
    the young camels of Midian and Ephah;
    all those from Sheba shall come.
They shall bring gold and frankincense
    and shall proclaim the praise of the LORD.
⁷ All the flocks of Kedar shall be gathered to you;
    the rams of Nebaioth shall minister to you;
they shall be acceptable on my altar,
    and I will glorify my glorious house.

⁸ Who are these that fly like a cloud
    and like doves to their windows?
⁹ For the coastlands shall wait for me,
    the ships of Tarshish first,
to bring your children from far away,
    their silver and gold with them,
for the name of the LORD your God
    and for the Holy One of Israel,
    because he has glorified you.
¹⁰ Foreigners shall build up your walls,
    and their kings shall minister to you,
for in my wrath I struck you down,
    but in my favor I have had mercy on you.

*Isaiah 60:1–22*

<sup>11</sup> Your gates shall always be open;
>    day and night they shall not be shut,
so that nations shall bring you their wealth,
>    with their kings led in procession.
<sup>12</sup> For the nation and kingdom
>    that will not serve you shall perish;
>    those nations shall be utterly laid waste.
<sup>13</sup> The glory of Lebanon shall come to you,
>    the cypress, the plane, and the pine,
to beautify the place of my sanctuary,
>    and I will glorify where my feet rest.
<sup>14</sup> The descendants of those who oppressed you
>    shall come bending low to you,
and all who despised you
>    shall bow down at your feet;
they shall call you the City of the LORD,
>    the Zion of the Holy One of Israel.
<sup>15</sup> Whereas you have been forsaken and hated,
>    with no one passing through,
I will make you majestic forever,
>    a joy from age to age.
<sup>16</sup> You shall suck the milk of nations;
>    you shall suck the breasts of kings,
and you shall know that I, the LORD, am your Savior
>    and your Redeemer, the Mighty One of Jacob.

<sup>17</sup> Instead of bronze I will bring gold;
>    instead of iron I will bring silver;
instead of wood, bronze;
>    instead of stones, iron.
I will appoint Peace as your overseer
>    and Righteousness as your taskmaster.
<sup>18</sup> Violence shall no more be heard in your land,
>    devastation or destruction within your borders;
you shall call your walls Salvation
>    and your gates Praise.

286                                                                    *Commentary*

¹⁹ The sun shall no longer be your light by day,
            nor for brightness shall the moon give light to you by night,[794]
but the LORD will be your everlasting light,
            and your God will be your glory.
²⁰ Your sun shall no more go down
            or your moon withdraw itself,
for the LORD will be your everlasting light,
            and your days of mourning shall be ended.
²¹ Your people shall all be righteous;
            they shall possess the land forever.
They are the shoot that I planted,
            the work of my hands, so that I might be glorified.[795]
²² The least of them shall become a clan
            and the smallest one a mighty nation;
I am the LORD;
            in its time I will accomplish it quickly.

As a whole, this poem stands in stark contrast to the three poems immediately preceding it, each of which focused on correcting the audience's iniquity. In two of them a contrast between light and darkness imagery reinforces the charges of wickedness and its outcomes (58:10; 59:9).[796] In Isaiah 60, light, restoration, and rejoicing are central and iniquity and transgression do not appear. This poem does not articulate conditions for such blessing.[797] Instead, it dramatically elaborates promises of restoration that have already been made. The focus is on the lavishness of this restoration and the LORD's ability to accomplish it entirely. It creates an encounter with a voice that enacts exuberant reassurance and reversal.[798]

---

[794] I am departing from the NRSV^ue's lineation here. Parallelism suggests a single couplet.

[795] I am departing from the NRSV^ue's lineation here and following MT. This division of the line pair's elements better reflects the balance of the elements in the Hebrew.

[796] See also J. Muilenburg, "Isaiah 40–66" (1956), 5:697, on the contrast between Isa 60 and what precedes.

[797] Note the absence of divisions within the community here. Christopher M. Jones, "'The Wealth of Nations Shall Come to You': Light, Tribute, and Implacement in Isaiah 60," *VT* 64 (2014): 613, observes that this absence is a significant element in the argument that Isa 60–62 form the "compositional core" of 56–66.

[798] An interesting case drawing on spatial theory is made by C. M. Jones, "Wealth" (2014), 612, to argue that "The imagery is spectacular, sublime, and utterly outside the realm of historical plausibility. Its purpose, I argue, is not to convince its audience that contemporaneous historical events will lead to Jerusalem's restoration; it is rather to

*Isaiah 60:1–22*

287

The poem expansively picks up motifs of restoration that are already familiar to the reader of the whole book of Isaiah (see further A Closer Look: The Final Form and the Former Things and A Closer Look: "Third Isaiah" as "Under-Rated" Poet). Two main images of restoration dominate this poem: light and an influx of people from far away. The association of light with deliverance or blessing (e.g., Ps 27:1; 97:11; Job 30:26) and darkness with punishment (e.g., Jer 13:16; Ezek 32:8; Joel 2:2, Micah 3:6) is not unusual in the Hebrew Bible, nor is the parallel drawn between these images (see, e.g., Isa 45:7, 59:9; Amos 5:18, 20; Lam 3:2). Here, light as image of blessing is joined to the image of peoples flooding into the restored city through juxtaposition. Such a correlation is implied, though not developed or explicitly expressed, in Isaiah 2. There the future is envisioned as one in which nations will be drawn to "the mountain of the LORD's house" because of the teaching that will go out from there (2:2–3) and this image stands alongside a plea to the people to "walk in the light of the LORD" (2:5).[799] Light dawning on "a land of deep darkness" is also offered as an image of "the latter time" of "joy" and deliverance from the "oppressor" (9:1–4).[800] In Isaiah 60's exuberant expansion of the motif of restoration as light, the opening lines parallel light to the LORD's "glory," which stands in dramatic contrast to the "thick darkness" of the surrounding world (60:2). Out of their darkness, the nations are drawn to the light of the divine glory that has settled upon Jerusalem.[801]

Toward the end of the poem, this motif reappears, significantly more expanded and directly associated with imagery of the rebuilt city. The

---

persuade them of Yhwh's power to subvert history itself in the city's favor." On "reversal," see Gary Stansell, "The Nations' Journey to Zion: Pilgrimage and Tribute as Metaphor in the Book of Isaiah," in *The Desert Will Bloom: Poetic Visions in Isaiah*, (ed. A. Joseph Everson and Hyun Chul Paul Kim; Atlanta: Society of Biblical Literature, 2009), 239, who highlights the "reversal" where Zion gains wealth having been "despoiled" and "oppressors will assume the position of the servant class."

[799] H. G. M. Williamson, *Book Called Isaiah* (1994), 148–149, discusses thematic resonances between Isa 60 and Isa 2:2–4.

[800] B. S. Childs, *Isaiah* (2001), 496, notes some of these resonances but does not develop the observation in detail. See also Carol J. Dempsey, "From Desolation to Delight: The Transformative Vision of Isaiah 60–62," in *The Desert Will Bloom: Poetic Visions in Isaiah* (ed. A. Joseph Everson and Hyun Chul Paul Kim; Atlanta: Society of Biblical Literature, 2009), 230.

[801] The association of the place of restoration and the city is not explicit in the opening lines but becomes clear as the rebuilding and return of children images develop in the following verses.

288                                                                    *Commentary*

poem envisions a city in which the heavenly lights, assigned to their roles
by the LORD at creation (see Gen 1:14–18), are no longer needed because
the LORD's own presence obliterates the darkness permanently.[802] The
pattern of "day" and "night," with their periods of light and darkness, are
contrasted with the "everlasting" quality of this light of the divine
"glory" (60:19–20).

More extravagantly expanded are the images of an influx of people
(60:4–16), which appear between the occurrences of the light motif
(60:1–3, 19–20). These gathering multitudes are worshippers (60:6–7)
coming to the "mountain of the LORD's house" (2:2–3).[803] They are
"nurses" bringing back exiled "children" (60:4, 9; see 49:22). They are
rebuilders (60:10; see 49:17).[804] They are tribute bearers bringing lavish
gifts: their "wealth" (60:5, 11), "gold and frankincense" (60:6), livestock
(60:6, 7), and trees for building materials (60:13) (see further A Closer
Look: The Reforestation Imagery of Isaiah 40–66 in the Context of the
Book of Isaiah). They are former oppressors transformed into servants
(60:12; cf. 14:2 where NRSV[ue] translates "slaves") who "bow down"
(60:14).[805] Isaiah 55 had proclaimed that "nations that you do not know"
would come (55:5). In expressive expansion of this and Isaiah 2's general
reference to "nations," Isaiah 60 names specific nations both familiar
(Midian, v. 6; Sheba, v. 6; Kedar, v. 7; Lebanon v. 13; Tarshish, v. 9)[806]

---

[802]  See also J. Muilenburg, "Isaiah 40–66" (1956), 5:706.

[803]  J. Muilenburg, "Isaiah 40–66" (1956), 5:698, helpfully points out that the items brought
by the nations can be connected to Temple worship. In addition, the absence of
reference to human drivers of the flocks of animals contributes to the sense of "self-
sacrificing" offerings. See this language in Roy D. Wells, "'They All Gather, They Come
to You': History, Utopia, and the Reading of Isaiah 49:18–26 and 60:4–16," in *The Desert
Will Bloom: Poetic Visions in Isaiah*, (ed. A. Joseph Everson and Hyun Chul Paul Kim;
Atlanta: Society of Biblical Literature, 2009), 207, though his depiction of "singing
camels" does not appear supported by the text.

[804]  B. S. Childs, *Isaiah* (2001), 496, sees Isa 49 as "provid[ing] the context for the entire
chapter." See also C. W. Jones, "Wealth" (2014), 617; and R. Alter, *Hebrew Bible*
(2019), 823.

[805]  J. Muilenburg, "Isaiah 40–66" (1956), 5:702, points out the reversal "As once foreigners
destroyed the city, foreigners will rebuild it."

[806]  Each of these nations appear numerous times in the Hebrew Bible in a number of
contexts. Midian is an enemy during Gideon's leadership period (Judg 6–9) and
collaborates with Moab to hire Balaam to curse Israel during the wilderness
wanderings (Num 22). Moses' father-in-law was a Midianite (Exod 2:15–22). Sheba is
known for its queen who visited Solomon in 1 Kgs 10. Kedar appears in a number of
prophetic and poetic texts (e.g. Isa 21:16, 17; 42:11, Jer 2:10; 49:28; Ezek 27:21; Ps 120:5).

# Isaiah 60:1–22

and unfamiliar (e.g., Ephah, v. 6; Nebaioth, v. 7),[807] those near (Lebanon)[808] and those far off (Tarshish),[809] those that have brought these gifts or supplies in the past (Sheba, Lebanon)[810] and those who have been traditional enemies (Midian).[811] The specific names of these places and the lavishness of their specific gifts expands and underscores the grandness of this vision of exaltation and restoration. Details highlight the expansiveness of the vision.

Alongside the lavishness of this image, the reuse of previous imagery underscores this restoration's security. In a line that picks up the language of the definitive turn from wrath to mercy in Isaiah 54:7–8, this poem sets that turn from "wrath" (*qeṣep*, 54:8; *qiṣpî*, 60:10) to "mercy" (*riḥamtîk* 54:8; cf. NRSV[ue] "compassion"; *riḥamtîk*, 60:10; cf. NRSV[ue] "mercy") into the midst of promises of rebuilding and foreign tribute. So secure is the promise of peace that there is no need to shut the gates. Instead, these typically defensive city structures are left open to allow the gifts of the nations to flood in at all times (60:11).[812]

The references to "kings" also surround and underscore the security and exuberance of the promise of the reversal from wrath to restoration.[813] In the ancient Near East, these figures represent not just might and political authority but military force as well. Kings led armies and a king's

---

Lebanon appears frequently as a place name (e.g., Deut 1:7; 3:25; 11:24; Josh 1:4; 9:1; 11:17; 12:7; Judg 3:3).

[807] Ephah occurs only here and in Gen 25:4, 1 Chron 1:33, and 1 Chron 2:46–47 each of which are genealogies. Nebaioth occurs in genealogies in Gen 25:13, Gen 36:3, and 1 Chron 1:29 as well as in a brief account of Esau taking an additional wife in Gen 28:9. Blenkinsopp's claim that all represent "established Arabian trade partners" (J. Blenkinsopp, *Isaiah 56–66* [2003], 213) requires subsuming Ephah into Midian and Nebaioth into Kedar.

[808] Lebanon is referenced in the description of the Israelites' destination when they are to journey to the promised land (Deut 1:7)

[809] Tarshish is commonly an image of a distant seafaring people. It is to Tarshish that Jonah attempts to go when sent to Nineveh (Jonah 1:3). See BDB, 1076–1077, "a distant port." As J. Blenkinsopp, *Isaiah 56–66* (2003), 215, notes "it is quite possible that the author was as uncertain of its precise location as we are."

[810] The Queen of Sheba honored Solomon with "gold" and "spices" 1 Kgs 10:10, Lebanon supplied wood for the Temple's construction 1 Kgs 5:1–12.

[811] See especially Judg 6–9 and note C. J. Dempsey, "From Desolation to Delight" (2009), 221.

[812] Contra B. S. Childs, *Isaiah* (2001), 497, these elements of peace and inflowing wealth do not require a choice between them. The open gates convey both elements poetically. C. Westermann, *Isaiah 40–66* (1969), 360, holds these elements together.

[813] See G. Stansell, "Nations" (2009), 239, on reversal.

dominance over surrounding nations was secured on the battlefield (e.g., 1 Sam 8:20; 2 Sam 11:1; 1 Kgs 22:31). Standing in parallel to the promise that the defensive structures of the walls will be rebuilt by those of other nations, the image of kings both rendering service (60:10)[814] and bringing tribute (60:11) conveys the absence of any military threat from those who would be responsible for bringing it. The poem reinforces the totality of this security through a sound play between the verbs "serve" (root ʿbd, 60:12) and "perish" (root ʾbd, 60:12). Those who will not do the former, will experience the latter.[815] The idea of such security had reinforced the initial promise of the definitive turn from wrath in Isa 54, where "the heritage" of the LORD's "servants" included the ineffectiveness of any "weapon" and the promise that anyone who brought contention against them would "fall" on account of them (54:15–17). Here, such a promise is incorporated into the vision of lavish security and tribute.

The kings reappear in a puzzling image that intensifies the turn from "forsaken" to richly blessed. The poem takes up the language of exilic suffering, "forsaken" (ʿăzûbâ, 60:15; cf. 49:14; 54:6), overturning it with honor (gě'ôn, NRSV[ue]: "majestic" 60:15. See, e.g., 2:10, 19, 21; 4:2; 24:14) and "joy" (měśôś, see, e.g., 24:8, 11; 32:13, 14). Language dominant in the response to the exiles (40–55) stands parallel to language that appears in the warnings offered to those before the exile. It is in that context that the people are promised "You shall suck the milk of nations; you shall suck the breasts of kings" (60:16). The absence of sufficient sustenance for nursing children was one expression of the severe suffering of the residents of Jerusalem in the aftermath of its fall to Babylon (Lam 4:3–4).[816] In the

---

[814] The verb employed here from the root šrt can refer either to service in the worshipping community, i.e., ministry in the Temple (e.g., 1 Kgs 8:11; Deut 10:8; 17:12) or a position of service in the household or royal court, i.e., the activities of a "servant" (e.g., Gen 39:4; 40:4; 2 Sam 13:17; Est 1:10). The latter seems more likely the connotation here in the context and in light of the use of the verb more closely connected with the work of a servant or slave in v. 12.

[815] B. S. Childs, *Isaiah* (2001), 497–498, rejects the "nationalism" some scholars attribute to this verse. He points out that "the polarity, which is consistent throughout Third Isaiah, is between those who turn to Yahweh, including foreigners, and those who resist God's will." Here, however, the nations are clearly in view and, as noted above, the polarity of righteous and wicked is absent in this chapter (see further Bridging the Horizons: "Third Isaiah" and the Divided Society). The text's exuberance in restoration expresses Zion's reversal of fortunes from oppressed servant of the oppressor to the recipient of the former oppressors' service. See G. Stansell, "Nations" (2009), 239.

[816] See K. M. Heffelfinger, "I Am He" (2021), 91–95.

# Isaiah 60:1–22

restoration imagery, the role of "kings" in supporting Zion's children stood in parallel to the use of "their queens" as "nursing mothers" (49:23). This image intensifies that one, not merely supplying the physical needs of the most vulnerable of society but explicitly feminizing the warrior-leaders of the other nations. Milk, which is only present by implication in the nursing imagery of Lamentations and Isaiah 49 but stands in parallel to it here, is both an image of the emptiness of land in its destruction (7:22) and of the lavish provision of restoration (55:1). Together, the promise of the "milk of nations" and the "breasts of kings" envision an extravagant reversal of suffering and subjugation that goes beyond what is naturally conceivable (see further A Closer Look: Birth and Breastfeeding Imagery in Isaiah 40–66).[817]

This extravagant restoration comes from the hand of the LORD. It is the LORD whose glory lightens the city and draws the nations (60:1, 3). It is for the sake of "the name of the LORD your God" that "children," "gold," and "silver" are brought (60:9). The divine voice promises to replace metals and wood with more precious items (60:17). In that context, two compelling sets of personifications appear. While the poem has elaborately depicted the removal of human overlords, the people are not to be left without oversight. Instead, the LORD will be the one to put "Peace" and "Righteousness" in charge of them. Rather than a human figure whose role it is to bring about these things, and who is charged with doing them (cf. Ps 72:3), the poem personifies these attributes offering a vision of a city in which Peace itself rules and Righteousness determines the work.[818] In a parallel image, the boundaries of the city ("your walls" *ḥômōtayik* and

---

[817] J. Blenkinsopp, *Isaiah 56–66* (2003), 216, reads the images as "a metaphor for 'milking' the resources of the Gentiles and their rulers." While the image is certainly metaphorical, "translation" into an economic idiom is but one element of its potential meaning. It is also consistent with Isaian modes of deploying reversal imagery (e.g., 49:26). See also R. D. Wells, "They All Gather" (2009), 213. The apparently impossible nature of the image carries the freight of the shocking and overwhelmingly transformative nature of the reversal.

[818] The word translated "taskmaster" here is used of those who oversaw the work of the Hebrews in their labor for Pharoah in the book of Exodus (see e.g., Exod 3:7; 5:6, 10, 13, 14 where NRSV[ue] translates "taskmaster"). It seems at times to convey "oppressor" as in Isa 3:12; 14:4; Zec 9:8. NRSV[ue] translates "oppressor" in each of these cases. See BDB, 620. J. Blenkinsopp, *Isaiah 56–66* (2003), 216, notes its "strong negative connotations." See also B. S. Childs, *Isaiah* (2001), 498.

"your gates" *šĕʿārayik*, 60:18), whose associations have shifted away from defense in the poem's earlier imagery, are renamed "Salvation" (*yĕšûʿâ*) and "Praise" (60:18). Echoing and intensifying the imagery of Isaiah 26:1–2, the "walls" (*ḥômôt*, 26:1) and "gates" (*šĕʿārîm*, 26:2) which there were established for deliverance, or salvation (*yĕšûʿâ*; NRSV[ue]: "as a safeguard," 26:1), are now imagined as so fully fulfilling that role that this becomes their name. The LORD is bringing about a restoration that aligns with the expectations created by the poems that have preceded this one in the book but that astoundingly surpasses them. The final line of the poem reemphasizes the insistence that all of this comes from the LORD, adding an expectation of imminent accomplishment to the already established themes of security and abundance.

This poem invites the audience into an overwhelmingly positive vision of their future. In light of the final form of the book of Isaiah as a whole, they have been warned of the consequences of their injustice and social evil and their turning away from faithful worship. They have also been responded to in compassion, comfort, and reconciliation in the aftermath of those consequences. For an audience sitting in the post-return restoration community, who have apparently fallen short of the ideal response to God's mercy, this vision gathers ancient promises and weds them to a vision of a renewed and restored future. They have again been called to repentance (Isa 57–59) and they are reminded of the journey of waywardness and return that has already been traveled. The promise of hope and reconciliation continues in another time and place.

### BRIDGING THE HORIZONS: "THIRD ISAIAH" AND THE DIVIDED SOCIETY

At times, the world of Isaiah 56–66 seems eerily familiar. It is a world where "truth stumbles in the public square" (59:14), where "No one brings suit justly; no one goes to law honestly" (59:4), where pursuing your "own gain" (56:11), "serving your own interests" (58:13), and choosing your "own ways" (57:17, 58:13; 66:3) and "own devices" (65:2) seem to be persistent problems, where foreigners apparently fear exclusion (56:3) and where a clear line appears drawn between opposing groups (65:13–15). Our own moment is evidently one of isolation, of divisiveness, intense competition,

# Bridging the Horizons: "Third Isaiah" and the Divided Society 293

suspicion, and lack of trust.[819] Today's reader might reasonably feel wary of a text that appears to deal with the problems of its own day by envisioning society's flourishing as involving the blessing of the servants and the destruction of enemies (e.g., 66:14–16). These words address their own moment and its struggles, and they must be read and interpreted with care. It would not be helpful, nor an appropriate application of this text, to claim the position of "servants" for those we agree with, for example, and to apply a corresponding dismissal to our rivals. Indeed, this would be essentially to read against the text's own insistence that serving our own interests is damaging.

It seems no accident that a fragmented and fractured society might be addressed by poems like these. Poems shape their hearers' internal disposition. They shape attitudes and orientations and in this way powerfully impact behaviors (see Bridging the Horizons: On Loving Poetry and Poetry's Loves). By remaining attuned to them, readers practice mental habits that have the potential to shape habits of being. That is, they can help produce greater attentiveness, empathy, humility, and creative synthesis.

Arguably, genuine, empathetic, sustained attention both merits practice in our cultural moment and undercuts our tendency toward divisiveness. Where our attention is fleeting, reductive, or commodifying, it prevents the kind of human engagement that allows relationships to flourish.[820] Shortened, unfocussed attention alongside profound levels of loneliness appear as both symptoms and further causes of the divisiveness of much of the contemporary West.[821] When poems like these, by enacting an encounter with a complex and difficult voice, force their audience to give and practice extended, focused attention, they may, over time, produce the kind of patience that must flourish for us to hear one another fully, to encounter

---

[819] See, e.g., the description in J. Sacks, *Morality* (2020), esp. 1–10.

[820] As J. Blake Couey and Elaine T. James, "Introduction," in *Biblical Poetry and the Art of Close Reading* (Cambridge: Cambridge University Press, 2018), 11, put it, "Sustained attention – to a poem, a painting, nature, another person – grows out of a kind of commitment in short supply in a society that values multitasking over intense focus, casual encounters over committed relationships, click-bait over sustained analysis."

[821] See the description of contemporary loneliness and its impact in J. Sacks, *Morality* (2020), 25–37, and the description of studies of attention span in J. Sacks, *Morality* (2020), 53.

others as people, and to move beyond divisive argumentative relationships.[822]

Similarly, poetic ambiguity produces humility, another essential character trait for healing divisive relationship breakdown. These poems are difficult. They invite their audience to be unsettled by their strangeness and in so doing have the potential to produce a willingness to admit to one's own uncertainty.[823] In order for mutual and enriching relationships to develop, human beings must be able to embrace the truth that there is more to know than what they already hold and that the experience and life of another will inevitably include things that they do not understand. The tendency toward reinforcement of one's own viewpoint through increasingly limited interactions with those who differ is a well-documented phenomenon and a strong contributor to personal isolation and polarization of viewpoints.[824] The cultivation of genuine relationships across lines of significant difference might be one of the most practical responses that people disturbed by the polarization of the contemporary world can make.[825] The skills for developing those relationships can be practiced with ancient poems like these.[826]

Finally, Isaiah 56–66 shows a particular fondness for drawing together divergent or disparate motifs into a new synthesis (see Bridging the Horizons: "Third Isaiah" as "Under-Rated" Poet). This ability is also one that may well pose possibilities in its very way of being for our own context of disparate apparent opposites. Where we learn creative synthesis we learn to look for such possibilities, and we may well find them in places and situations that seem beyond reconciling.

Isaiah 56–66 does not always look for reconciliation of all perspectives. It has some exclusive views and paints the future in stark colors for its

---

[822] See K. M. Heffelfinger, 'Truth and Hidden Things' (2023), 172–173.

[823] See K. M. Heffelfinger, 'Truth and Hidden Things,' (2023) 159–160.

[824] J. Sacks, *Morality* (2020), 168–169.

[825] An interesting example of listenitng is the "One Small Step" project from StoryCorps, which presents its approach to pairing politically opposed Americans for story sharing about their lives as a response to current "divisions" and as developing out of "contact theory." See https://storycorps.org/discover/onesmallstep.

[826] Jacobs, *Breaking Bread* (2020), 36, suggests that the kind of "reckoning with otherness" that attention to literature can offer can be "useful in helping me learn to deal with my actual 'on-the-ground' neighbors," though the development of this skill through such reading is not "inevitable."

*Isaiah 61:1–11* 295

audience to imagine. However, its form does not suggest that such a separation is one to arrive at lightly. Rather, through wrestling and struggling toward the best possible engagement, through the development of empathy, through honest humility and through the practice of creative synthesis, it may form readers in habits of the mind that enable them to slowly, carefully, and with great patience learn to do the very difficult work of finding a home in a world of constantly competing tensions.

The impact of the poetic form in shaping humility, attention, empathy, and creative synthesis collaborates with the more overt aims of these poems' persuasion. They aim to shape their hearers into "servants" (see A Closer Look: From Servant to Servants). If we read for the attitudes, dispositions, and habits that the poems seek to form we discover humility, contrition, and fidelity to the ways of the LORD. These become appealing precisely because they are part of a flourishing world. Here we see a world that thrives when traditional barriers are set aside in favor of fidelity to the ways of God and people are defined not by their origins or experiences but by their obedience (56:3–8). Here is a world where "delight" is found precisely in setting aside self-interest and embracing generosity, justice, and the rejection of oppression (58:6–14), and an orientation toward humility and contrition characterizes the people with whom God chooses to "dwell"(57:15). This is a world in which human behavior embraces the ways of the righteous one (e.g., 64:5) and self-interest is set aside for divine interest (e.g., 58:13). This is the context in which the "wolf and lamb" can "feed together" (65:25), truly a "new heavens" and "new earth" (65:17; 66:22).

ISAIAH 61:1–11

¹ The spirit of the Lord GOD is upon me
  because the LORD has anointed me;
he has sent me to bring good news to the oppressed,
  to bind up the brokenhearted,
to proclaim liberty to the captives
  and release to the prisoners,
² to proclaim the year of the LORD's favor
  and the day of vengeance of our God,

to comfort all who mourn,[827]
 ³ to provide for those who mourn in Zion –
to give them a garland instead of ashes,
  the oil of gladness instead of mourning,
  the mantle of praise instead of a faint spirit.
They will be called oaks of righteousness,
  the planting of the LORD, to display his glory.
⁴ They shall build up the ancient ruins,
  they shall raise up the former devastations;
they shall repair the ruined cities,
  the devastations of many generations.

⁵ Strangers shall stand and feed your flocks;
  foreigners shall till your land and dress your vines,
⁶ but you shall be called priests of the LORD;
  you shall be named ministers of our God;
you shall enjoy the wealth of the nations,
  and in their riches you shall glory.
⁷ Because their shame was double
  and dishonor was proclaimed as their lot,
therefore in their land they shall possess a double portion;
  everlasting joy shall be theirs.

⁸ For I, the LORD, love justice,
  I hate robbery and wrongdoing;
I will faithfully give them their recompense,
  and I will make an everlasting covenant with them.
⁹ Their descendants shall be known among the nations
  and their offspring among the peoples;
all who see them shall acknowledge
  that they are a people whom the LORD has blessed.

---

[827] My analysis of the lines differs from NRSV^ue here. The two lines concerned with mourners seem best understood as a couplet. This decision impacts the lineation for the next several lines, continuing until "They will be called oaks of righteousness," where my lineation re-joins that of NRSV^ue.

*Isaiah 61:1–11* 297

<sup>10</sup> I will greatly rejoice in the LORD[828]
  my whole being shall exult in my God,
for he has clothed me with the garments of salvation;
  he has covered me with the robe of righteousness,
as a bridegroom decks himself with a garland
  and as a bride adorns herself with her jewels.
<sup>11</sup> For as the earth brings forth its shoots
  and as a garden causes what is sown in it to spring up,
so the Lord GOD will cause righteousness and praise
  to spring up before all the nations.

In this poem, the audience encounters a voice fully embracing and expressing a divine commission. The imagery closely echoes the Servant personification developed in Isaiah 40–55 (see A Closer Look: The Servant and His "Songs"). Here, a singular, anonymous speaker draws the audience into the expression of and embrace of the commission to comfort and restore. Associations with the personification into which the earlier poems aimed to transform its own audience are strong and the poem's inexplicitness about that association makes the audience overhear and recognize the appealing figure. Imagery is both echoed and reoriented as the audience are moved to envision further a context in which embrace of the Servant's willingness to proclaim God's restoration is not enough. They must unite this commission with its purposes for justice.

In lines that closely parallel his words here, the Servant had been addressed by the LORD with his commission (42:6–7) and had reported what the divine voice had said to him about what he was called to do (49:8–9).[829] Here, while it is still clear that the call comes from God, the

---

[828] The change back to the original voice speaking this poem indicates a new stanza, contra NRSV<sup>ue</sup>.

[829] See B. S. Childs, *Isaiah* (2001), 505; C. Westermann, *Isaiah 40–66* (1969), 365; J. Blenkinsopp, *Isaiah 56–66* (2003), 221; and J. L. McKenzie, *Second Isaiah* (1968), 180. McKenzie is among those who view the poem as spoken by the prophet who "thinks of himself as fulfilling the mission of the Servant." However, it is not necessary to assign the speaker so precisely. Instead, the poetic ambiguity has rhetorical power. As B. S. Childs, *Isaiah* (2001), 503, helpfully comments, "the interpreter's task is to determine the subtle connection that is made between his [the speaker's] mission and that of the servant of Second Isaiah. It is necessary not too quickly to identify the speaker with the servant or with a personal prophetic call of Third Isaiah."

298                                                                      *Commentary*

voice has embraced the call for itself. He speaks about it in his own voice
and as the poem progresses, he enacts the call to "proclaim."

The voice first proclaims that calling in phrases that closely mirror the
form of the Servant's original commission, employing a chain of infinitives
"to bind up," "to proclaim," "to comfort," "to provide" (61:1–3) and referring to the beneficiaries in the third person (61:3–4). However, he then
enacts the commission to "proclaim" restitution to his audience turning to
them as "you" (61:5–7). Without introduction, the divine voice speaks lines
that correspond in their promises and tone with the voice's proclamation
(61:8–9), adding support to its claim to speak at the LORD's instigation
(61:1). Finally, the voice "exult[s]," adding an expression of praise to its
further announcement of the good things that the LORD has done and will
do (61:10–11).[830]

However, this poem does more than return to and continue the Servant
motif of earlier poems. The Servant personified an exemplary response to
the reconciliation that the divine voice offered to the exiles and stood in
contrastive juxtaposition to the voice that most nearly expressed their own
perspective (see A Closer Look: Lady Zion and the Suffering Servant, the
Rhetorical Power of Juxtaposition). Here, the Servant-like voice also
employs motifs that are familiar from the divine voice's words to Zion.
Her "double" punishment (40:2) is named as humiliation, which had been
"double" (*mišneh*, 61:7) and is overturned by a "double" (*mišneh*, 61:7)
allotment[831] and "everlasting joy."[832] The poem's garment imagery (61:10)

---

[830]  Along with B. S. Childs, *Isaiah* (2001), 506, I think the final verses return to the voice
that began the poem. The poetic ambiguity returns and the point of view of this speaker
is that of a voice for whom the divine commission has brought about a new reality.

[831]  As J. Blenkinsopp, *Isaiah 56–66* (2003), 226, points out, the "double" provision is
explicitly "in their land."

[832]  See also C. Westermann, *Isaiah 40–66* (1969), 370. As a number of commentators point
out, there is some difficulty in the translation of verse 7 in light of the mixture of second
and third person pronouns in the Hebrew. NRSV[ue] translates all of them as third
person. J. Blenkinsopp, *Isaiah 56–66* (2003), 218, also handles the difficulty in this way
while C. Westermann, *Isaiah 40–66* (1969), 368, translates with second person pronouns
throughout the verse. A distinction such as that which J. D. W. Watts, *Isaiah 34–66*
(2005), 304, draws between "you" as priests and "them" as the people is not necessary.
The "your" which is the Hebrew pronoun in the first occurrence follows the addressee of
the preceding lines, while "their" in the remaining occurrences matches what follows.
Both contexts point toward blessings and covenant with the restored whole people of
God. Such juxtapositions are not uncommon in exilic Isaiah poems and here it seems
best to view the line as offering the audience a vision of promised well-being, despite the
perplexing pronoun shift within a single couplet.

*Isaiah 61:1–11* 299

takes up the motifs of the reclothing of Zion (52:1) and especially her putting on jewels like a bride (49:18; 61:10). However, here the image is elaborated into "garments of salvation" and "robe of righteousness" (61:10) as well as special celebratory accessories for both bride and groom. The imagery is extravagant and joins imagery for Zion's restoration directly with imagery for the Servant's commission. The proclamation of comfort, the imagery of reconciliation, and the insistence upon justice appear together in this poem, which offers an expression of the embrace of the LORD's intentions for the audience. The juxtaposition between competing responses is no longer needed. Now the images that did this work are employed together to express the desired response. Much like the joining of the "servants" and their "heritage" (54:17) with Zion's restoration in Isaiah 54, this poem interweaves Zion and Servant motifs to push beyond embrace of reconciliation with the LORD toward enacting a righteous and worshipful response.

The voice's claim to have received "the spirit of the LORD" (61:1) reiterates and interprets the divine voice's statement "I have put my spirit upon him; he will bring forth justice to the nations" (42:1). Justice, which figured heavily in the LORD's description of the Servant's purpose (42:1, 3, 4), is here illustrated through repeated images of the reversal of suffering, as well as the "vengeance of our God." This retributive form of justice, "vengeance" (*nāqām*, 61:2), stands by parallelism and sound play alongside the intention "to comfort" (*lěnaḥēm*, 61:2). The voice's commission to "bind up the brokenhearted" and to announce "release to the prisoners" is an embrace of the LORD's intentions to overturn the conditions of suffering and to bring about the radical reversal of the audience's subjection. No longer will they be "slave[s] of rulers" (49:7). Instead, kings will bring them tribute (60:11). This reversal carries strong resonances of economic and social transformation. As Blenkinsopp points out, the "poor" and the "broken hearted" here relate directly to societal conditions including debt slavery as known from Nehemiah.[833] The imagery of overturning, as Childs and others highlight, draws upon the imagery and language of the Levitical Year of Jubilee, which, among other things, included the return of those in debt servitude to their own ancestral lands

---

[833] J. Blenkinsopp, *Isaiah 56–66* (2003), 223–225.

300          *Commentary*

in freedom.[834] Thus, this restoration, even as it envisions glorification of the whole of the people Israel,[835] is grounded in an expectation that such glorification will include the transformation of the material conditions of the poor.[836] Significantly, however, such socioeconomic realities are enveloped within a vision of societal restoration that images the end of exile and return to the land as the remission of debt slavery and a return of Jubilee.[837] The imagery resonates on both levels simultaneously. The economic realities are envisioned as transformed, even as that same imagery is applied to the people's exile.

The sound of the poem conveys the reversal underway. They are to be given a "garland" (*pĕʾēr*) rather than "ashes" (*ʾēper*).[838] Their "mantle" (*maʿăṭēh*), which is "of praise," carries the sounds of another image of what they are, "the planting (*maṭṭaʿ*) of the LORD" (61:3).[839] In addition to these inversions of the orders of sounds, the poem repeats "instead of" (*taḥat*) three times in the short space of three lines, emphatically reiterating this word for reversal, which is already familiar in the book as an image of God's transformation. Similar repetitions of this word expressed the change from thorns to trees in Isaiah 55:13 and conveyed the LORD's replacement of materials with more precious ones in Isaiah 60:17. Through these sounds and repetitions, the poem underscores the claim that the LORD is already enacting the reorienting of the world.

Standing immediately juxtaposed to the preceding poem's repeated insistence that the "kings" would honor (60:10), bring gifts to (60:11), and nourish (60:16) the restored people, this poem's declaration has regal overtones. The "spirit" is "upon" this voice because the LORD has "anointed" (*māšaḥ*, 61:1) him. In addition to being the standard

---

[834]  B. S. Childs, *Isaiah* (2001), 505. See also B. D. Sommer, *A Prophet Reads Scripture* (1998), 142; J. Muilenburg, "Isaiah 40–66" (1956), 5:710; J. D. W. Watts, *Isaiah 34–66* (2005), 303; and M. A. Sweeney, *Isaiah 40–66* (2016), 325. Cf. J. Blenkinsopp, *Isaiah 56–66* (2003), 225, who ties it to the seventh year.

[835]  See J. Blenkinsopp, *Isaiah 56–66* (2003), 224.

[836]  See J. Blenkinsopp, *Isaiah 56–66* (2003), 223, on the "moral" contribution of the prophets regarding the treatment of the poor.

[837]  See Bradley C. Gregory, "The Postexilic Exile in Third Isaiah: Isaiah 61:1–3 in Light of Second Temple Hermeneutics," *JBL* 126 (2007): 484–485, especially his discussion of the connection to Isaiah 40. See also B. D. Sommer, *A Prophet Reads Scripture* (1998), 141.

[838]  See J. Blenkinsopp, *Isaiah 56–66* (2003), 226; and R. Alter, *Hebrew Bible* (2019), 827.

[839]  See C. Westermann, *Isaiah 40–66* (1969), 367; J. D. W. Watts, *Isaiah 34–66* (2005), 300; J. Muilenburg, "Isaiah 40–66" (1956), 5:711.

*Isaiah 61:1–11* 301

terminology for the making of Israel's kings (see, e.g., 1 Sam 10:1; 15:1; 16:13; 2 Sam 2:4; 1 Kgs 1:34; 2 Kgs 9:3),[840] this term in parallel to the "spirit . . . is upon me" evokes the "last words of David" (2 Sam 23:1)[841] who is called "the anointed of the God of Jacob" (2 Sam 23:1) and who opens his poem: "The spirit of the LORD speaks through me" (2 Sam 23:2). This connection between the "spirit" and anointing may reflect the tradition reflected in 1 Sam 16:13 that when Samuel anointed David "the spirit of the LORD came mightily upon David from that day forward." David's poem uses images of "sun rising" and "light" (2 Sam 23:4; cf. Isa 60:1–3, 19–20) to depict a just ruler (2 Sam 23:3) and contrasts God's "everlasting covenant" (2 Sam 23:5) with him to the disposal of the "godless" as "like thorns" (2 Sam 23:6) devoured by "fire" (2 Sam 23:7). David's name has appeared only once in the exilic and postexilic portions of Isaiah. There the promise of "an everlasting covenant" was supported by the enigmatic statement "my steadfast, sure love for David" (55:3) and the thorns were replaced by trees (55:13). Earlier in the canonical book of Isaiah, the expectation of a just ruler who would bring about peace and restoration is associated with David's name (see, e.g., 9:6–7; 16:5). Now this Servant-echoing voice, whose words echo David's, speaks a poem in which the people are to be "oaks of righteousness" (61:3) and that is interrupted by the divine voice, which, among other things, proclaims "an everlasting covenant with them" (61:8).[842]

If the Servant personifies willing and enthusiastic embrace of the LORD's mission for the audience, then this figure's words reiterate that calling for a new time and set of circumstances. The returnees are lifted up as regal figures to whom the surrounding nations offer service. They are also, as McKenzie points out, explicitly here priests (61:6), whose needs are

---

[840] The term is also used of the institution of prophets (e.g., 1 Kgs 19:16) and priests (e.g., Exod 28:41; 30:30; Lev 6:20; 8:12; 16:32; Num 3:3). However, the term has a strong association with kingship and here in light of the other connections to David, that seems the most probable nuance. Cf. J. Blenkinsopp, *Isaiah 56–66* (2003), 222–223, who sees anointing as connected with "priests . . . and kings . . . but not with prophets." His understanding of the voice here as a prophetic figure leads him to conclude that "therefore, the anointing is metaphorical" (223). While the anointing is indeed metaphorical, that is not for its lack of resonance with the kingly and priestly anointings, both of which here are significant bearers of the meaning of this anointing.

[841] See also C. Westermann, *Isaiah 40–55* (1969), 365; and J. Muilenburg, "Isaiah 40–66" (1956), 5:709.

[842] See J. Blenkinsopp, *Isaiah 56–66* (2003), 229.

302  *Commentary*

met, as would be appropriate, by the people for whom they stand as mediators of the LORD.[843] Such glorification comes with responsibilities. They, like David, must act justly. In light of the indictments of the preceding poems (Isa 57–59), there is a new calling. Those who have returned and embraced the reconciliation announced by the LORD's voice, must now fulfil the mission of "a leader and commander for the peoples" (55:4). They must honor the God who "love[s] justice" and who "hate[s] robbery and wrongdoing" (61:8). The promise of "recompense" is not without its warning. For those whose deeds merit punishment, the LORD has already demonstrated willingness to enact it.

ISAIAH 62:1–12

¹ For Zion's sake I will not keep silent,
    and for Jerusalem's sake I will not rest,
until her vindication shines out like the dawn
    and her salvation like a burning torch.
² The nations shall see your vindication
    and all the kings your glory,
and you shall be called by a new name
    that the mouth of the LORD will give.
³ You shall be a beautiful crown in the hand of the LORD
    and a royal diadem in the hand of your God.
⁴ You shall no more be termed Forsaken,
    and your land shall no more be termed Desolate,
but you shall be called My Delight Is in Her
    and your land Married,
for the LORD delights in you,
    and your land shall be married.
⁵ For as a young man marries a young woman,
    so shall your builder marry you,
and as the bridegroom rejoices over the bride,
    so shall your God rejoice over you.

---

[843] J. L. McKenzie, *Second Isaiah* (1968), 182. See also J. Blenkinsopp, *Isaiah 56–66* (2003), 226 and B. D. Sommer, *A Prophet Reads Scripture* (1998), 146.

*Isaiah 62:1–12*                                                     303

⁶ Upon your walls, O Jerusalem,
        I have posted sentinels;
all day and all night
        they shall never be silent.
You who remind the LORD,
        take no rest,
⁷ and give him no rest
        until he establishes Jerusalem
        and makes it renowned throughout the earth.
⁸ The LORD has sworn by his right hand
        and by his mighty arm:
I will not again give your grain
        to be food for your enemies,
and foreigners shall not drink the wine
        for which you have labored,
⁹ but those who harvest it shall eat it
        and praise the LORD,
and those who gather it shall drink it
        in my holy courts.

¹⁰ Go through, go through the gates;
        prepare the way for the people;
build up, build up the highway;
        clear it of stones;
        lift up an ensign over the peoples.
¹¹ The LORD has proclaimed
        to the end of the earth:
Say to daughter Zion,
        "Look, your savior comes;
his reward is with him
        and his recompense before him."
¹² They shall be called, "The Holy People,
        The Redeemed of the LORD,"
and you shall be called, "Sought Out,
        A City Not Forsaken."

This is a poem of "until" (62:1, 7). This contingency, this sense that what is
expected has not occurred yet, but will, offers the context for both the

304 Commentary

poem's recollections of restoration imagery already familiar from previous poems and its instructions to the audience to embrace activities of response to that expectation.

An anonymous poetic voice opens the poem with a resolution to be vocal and not to rest. The parallelism of the opening couplet is remarkably precise. The four terms of the first line appear in the same order with the second line employing either the same term (*lĕma'an*, i.e., "for the sake of," *lō'*, i.e., "no"/"not") or a synonym (Zion/Jerusalem, *'eḥĕšeh*, i.e., "keep silent"/*'ešqôṭ*, i.e., "rest") in alternation. The same ideas reappear elaborated in the lines related to the sentinels. The claim that they will not "be silent" (*yeḥĕšû*, 62:6) stands within a parallelistic couplet that emphasizes the perpetual nature of this refusal to be quiet ("all day and all night"/ "never," 62:6).

The idea of "rest" reappears employing a different word (*dŏmî*) and relating the sentinels' lack of "rest" to the "rest" they will not give to the LORD (62:6–7). Again, the word order and syntax highlight the parallelism with the conjunction ("and"), the addition of the verb ("give"), and the change of person for the object (from "you" to "him") being the only alterations of otherwise identical lines. That which the speaker has invoked as self-commitment and enjoined the sentinels to undertake is what is to be done to the LORD as well.

Each of these commitments to perpetual and rest-less lifting up of the voice precede the limitation "until" (62:1, 7). This term ('*ad*) establishes the expectation. In each instance, the expectation is of that which has been promised to Jerusalem – restoration. The emphasis that this poem places upon the ongoing expectation of that restoration is one indication that the context of the addressees has shifted somewhat since Isaiah 54. There the emphasis fell upon convincing the audience that the wrath of the LORD had passed and that they should entrust themselves to the promises of restoration. Here, the sentinels are urged to persist in expecting that which has been promised and to "remind" (62:6) the LORD of what the LORD has "sworn" to do (62:8).[844]

Frequent allusions join this poem's expectation to that which was promised in Isaiah 54. The paralleled terms "Forsaken" ('*ăzûbâ*) and

---

[844] As J. Muilenburg, "Isaiah 40–66," 720, points out, their role is "to pray." See also J. L. McKenzie, *Second Isaiah* (1968), 185.

*Isaiah 62:1–12*                                                                 305

"Desolate" (*šĕmāmâ*)[845] (62:4), which are here names that are to be replaced by a "new name" (62:2), were descriptors of personified woman Zion's distress in Isaiah 54. There she was called "desolate woman" (*šômēmâ*, 54:1) and "like a wife forsaken" (*kĕ'iššâ 'ăzûbâ*, 54:6). The first term in each of these transformations, "Forsaken" and "My Delight is in Her" are names drawn from Judean history. As several commentators observe, Azubah ("Forsaken") was the name of Jehoshaphat's mother (1 Kgs 22:42) and Hephzibah ("My Delight is in Her") was the name of Manasseh's mother (2 Kgs 21:1).[846] As Halpern observes, "The odds that the names of two queen mothers should appear accidentally juxtaposed in a poetic passage as descriptors of something other than the persons themselves is infinitessimally small."[847] Here, the name changes appear in a context of crown imagery (62:3). While it is improbable that the focus is intended to be upon Jehoshaphat and Manasseh, it does seem likely that the prophetic poet is enhancing the regality of the imagery applied to the city here by drawing upon queen mother names whose meaning conveys the reversal of conditions that the poem depicts.[848]

This promise of the replacement of these names "Forsaken" and "Desolate" begins a pattern of couplets whose lines alternate promises to "you" and to "your land" (62:4). The pattern intensifies in v. 5 where the first line offers the analogy "as a young man marries a young woman"/ "as the bridegroom rejoices over the bride" and the second connects that analogy to the relationship between the LORD and the addressees employing "your" and "you" (62:5) together in the second line. The metaphor of marriage to represent the relationship between the LORD and Zion dominates these lines. From the opening allusion to the "wife" who was "forsaken" and the "desolate woman" of Isaiah 54, the imagery continues

---

[845] A number of commentators, e.g., C. Westermann, *Isaiah 40–66* (1969), 371; and J. Muilenburg, "Isaiah 40–66" (1956), 5:719, suggest emending the vowels in line with Isa 54:1 here. Such a move is unnecessary. The feminine noun carries the meaning and sufficiently echoes Isa 54:1.

[846] See C. Westermann, *Isaiah 40–66* (1969), 376; J. Muilenburg, "Isaiah 40–66" (1956), 5:719; and J. Blenkinsopp, *Isaiah 56–66* (2003), 236.

[847] Baruch Halpern, "The New Names of Isaiah 62:4: Jeremiah's Reception in the Restoration and the Politics of 'Third Isaiah,'" *JBL* 117.4 (1998): 638.

[848] See further the argument of B. Halpern, "New Names" (1998), 639–641. Halpern thinks "it would be an error to read too much into his choice of specific ancestral figures" (639) and points to the way that "the names of that queen mothers assume a meaning that *conforms* to their semantic content (641)."

echoing the noun "Married" (*bĕ'ûlâ*, 62:4) with three occurrences of verbal forms of the same word (root *b'l*, 62:4–5).[849] This imagery is also explicit in Isaiah 54, where the LORD is directly called "your husband" (*bō'ălayik*, 54:5). Here the poem repeatedly elaborates the metaphor using the heavily alliterated image of a "young man" (*bāḥûr*, 62:5) and "young woman" (*bĕtûlâ*, 62:5) marrying (*yib'al*)[850] as well as referring to both "bridegroom" and "bride." By alluding both to the distress and to the response that employs the metaphor of marriage, the poem closely links the poet's expectation of restoration with prior promises.[851] However, here the marriage imagery that portrays the restoration dramatically overwhelms the images of distress. The expectation of restoration takes the central place of prominence in this poem eclipsing the imagery of that which is to be overcome.

Similarly, the poem elaborates and expands the imagery of the LORD swearing that the punishment was finished and unrepeatable (54:9). While the divine voice speaks words claiming to have sworn "not [to] be angry with you" and comparing that instance of having sworn with the prior promise never to repeat the flood (*nišba'tî*), here the poet announces that the LORD has "sworn" (*nišba'*) and proceeds to offer two parallel oaths. Two open-ended conditional statements (woodenly: "If I give ... If they

---

[849] S. Moughtin-Mumby, *Sexual and Marital* (2008), 150–151, points out the textual difficulty discussed by commentators here in 62:5. The Hebrew text reads *yib'ālûk bānāyik*, i.e., "your sons will marry you." A common proposal, attributed to Robert Lowth (see the discussion in Paul V. Niskanen, "Who Is Going to Marry You? The text of Isaiah 62:5," *CBQ* [2015]: 657), accords with how NRSV[ue] has translated here, namely emending "your sons" to the similar sounding "your builder." Commentators who take this option include J. L. McKenzie, *Second Isaiah* (1968), 185; J. Muilenburg, "Isaiah 40–66" (1956), 5:720; and C. Westermann, *Isaiah 40–66* (1969), 372. A similar possible overlap of these words appears in Isaiah 49:17. There, as here, word play seems likely. See further K. M. Heffelfinger, *I Am Large* (2011), 229. See also J. Blenkinsopp, *Isaiah 56–66* (2003), 233, 237, who notes "It seems that the writer has borrowed the play on words *bānîm/bōnîm* ('children/builders') from 49:17" (237). On the occurrence in 62:5, see S. Moughtin-Mumby, *Sexual and Marital* (2008), 151, who describes the way the verb plays with multiple meanings of "marry" as well as live in, and "to rule over." Interestingly, P. V. Niskanen, "Who Is Going to Marry" (2015), 665, drawing on wedding practices observes that "The imagery is that of movement in procession to a common dwelling."

[850] B. Halpern, "New Names" (1998), 624, observes in the line "For as a young man marries a young woman, so shall your builder marry you," "an alliterative frenzy."

[851] See further S. Moughtin-Mumby, *Sexual and Marital* (2008), 149, who sees this imagery as "almost certainly inspired by 54:5."

*Isaiah 62:1–12*  307

drink ..." 62:8; cf. NRSV[ue] "I will not again give ... foreigners shall not drink") leave the self-invoked penalty for failure to uphold the condition unspecified, a particularly strong expression of the oath formula.[852] Each of the oaths overturn covenant curses (cf. Deut 28:30–31, 33) with promises that the beneficiaries will praise the LORD in response (62:9).

The final stanza's repeated double plural imperatives evoke the opening lines of Isaiah 40 and the doubled commands in Isaiah 51–52. The announcement is not new. It is, as has been clear throughout the analysis of this poem, a return to and reiteration of the announcement of deliverance begun in Isaiah 40.[853] The people's situation has apparently changed. Jerusalem has "gates" (62:10) and "walls" (62:6), yet all is not yet restored.[854] There is still expectation and the need to cry out to God "until" all is accomplished. Jerusalem's "vindication" (*ṣidqāh*) "and salvation" (*wîšûʿātāh*) are still awaited (62:1). A series of exclamations (*hinnēh*, v. 11, 3 times)[855] announce with increasing urgency that salvation (*yišʿēk*, i.e., "your salvation"; cf. NRSV[ue] "your savior") is coming, a personified expression of deliverance bringing "reward," "recompense," and new names for both people and city.

This poem draws upon familiar imagery to reiterate and expand the vision of coming restoration. It speaks into a context in which it appears that the return and the delay of full restoration have combined to create either actual or potential discouragement. The audience are urged to embrace and enact the deliverance they have come to expect. They must both continue to call out to God for the full restoration promised and prepare the way for the people (cf. "prepare the way of the LORD," 40:3) as they eagerly expect transformation of both themselves and their city.

---

[852] See further J. D. W. Watts, *Isaiah 34–66* (2005), 319.

[853] B. S. Childs, *Isaiah* (2001), 513, points out that "It has often been observed that these three verses [10–12] constitute a virtual catena of verses from Second Isaiah."

[854] Cf. J. Muilenburg, "Isaiah 40–66" (1956), 5:720, who thinks the walls "now lie in ruins." However, the line itself seems to envision them as something upon which watchmen could be positioned.

[855] J. Muilenburg, "Isaiah 40–66" (1956), 5:722, observes this repetition but concludes that "the climax ... falls on the people." Arguably, the repetition of *hinnēh* (i.e., "behold," 3 times; cf. NRSV[ue] "Look" 1 time v. 11) calls attention to the appearance of salvation which leads on to the two renamings signaled by "be called" in v. 12. These are of the people and the city respectively. Thus, the focus remains on the restoration that comes about with the arrival of divinely instituted deliverance.

## ISAIAH 63:1–6

[1] "Who is this coming from Edom,
      from Bozrah in garments stained crimson?
Who is this so splendidly robed,
      marching in his great might?"

"It is I, announcing vindication,
      mighty to save."

[2] "Why are your robes red
      and your garments like theirs who tread the winepress?"

[3] "I have trodden the winepress alone,
      and from the peoples no one was with me;
I trod them in my anger
      and trampled them in my wrath;
their juice spattered on my garments,
      and I stained all my robes.
[4] For the day of vengeance was in my mind,
      and the year for my redeeming work had come.
[5] I looked, but there was no helper;
      I was abandoned, and there was no one to sustain me,
so my own arm brought me victory,
      and my wrath sustained me.
[6] I trampled down peoples in my anger;
      I crushed them in my wrath,
      and I poured out their lifeblood on the earth."

This distinctively dialogic poem departs from the expectation that questions in these chapters will be rhetorical. An imagined exchange between the LORD and the questioning voice links this passage's central compelling image for the wrath of God with other poems that announce the coming vindication of Zion's suffering. The LORD is not named here as speaker.[856] However, clear development of the imagery of Isaiah 59 (see further below)

---

[856] This ambiguity allows J. D. W. Watts, *Isaiah 34–66* (2005), 317, to propose the Persian general Megabyzus. This suggestion is unnecessary. The poem implies that the figure is the LORD.

# Isaiah 63:1–6

ties this imagery to the divine voice. Its unnamed quality makes the association potentially more ominous. "Who is this" (v. 1) is not answered, except by the speaking "I" (v. 1). That "I" is sufficient, associated with dramatic and violent deliverance and enacting justice all alone conveys a singular divine majesty.[857] The encounter this poem offers is with the commanding, powerful, and justice-wielding presence of the LORD.

The opening questions inquire about the identity of a glorious figure. The direction from which this one is "marching" is given, as are observations about the figure's clothing. The pair "garments" and "robed" (cf. "robes" and "garments" in vv. 2, 3), which will appear throughout this short poem, introduces the poem's central motif. The robes will continue to attract attention. The one asking will continue to inquire about the appearance of the figure's clothing, while the response from the LORD emphasizes deliverance, paralleling "vindication" (*ṣĕdāqâ*) and salvation ("to save").

On their own, the opening lines do not yet make it clear that the image is an ominous one. Alongside the ambiguity created by the question about the identity of the one who approaches, the words about their appearance are quite open. The NRSV[ue] translates "crimson" (63:1), but it is not clear what the word that occurs only here in the Hebrew Bible means. It is in parallel to a term that conveys splendor (NRSV[ue]: "splendidly").[858] The spattered clothing will certainly come to clearly represent bloodstains later in the poem; but in Isa 63:1, the words merely call attention to the appearance of the figure being addressed. It is not yet clear what draws this speaker's attention.[859] The poem's opening ambiguity engages its addressees' imagination drawing them into the poem.

---

[857] As B. S. Childs, *Isaiah* (2001), 517, puts it, "God's identity is obvious to all by the characteristic of his self-predicative speech." See similarly C. Westermann, *Isaiah 40–66* (1969), 381.

[858] BDB, 213–214.

[859] A number of scholars treat these lines as clearly spoken by a sentry figure. See, e.g., C. Westermann, *Isaiah 40–66* (1969), 380–381; J. Muilenburg, "Isaiah 40–66" (1956), 5:726. However, the ambiguity is pervasive here. The poem does not name the speaker and reconstructions of an imagined speaker work against the poem's thorough initial ambiguity. The focus is not on the unnamed speaker but on the one toward whom their words point, the vividly appearing and rapidly disambiguating, retribution enacting divine presence. See also B. S. Childs, *Isaiah* (2001), 515.

310                                                                                    *Commentary*

However, if these opening lines are read with awareness of the whole of the final form of the book of Isaiah, the reference to Edom and Bozrah creates an expectation of violence. These two, one of Israel's neighboring nations (Edom) and a city within it (Bozrah), appear together only one other time in the book of Isaiah.[860] In a passage that voices the LORD's anger against "all the nations" (34:2), Edom is the place that the LORD will enact "judgment" after the LORD's "sword has drunk its fill in the heavens" (34:5). The passage makes repeated reference to "blood" (34:3, 6, 7) in portraying a judgment that is extensive and violent.

Edom appears in a number of exilic and postexilic texts. They seem to have benefited from Jerusalem's destruction and the Judeans accuse them of rejoicing over Jerusalem's downfall (see, e.g., Ezek 36:5; Ps 137:7). Thus, they appear in exilic and postexilic texts as enemies who merit retribution (see, e.g., Ps 137:7; Jer 49:7–22; Obad; Lam 4:21–22).[861] However, as a number of commentators point out, here Edom is the place from which the avenger returns, the place of vengeance taking.[862] "Peoples" (plural, 63:6) are judged. The ambiguity here conveys a potentially expansive vision of divine wrath. If, as Lynch argues, Edom comes to stand for nations that take advantage of Zion's weakness, and if Zion comes to include an idea of protection of the vulnerable, then the retribution figured here may convey God's commitment to justice for the oppressed and vulnerable.[863]

Blood does not appear in this passage. Instead, the poem employs vivid imagery to portray this violence indirectly but perhaps even more intensely. Edom means "red" and the association between the color and the name is strong in Israelite literature, including the birth story of their ancestral figure, Esau (see Gen 25:25; 36:1). Here, the question "Why are your robes red ('ādôm, 63:2)" echoes the name Edom. The imagery of red-soaked clothing fuses the grapes of the wine-making process with the peoples being trampled in the LORD's wrath. Grapes are not mentioned, making the connection between "their juice" (niṣḥām, v. 3) and the blood of the "peoples" that have been "trampled" more direct and intense (63:3, see 6 where NRSV[ue]'s "lifeblood" is also niṣḥām). Instead of the "sword"

---

[860] B. S. Childs, *Isaiah* (2001), 516, observes the uniqueness of this combination in the two passages.

[861] See, e.g., J. Muilenburg, "Isaiah 40–66" (1956), 5:726.

[862] E.g., J. L. McKenzie, *Second Isaiah* (1968), 187.

[863] M. J. Lynch, "Zion's Warrior" (2008), 259, see also 255–256.

*Isaiah 63:1–6*

through which the LORD enacted vengeance in Isa 34, this image is of direct, unmediated violence (i.e., trampling), with an emphasis on "anger" (63:3, 6) and "wrath" (63:3, 5, 6). Alongside the depiction of juice running into the earth (63:6), the more indirect imagery of splattered clothing is perhaps even more threatening.

However, this is not violence threatened against the audience. Given that the nation who is to be the recipient of this violence is one they regard as enemy and as one who profited from their demise, the poem's emphasis on "vengeance" (63:4) significantly shapes how the original audience would have heard this poem. The divine avenger here dramatically overturns Zion's destruction, picking up and reversing Lamentations' motifs. While people defiled by blood with untouchable "garments" conveyed Zion's desolation (Lam 4:14), the divine voice claims to have splattered (the same verb, the root *g'l*) its own "garments" (Isa 63:3). Lamentations' community looked for but did not find a helper (Lam 4:17), an expression of their sense of abandonment. The LORD accomplishes this vindication alone, without a "helper" (a participle from the same root *'zr*) expressing majestic divine power (Isa 63:5). Lamentations complained that the LORD had trampled Zion "as in a winepress" (Lam 1:15).[864] Here the LORD tramples peoples in the "winepress" (63:3) as an action of "vengeance" and redemption. As though the poem takes up Zion's plea "All my enemies heard of my trouble; they are glad that you have done it. Bring on the that day you have announced, and let them be as I am" (Lam 1:21), the "day of vengeance" (Isa 63:4) this text announces brings about a passing of the "cup" into the hand of Edom (Lam 4:21), an answer to the desperate pleas of the community in the destruction of exile.

The LORD is presented as having looked for one to assist but finding none. This motif picks up the language of Isaiah 59:16–17, where the LORD was "displeased" by there being "no one" to bring about justice and where the LORD's arm accomplished "victory" (root *yš'*) and "his righteousness" (*ṣidqātô*) sustained him. Garment imagery appears here as well, with the

---

[864] See C. Westermann, *Isaiah 40–66* (1969), 382. B. D. Sommer, *A Prophet Reads Scripture* (1998), 218, proposes that this overlap of terminology and imagery "may well be coincidental." While that suggestion is certainly possible, it seems that the number of potential connections between the imagery of Lamentations and Isaiah 63:1–6, alongside the echoing of Lamentations elsewhere in exilic Isaiah, supports the likelihood of an echo here.

312  Commentary

LORD wearing "righteousness" (*ṣidāqâ*, 59:17). In the near repetition of the helper-less gaining of deliverance by the divine arm, now stated in the first person, "righteousness" has been replaced by "wrath" (*ḥămātî*, 63:5). In Isaiah 63, "vengeance" picks up the "day of vengeance" (*yôm nāqām*) language of Isaiah 34:8,[865] but here vengeance stands parallel to redemption (*gĕʾûlay*, 63:4) rather than "vindication." These two citations with alterations highlight the import of this violent imagery.[866] The LORD is enacting justice for Zion by visiting punishment upon her enemies.

Redemption (root *gʾl*) belongs to the world of bloodguilt retribution and the boundaries placed upon it in Israelite law as Blenkinsopp points out.[867] The *gōʾēl*, that is, redeemer (NRSV[ue] "avenger," Num 35:19), is the one with responsibility for enacting the death sentence on a murderer (Num 35:19). Unintentional killing without malice is explicitly excluded from this punishment (Num 35:22–28) and provision is made for the perpetrator's safety from the avenger in these cases. That Isaiah 63:1–6 is developing the avenger image is further reinforced by the sound play between vengeance *gĕʾûlay* (v. 4) and *ʾegʾāltî* (root *gʾl*) with the less common meaning "defile" (NRSV[ue] "stained") in v. 3's description of the "stained" clothing.[868] Isaiah 63's use of this imagery conveys significant implications. The LORD, as the people's avenger, appears to act against those who are guilty of malicious or intentional violence. For the audience this is an element of

---

[865] See also B. S. Childs, *Isaiah* (2001), 516.

[866] See further J. Blenkinsopp, *Isaiah 56–66* (2003), 248–249; and B. S. Childs, *Isaiah* (2001), 515, each of whom discuss connections between these passages. One significant element of scholarly attention to the relationship between Isaiah 59:15–21 and 63:1–6 has been the proposal that these two warrior passages form an intentionally constructed frame around a unit focused on Zion's restoration (60–62). See, e.g., J. Blenkinsopp, *Isaiah 56–66* (2003), 248. While this commentary focuses primarily on the text in its final form, the contrasts produced by this structure are meaningful. Judgment and punishment of her enemies conveys divinely offered security elsewhere in Zion focused poems, see, e.g., 49:22–26. Here, the extended juxtaposition may contrast arrogant actions to "persecute Zion's weak" with "humble (and perhaps humiliating) pilgrimage" so M. J. Lynch, "Zion's Warrior" (2008), 258.

[867] J. Blenkinsopp, *Isaiah 56–66* (2003), 251, makes this connection linking the imagery to the Jubilee year legislation.

[868] B. S. Childs, *Isaiah* (2001), 517, notes the word play but does not see it as pointing to "blood wrath" here. While he says it "distorts the context of chapter 63," it appears rather to convey elements of the vindication being imaged. For *gʾl* as "defile," see BDB, 146.

*Bridging the Horizons: Isaiah 56–66 and the New Testament* 313

restoration.[869] Justice, by means of violent retribution against those who have perpetrated violence, is what the LORD, their vindicator, has accomplished, not with human help but by the LORD's own "arm" (63:5).

The absence of a "helper" for the LORD in this enactment of vengeance resonates with the depiction of the LORD seeking someone to intervene in the absence of justice in Isaiah 59:15–16.[870] The violent encounter with the divine redeemer acting alone, juxtaposed with the intervening imagistic encounter with deliverance and restoration invite the community addressed to consider their own place within a context of division between righteous and wicked (Isa 57), consuming self-interest (Isa 58), and communal injustice (Isa 59). Division is in view here as well[871] and the vivid judgment and retribution motif reinforces the poetry's rhetorical urging to reject a grouping that persists in the actions it so strongly condemns.

The violence of this imagery is disturbing, undoubtedly. This passage is far from alone among the prophets in depicting the violent wrath of God. It is important to emphasize that this passage does not call upon its audience to right the wrongs committed against them through violence. However, it is also noteworthy that the idea of justice does not neglect the suffering of those who have been wronged by others and the Hebrew Bible presents the LORD as far from indifferent to such human suffering. As such it offers a challenge to contemporary readers to take seriously the recognition that oppression, injustice, and the willingness to profit from them are appalling to the LORD.

BRIDGING THE HORIZONS: ISAIAH 56–66 AND THE
NEW TESTAMENT

Alongside Luke's programmatic inauguration of Jesus' public ministry[872] by reading from Isaiah in the synagogue at Nazareth (Luke 4:16–20), with

---

[869] As J. Blenkinsopp, *Isaiah 56–66* (2003), 250, helpfully articulates, "To execute vengeance was a way of obtaining redress, of righting a lost balance and restoring the damaged integrity of the kinship group."

[870] See also B. S. Childs, *Isaiah* (2001), 517.

[871] With M. J. Lynch, "Zion's Warrior" (2008), 258, it is clear that the poem participates in the expectation that the LORD's righteous judgment produces division.

[872] Bart J. Koet, "Isaiah in Luke-Acts," in *Isaiah in the New Testament* (eds. Steve Moyise and Maarten J. J. Menken; London: T&T Clark, 2007), 85, comments, "Luke gives an outline of the entire ministry of Jesus by means of the Isaiah quotation."

314                                                                    *Commentary*

which many New Testament readers will be familiar, Isaiah 56–66's imagery is taken up in New Testament texts in several fascinating ways. Only a small sampling of these can be examined here. The aim of these short engagements is to show that readings of New Testament passages are expanded by careful attention to the details of the texts from Isaiah to which they allude and that the New Testament authors' use of Isaiah displays a more sophisticated approach than simple equation with Jesus. Instead, these authors redeploy biblical imagery to announce their claims about the meaning of Jesus and the Christian message for their own audiences.[873]

Importantly, New Testament scholar Richard Hays reminds us that this type of work was "retrospective."[874] As he puts it "After the resurrection, the community of Jesus' followers returns to reread Scripture under the guidance of the Spirit and experiences, again and again, an 'Aha!' reaction."[875] That is, in order for Christian readers to claim that Isaiah illuminates their understanding of Jesus and of their faith, it is not necessary to claim that prediction of Jesus was in the mind of the exilic and postexilic period authors. It is also not necessary to claim either that the exilic and postexilic period meanings of these poems, nor other later readings of them, are negated by the experience of having one's understanding of Jesus expressed, illuminated, or expanded by them (see Bridging the Horizons: Seeing Jesus and Seeing the Suffering Servant Today).[876]

Matthew's "magi from the east" (Matt 2:1) "knelt down" and brought gifts of "gold, frankincense, and myrrh" (Matt 2:11) in what may be an echo of Isaiah 60's imagery of "the wealth of nations" (60:5).[877] There peoples

---

[873] Extended analysis of the various techniques and approaches of each Gospel writer in their use of Hebrew Bible imagery, language, citation, and allusion in general and not just with reference to Isaiah appears in Richard B. Hays, *Reading Backwards: Figural Christology and the Fourfold Gospel Witness* (Waco, TX: Baylor University Press, 2014). Useful resources for readers interested in further examining the reuse of Isaiah in New Testament contexts include Steve Moyise and Maarten J. J. Menken, eds. *Isaiah in the New Testament* (London: T&T Clark, 2007) and Ben Witherington III, *Isaiah Old and New: Exegesis, Intertextuality, and Hermeneutics* (Minneapolis: Fortress Press, 2017).

[874] R. B. Hays, *Reading Backwards* (2014), 106.

[875] R. B. Hays, *Reading Backwards* (2014), 105.

[876] For discussion of the various ways in which the idea of God speaking might apply to the concept of Scripture, see Nicholas Wolterstorff, *Divine Discourse: Philosophical reflections on the claim that God speaks* (Cambridge: Cambridge University Press, 1995).

[877] J. F. A. Sawyer, *The Fifth Gospel* (1996), 34; and Daniel J. Harrington, S.J., *The Gospel of Matthew* (Sacra Pagina 1; Collegeville, MN: The Liturgical Press, 1991), 44. See also

*Bridging the Horizons: Isaiah 56–66 and the New Testament*  315

will "bring gold and frankincense" (60:6), and former oppressors' offspring "bow down" (60:14). Christians who perceive these resonances must take care in their presentation of them to avoid giving the impression that the promise has been transferred to them in any way that negates the original meaning of the promise to the collective people Israel (see Bridging the Horizons: "God's Sovereign Choice"). Here, the first-century Jewish child Jesus is an inheritor of such promises made to his ancestors. Matthew's redeployment of Isaian imagery here invites those who perceive it to see resonances between Jesus and the community of servants that Isaiah 56–66 shapes.[878] It offers a glimpse of the generous and miraculous triumph of God in a new time and place (see commentary on Isaiah 60:1–22). It announces that for Matthew, God is, in the birth of the infant Jesus, once again with lavish abundance liberating and restoring God's people.

The oppressor in Matthew's text is Herod whose presentation in this passage seems designed to evoke the Pharoah of the Exodus.[879] Care should also be taken in the mode of denouncing Herod's tyranny. This ruler is depicted as carrying out atrocities against his own people, which should be lamented as human abuses of power, not as elements of a contest between Jewish and later Christian modes of rulership.[880] As a point of fact, Herod is not called "king of the Jews" in the Matthew passage, only the child Jesus is (Matt 2:2), and in this passage only on the lips of the "magi."[881] Herod himself was a "client king" of the Romans and is depicted

---

J. Nolland, *Matthew* (2005), 117, who notes "An allusion to Is 60:6 is possible" while also recognising other appearances of various combinations of some of the gift items in other texts.

[878] Clearly Matthew is drawing on other biblical texts alongside and in concert with any allusion to the Isaiah text here, as the citation of Jeremiah 31:15, as well as the apparent connection to the Exodus story indicate.

[879] R. B. Hays, *Reading Backwards* (2014), 38.

[880] See Amy-Jill Levine, "Gospel of Matthew," in *Women's Bible Commentary* (20th Anniversary ed.; Carol A. Newsom, Sharon H. Ringe, and Jaqueline E. Lapsley, eds.; Louisville: Westminster John Knox Press, 2012), 468, who observes that "The story is not about 'evil Jews' (Herod and Jerusalem) vs. 'good Gentiles' (the magi), but about earthly power vs. divine power."

[881] See Eugene Eung-Chun Park, "Rachel's Cry for Her Children: Matthew's Treatment of the Infanticide by Herod," *CBQ* 75 (2013): 475, for discussion of how the literary context of the mention of Herod's rulership signals "implicit criticism revealing the illegitimacy of Herod as the vassal king of the Roman Empire."

as power hungry and ruthless in the historical record.[882] As Park observes, "In the context of a powerful empire and its subjugated world, in which unjust acts by the ruling elites went largely unchecked, relating an incident of abuse of power by a vassal king could in itself be a form of implicit criticism."[883] That Matthew makes such an application is suggestive for later readers. Isaiah's wealth of nations invites thoughtful and ethically attuned reflection. Power and prestige historically and seemingly inevitably invite corruption and abuse.[884] For contemporary, wealthy, Western readers and for Christians in dominant social positions, the poem and its reappropriation invite careful and potentially challenging self-examination.

The imagery of the divine warrior who "trampled" the "winepress" in "wrath" is familiar, though perhaps more from the lyrics of the *Battle Hymn of the Republic* and from Steinbeck's novel's title than from Isaiah 63 or its echoes in Revelation. Appropriately enough, each of these cultural adaptations of the motif apply its imagery to issues of social justice. The *Battle Hymn*, in particular, appears to be reading the imagery of the divine warrior through the lens of Revelation 19, which applies the imagery of one who "tread[s] the winepress of the fury of the wrath of God the Almighty" along with "a sharp sword with which to strike down the nations" coming from "his mouth" (Rev 19:15) to a figure who represents Christ. This one is "called Faithful and True" (Rev 19:11). He is named "The Word of God" and is said to judge "in righteousness" (Rev 19:11, 13). In the immediate context, the "servants" of God are invited to praise him (Rev 19:5) and the "angel" who describes himself as "a fellow servant" pronounces an invitation "to the marriage supper of the Lamb" (Rev 19:9–10).

Here the sharp dichotomy between the "servants" and the oppressive wicked familiar from Isaiah 56–66 is cast into the cosmic sphere. The

---

[882] See further Everett Ferguson, "The Herodian Dynasty," in *The World of the New Testament: Cultural, Social, and Historical Contexts* (eds. Joel B. Green and Lee Martin McDonald; Grand Rapids, MI: Baker Academic, 2013), 56–65, citation 58. As Stanley P. Saunders, "Matthew," in *Theological Bible Commentary* (eds. Gail R. O'Day and David L. Petersen; Louisville: Westminster John Knox, 2009), 294, observes "Herod the Great ... ruled over and exploited the Jewish people as a 'client king' in service to Rome."

[883] E. E. Park, "Rachel's Cry" (2013), 485.

[884] Compare the observations of Lord Acton in his "Letter to Archbishop Mandell Creighton" dated April 5, 1887, history.hanover.edu/courses/excerpts/165acton.html.

*Bridging the Horizons: Isaiah 56–66 and the New Testament* 317

exalted Christ figure enacts divine justice through judgment, now not "alone" (Isa 63:3) but with the support of an army (Rev 19:14).[885] Drawing together the winepress of Isaiah 63 with the imagery of a "mouth like a sharp sword" (Isa 49:2),[886] the text depicts the victory of God's righteous judgment as an invitation to a feast in dramatic and graphic terms. This passage from Revelation reactivates the stark choices about allegiance and obedience with which Isaiah closes (Isa 65–66).

In doing so, it reappropriates for another time and another place the radical expression of God's intention to definitively deal with injustice, God's commitment to righteousness, and God's profound rage against evil and oppression. As Witherington comments about Isaiah 63's emphasis on God's action "all alone," "only divine intervention can finally deal with injustice everywhere."[887] Here, on a cosmic plane, the text once again reengages the ancient conception of God as righteously reorienting the world to justice. It serves as an intense reminder of the seriousness with which God as presented in the Bible takes corruption, wickedness, and sin that brings suffering and sorrow. As with all stark texts, it must be handled with care and discernment bearing in mind that God's righteous wrath is ultimately also an expression of the God who "is love" (1 John 4:8) and whose love responds to the brokenness of human brutality and depravity. Righteousness and justice, grace and mercy dwell together in the nature of God (see especially Exod 34:6–7).[888]

---

[885] Craig R. Koester, *Revelation* (AB 38A; New Haven: Yale University Press, 2014), 757, discusses the possibilities for reading this army as composed of "saints" or "angels" or a combination of both.

[886] David Mathewson, "Isaiah in Revelation," in *Isaiah in the New Testament* (eds. Steve Moyise and Maarten J. J. Menken; London: T&T Clark, 2007), 194; and B. Witherington, *Isaiah Old and New* (2017), 319. See also David E. Aune, *Revelation 17–22* (WBC 52c; Grand Rapids: Zondervan, 1998), 1048–1050, 1060–1062, for discussion of other ancient texts that might have played a role in developing the interpretation Revelation 19 presents.

[887] B. Witherington, *Isaiah Old and New* (2017), 318.

[888] Christopher C. Rowland, "Revelation," in *New Interpreters Bible Commentary* (Vol 12; eds. Leader E. Keck et al.; Nashville: Abingdon Press, 1998), 701, comments "Balancing justice and love lies in the depths of both Jewish and Christian wrestling with the character of God. No theodicy can answer the problem merely by showing revulsion at the consequences of justice. Love's ability to cover a multitude of sins in a vision of eternal inclusion is in danger of baptizing the status quo of this world's injustice, as the kings, magnates, and captains ride into the kingdom on the tide of the love of God. That sentimentality is ruthlessly challenged by the apocalyptic vision."

318                                                                    *Commentary*

Likely more familiar from its New Testament appearances than the preceding example is the imagery of the divine warrior's garments taken up from Isaiah 59:16–17 in Ephesians 6:10–17. While Revelation applied Isaiah's imagery to Jesus, depicting him as the divine warrior who accomplishes the vanquishing of injustice and the enemies of God's purposes, Ephesians applies divine warrior imagery instead into the life of the believer addressed by the letter itself. There, urging its audience to "stand firm" (Eph 6:13), made more powerful by the repetition of forms of the word "stand" (Eph 6:11, 13, 14),[889] believers are told to "take up the whole armor of God" (Eph 6:13). This is the armor that God puts on in Isaiah 59, including both the "righteousness like a breastplate" and "a helmet of salvation" (Isa 59:17).[890] The armor imagery is more expansive in Ephesians than Isaiah 59 with the addition of the "belt ... [of] truth" (Eph 6:14), which may be drawn in from Isaiah 11:5,[891] feet ready "for the gospel of peace" (Eph 6:15),[892] "the shield of faith" (Eph 6:16), and "the sword of the Spirit, which is the word of God" (Eph 6:17).[893] This last occurrence may depend at least in a small way on the same "mouth like a sharp sword" (Isa 49:2) imagery discussed above in connection with Rev 19.[894] Similarly, Isaiah 52:7 celebrates the beauty of the "feet of the messenger who announces peace, who brings good news," corresponding closely to the idea of "the gospel [i.e., good news] of peace" (Eph 6:15).[895]

---

[889] On the grammatical construction here, see Andrew T. Lincoln, *Ephesians* (WBC 42; Grand Rapids: Zondervan, 1990), 431. See also Lincoln's discussion of the exhortative function of the structure employed (432–434).

[890] See A. T. Lincoln, *Ephesians* (1990), 437, 440–441, for discussion of how the application of the divine armor to the believers works to build confidence in the writer's claims and exhortation.

[891] See B. Witherington, *Isaiah Old and New* (2017), 300; and A. T. Lincoln, *Ephesians* (1990), 436.

[892] The whole phrase in NRSV[ue] is "lace up your sandals in preparation for the gospel of peace," but note that the Greek includes reference to "feet" here.

[893] B. Witherington, *Isaiah Old and New* (2017), 300–301, examines these details pointing out significant similarities here with Wisdom 5:17–20 stating that "Paul is not just drawing on Isaiah, he is drawing on the use of Isaianic material in Wisdom 5:17–20."

[894] See A. T. Lincoln, *Ephesians* (1990), 436, who sees a link between Isa 11:5 and Isa 49:2 at work and observes both similarities and differences in the use of this material in Ephesians and Revelation (451).

[895] See B. Witherington, *Isaiah Old and New* (2017), 300; and A. T. Lincoln, *Ephesians* (1990), 436. See especially A. T. Lincoln, Ephesians (1990), 448, which observes that the author of Ephesians "does not refer directly to the footwear and instead talks of the feet

*Isaiah 63:7–64:12*  319

Here, it is explicitly the believer who is to put on the divine battle garments, but the task at hand is not the requital of God's human adversaries whose "feet run to do evil" and who "rush to shed innocent blood" (Isa 59:7). Instead, it is against "spiritual forces of evil" rather than those of "blood and flesh" (Eph 6:12)[896] that the believer is to take up these "offensive" and "defensive" weapons.[897] The battle with evil continues and the divine battle array is redeployed again, this time in a spiritual manner.

Each of these instances demonstrate that New Testament writers use the language and imagery of Isaiah 56–66, applying and interpreting it along the way, in order to proclaim the message that they present. Each seems, in some way, to draw on the larger context and to craft new imagery by drawing together threads from other passages in Isaiah as well as other sources and interpretations. Awareness of Isaiah's imagery illuminates what each author is doing when they apply it, and this kind of work has the potential to enrich readers' understanding.

## ISAIAH 63:7–64:12

⁷ I will recount the gracious deeds of the LORD,
     the praiseworthy acts of the LORD,
because of all that the LORD has done for us
     and the great favor to the house of Israel
that he has shown them according to his mercy,
     according to the abundance of his steadfast love.
⁸ For he said, "Surely they are my people,
     children who will not act deceitfully,"
and he became their savior
     ⁹ in all their distress.
It was no messenger or angel
     but his presence that saved them;

---

being fitted or shod, showing again that he is primarily influenced by the language of an OT passage which mentions feet in connection with proclaiming the gospel of peace."

[896] B. Witherington, *Isaiah Old and New* (2017), 301.

[897] See A. T. Lincoln, *Ephesians* (1990), 451, on both "offensive" and "defensive" weapons here.

320           *Commentary*

in his love and pity it was he who redeemed them;
      he lifted them up and carried them all the days of old.
[10] But they rebelled[898]
      and grieved his holy spirit;
therefore he became their enemy;
      he himself fought against them.
[11] Then they remembered the days of old,
      of Moses his servant.

Where is the one who brought them up out of the sea[899]
      with the shepherds of his flock?
Where is the one who put within them
      his holy spirit,
[12] who caused his glorious arm
      to march at the right hand of Moses,
who divided the waters before them
      to make for himself an everlasting name,
      [13] who led them through the depths?
Like a horse in the desert,
      they did not stumble.
[14] Like cattle that go down into the valley,
      the spirit of the LORD gave them rest.
Thus you led your people,
      to make for yourself a glorious name.
[15] Look down from heaven and see,
      from your holy and glorious habitation.
Where are your zeal and your might?
      Your great pity and your compassion are withheld from me.

[16] For you are our father,[900]
      though Abraham does not know us
      and Israel does not acknowledge us;

---

[898] My stanza breaks depart from NRSV[ue]. This first unit includes the historical recital up to the point of the first question.

[899] This stanza begins and ends with rhetorical questions, marking it out as a stanza. This delineation of both the beginning and end of the stanza differs from NRSV[ue].

[900] This stanza is framed by the "you are our father" refrain, contra the stanza delineation of NRSV[ue].

*Isaiah 63:7–64:12*

you, O LORD, are our father;
    our Redeemer from of old is your name.
¹⁷ Why, O LORD, do you let us stray from your ways
    and let our heart harden, so that we do not fear you?
Turn back for the sake of your servants,
    the tribes that are your heritage.
¹⁸ Your holy people took possession for a little while,
    but now our adversaries have trampled down your sanctuary.
¹⁹ We have long been like those whom you do not rule,
    like those not called by your name.
64:1 O that you would tear open the heavens and come down,
    so that the mountains would quake at your presence –
² as when fire kindles brushwood
    and the fire causes water to boil –
to make your name known to your adversaries,
    so that the nations might tremble at your presence!
³ When you did awesome deeds that we did not expect,
    you came down; the mountains quaked at your presence.
⁴ From ages past no one has heard,
    no ear has perceived,
no eye has seen any God besides you,
    who works for those who wait for him.
⁵ You meet those who gladly do right,
    those who remember you in your ways.
But you were angry, and we sinned;
    because you hid yourself we transgressed.
⁶ We have all become like one who is unclean,
    and all our righteous deeds are like a filthy cloth.
We all fade like a leaf,
    and our iniquities, like the wind, take us away.
⁷ There is no one who calls on your name
    or attempts to take hold of you,
for you have hidden your face from us
    and have delivered us into the hand of our iniquity.
⁸ Yet, O LORD, you are our Father;
    we are the clay, and you are our potter;
    we are all the work of your hand.

322  *Commentary*

⁹ Do not be exceedingly angry, O LORD,⁹⁰¹
    and do not remember iniquity forever.
    Now consider, we are all your people.
¹⁰ Your holy cities have become a wilderness;
    Zion has become a wilderness,
    Jerusalem a desolation.
¹¹ Our holy and beautiful house,
    where our ancestors praised you,
has been burned by fire,
    and all our pleasant places have become ruins.
¹² After all this, will you restrain yourself, O LORD?
    Will you keep silent and punish us so severely?

This poem of fervent longing implores the LORD to act on the people's behalf.[902] It engages memory, expresses confession, and pleads directly. The imagery mixes echoes of narratives from Israel's past with poetic allusions to Lamentations and other parts of Isaiah. As the poem draws to a close, it echoes Lamentations strongly, reiterating rather than reversing its message as poems in Isaiah 40–55 had done. The poem's longing and its return to Lamentations' pleadings as live and ongoing concerns complicates a straightforward trajectory for the Isaian literature from warning to punishment to restoration (see A Closer Look: "Third Isaiah" as "Under-Rated" Poet).

This poem, with its recurrent actions of reminding the LORD of the past and its repeated reference to remembering (63:11; 64:5, 9 and 63:7 where NRSV[ue] "recount"), resonates with the characterization of the sentinels in Isa 62:6, "You who remind the LORD." While "sentinels" are never named here and the anonymized voice shifts from singular "I will recount" (63:7) to plural "you are our Father" (63:16), the poem itself enacts a response to the insistence that those "who remind the LORD, take no rest" (62:6).

The opening line of the poem expresses a voice's intention to "recount" (*'azkîr*) and goes about it by emphasizing the compassion and faithfulness of the LORD (63:7) and by apparent allusion to deliverance in the time of

---

⁹⁰¹ This final stanza is framed by the expressions *'ad-mĕ'ōd* ("exceedingly"/"severely") echoing Lamentations 5:22. This division of stanzas differs from that of NRSV[ue].

⁹⁰² The description by J. Blenkinsopp, *Isaiah 56–66* (2003), 258, of how this passage compares with communal lament Psalms is apt.

*Isaiah 63:7–64:12*                                                                    323

the Patriarchs. The couplet that follows the perplexing reference to "no messenger or angel (*mal'ak*) but his presence" employs a word for "pity" (*běhemlātô* "in his . . . pity," 63:9) that occurs only here and in Gen 19:16,[903] where it describes "the LORD being merciful to" Lot, an act of merciful deliverance that is carried out by a pair of angelic figures (*hammal'ākim*, Gen 19:1, where NRSV[ue] translates "The . . . angels").[904] That particular deliverance narrative seems pertinent to a situation in which the poetic voice is about to plead for divine intervention. These angelic figures went to Sodom to bring Lot and his family out after Abraham had pleaded with God in an extended exchange. It was not an exchange that denied the sinfulness of the cities that were about to be destroyed but one that sought the deliverance of the city for the sake of the few righteous people within it (Gen 18:23–33). Similarly, this poem repeatedly admits wrongdoing (63:10, 17; 64:5, 6, 7) but implores God not to "be exceedingly angry" and reminds the LORD "we are all your people" (64:9). This potential subtle echo of a prior deliverance that expressed divine mercy in the face of iniquity for the sake of one who pleaded the cause of others provides a fascinating potential context for the pleading that follows.

The poem's second recollection, signposted with the word "remembered" (*wayyizkōr*) and reappearance of the phrase "days of old" (*yěmê-'ôlām*, 63:11), which had concluded the recollection of deliverance in 63:9, launches a recital of the mighty deeds of the LORD in the deliverance from Egypt. By framing this recital with questions (63:11, 15), the poetic lines transform this recital from a thankful recounting to a plea for the God who delivered Israel out of Egypt to again act on the people's behalf.[905] These

---

[903] C. Westermann, *Isaiah 40–66* (1969), 388, also note this occurrence but does not develop the observation further.

[904] The NRSV[ue]'s "angel" here indicates one sent by God. While it is true that much of the developed thinking about angels familiar to readers of the New Testament postdates both of these passages, it seems clear that in the Genesis narrative the figures named by the term *hammal'ākim* (Gen 19:1) act as carriers of God's messages and agents who bring about the LORD's intentions (Gen 19:13), that they have the ability to do things that the human actors cannot (Gen 19:11), and that they have the ability to negotiate the details of the intended destruction directly (Gen 19:21). The other term, *ṣār*, is probably best taken from *ṣîr* (i.e., "messenger") and has either been modified to create a sound play with "their distress" (*ṣārātām*) in the preceding line (v. 9) or has been altered by the textual pressure of that preceding and very similar sounding word.

[905] The poetry employs language from both the narrative account (e.g., "divided the waters" *bôqēa' mayim*, Isa 63:12; cf. Exod 14:21) and the poetic account (e.g., "through the

324                                          *Commentary*

lines reorient two modes of reassurance familiar from Isaiah 40–55. There rhetorical questions spoken by the divine voice and participles extolling God's activities reinforced the claims that the one speaking and announcing deliverance would bring it about. Here, the questions are relocated into the human voices. They ask God "where" (63:11 twice, 15) God is and develop that query by describing the LORD in participles "who brought them up" (63:11), "who put within them" (63:11), "who caused . . . to march" (63:12), "who divided" (63:12), "who led" (63:13). The questions both plead for deliverance and strengthen their plea by recalling the promises of the certainty of that deliverance in Isaiah 40–55.[906]

The movement from recollection to petition is clear in the imperatives imploring the LORD to observe (63:15) that immediately precede the questions that conclude this recital. The idea that the LORD must "Look down" (63:15) to observe the speaker's distress conveys a sense of alienation from the LORD, which is further reinforced by the answer the speaker gives to their own question. Having asked where the delivering power and mercy of God are, the voice concludes they "are withheld from me" (63:15).[907]

The refrain "you are our father" (63:16; 64:8 Eng., 64:7 Heb.)[908] frames the next sequence of lines, which is both confessional and accusing. The "we" who voice these lines do not dispute their guilt. Indeed, they offer vivid depictions of the worthlessness of their attempts at righteousness. In lines that seem to expand an allusion to Lamentations' description of daughter Zion as one whose "uncleanness was in her skirts" (Lam 1:9)[909] to parallel claims that those speaking are "all . . . unclean" and that their righteousness compares to clothing stained with menstrual blood, the "we"

---

depths" *batĕhōmôt*, Isa 63:13; cf. Exod 15:5, 8; and the "horse" reference *sûs*, Isa 63:13; cf. Exod 15:1).

[906] See J. Muilenburg, "Isaiah 40–66" (1956), 5:734, who points to "the intensity of the writer's mood" indicated by the "fervent and anxious repetition" of the questions, "the length of the sentence . . . and the repeated allusion to the crossing of the sea."

[907] See also J. Muilenburg, "Isaiah 40–66" (1956), 5:734, who notes, commenting on v. 11, "in the present situation God seems absent or silent"; and J. Blenkinsopp, *Isaiah 56–66* (2003), 262, who identifies the "feeling . . . that God had moved away from his people" as prevalent in Isa 56–66.

[908] Isaiah 63:16 contains an additional near repetition of the phrase: "you, O LORD, are our father."

[909] J. Blenkinsopp, *Isaiah 56–66* (2003), 266, points out the connection to menstrual blood in Lam 1:17.

*Isaiah 63:7–64:12* 325

explicitly name their state and the impact of their "iniquities" (64:6) upon them.[910]

However, the father language also stands juxtaposed to complaints that the LORD has brought about the people's waywardness (63:17; 64:7). A couplet launched by the question "Why" draws a parallel between the people's tendency to turn from the LORD's ways to the LORD's activity in bringing about Pharaoh's resistance to the people's deliverance in Exodus (63:17). The claim that the LORD "make[s] us stray" (NRSV)[911] and that the LORD "harden[s] our heart" (NRSV)[912] (Isa 63:17; cf. Exod 7:3) is not offered as an impossibility but as an expression of being "like those whom you do not rule" (63:19). It does not appear that these lines charge God with wrongdoing. Rather, the people voice in vivid terms their sense that they have become like the LORD's "enemy" (63:10) and put themselves on the same level as the ancient enemy of the LORD, Pharaoh. It is an image of being a foreign people, rather than the people to whom the LORD is Father. Standing juxtaposed to the repeated reminders that "you are our father"[913] and the claim "we are all your people" (64:9), this image serves to implore God to reverse the extreme alienation that the people experience, and which they admit is the result of their wickedness.

---

[910] NRSV^ue's "filthy cloth" obscures the possible force of *kĕbeged 'iddîm* (Eng. Isa 64:6, Heb. 64:5), which may mean, woodenly translated, "like garments of menstruation." The word potentially meaning menstruation in that phrase occurs only once in the Hebrew Bible so, while this is the most likely reading it remains somewhat unclear. See also J. Blenkinsopp, *Isaiah 56–66* (2003), 264. This image may both interpret Lam 1:9 and seemingly associate the people's righteousness with something regarded as "unclean." See Lev 15:19–24, which uses different terms to refer to menstruation but does connect it to uncleanness using the same terms as here. The Hebrew versification system differs at the chapter break. Throughout chapter 64, the Hebrew numbering differs from NRSV^ue by one verse. For further details, see B. S. Childs, *Isaiah* (2001), 525.

[911] Cf. NRSV^ue "let us stray." The verb is a *hip'il* (causative) form. The "permissive" rendering here and in the reference to "hardening" the "heart" is not necessary to avoid theological difficulty. As described in the comment above, this statement is not an abstract theological claim but a complaint that represents the perception of the one offering it.

[912] Cf. NRSV^ue "let our heart harden." Again, the Hebrew is *hip'il* (causative) and there does not seem to be a compelling reason in this case to overturn the more naturally causative meaning.

[913] The repetition is particularly noteworthy given its relative rarity in the Hebrew Bible as pointed out by Paul Niskanen, "Yhwh as Father, Redeemer, and Potter in Isaiah 63:7–64:11," *CBQ* 68 (2006): 397–398.

326                                                                    *Commentary*

As indicated by Niskanen, the father language resonates with the expressions of alienation from Abraham and Isaac, connecting this imagery to the "Redeemer" language that also appears in this passage (63:16). Niskanen puts it this way, "as their kinsman of the most intimate degree, Yhwh has not only the right to be honored and respected as the head of the clan but also the responsibilities to protect, defend, and redeem his children."[914] The repetition of "all," which appears in this confession and pleading (64:6, three times, 8, 9, 12), underscores its corporate interest. This poem calls for the LORD's restoration for "all."[915] The "we" cry out for deliverance, and they envision an encompassing restoration.

The relationship between the people's resistance and God's distance comes through more directly in the claim that "no one" seeks the LORD "for you have hidden your face from us and have delivered us into the hand of our iniquity" (64:7). It is a depiction of the LORD allowing the people's sin to accomplish its own results. Elsewhere in Isaiah, the LORD has been portrayed as "hiding" (e.g., 8:17) and as "wait[ing] to be gracious to you" (30:18; cf. "those who wait for him," 64:4 NRSV[ue]).[916] In those instances, the prophet was urged to protect the prophecy for a future time (8:16; 30:8) in light of a culture that suppressed true speech on behalf of the LORD (8:19; 30:9–10). Resistance to reliable instruction about the ways of the LORD seems one factor in the people's situation of being estranged and distant from the LORD.[917] The "we" together bring both their confession of their own lack of righteousness and their plea to God to draw near.

---

[914]  P. Niskanen, "Yhwh as Father" (2006), 401.

[915]  As P. Niskanen, "Yhwh as Father" (2006), 406, points out, in context this "all" is the whole people of Israel in the postexilic context, not a universal expression. It is an "all" spoken by the poem's "we."

[916]  Each of these passages employ the term "wait," which appears in 64:4.

[917]  The couplet which the NRSV[ue] translates "But you were angry, and we sinned; because you hid yourself we transgressed" does not factor in my discussion of this motif because the translation does not seem to reflect the Hebrew text here. It appears to depend upon the Septuagint, which was interpreting an admittedly difficult text. However, there is no clear reference to either transgression or hiding in the second line of this couplet. It is preferable to read the difficult text as it stands, which results in a second line that reads something such as "we are delivered in them of old." See J. D. W. Watts, *Isaiah 34–66* (2005), 326, who also takes this position and translates similarly. The connection between divine anger and human sin in the first line could involve causation, as in 63:17 and 64:7 (see discussion above), but the grammar does not demand it and it is possible to read it as simply expressing sequence. B. S. Childs, *Isaiah* (2001), 525, points out that the sequence first highlights divine anger and then human sin, reversing expectation. While the sequence does reverse expectation, this need not necessarily

*Isaiah 63:7–64:12* 327

That desire for the LORD to draw near is figured as a ripping apart of the heavens. A violent transformation of the earth and trembling among the people accompanies such an appearance. These speakers are in no doubt both about their own human frailty and the divine majesty. The LORD whom they beg to appear is one whose appearance makes "mountains" tremble (64:1, 3). They are likened to mere leaves, blown about by a breeze (64:6). They have recounted God's deeds of the past and they long for the promised restoration.

The final verses of the poem express the situation from which they beg deliverance. The final frame of this poem depicts the severity of the LORD's wrath while alluding to the closing lines of Lamentations.[918] They beg "Do not be exceedingly angry" (*'al-tiqṣōp* ... *'ad-mĕ'ōd*, Isa 64:9 Eng; Heb. 64:8) and "Will you ... punish us so severely" (*ûtĕ'annēnû 'ad-mĕ'ōd*, Isa 64:12 Eng.; Heb. 64:11). Lamentations had concluded "Restore us to yourself, O LORD, that we may be restored; renew our days as of old – unless you have utterly rejected us and are angry with us beyond measure (*qāṣāptā 'ālênû 'ad-mĕ'ōd*)" (Lam 5:21–22). The conditions this poem describes, where "wilderness" and "desolation" and destruction by "fire" are the reality of life in the land (64:10–11), hearken back to Lamentations' description of the aftermath of the siege of Jerusalem. The temple, here called "our holy and beautiful house" is burned and "our pleasant places" (*mahămaddênû*, Isa 64:11 Eng.; Heb. 64:10; cf. Lam 1:7, 10, 11; 2:4) are destroyed. The voices of this poem exhort the LORD to bring about restoration, casting their circumstances as those of the immediate aftermath of Babylonian destruction. They beg for the LORD to make Jerusalem's "vindication ... like the dawn" (62:1) in the strongest possible terms.

They ask again the question left open by the end of Lamentations.[919] They reopen the cries for the LORD to restore that had been answered by the divine voice in Isaiah 40–55. While the divine voice treated the

---

imply a causal link. Read this way, the couplet appears less a part of the "hardening heart" motif and more a part of the plea to God to recall that the past has included both sin and restoration.

[918] See J. Blenkinsopp, *Isaiah 56–66* (2003), 265–266, who adds further points of connection.

[919] See Tod Linafelt, "The Refusal of a Conclusion in the Book of Lamentations," *JBL* 120 (2001): 340–343, who describes the incomplete conditional statement as "a willful *non*ending" (343, emphasis original).

328                                                                    *Commentary*

hiddenness of God as "a moment" (54:8) and proclaimed glorious restoration (54:11–17) and security as the "heritage" (*naḥălat*) of the "servants" (*ʿabdê*, 54:17), this poem expresses the people's anguish as an experience of the ongoing turmoil of destruction.[920] They plead with the LORD to bring about restoration "for the sake of your servants, (*ʿăbādeykā*) the tribes that are your heritage (*naḥălāteka*)" (63:17)[921] (see further A Closer Look: From Servant to Servants).

This is a poem of urgent and eager longing. It is a poem that confesses guilt and pleads with God for intervention. Drawing together Israel's past and its present, the poem returns to the lament, reopening the expression of a strained relationship between the people and the LORD. In so doing it contests the resolution of Isaiah 40–55, reinterpreting those promises as ongoing and awaiting fulfilment in the audience's own time.

ISAIAH 65:1–25

¹ I was ready to be sought out by those who did not ask,
        to be found by those who did not seek me.
I said, "Here I am, here I am,"
        to a nation that did not call on my name.
² I held out my hands all day long
        to a rebellious people,
who walk in a way that is not good,
        following their own devices;
³ a people who provoke me
        to my face continually,
sacrificing in gardens

---

[920]  Commentators work to assign a date in the postexilic period that accords with this description. See the summary in J. Blenkinsopp, *Isaiah 56–66* (2003), 258–259. However, the reopening of Lamentations' plea through allusion here and its overturning of Isa 54's resolution suggest that the postexilic experience is being re-framed as a continuation of exile here. See Martien A. Halvorson-Taylor, *Enduring Exile: The Metaphorization of Exile in the Hebrew Bible* (VTSup 141; Leiden: Brill, 2011), 149. Her discussion points out that "Isa 56–66 suggests that its predecessor's promises about the end of exile still await realization decades after the return." Reading in this way it is not necessary to suggest any new historical context of destruction.
[921]  J. D. W. Watts, *Isaiah 34–66* (2005), 334, also highlights the repetition of Isaiah 54:17's terms here.

*Isaiah 65:1–25*

and offering incense on bricks;
⁴ who sit inside tombs
　　and spend the night in secret places;
who eat the flesh of pigs,
　　with broth of abominable things in their vessels;
⁵ who say, "Keep to yourself;
　　do not come near me, for I am too holy for you."
These are a smoke in my nostrils,
　　a fire that burns all day long.
⁶ See, it is written before me:
　　I will not keep silent, but I will repay;
I will indeed repay into their laps
　　　⁷ their iniquities and their ancestors' iniquities together,
　　says the LORD;[922]
because they offered incense on the mountains
　　and reviled me on the hills,
I will measure into their laps
　　full payment for their actions.
⁸ Thus says the LORD:
As the wine is found in the cluster,
　　and they say, "Do not destroy it,
　　for there is a blessing in it,"
so I will do for my servants' sake
　　and not destroy them all.
⁹ I will bring forth descendants from Jacob
　　and from Judah inheritors of my mountains;
my chosen shall inherit it,
　　and my servants shall settle there.
¹⁰ Sharon shall become a pasture for flocks
　　and the Valley of Achor a place for herds to lie down,
　　for my people who have sought me.
¹¹ But you who forsake the LORD,
　　who forget my holy mountain,
who set a table for Fortune

---

[922] I have treated "says the LORD" as a line within the poetic triplet. This arrangement differs from that offered by NRSV[ue].

330 Commentary

and fill cups of mixed wine for Destiny,
¹² I will destine you to the sword,
and all of you shall bow down to the slaughter;
because, when I called, you did not answer,
when I spoke, you did not listen,
but you did what was evil in my sight
and chose what I did not delight in.

¹³ Therefore thus says the Lord GOD:[923]
My servants shall eat,
but you shall be hungry;
my servants shall drink,
but you shall be thirsty;
my servants shall rejoice,
but you shall be put to shame;
¹⁴ my servants shall sing for gladness of heart,
but you shall cry out in pain of heart
and shall wail in anguish of spirit.
¹⁵ You shall leave your name to my chosen to use as a curse,
and the Lord GOD will put you to death,
but to his servants he will give a different name.
¹⁶ Then whoever invokes a blessing in the land
shall bless by the God of faithfulness
and whoever takes an oath in the land
shall swear by the God of faithfulness;
because the former troubles are forgotten
and are hidden from my sight.

¹⁷ For I am about to create new heavens
and a new earth;
the former things shall not be remembered
or come to mind.
¹⁸ But be glad and rejoice forever
in what I am creating,

---

[923] It seems best to regard this line as the beginning of a new stanza. The patterning of the lines sets them off somewhat from what has preceded. NRSV[ue] does not create a stanza break here.

*Isaiah 65:1–25*                                                                                    331

for I am about to create Jerusalem as a joy
    and its people as a delight.
[19] I will rejoice in Jerusalem
    and delight in my people;
no more shall the sound of weeping be heard in it
    or the cry of distress.
[20] No more shall there be in it
    an infant who lives but a few days
    or an old person who does not live out a lifetime,
for one who dies at a hundred years will be considered a youth,
    and one who falls short of a hundred will be considered accursed.
[21] They shall build houses and inhabit them;
    they shall plant vineyards and eat their fruit.
[22] They shall not build and another inhabit;
    they shall not plant and another eat,
for like the days of a tree shall the days of my people be,
    and my chosen shall long enjoy the work of their hands.
[23] They shall not labor in vain
    or bear children for calamity,
for they shall be offspring blessed by the LORD –
    and their descendants as well.
[24] Before they call I will answer,
    while they are yet speaking I will hear.
[25] The wolf and the lamb shall feed together;
    the lion shall eat straw like the ox,
    but the serpent – its food shall be dust!
They shall not hurt or destroy
    on all my holy mountain, says the LORD.[924]

Standing immediately juxtaposed to the revoicing of Lamentations'
complaint at the end of the previous poem, this poem offers an encounter
with the answering divine voice.[925] It is a voice that is so responsive that it

---

[924] In contrast to the lineation of NRSV[ue], I am treating "says the LORD" as part of the
second line.
[925] The idea of this poem as a response to the preceding unit understood in terms of lament
is widely held. See J. L. McKenzie, *Second Isaiah* (1968), 195; J. Muilenburg, "Isaiah

332  Commentary

offers a reply to those who would not ask and responds before called upon. As if offering proof of this prior attentiveness, the response reiterates and expands the vision of restoration drawing on previous texts both reversing curses and reiterating and recasting depictions of blessing. While the people's voices had urged the LORD to deliver "all" for the sake of the servants, this poem continues the sharp distinction familiar in Isaiah 56–66 between the servants and those who continue to practice idolatry and to rebel against the LORD's ways.[926]

The poem employs two central contrasts. The LORD, the dramatically and preemptively responsive one, is contrasted with people who rebel and resist. Similarly, the servants, those people who "have sought" (65:10) the LORD, stand in stark contrast to those who "forsake the LORD" (65:11).

The poem opens with a vivid image of the responsive deity. Repeatedly, the parallelism contrasts the LORD's action ("I was ready to be sought," "[I was ready] to be found," "I held out") and the people's inaction ("did not ask," "did not seek," "did not call," 65:1–2). Both vocal and physical images of openness to the people appear. The idea of the LORD calling out "here I am"[927] and not being acknowledged stands alongside the depiction of "hands" being "held out (65:1–2).[928] The divine voice emphasizes its continuous availability ("all day long") and contrasts this with the people's behavior, which provokes the LORD "continually" (65:3). The provocation is two-fold. It is both transgressive worship practices (65:3–4) and the misperception that they constitute holiness (65:5).

The motif of contrast between the LORD's attentiveness and the people's reappears in verse 12. Here again the LORD is active "I called"

---

40–66" (1956), 5:744; and the helpful summary of positions in Michael J. Chan, "Isaiah 65–66 and the Genesis of Reorienting Speech," *CBQ* 72 (2010): 445–446 n. 2, and details, 457. See B. Schramm, *Opponents* (1995), 155, who comments, "The primary function of 65.1–25 is to attack the fundamental presuppositions of the speaker of the lament."

[926] See B. S. Childs, *Isaiah* (2001), 535; J. Blenkinsopp, *Isaiah 56–66* (2003), 268; and B. Schramm, *Opponents* (1995), 155.

[927] See B. D. Sommer, *A Prophet Reads Scripture* (2008), 250, on this image of divine activity as distinctively Isaian.

[928] See J. Blenkinsopp, *Isaiah 56–66* (2003), 270, on the inversion implied in this image. He notes hands outstretched is a "typical attitude of the one praying." Here it is the LORD, not the people who stretches out hands. M. J. Chan, "Isaiah 65–66" (2010), 448, adds to this understanding of the LORD as "supplicant" here writing, "The metaphor is radical, envisioning Yhwh in a state of vulnerability, even as one whose future lies in the hands of another." See also R. Alter, *Hebrew Bible* (2019), 837.

*Isaiah 65:1–25*  333

(root *qr'*) and "I spoke" (root *dbr*) while the addressee's activity stands in contrastive parallel "did not answer" (root *'nh*) and "did not listen" (root *šm'*). The same words are used in the final expression of the motif (65:24) but without the negation. Now voicing extreme and anticipatory attentiveness, the divine voice "will answer" (root *'nh*) and "will hear" (root *šm'*) even "Before they call" (root *qr'*) and "while they are yet speaking" (root *dbr*). The contrast is dramatic, specific, and is itself responsive to the people's complaint. The preceding poem had lamented the hiding of God's "face" (64:7 Eng., 64:6 Heb.).[929] Here, the LORD expresses presence through hands held out to people who provoke God to God's "face" (65:2–3). The people have begged the LORD not to "keep silent" (*teḥĕšeh*)" (64:12 Eng.; 64:11 Heb.). Here the LORD announces, "I will not keep silent" (*'eḥĕšeh*, 65:6),[930] employing the same verb.[931]

The second dominant contrast differentiates between groups within the audience. Those "who walk in a way that is not good" (65:2) are accused of idolatrous actions.[932] This motif reappears throughout the poem. Worship in outdoor spaces, particularly among trees, in "gardens" (65:3) and on high places (65:7) appears in association with the worship of other gods (e.g., Isa 1:29; 1 Kgs 14:23; Jer 2:20; 3:6).[933] Association with spirits of the dead may be implied in the reference to tombs, another practice that was problematic within Israelite religion (Isa 8:19; Deut 18:11).[934] Eating pork is specifically forbidden in Leviticus (e.g., Lev 11:7).[935] This last specific

---

[929]  See J. Muilenburg, "Isaiah 40–66" (1956), 5:747.

[930]  I am reading here with the editors of *BHS* who cite support in manuscript evidence for *š* here as opposed to *ś*. This is also the decision that appears to underlie NRSV[ue]'s translation.

[931]  J. Muilenburg, "Isaiah 40–66" (1956), 5:745, names this connection and additional points of connection.

[932]  My position is contrary to that of C. Westermnann, *Isaiah 40–66* (1969), 402, who argues that "There is no suggestion of apostasy to other gods, but only of illicit cultic practices." His assessment applies only to vv. 1–7. He does identify idolatry in v. 11. See the discussion of locations and pork eating below. The incense description is unclear and has caused difficulties to commentators. See J. Blenkinsopp, *Isaiah 56–66* (2003), 271, for a helpful description. In the context of the other charges it seems best to regard it as referring to inappropriate and potentially idolatrous worship of some sort.

[933]  See J. Blenkinsopp, *Isaiah 56–66* (2003), 270, who connects this imagery potentially with the worship of the goddess Asherah.

[934]  See J. Blenkinsopp, *Isaiah 56–66* (2003), 271–272; and J. D. W. Watts, *Isaiah 34–66* (2005), 343.

[935]  C. Westermann, *Isaiah 40–66* (1969), 401, makes the same point citing Lev 17:11; while J. Blenkinsopp, *Isaiah 56–66* (2003), 272, cites Lev 11:7 and Deut 14:8. See further Andrew

334  Commentary

prohibition stands in ironic contrast to the claim "I am too holy for you" (Isa 65:5).

The charge against those who "forsake" and "forget" (65:11), when read within the final form of the book of Isaiah, resonates with other Isaian imagery for the LORD's impending restoration of the people. Those who "forget" the "holy mountain" and who worship other gods there with offerings of food and drink (65:11) contrast with the announcement that the LORD intends to offer a "feast of rich food" and "well-aged wines" on "this mountain" (25:6).[936] In direct contrast to those who are the LORD's "chosen" (65:9), who have "sought" (65:10) the LORD and who will benefit from the coming blessings, these who worship other gods "chose" (65:12) the things that provoke the LORD's wrath.

In the preceding poem, the "we" had implored the LORD to turn to them again "for the sake of your servants" (*lĕmaʿan ʿăbādêkā*, 63:17) and had emphasized the corporate nature of the need ("all," e.g., *kullānû*, 64:9 Eng., 64:8 Heb.) (see comment on Isa 63:7–64:12). This poem is directly responsive to that petition but draws a distinction between those who will be restored and those who will be destroyed.[937] Picking up both the "all" (*hakkōl*, 65:8) and the "servants' sake" (*lĕmaʿan ʿăbāday*, "my servants' sake," 65:8), the promise is now that not all will be destroyed for the sake of the servants. Not everyone will be delivered on account of the servants, as is probably the implication of "consider, we are all your people" (64:9). However, neither will "all" be destroyed.

---

T. Abernethy, "Feasts and Taboo Eating in Isaiah: Anthropology as a Stimulant for the Exegete's Imagination," *CBQ* 80 (2018): 401–407, for a helpful summary of anthropologically informed discussion.

[936] Isa 25 is usually considered to be a later text than the eighth-century context generally given for large portions of Isa 1–39, and possibly later than Isaiah 56–66, see J. Stromberg, *Isaiah after Exile* (2011), 249–250. So, it is not clear that the author of this passage knew Isaiah 25. However, within a final form reading, it is not inappropriate to observe resonances between these chapters as they stand in the final book of Isaiah. On the final form see further A Closer Look: The Final Form and the Former Things. On the vision offered by Isa 25, see the fascinating insights of A. T. Abernethy, "Feasts and Taboo Eating" (2018), 399, who writes, "The feast of Isa 25:5–6 projects a 'world' where there is a powerful and welcoming king upon Mount Zion who has a place at his table for people from all nations and who has the power to abolish the greatest of threats to the well-being of the world, even death." Abernethy is not here claiming any connection between Isaiah 25 and 65. However, his illumination of Isa 25 is instructive.

[937] See J. Blenkinsopp, *Isaiah 56–66* (2003), 275, who points out "The author of the lament psalm protested that 'we are all your people' (64:8), but this must be qualified, because now the promises are restricted to 'my people who seek me' (65:10b)."

*Isaiah 65:1–25* 335

The poetry dramatically reinforces the distinction between the "servants" who will be blessed and the evil-doers (65:12) through repetitive and precise parallelistic contrasts between them. Four times the LORD announces, "my servants shall" with an introductory exclamation (*hinnēh 'ăbāday*, 65:13–14)[938] and contrasts this in the following line by "but you" (*wĕ'attem*). The contrasts oppose food, "drink," joy, and "gladness" to hunger, thirst, "shame," and "pain." The food and drink imagery may echo the feast that the idolators have forgotten (25:6) and certainly takes up the images of hunger (e.g., Lam 4:5; 5:9) and abundant food and drink (55:1) that have expressed both the suffering of destruction and the fullness of restoration.

Neatly matched couplets opposing the servants and "you" give way to an expansion of the suffering of those who are to be judged in a triplet (65:14). Here a single expression of "gladness of heart" stands in contrast to the "pain of heart" and "anguish of spirit," further underscoring the poem's intense emphasis on this judgment. The final contrast, also a triplet, reorients the poem's attention. In each of the prior expressions of the contrast, the blessing of the servants has come before the punishment of the "you." Here, the notice that the "name" of these who practice idolatry is going to be left for use as a curse comes first and the direct juxtaposition of their fate with that of the servants is interrupted by the notice that they will be "put . . . to death" (65:15). This concern over the survival of their name as a curse perhaps offers an intensification of the punishment that results in the loss of memory of one's name (e.g., Deut 29:20, Heb. 29:19; Job 18:17).[939] By contrast, the "servants" will be the recipients of a "different name," picking up the motif of renaming as restoration that appeared in Isaiah 62:2.

From here onwards the poem will no longer focus on those who "forget my holy mountain" (65:11) as it envisions and re-expresses the coming restoration that has been promised (e.g., 54:11–17) and for which the sentinels were commanded to call out (62:6–7). Now the "former" sufferings are to be "forgotten" and "not . . . remembered" (65:16–17) and what

---

[938] The NRSV[ue] leaves *hinnēh* here untranslated. However, the exclamation provides an element of the repetition that draws attention to the intensity of the contrast. See also B. S. Childs, *Isaiah* (2001), 537.

[939] J. Blenkinsopp, *Isaiah 56–66* (2003), 282, points to a number of biblical examples of the use of the name as a curse highlighting Jer 29:21–23; Ps 102:9 (8 Eng.); and Num 5:21.

336                                                                                    *Commentary*

hides is no longer the LORD's face but the memory of these struggles (see
further A Closer Look: Conflicted Commands and Competing Contentions
in the Memory Motif and A Closer Look: A God Who Hides Himself).

The vision of "new heavens" and "new earth" draws together biblical
imagery from a number of sources to present a vision of restoration that
answers the people's longing (e.g., 64:1) and responds to the sense that the
fullness of restoration has not yet come (62:1, 6–7). The lines call attention
to the LORD's creative work repeating the participle "creating" (*bôrē*', Isa
65:17, 18 twice).[940] The force of this verbal form in this context is to imply
imminent and ongoing action, as the NRSV[ue]'s translation "about to
create" conveys.[941] While the human voices of these chapters have hinted
that the promised restoration has not yet happened, the divine voice not
only reiterates the promise of restoration but presents it as imminent and
not yet complete. Images of rejoicing (65:18, 19), both divine and human,
stand juxtaposed to promises of the elimination of sorrow and untimely
death (65:19–20) perhaps again picking up the imagery of God's mountain
feast in Isaiah 25, where the elimination of death stands alongside the
promise that God will "wipe away the tears" (25:8).[942] Futility curses,
familiar from Deuteronomy 28:30, 33, are explicitly reversed emphasizing
both security and provision of food.[943] As Sommer points out, the reversal
takes up and overturns Jeremiah's instruction to the exiles to settle themselves in Babylon drawing on Jeremiah's words closely.[944] Through word
play, this poem announces that exile has ended, "exultation" has begun.[945]

---

[940]  As B. S. Childs, *Isaiah* (2001), 537, points out, this is an important way of portraying God
in Isa 40–55.

[941]  J. Blenkinsopp, *Isaiah 56–66* (2003), 286, also translates in this way. NRSV[ue] renders two
of these three occurrences "about to create."

[942]  While Isaiah 65 does not directly cite this text here and the relationships are loosely and
thematically allusive rather than quotations of vocabulary, it seems likely that such
echoes are discernible. The Book of Revelation much more explicitly joins Isaian
restoration imagery, particularly that of Isa 65:17, 19 with apparent quotation of Isa
25:7–8 (see Rev 21:1, 4). Thus, it seems likely that early Christian readers saw the images
as related. See C. Westermann, *Isaiah 40–66* (1969), 408–409.

[943]  See also Richard L. Schultz, "Intertextuality, Canon, and 'Undecidability':
Understanding Isaiah's 'New Heavens and New Earth' (Isaiah 65:17–25)," *BBR* 20.1
(2010): 33.

[944]  B. D. Sommer, *A Prophet Reads Scripture* (1998), 41–43.

[945]  B. D. Sommer, *A Prophet Reads Scripture* (1998), 43, notes the sound play between
*haggôlâ* (NRSV[ue] "the exiles") in the Jeremiah source text (29:4) and *gîlâ* ("exultation,"
NRSV[ue] "a joy") in Isa 65:18. "Exultation" is Sommer's translation.

*Isaiah 65:1–25* 337

The divine voice cites its own prior speech, dramatically underlining the promise "Before they call I will answer." The lines "the lion shall eat straw like the ox" and "They shall not hurt or destroy on all my holy mountain" are perfect citations of portions of Isaiah 11:7 and 9. This citation interprets the tradition it recalls. The opening line that recalls Isaiah 11 is not a quotation but an adaptation. The "wolf" appears in Isaiah 11:6 but there it "live[s] with the lamb," and the word for lamb differs between Isaiah 11 and Isaiah 65. Since the poet responsible for Isaiah 65 clearly knows Isaiah 11, the difference is hardly accidental. Instead, it is notable that while Isaiah 11 juxtaposes images of dwelling together (11:6) with images of feeding together (11:7) for the apparent aim of demonstrating harmony and lack of danger, Isaiah 65 selects the feeding images from these lines.[946] Echoing both the imagery of eating from one's own planting in the reversal of the covenant curses (65:21–22) and the contrast between the servants who will "eat" and "drink" and the idolators who will be "hungry" and "thirsty" (65:13), this reiteration of an earlier Isaian vision of what is sometimes called "the peaceable kingdom"[947] emphasizes the abundance of restoration and the limits to sharing in that abundance.[948] As Chan points out, this poem's inclusion of the nonhuman world in its vision of restoration is far from incidental. Instead, it reflects the grand vision of the LORD as creator and appropriately overturns the negative impact of sin on all creation as imaged in Isaiah.[949]

The statement about the "food" of the "serpent" underscores the boundaries about who will share in the abundance of this vision. This is a significant difference between Isaiah 65 and Isaiah 11. There are references to snakes in Isaiah 11. However, the more specific terms "asp" (*pāten*) and "adder" (*ṣip'ônî*) are used there rather than "serpent" (*nāḥāš*) as in Isaiah 65.[950] Additionally, no mention is made in Isaiah 11 of what these creatures will eat. They are present as non-threats to the child who plays near their

---

[946] See further Daniel J. Stulac, "Rethinking Suspicion: A Canonical-Agrarian Reading of Isaiah 65," *JTI* 9.2 (2015): 188.

[947] See, e.g., Gene M. Tucker, "The Book of Isaiah: Introduction, Commentary and Reflection," *NIB* (Nashville: Abingdon, 2001), 6:140.

[948] See D. J. Stulac, "Rethinking Suspicion" (2015), 194, who comments, "Isa 65 extends a historically rooted typology of hunger and satiety toward the identification of righteous and wicked groups."

[949] M. J. Chan, "Isaiah 65–66" (2010), 458.

[950] See also R. L. Schultz, "Intertextuality" (2010), 34.

338  *Commentary*

homes. The idea that the serpent's food is "dust" appears in Gen 3:14.[951] In Genesis 3, the serpent is condemned to eat dust as punishment for its deception of the first human couple. Interestingly, the potential Eden connection also illuminates the vision of restoration as one in which the Servants will eat and the rebels will hunger (65:13). Not only is the tempter fed dust, an ephemeral, unsatisfying meal, Eden is, as Stulac points out, "a place whose soil humans serve and from which they eat."[952] This connection to a story about sin and alienation from God in the vision of restoration reiterates the distinction that the poem has repeatedly drawn between the LORD's servants, who will be blessed in the coming restoration, and those who rebel, who will be punished.

By citing previous promises and responding directly to the complaint of Isaiah 63:7–64:12, the divine voice presents a vision of future restoration on its own terms. The people had pleaded for "all," but those who refuse to acknowledge the ways of the LORD are not envisioned as participating in this future abundance. This restoration is not a return to the original Eden.[953] Death remains but is delayed. Sin remains and continues to be punished. A distinction is drawn between those who will benefit, that is, the servants, and those who will be punished. The complaint of alienation from the LORD is directly addressed with renewed promises of attentiveness that responds before being called upon (65:24)[954] and which eliminates hunger, thirst, and destruction from the holy city. The scarcity, alienation, and vulnerability of Lamentations are again overwhelmed in provision of presence and abundance (cf. Isa 55).

A CLOSER LOOK: CONFLICTED COMMANDS AND COMPETING
CONTENTIONS IN THE MEMORY MOTIF

Conflict and paradox convey Isaiah 40–66's engagement with its audience, particularly in light of their embedded complaints. Twice in Isaiah 40–55,

---

[951] See also B. S. Childs, *Isaiah* (2001), 538; J. Blenkinsopp, *Isaiah 56–66* (2003), 290; J. Muilenburg, "Isaiah 40–66" (1956), 5:757; R. Alter, *Hebrew Bible* (2019), 841; and J. Stromberg, *Isaiah after Exile* (2011), 104–105.

[952] D. J. Stulac, "Rethinking Suspicion" (2015), 193.

[953] Cf. J. Blenkinsopp, *Isaiah 56–66* (2003), 290, who does call it a "return to the first creation" while noting the serpent's exclusion.

[954] See also J. Muilenburg, "Isaiah 40–66" (1956), 5:757.

# A Closer Look: Conflicted Commands and Competing Contentions 339

voices closely tied to the audience are cited within the poetry. The central motifs of their complaints, that their way is "hidden" (*nistěrâ*; Jacob-Israel, 40:27) and that they are "forsaken" and "forgotten" (*ʿăzābanî, šěkēḥānî*; Zion, 49:14) are each taken up repeatedly in the poems, are problematized, and are embraced by the divine voice in complex ways.

Memory is unsurprising as a contested motif in these chapters, given the tension that the exiles would almost certainly experience between their past experience, present reality, and future hopes (see Bridging the Horizons: Isaiah 40–66 and Human Migration).[955] The divine voice's citation of Zion's complaint contests it on several levels. Not only does the divine voice immediately refute the charges of forgetfulness (49:15), but it implicitly indicts Zion as forgetful (49:21, see further the comment on Isaiah 49:14–50:3) and exhibits a profoundly detailed memory of Zion, taking up and citing her words as expressed in Lamentations 5:20.[956] Similarly in the case of Jacob-Israel's complaint, at the opening occurrence of this theme a voice representing the divine perspective rejects the complaint straightforwardly and passionately (On the language of Jacob-Israel's complaint, see A Closer Look: A God Who Hides Himself).[957] However, in each of these cases, the words that convey the human voice's complaint are heavily conflicted elsewhere in the poems.

The most obvious tension expressed through these motifs appears in the contradictory commands to the audience to both remember (46:9) and not remember (43:18) the "former things." The former things themselves appear as an enigmatic image sometimes referring to things predicted or to be predicted as evidence of divine reliability or a rival's unreliability (e.g., 41:22; 43:9; 48:3) and at other times they appear to refer to events of the ancient or more recent past (e.g., 42:9, 43:18; 65:16–17). They seem in some places to play a role in tying the ministry of the exilic voice to the prophetic work of Isaiah of Jerusalem (see A Closer Look: The Final Form and the Former Things). Despite the sense that the language of "former things" carries different shades of meaning in Isaiah 40–66, the diametrically

---

[955] See further L. Stulman and H. C. P. Kim, *You Are My People* (2010), 54–55, who consider Jacob and Zion's complaints in the context of discussion about "forced relocation."

[956] See T. Linafelt, *Surviving Lamentations* (2000), 74; Lena-Sofia Tiemeyer, "Geography and Textual Allusions: Interpreting Isaiah xl-lv and Lamentations as Judahite Texts," *VT* 57 (2007), 375; and K. M. Heffelfinger, "I am He" (2021), 89–90.

[957] Regarding the potential ambiguity of speaker here, see the comment on Isaiah 40:1–31.

opposed ways in which the commands to remember and to not remember are phrased is striking. As is common in these chapters, the poetry juxtaposes counter-positions and allows the tension between them to produce meaning, not least by wrestling emotionally toward a resolution that responds to the audience's complaint without minimizing or trivializing it.

The contested memory of the past relationship between the LORD and the people comes out in the ways that their various memories are depicted by the divine voice. Memory language appears in charges that the audience have "forgotten" the LORD (51:13) and the promise that Zion will "forget" (*tiškāḥî*) and not recall (*lō' tizkĕrî*, i.e., "not remember") the shame of the past (54:4). The divine voice both promises to forget sins (43:25) and invites the audience to remind the LORD (43:26). In these chapters "forsaken" is an expression of what the LORD will not do (41:17; 42:16), a characterization of Zion herself (54:6), and a call to repentance for the wicked (55:7).

In a pair of couplets that draw together the terms of both Zion's and Jacob-Israel's complaint, the divine voice appears to overturn its prior refutation of the complaints, admitting "For a brief moment I abandoned you (*'ăzabtîk*) .... In overflowing wrath for a moment I hid (*histartî*) my face from you" (Isa 54:7–8). The emphasis on brevity here takes up and reverses the contexts of the original complaint as cited from Lamentations 5:20. There the people ask "Why have you forgotten us (*tiškāḥēnû*) completely? Why have you forsaken us (*ta'azbēnû*) these many days?" Interestingly, in Isa 54 the divine voice embraces the language of having "forsaken" (*'ăzabtîk*) the people, overturning the length contention but allowing the forgotten language to go unmentioned. It was precisely forgetfulness that the divine voice directly refuted in Isaiah 49. Instead, here the divine voice joins forsakenness not with the forgottenness of Zion's complaint but with the charge of having been hidden from divine attention in Jacob-Israel's (40:27). This language is intensified from the passive voice "My way is hidden" (40:27) to the direct action of the deity "I hid my face from you" (54:8). The reiteration of these motifs transforms them. Here they offer embrace of the details of the complaint that cannot be equated with forgetfulness. Rather, having heard and remembered the people, the divine voice reverses their expression of the enduring, ongoing, endless nature of their struggle by speaking restoration, brevity, and completion (see further the comment on Isaiah 54:1–17).

*Isaiah 66:1–24*

341

As with the hiddenness motif, the apparent resolution of tension about memory achieved in Isaiah 54 is recomplicated in Isaiah 56–66. Both "forsaken" and "forgotten" reappear in these chapters. The hint in Isaiah 55:7 that what needs to be forsaken is the way of the wicked develops alongside Isaiah 56–66's differentiation between those who follow in the LORD's way and those who do not (see A Closer Look: From Servant to Servants). In Isaiah 58, the idea of the LORD's "ways" stands alongside references to justice, another key element of what Jacob claimed was overlooked. Both justice and the LORD's ways are now what those charged with "rebellion" are said to "forsake" (58:1–2). The people's voice again expresses alienation through these key motifs of memory and hiding. They charge the LORD with hiding (64:5, 7) and plead with God to decide against remembering their transgressions indefinitely (64:9) again echoing the imagery of Lamentations 5 (See the comment on Isa 63:7–64:12). Both "forget" and "forsake" become charges against those whose practices merit punishment (65:11), while the promise for those who are "my servants" (65:14) includes both forgetfulness and hiddenness of "the former troubles" (65:16) and the promise that the "former things shall not be remembered" (65:17). In line with Isaiah 56–66's distinction between the wicked and the LORD's servants, this new depiction of the redemption of the audience's memories achieves a new resolution, but it is one that creates a distinction between those who forget and are the recipients of wrath and those who are blessed and so will forget.

## ISAIAH 66:1–24

¹ Thus says the LORD:
Heaven is my throne,
> and the earth is my footstool;
so what kind of house could you build for me,
> and what sort of place for me to rest?
² All these things my hand has made,
> so all these things are mine, says the LORD.[958]

---

[958] I am departing from the NRSV^ue's lineation by keeping "says the LORD" with the rest of the line as does the lineation of MT.

342                                                                  *Commentary*

But this is the one to whom I will look,
>     to the humble and contrite in spirit
>     who trembles at my word.
³ Whoever slaughters an ox is like one who kills a human,
>         whoever sacrifices a lamb like one who breaks a dog's neck,
whoever presents a grain offering like one who offers pig's blood,
>         whoever makes a memorial offering of frankincense like one
>             who blesses an idol.
Just as these have chosen their own ways
>     and in their abominations they take delight,
⁴ so I will choose their punishments
>     and bring upon them what they fear,
because, when I called, no one answered,
>     when I spoke, they did not listen,
but they did what was evil in my sight
>     and chose what did not please me.

⁵ Hear the word of the LORD,
>     you who tremble at his word:
Your own people who hate you
>     and reject you for my name's sake
have said, "Let the LORD be glorified,
>     so that we may see your joy,"
>     but it is they who shall be put to shame.

⁶ Listen, an uproar from the city!
>     A voice from the temple!
The voice of the LORD,
>     dealing retribution to his enemies!⁹⁵⁹
⁷ Before she was in labor
>     she gave birth;

---

⁹⁵⁹ NRSVᵘᵉ includes a stanza break after v. 6. The lineation offered here differs and treats the birthing imagery (v. 7) and the roar from the Temple (v. 6) together. The patterning of the lines in Hebrew seems to support reading them together. The first three lines of the pair of couplets in v. 6 begin with the word "voice" *qôl*, while the first line of each couplet in v. 7 begins with "before" *bĕṭerem*, a poetic pattern shared between these verses reinforcing their connection to one another.

*Isaiah 66:1–24*

before her pain came upon her
>she delivered a son.
⁸ Who has heard of such a thing?
>Who has seen such things?
Shall a land be born in one day?
>Shall a nation be delivered in one moment?
Yet as soon as Zion was in labor
>she delivered her children.
⁹ Shall I open the womb and not deliver?
>says the LORD;
shall I, the one who delivers, shut the womb?
>says your God.

¹⁰ Rejoice with Jerusalem, and be glad for her,
>all you who love her;
rejoice with her in joy,
>all you who mourn over her –
¹¹ that you may nurse and be satisfied
>from her consoling breast,
that you may drink deeply with delight
>from her glorious bosom.

¹² For thus says the LORD:
I will extend prosperity to her like a river
>and the wealth of the nations like an overflowing stream,
and you shall nurse and be carried on her arm
>and bounced on her knees.
¹³ As a mother comforts her child,
>so I will comfort you;
>you shall be comforted in Jerusalem.

¹⁴ You shall see, and your heart shall rejoice;
>your bodies shall flourish like the grass,
and it shall be known that the power of the LORD is with his servants,
>and his indignation is against his enemies.
¹⁵ For the LORD will come in fire
>and his chariots in a whirlwind,
to vent his anger in fury

344                                                                  *Commentary*

and his rebuke in flames of fire.
[16] For by fire will the LORD execute judgment,
and by his sword on all flesh;
and those slain by the LORD shall be many.
[17] Those who sanctify and purify themselves to go into the gardens,
following the one in the center,
eating the flesh of pigs,
vermin, and rodents,
shall come to an end together, says the LORD.[960]

[18] for I know their works and their thoughts. I am coming to gather all
nations and tongues, and they shall come and shall see my glory, [19] and
I will set a sign among them. From them I will send survivors to the
nations, to Tarshish, Put, and Lud, to Meshech, Tubal, and Javan, to the
coastlands far away that have not heard of my fame or seen my glory,
and they shall declare my glory among the nations. [20] They shall bring
all your kindred from all the nations as an offering to the LORD, on
horses, and in chariots, and in litters, and on mules, and on
dromedaries, to my holy mountain Jerusalem, says the LORD, just as
the Israelites bring a grain offering in a clean vessel to the house of the
LORD. [21] And I will also take some of them as priests and as Levites,
says the LORD.

[22] For as the new heavens
and the new earth, which I will make,[961]
shall remain before me, says the LORD,
so shall your descendants and your name remain.
[23] From new moon to new moon
and from Sabbath to Sabbath,
all flesh shall come

---

[960] NRSV[ue] treats v. 17 as prose. However, the parallelism continues and the MT lineates.
This departure from NRSV[ue]'s lineation also impacts the beginning of v. 18, which
I have kept together with what follows while NRSV[ue] has a paragraph break within v.18.
My treatment of v. 18 follows MT.

[961] My lineation differs from the NRSV[ue] and follows the lineation of MT here. Dividing
the couplet in this way creates more balanced lines in terms of length and more closely
echoes the preceding reference to "new heavens" and "new earth" where these ideas
stood in parallel lines (65:17).

*Isaiah 66:1–24* 345

> to worship before me, says the LORD.[962]
> [24] And they shall go out and look at
> > the dead bodies of the people who have rebelled against me,
> for their worm shall not die,
> > their fire shall not be quenched,
> > and they shall be an abhorrence to all flesh.[963]

The contrast that has appeared in Isaiah 56–66 between those comforted and those judged continues right to the end of the book. That contrast revolves around their attitude to the word, ways, and worship of the LORD. Again drawing upon themes familiar from both Isaiah 1–39 and 40–55, this poem repeatedly juxtaposes coming comfort with just judgment, making the restoration of the LORD's servants and the destruction of the LORD's enemies the same event. The book closes having negotiated the tension between judgment and comfort by apportioning these on the basis of response to the LORD.

This poem initially appears to reject worship practices that are elsewhere given to the Israelites by divine instruction. As the NRSV[ue] translates Isa 66:3, an unfavorable comparison is drawn between one who "slaughters" (*šôḥēṭ*; cf. Lev 9:18, where Aaron does this action to an ox at Moses' instruction), "sacrifices" (*zôbēaḥ*; cf. Deut 17:1, which indicates sheep with defects may not be sacrificed, implying that they are otherwise acceptable), brings a "grain offering" (*minḥāh*, instructions for this offering are included in Lev 2), and offers a "memorial offering" (*mazkîr*, the inclusion of frankincense with this offering is detailed in Lev 2:16).[964] However, the lines in Hebrew contain no word for this comparison. Instead, they could as easily be read as indicating that the ones who are participating in these sacrifices as known from Leviticus and elsewhere are also doing the detestable things listed.[965]

---

[962] I am following MT in keeping "says the LORD" with the preceding line and breaking the verse instead after "all flesh" as MT does in contrast to the NRSV[ue]'s lineation.

[963] The final verse of the book continues in poetic parallelism, contra the prose representation of the NRSV[ue] and in agreement with MT.

[964] See J. Muilenburg, "Isaiah 40–66" (1956), 5:762, for references in Lev 2 and 24 and see further J. Blenkinsopp, *Isaiah 56–66* (2003), 298.

[965] This understanding of the lines appears to underlie the translations of both NET "The one who slaughters a bull also strikes down a man" and JPS *Tanakh* "those who slaughter oxen and slay humans." J. D. W. Watts, *Isaiah 34–66* (2003), 356, rejects reading these lines "as the one doing this also does that" as "an accusation of

346                                                              *Commentary*

Such an interpretation would make sense of the apparently positive treatment of "offering" (*minḥāh*, 66:20) later in the passage and suits the depiction of those indicted elsewhere in these chapters. They are accused of calling themselves "holy" (65:5) while engaging in forbidden practices, including eating "the flesh of pigs," (65:4). The term for pigs (*haḥăzîr*, 65:4; cf. 66:3) that appears in these accusations is employed to depict those who "provoke" the LORD in Isaiah 65.[966] Elsewhere those who are accused "fast," expecting that to bring a response from the LORD but are in fact oppressing others (58:3–4). Such imagery resonates with the first chapter of the book of Isaiah where the rejection of the people's worship is accompanied by the accusation "your hands are full of blood" and the imperative to "seek justice" (1:11–17). Here, it appears that the rejection is of those who practice piety alongside wickedness.[967]

The imagery that follows the list of offerings further supports such a reading. The ones to be judged are characterized in ways that draw direct connections with earlier depictions. The poetry juxtaposes what they have "chosen" (*bāḥărû*, 66:3) with what the LORD says "I will choose" ('*ebḥar*, 66:4).[968] What they "delight" in (*ḥāpēṣāh*, 66:3) is what does "not please" (*lō'-ḥāpaṣtî* 66:4) the LORD.[969] Those who are indicted in the preceding poem "chose (*bĕḥartem*) what I did not delight (*ḥāpaṣtî*) in" (65:12). Here,

---

syncretism" implausible in this context. However, rejection of Temple and cultic worship, per se, seems much less plausible in Isaiah 56–66 and the combination of pious and impious deeds is in harmony with depictions of those rejected elsewhere in these chapters (e.g., chs. 58 and 65). Indeed, B. Schramm, *Opponents* (1995), 178–182, argues for syncretism as a part of the historical mainstream cult as part of the primary force against which Third Isaiah sets itself. Thus, a both/and meaning seems more likely than a condemnation of otherwise acceptable worship practices here. See also J. Muilenburg, "Isaiah 40–66" (1956), 5:761–762; J. Blenkinsopp, *Isaiah 56–66* (2003), 294, 297; and R. Alter, *Hebrew Bible* (2019), 842. B. Schramm, *Opponents* (1995), 166–168, describes the possibilities and points to Rofé's proposal that the first portion "one who slaughters" and its parallels are descriptors for the person undertaking the action.

[966] See also the sound play between "frankincense" *lĕbōnâ* 66:3 and *hallĕbēnîm* the "bricks" in 65:3.

[967] Against J. L. McKenzie, *Second Isaiah* (1968), 203, who sees this passage as "hostile to the cult" and divergent from Isaiah 56–66's perspective, if read as combined pious and aberrant behaviors rather than comparison, the description is in harmony with those elsewhere in Isaiah 56–66.

[968] J. Muilenburg, "Isaiah 40–66" (1956), 5:763, notes that "the contrast is emphatic," highlighting the personal pronouns. See also M. A. Sweeney, *Isaiah 40–66* (2016), 373.

[969] In contrast the promise of a name is made to the eunuchs who "choose (*bāḥărû*) the things that please me (*ḥāpāṣtî*, 56:4)."

*Isaiah 66:1–24* 347

their choice is for "their own way" (66:3; cf. 57:17). The LORD's choice is "their punishments" (66:4). The charge that they have "not answered" when the LORD "called" is repeated from the preceding poem (66:4; cf. 65:12).[970] By these means, Isaiah 66 draws together the preceding indictments with its own expression of coming wrath.

In this poem, as elsewhere in these chapters, an element of the judgment is the charge of idolatry, but here the emphasis lies on doing what the LORD rejects. Like those who called themselves "too holy for you" (65:5) while engaging in forbidden worship, these figures "purify themselves" to do these things (66:17) and the location of these practices in "gardens" suggests worship of other gods (see further comment on Isaiah 65:1–25).[971] Like the depiction of those who fast and look for divine favor but act unjustly, the imagery is of those who present themselves as holy but whose actions are the very opposite of holiness. These, the poem insists, are destined for judgment.

That judgment comes from the Temple (66:6). The Temple appears to function in this poem as a place that the LORD does not reject but from which the LORD dispenses judgment. The image of nations coming and the LORD choosing some of them for priestly service fits with a concept of the Temple as a continuing place of worship (66:21).[972] This imagery echoes the depiction of the LORD offering a place "in my house" (56:5) to the eunuchs who "choose the things that please me" (56:4).[973] Those who have thought themselves pure (66:17) have chosen "what did not please me" (66:4) and will find themselves an exhibit of defilement (66:24). Their bodies will be on display to "all flesh" (66:23–24) who come to worship the LORD in direct contrast to those who will "see" and "rejoice" and whose "bodies" will "flourish" (66:14). Thus, the imagery underscores a contrast between those who will be delivered and those who face judgment. It also demonstrates how this closing poem draws together themes from Isaiah as a whole. In Isaiah 40, the "glory" of the LORD was announced as being

---

[970] See also B. S. Childs, *Isaiah* (2001), 540.

[971] See J. D. W. Watts, *Isaiah 34–66* (2005), 364.

[972] See further J. D. W. Watts, *Isaiah 34–66* (2005), 365, on the inclusion of "believers from everywhere" and B. D. Sommer, *A Prophet Reads Scripture* (1998), 148, who notes ambiguity but thinks of the options the "more likely" is "that the prophet does anticipate priestly service performed by foreigners."

[973] See B. S. Childs, *Isaiah* (2001), 542.

348                                                                  *Commentary*

"revealed" and "all flesh" (*kol- bāśār*) would "see it together" (40:5).[974] Now the glory of God is to be seen by "all nations" (66:18). It is precisely "all flesh" (*kol-bāśār*) who will "worship" (66:23) and who will abhor (66:24) the "bodies" of the rebels.[975]

It is not just the LORD who stands starkly against those who are to be judged. There are clear indicators that the audience experience these figures as enemies. Thus, their demise is presented as part of the audience's deliverance. A key difference between these figures appears to be their attitude toward the divine word. While those who are to be judged ignored when the LORD "spoke" (*dibbartî*, 66:4), their opposites are twice called one "who trembles at my word" (*ḥārēd 'al-dēbārî*, 66:2; cf. 66:5). These tremblers are the ones addressed "Hear the word of the LORD" (66:5). These who "tremble" are afflicted ( *'ānî*, NRSV[ue]: "humble," 66:2), using the same adjective as described the "homeless poor" (58:7) in the condemnation of unjust fasting. They are "contrite" (66:2) in spirit using a form of the verb that described the actions of violent "fist[s]" (58:4) in that poem. While this depiction may be an indication of their humility, there are suggestive hints that they are their neighbors' victims as well.[976] Those hints become much clearer in the second occurrence of those "who tremble at his word" (66:5). Here their "own people" are the ones "who hate" and "reject" them because of their faithfulness to the LORD.[977]

The restoration that the poem envisions draws together further expansions of previous imagery for divinely offered comfort. Birth and nursing

---

[974] See J. Stromberg, *Isaiah after Exile* (2011), 115, who connects this imagery to 66:18–19.

[975] The people who flourish like grass also pick up imagery, but not precise wording, from Isaiah 40. There the voice had proclaimed human grassiness repeatedly (40:6–8) as expressions of the contrast between human limitation and the divine word. Here, those who tremble at the divine word (66:5) are those who flourish like vegetation. See J. D. W. Watts, *Isaiah 34–66* (2005), 364, who notes the "metaphor . . . reverses the intention of 40:6–8" and Chris A. Franke, "'Like a Mother I Have Comforted You': The Function of Figurative Language in Isaiah 1:7–26 and 66:7–24," in *The Desert Will Bloom: Poetic Visions in Isaiah* (eds. A. Joseph Everson and Hyun Chul Paul Kim; Atlanta: SBL, 2009), 47: "The contrast between the image in 40:6–7 and 66:14 is extreme. The latter is awash with images of abundant fertility most associated with life-giving liquids of milk and water."

[976] While thematically divine attention to the "humble and contrite in spirit" sounds very much like the contrition that the LORD "will not despise" in Psalm 51:17, the words used here do not directly echo the Psalm and do relate to Isaiah 58. J. D. W. Watts, *Isaiah 34–66* (2005), 355, points out the appearance of this language in Isa 57:15.

[977] See further J. D. W. Watts, *Isaiah 34–66* (2005), 356–357; and B. Schramm, *Opponents* (1995), 170.

*Isaiah 66:1–24* 349

imagery further develop the maternal imagery of Isaiah 49 and 54 (see further A Closer Look: Birth and Breastfeeding Imagery in Isaiah 40–66). Restoration has already been depicted in this way, offering a vision of those comforted nursing at the "breasts of kings" (60:16). Here Zion nourishes her children directly in this way (66:11). Imagery of children being carried using the phrase *'al-ṣad*, that is, "on an arm" (60:4 NRSV[ue]: "in ... arms"; 66:12 NRSV[ue]: "on ... arm") underscores the resonance between the two poems. This movement follows the same trajectory as the maternal images in Isaiah 49 and 54. There royal figures as "foster" parents (49:23)[978] finds an echo in poems that depict Zion offering maternal comfort directly. The trajectory continues even further in Isaiah 66 as the movement from kings to Zion culminates in the LORD comforting the addressees "As a mother comforts her child" (66:13).[979]

The maternal imagery conveys significant meaning through the metaphor. The imagery of Jerusalem nursing the addressees appears in parallel couplets that employ expansive imagery emphasizing satiety, comfort (NRSV[ue]: "consoling"), "delight" (*hit'annagtem*), and abundance (66:11).[980] The depiction picks up both the "comfort" assurances that appeared throughout Isaiah 40–55 and the richness of provision that appeared in Isaiah 55. There the people were invited to "delight" (*tit'annag*) themselves with "rich food" (55:2). Expanding earlier imagery of the city's fertility, this poem depicts "birth" that precedes "labor" and "pain" (66:7). While earlier imagery moved from a mother who did not know who had borne her children (49:21) to one who did not "labor" but has many children (54:1), this poem progresses the imagery further, expansively announcing both the speed (66:7–8) and certain accomplishment of these blessings at the divine hand (66:9). If the miraculous expansion of Mother Zion's family in Isaiah 40–55 offered a vision of return and restoration for exiles listening as her "children," to a beleaguered and apparently oppressed segment of the returnee community still awaiting the fullness

---

[978] See J. D. W. Watts, *Isaiah 34–66* (2005), 363; and C. Westermann, *Isaiah 40–66* (1969), 419.

[979] See also J. L. McKenzie, *Second Isaiah* (1968), 209; and J. Blenkinsopp, *Isaiah 56–66* (2003), 305–306.

[980] The term translated "glorious" (NRSV[ue]) can convey glory but may also mean heavy. See *HALOT*, 1:457. In this context either "glorious" or "heavy" carries with it the idea of abundance.

350                                                                    *Commentary*

of the restoration vision, this swift and certain accomplishment at the divine hand further transforms and applies the expectation to their moment, offering them a vision of response to and transformation of their need. It is abundant, overflowing, and divinely provided.[981] As Franke points out, the divine voice takes up the maternal image and offers it using the word for comfort that opened Isaiah 40.[982] The problem of comfort and the expressed need for restored relationship with the LORD is answered again in a new moment and circumstance.

The contrast between blessing and judgment is stark in this poem. It takes up the condemnation of worship by those who practice evil (e.g., Isa 1:11–17)[983] and juxtaposes it with overwhelming consolation (e.g., 54–55). Those who are oppressed by the unrighteous (66:5) will witness their downfall (66:24) as will worshippers that the LORD will bring from other nations (66:20–21, 24).[984] The promise of "new heavens" and a "new earth" (66:22) with their stability combine dramatically with the closing image of perpetual punishment for those "who have rebelled" (66:24).[985] As Blenkinsopp points out, the servants are here promised a perpetual name (66:22), picking up the promises to the eunuch (56:5) and to the exiles (48:19).[986] In contrast, the name of those condemned was to remain as a curse (65:15, see comment there). The imagery is stark and effective. This abrupt ending suits a book that has been filled with tension and juxtaposition throughout. In significant measure, the final poems resolve this tension in terms of allocation of judgment and comfort to different groups in its audience.[987] By interweaving and intensifying imagery that

---

[981]  C. A. Franke, "Mother" (2009), 46.

[982]  C. A. Franke, "Mother" (2009), 45. See also R. Alter, *Hebrew Bible* (2019), 844.

[983]  See also M. A. Sweeney, *Isaiah 40–66* (2016), 380.

[984]  See further details in J. Blenkinsopp, *Isaiah 56–66* (2003), 314–315.

[985]  See B. S. Childs, *Isaiah* (2001), 542. See also B. D. Sommer, *A Prophet Reads Scripture* (1998), 251, on Isa 1:28–30 and the emphasis in both places "that the evildoers will receive punishment." On the connection to chapter 1 see further J. Blenkinsopp, *Isaiah 56–66* (2003), 316; and R. Rendtorff, "Isaiah 56:1" (1993), 187.

[986]  J. Blenkinsopp, *Isaiah 56–66* (2003), 315–316.

[987]  B. D. Sommer, *A Prophet Reads Scripture* (1998), 246, highlights the widespread discomfort among commentators with the final verses. He notes, "the verses flow naturally from what precedes them. They complete the thoughts expressed earlier in the chapter and in the last part of 40–66 – viz., that there are good and evil people among both the Judeans and the nations; the evil will be punished."

# A Closer Look: Birth and Breastfeeding Imagery in Isaiah 40–66          351

has appeared throughout the book, this poem gathers the promises and warnings of the book of Isaiah into its final poetic lines.[988]

## A CLOSER LOOK: BIRTH AND BREASTFEEDING IMAGERY IN ISAIAH 40–66

The divine voice in Isaiah 40–66 applies to itself some unusual feminine imagery.[989] By means of images comparing itself both to a laboring woman and to a breastfeeding mother, the divine voice creates identification with Zion. The other of the two driving personifications in Isaiah 40–55, the Servant, increasingly speaks like the divine voice (see further A Closer Look: The Majestic Divine Speaker and A Closer Look: The Servant and His "Songs"). However, the correlation between Zion and the LORD also increases as the poems progress and in this instance the movement toward drawing those comparisons comes from the divine voice.

The divine voice introduces several comparison partners for itself drawn from the sphere of birth and breastfeeding. In Isaiah 42:14, the LORD compares the impending "cry" of the divine voice to "a woman in labor," an image that interestingly stands juxtaposed to warrior language applied to the LORD by another voice (42:13). In this instance, the emphasis on the voice and breath and the immediate context of parching of the land suggest a relationship to the "breath of the LORD" and its power (40:7).[990] In a

---

[988] See also B. S. Childs, *Isaiah* (2001), 539, who acknowledges the discussion of this poem as a heavily edited group of elements but focusses instead on the final form writing, "I would argue that the literary effect of chapter 66 along with chapter 65 is to bring the book of Isaiah as a whole to a conclusion by interweaving elements from First, Second, and Third Isaiah together." B. S. Childs, *Isaiah* (2001), 543, delineates relationships of shared imagery between 65–66 and Isa 40 and Isa 1:1–2:4, respectively. Some connections appear more persuasive than others. See also J. Blenkinsopp, *Isaiah 56–66* (2003), 316–317. See also B. Schramm, *Opponents* (1995), 173, who writes, "the final two verses reinforce the message with which the book began, that those who 'rebel' ... against YHWH will perish."

[989] K. P. Darr, "Like Warrior" (1987), 565, notes "like a travailing woman" is applied to the LORD only in Isa 42:14 "in all of Hebrew Scripture." See also Patricia K. Tull, "Isaiah," in *Women's Bible Commentary* (20th Anniversary ed.; Eds. Carol A. Newsom, Sharon H. Ringe, and Jacqueline E. Lapsley; Louisville: Westminster John Knox, 2012), 263, 265.

[990] On juxtaposition with warrior imagery as well as parching, see K. P. Darr, "Like Warrior" (1987), 567–570. Note however, that the emphasis on "the throat of God," which Darr identifies here, does not negate the sense in which this birthing imagery must necessarily be seen as also maternal in nature. See also C. Bergmann, "Like A Warrior" (2010), 48–49.

352                                                                    *Commentary*

second instance, the divine voice sarcastically rejects objections to its activity by querying whether one questions a laboring woman about what she is bringing to birth (45:10). Here, the female birthing imagery stands in parallelism to imagery of "fathering."

This imagery that the divine voice relates to itself, primarily in terms of its power and incomparability, begins to intersect directly with the Zion personification in Isaiah 49:15, initially with contrast. In Isaiah 49:14–15, the divine voice employs nursing mother imagery, paired with reference to "the child of her womb," to illustrate how intensely the divine care for Zion exceeds human care.[991] The tone of this passage indicts Zion herself as a forgetful mother and is one of the passages where Zion's personification is most compellingly rejected as one for the audience to imitate (see A Closer Look: Lady Zion and the Suffering Servant, the Rhetorical Power of Juxtaposition and the commentary on Isaiah 49:14–50:3).

Both labor and breastfeeding appear as images of restoration in the poems that follow. Isaiah 54:1 addresses Zion as one who has not labored and the passage goes on to celebrate her abundance of children (54:1–3). In a startling reversal that conveys the totality and overwhelming nature of divine restoration, Isaiah 66:7 depicts Zion as giving birth "Before she was in labor."[992]

The breastfeeding imagery follows a similar trajectory. In Isaiah 49:22–23, foreign rulers are depicted as carrying Zion's children, and the vision offers their queens as nurses. In much more emphatic imagery, Isaiah 60:16 proclaims, "You shall suck the milk of nations; you shall suck the breasts of kings." Here the "you" is Zion herself in the most immediate context, and this appears to be a place where the reference to Zion blends with the addressees figured as her children. Thus, this is one place that the poetry enacts identification between the people and the restored imagery of Zion.

This expansive nursing imagery finds its final expression within Isaiah 40–66 in the final chapter where Zion's "glorious bosom" is a place for

---

[991]  As S. Moughtin-Mumby, *Sexual and Marital* (2008), 136, helpfully observes, "The poetry stops short of directly portraying YHWH as a breast-feeding or pregnant mother, with the distinction between 'these' and 'I' insisting that YHWH is even more compassionate. Nevertheless, it comes startlingly close."

[992]  R. Alter, *Hebrew Bible* (2019), 843, observes "To give birth without labor is to reverse the curse on Eve in Genesis, and it also suggests the miraculous swiftness with which the redemption is to be realized."

# A Closer Look: Birth and Breastfeeding Imagery in Isaiah 40–66

"drink[ing] deeply with delight" (66:11), a profound reversal of the complaints of Lamentations in which Jerusalem's mothers failed to nurse their children in the context of the siege (Lam 4:3–4). Here, standing alongside the imagery of miraculous birth before labor, explicitly at the divine hand (66:7–9), the nursing imagery is also offered as an image of divine comfort.[993] In the immediate context of the people drinking from Jerusalem's comforting (*tanḥumêhā*) breast, the divine voice announces, "As a mother comforts (*tĕnaḥămennû*) her child, so will I comfort you ('*ănaḥemkem*)" (66:13). Here the divine voice's birth and breastfeeding imagery connects to the Zion personification, offering Zion in her restored state as an image of divinely offered comfort.

Thus, while it is certainly the case that the divine voice works to undermine Zion's objections, and presents the response of the Servant figure as an embodiment of the response it urges from its audience (see further A Closer Look: Lady Zion and the Suffering Servant, the Rhetorical Power of Juxtaposition), it is clear that the Zion personification is offered as a powerful vision of hope and promise in its own right. Her objections overwhelmed, Zion as miraculous mother (54:1; 66:7–8) and Zion as superabundant nourisher (66:11), stands as a personification of the divinely offered comfort. As the poems draw to a close, it is Zion imagery, maternal breastfeeding imagery, that depicts the comfort the divine voice enacts (66:13).

---

[993] W. A. M. Beuken, "Main Theme" (1990), 83, comments, "This is the only place where Zion itself grants consolation, Everywhere else the comfort comes from God."

# Glossary of Poetic Terminology

**Alliteration** – A sound device created through the repetition of the sounds of consonants.
**Chiasm** – A poetic pattern in which parallel elements form a set of frames. Brown glosses it as "concentric inverted parallelism,"[1] which describes the phenomenon well. In this structure, outer themes, motifs, or other patterns parallel each other while more central elements parallel each other and so on in a set of envelope structures nested within each other. Chiasm sometimes exhibits a central term or element which has no parallel within the structure. A pattern such as A-B-C-B'-A' is sometimes used to represent the structure and the relationship of its elements.
**Couplet** – A pair of lines bound together by parallelism.
**Gapping** – The omission of a word or part of speech in one or more lines of a group of lines where its meaning is implied through its appearance in another of the lines in the parallelistic relationship.[2]
**Inclusio** – A device that frames a section of text through the appearance of mirrored motifs, images, or words at the beginning and end of the section. Berlin discusses this construction as a type of parallelism which she notes carries the specific function of "provid[ing] cohesion and unity for the text as a whole."[3]

---

[1] W. P. Brown, *A Handbook* (2017), 341.
[2] See further J. Blake Couey, *Reading the Poetry of First Isaiah: The Most Perfect Model of the Prophetic Poetry* (Oxford: Oxford University Press, 2015), 32.
[3] Adele Berlin, *The Dynamics of Biblical Parallelism* (Rev and Exp ed.; Grand Rapids: William B. Eerdmans, 2008), 132.

**Line** – A group of words separated into a unit or segment,[4] forming "The primary formal unit in poetry."[5] The line is represented visually on the printed page by standing on its own horizontal line of text separated from what precedes and follows. As Dobbs-Allsopp notes, many biblical scholars use the term colon for this unit with the terms bicolon meaning the same unit as couplet and tricolon conveying the same unit as triplet.[6]

**Merism** – A poetic structure that employs opposites to express an encompassing reality.[7]

**Parallelism** – A structure binding two or more lines closely together. Parallelism is not simple repetition, but a "seconding"[8] or "dynamic movement from one verset to the next."[9] It frequently conveys development of ideas through modification of repeated forms or themes. Robert Alter helpfully describes "two basic operations of specification and heightening within the parallelistic line" or as James Kugel puts it the second, "carries it further, backs it up, completes it, goes beyond it."[10] In addition, parallelism can function on a broader level within poems and poetic units.[11]

**Parataxis** – A term that poetic theorists use to describe a style where ideas are juxtaposed rather than explicitly related to one another.[12] A paratactically styled poem will often shift theme, topic, or speaker suddenly and without explanation.

**Personification** – A poetic device that develops an inanimate object, animal, or idea in human terms.[13]

---

[4] See F. W. Dobbs-Allsopp, *On Biblical Poetry* (Oxford: Oxford University Press, 2015), 8.

[5] Mary Kinzie, *A Poet's Guide to Poetry* (Chicago: University of Chicago Press, 1999), 433.

[6] F. W. Dobbs-Allsopp, *On Biblical Poetry* (2015), 23.

[7] See the example that "'heaven' and 'earth' together designate the totality of creation" in Gen 2:4 as noted by W. P. Brown, *A Handbook* (2017), 155.

[8] James L. Kugel, *The Idea of Biblical Poetry: Parallelism and Its History* (London: Johns Hopkins University Press, 1981), 51.

[9] R. Alter, *Art* (1985), 10.

[10] R. Alter, *Art* (1985), 62; J. L. Kugel, *Idea* (1981), 52.

[11] See Dennis Pardee, *Ugaritic and Hebrew Poetic Parallelism: A Trial Cut ('nt and Proverbs 2)* (VTSup 39; New York: Brill, 1988), 66–67.

[12] See Michael Patrick O'Connor, "Parataxis and Hypotaxis," in *The New Princeton Encyclopedia of Poetry and Poetics* (eds. Alex Preminger and T. V. F. Brogan; Princeton: Princeton University Press, 1993), 879–880.

[13] See further, John Arthos and T. V. F. Brogan, "Personification," in *New Princeton Enyclopedia of Poetry and Poetics* (Eds. Alex Preminger and T. V. F. Brogan; Princeton: Princeton University Press, 1993), 902.

# Glossary of Poetic Terminology

**Stanza** – A group of lines that forms a larger unit.[14]

**Synecdoche** – A poetic device that uses a smaller part of something as a means of referencing the whole.

**Tone** – Tone, from a literary perspective, indicates the "attitude" that the speaker conveys toward its subject matter or audience.[15]

**Triplet** – A group of three lines held together as a unit by parallelism.

---

[14] See further F. W. Dobbs-Allsopp, *On Biblical Poetry* (2015), 434 n. 108, on the non-necessity of inferring any reference to meter or rhyme through the use of the term.

[15] I. A. Richards, *Practical Criticism: A Study of Literary Judgment* (New York: Harcourt, Brace and Company, 1929), 182. See also, T. V. F. Brogan and Fabian Gudas, "Tone," in *The New Princeton Encyclopedia of Poetry and Poetics* (eds. Alex Preminger ad T. V. F. Brogan; Princeton: Princeton University Press, 1993), 1293–1294.

# Author Index

Abernethy, Andrew T., 334
Ahn, John, 9, 18, 55, 56, 57, 246
Alter, Robert, 15, 16, 25, 27, 28, 39, 87, 88, 93, 109, 131, 134, 142, 151, 182, 259, 270, 280, 288, 300, 332, 338, 346, 350, 352, 356
Ames, Frank Ritchel, 55
Arnold, Bill T., 42, 140, 165
Arthos, John, 356
Askins, Kye, 60
Aune, David E., 317

Balentine, Samuel (E.), 133, 137, 138
Baltzer, Klaus, 2, 15, 72, 82, 92, 98, 99, 100, 110, 111, 113, 114, 117, 118, 123, 124, 126–127, 131, 133, 139, 140, 141, 142, 143, 144, 149, 150, 152, 153, 155, 159, 160, 161, 164, 165, 170, 171, 178, 180, 188, 189, 195, 201, 202, 203, 205, 209, 210, 211, 212, 214, 218, 223, 237, 243, 244
Barré, Michael L., 219
Beasley-Murray, George R., 228
Becker, Ewe, 6
Benedict XVI, 52
Berges, Ulrich (F.), 18, 32, 41, 251, 252, 253
Bergmann, Claudia, 81, 351
Berlin, Adele, 12, 16, 355
Beuken, Willem A. M., 19, 106, 185, 233, 253, 254, 353
Blenkinsopp, Joseph, 2, 8, 9, 15, 25, 27, 29, 31, 33, 35, 36, 39, 41, 42, 45, 47, 62, 63, 64, 66, 70, 71, 83, 96, 97, 98, 100, 104, 113, 116, 122, 123, 126–127, 129, 130, 131, 132, 141, 142, 144, 147, 149, 152, 154, 155, 158, 159, 164, 166, 170, 173, 179, 183, 188, 189, 191, 192, 195, 196, 197, 198, 201, 202, 207, 210, 212, 214, 243, 248, 249, 251, 252, 258, 263, 277, 281, 282, 283, 289, 291, 297, 298, 299, 300, 301, 302, 305, 306, 312, 313, 322, 324, 325, 327, 328, 332, 333, 334, 335, 336, 338, 341, 345, 349, 350, 351
Brettler, Marc, 19, 220, 224, 225, 228, 229
Briant, Pierre, 18, 41, 42, 140
Brisman, Leslie, 221
Brogan, T. V.F., 356, 357
Brown, William P., 145, 355, 356

Carvalho, Corrine, 183
Cerna, Lucía, 230
Chan, Michael J., 143, 332, 337
Childs, Brevard S., 11, 15, 36, 38, 48, 62, 64, 65, 66, 70, 76, 93, 96, 106, 112, 140, 143, 149, 150, 151, 158, 166, 170, 171, 183, 187, 188, 207, 211, 214, 217, 220, 221, 222, 233, 234, 237, 242, 243, 245, 249, 258, 259, 261, 262, 263, 270, 271, 273, 277, 278, 281, 283, 287, 288, 289, 290, 291, 297, 298, 299, 300, 307, 309, 310, 312, 313, 325, 326, 332, 335, 336, 338, 347, 350, 351
Choi, John H., 165
Clements, R. E., 78, 83
Clifford, Richard J., 2, 8, 19, 41, 106
Clines, David J.A., 218, 219, 222, 224
Couey, J. Blake, 16, 17, 293, 355
Culler, Jonathan, 4, 5

Dahood, Mitchell, 75
Dalberg, John Emerich Edward (Lord Acton), 316
Daniel, E. Valentine, 57
Darling, Jonathan, 60
Darr, Katheryn Pfisterer, 80, 81, 351
Day, Peggy L., 18, 155, 156
De Roche, Michael, 88

359

# Author Index

Dekker, Jaap, 220, 254, 261, 262, 263
Dempsey, Carol J., 287, 289
Dobbs-Allsopp, F. W., 7, 16, 17, 118, 156, 163, 356, 357
Donahue, John R., 227
Donelson, Lewis R., 228

Essex, Ryan, 56, 57
Exum, J. Cheryl, 2

Ferguson, Everett, 316
Fitzgerald, Aloysius, 155–156
Franke, Chris A., 150, 151, 348, 350
Freyne, Patrick, 59
Fried, Lisbeth S., 18, 122, 123

Geller, Stephen A., 26, 27, 29
Geyser-Fouchè, Ananda, 219, 221
Gill, Nick, 60
Gitay, Yehoshua, 2
Goldingay, John, 7, 8, 15, 27, 28, 29, 31, 37, 39, 41, 45, 49, 62, 63, 65, 67, 72, 75, 77, 81, 82, 83, 85, 86, 87, 92, 93, 94, 95, 96, 97, 98, 99, 100, 101, 102, 104, 105, 106, 109, 110, 111, 113, 114, 116, 117, 118, 122, 123, 124, 125, 126, 129, 130, 131, 132, 133, 141, 143, 144, 148, 149, 151, 152, 153, 154, 158, 159, 160, 161, 164, 165, 170, 171, 174, 178, 179, 181, 182, 183, 184, 187, 188, 189, 190, 192, 194, 195, 197, 198, 202, 203, 204, 205, 210, 211, 212, 214, 217, 225, 228, 233, 234, 235, 236, 237, 240, 242, 244
Gottwald, Norman K., 12, 189
Goździak, Elżbieta M., 59
Graham, M. Patrick, 76
Gregory, Bradley C., 300
Gudas, Fabian, 357

Hackett, Jo Ann, 156
Halpern, Baruch, 305, 306
Halvorson-Taylor, Martien A., 18, 328
Harrington, Daniel J., 227, 314
Hays, Christopher B., 17, 77
Hays, Richard B., 314, 315
Heffelfinger, Katie M., 1, 3, 5, 7, 11, 12, 34, 58, 101, 120, 171, 178, 179, 184, 185, 202, 203, 205, 209, 213, 217, 219, 225, 259, 261, 262, 264, 294, 306
Held, Shai, 50, 54
Hiraide, Lydia Ayame, 59

Holtz, Shalom E., 37
Hutton, Jeremy M., 202, 203, 204

Ignoffo, Mary Jo, 230

Jacobs, Alan, 120, 294
James, Elaine T., 16, 17, 293
Jameson, Jill, 56, 57
Jones, Christopher M., 286, 288
Jong, Matthijis J. de, 134

Kaiser, Barbara Bakke, 178
Kalocsányiová, Erika, 56, 57
Kaminsky, Joel S., 19, 50, 53, 54
Kim, Hyun Chul Paul, 19, 25, 55, 56, 57, 58, 67, 152, 339
King, Philip J., 245
Kinzie, Mary, 356
Knudsen, John Chr., 57
Koester, Craig R., 317
Koet, Bart J., 313
Korpel, Marjo C.A., 240, 243, 246
Kugel, James L., 16, 17, 356
Kuhrt, Amélie, 42

Laato, Antti, 41
Landy, Francis, 1, 25, 26, 27, 28, 29, 31
Lassalle-Klein, Robert, 229–230
Levine, Amy-Jill, 19, 220, 224, 225, 228, 229, 315
Lim, Bo H., 19, 55, 56, 221, 230
Linafelt, Tod, 12, 16, 17, 143, 153, 178, 327, 339
Lincoln, Andrew T., 318–319
Lindblad, Ulrika, 66, 71
Lowth, Robert, 306
Ludwig, Theodore M., 73
Lynch, Matthew J., 19, 59, 310, 312, 313

Macías, Daniel Vega, 59
Main, Izabella, 59
Markl, Dominik, 19
Mathewson, David, 317
McGilchrist, Iain, 60, 120, 225
McKenzie, John L., 2, 16, 68, 81, 88, 97, 98, 100, 113, 133, 135, 143, 144, 150, 164, 165, 166, 171, 189, 191, 202, 203, 207, 210, 221, 243, 259, 263, 270, 271, 273, 278, 283, 297, 301, 302, 304, 306, 310, 331, 346, 349
Melugin, Roy F., 5, 17
Mettinger, Tryggve N. D., 17, 66, 68, 218, 222

# Author Index

361

Michalowski, Piotr, 42
Moberly, R. W.L., 50, 54
Moughtin-Mumby, Sharon, 88, 89, 149, 150, 154, 155, 234, 251, 260, 261, 306, 352
Mtshiselwa, Ndikhokele, 272, 273
Muilenburg, James, 6, 16, 47, 62, 63, 67, 68, 73, 75, 76, 93, 96, 98, 100, 106, 109, 113, 114, 116, 118, 119, 123, 124, 125, 131, 132, 133, 140, 148, 149, 150, 158, 163, 164, 166, 170, 178, 184, 189, 191, 192, 195, 197, 198, 202, 203, 204, 210, 211, 214, 217, 223, 237, 242, 244, 251, 259, 264, 269, 271, 272, 273, 277, 279, 280, 283, 286, 288, 300, 301, 304, 305, 306, 307, 309, 310, 324, 331, 333, 338, 345, 346
Mullins, Matthew, 16, 17, 119
Munengwa, Thomas M., 219, 221

Nanos, Mark D., 50, 52
Newsom, Carol A., 8, 12
Niditch, Susan, 144
Nielsen, Kristen, 49, 245–246
Nihan, Christophe, 59
Niskanen, Paul V., 306, 325, 326
Nolland, John, 228, 315

O'Connor, Michael Patrick, 356
Olley, John W., 167, 219

Pardee, Dennis, 356
Park, Eugene Eung-Chun, 315–316
Payne, David, 7, 8, 15, 27, 28, 29, 31, 37, 39, 41, 45, 49, 62, 63, 65, 67, 72, 75, 77, 81, 82, 83, 85, 86, 87, 92, 93, 94, 95, 96, 98, 101, 102, 104, 105, 106, 109, 110, 111, 113, 114, 116, 117, 118, 122, 123, 124, 125, 126, 129, 130, 131, 132, 133, 141, 143, 144, 148, 149, 151, 152, 153, 158, 159, 160, 161, 164, 165, 170, 171, 174, 178, 179, 181, 182, 183, 184, 187, 188, 189–190, 192, 194, 195, 197, 198, 202, 203, 204, 205, 210, 211, 212, 214, 217, 225, 228, 233, 234, 235, 236, 237, 240, 242, 244
Pilkington, Christine, 133

Raabe, Paul R., 75, 76, 222
Rembaum, Joel E., 228, 229
Rendtorff, Rolf, 18, 77, 78, 79, 134, 143, 182, 265, 350
Richards, I.A., 357
Ricoeur, Paul, 3

Roberts, Kathryn R., 178, 179–180
Roche, Kathleen M., 59
Rowland, Christopher C., 317
Rudin, A. James, 225
Rumyantseva, Nataliya, 56, 57

Sacks, Jonathan, 199, 293, 294
Saunders, Stanley P., 316
Sawyer, John F.A., 19, 224, 228, 229, 314
Schaudig, Hanspeter, 140
Schipper, Jeremy, 220
Schmidt, Uta, 19, 69, 177, 178, 184, 185
Schramm, Brooks, 6–7, 10, 11, 19, 253, 263, 277, 278, 332, 346, 348, 351
Schultz, Richard L., 336, 337
Schwartz, Seth J., 59
Seufert, Matthew, 64
Sheringham, Olivia, 58, 59
Smillie, Gene R., 40, 67
Smith, Barbara Herrnstein, 118
Smith, James K.A., 120
Smith, Mark S., 174, 175
Smith-Christopher, Daniel L., 9, 19
Sommer, Benjamin D., 7, 11, 16, 17, 30, 67, 87, 166, 180, 183, 188, 189, 190, 192, 196, 211, 212, 214, 218, 219, 221, 224, 241, 242, 252, 259, 263, 264, 266, 278, 300, 302, 311, 332, 336, 347, 350
Soulen, R. Kendall, 51–52, 54
Spencer, Bradley J., 49
Stager, Lawrence, 245
Stansell, Gary, 287, 289, 290
Stern, Philip D., 47, 83, 100, 101, 222
Stewart, Anne, 19, 50, 53
Streitweiser, Bernhard, 59
Strine, C. A., 56
Stromberg, Jacob, 10, 18, 252, 253, 266, 334, 338, 348
Stulac, Daniel J., 337, 338
Stulman, Louis, 19, 25, 55, 56, 57, 58, 152, 339
Sweeney, Marvin A., 6, 12, 13, 14, 16, 37, 68, 140, 173, 174, 194, 233, 253, 255, 281, 300, 346, 350

Taylor, Helen, 58, 59
Tiemeyer, Lena-Sofia, 7, 196, 259, 339
Trible, Phyllis, 179
Tucker, Gene M., 337
Tull (Willey), Patricia K., 12, 13, 16, 17, 20, 25, 27, 32, 33, 69, 153, 178, 179, 180, 182, 185, 189,

190, 192, 193, 202, 203, 204, 208, 210, 212, 214, 217, 220, 222, 223, 235, 236, 237, 240, 351

Vanderhooft, David, 42

Walsh, Jerome T., 36, 38, 47, 48, 145
Watts, John D.W., 16, 30, 36, 37, 38, 41, 83, 93, 98, 104, 109, 113, 118, 123, 125, 141, 163, 164, 166, 182, 188, 195, 201, 202, 203, 204, 210, 251, 252, 273, 277, 283, 298, 300, 307, 308, 326, 328, 333, 345, 347, 348, 349
Wells, Roy D., 288, 291
Westermann, Claus, 16, 28, 31, 32, 35, 36, 39, 41, 48, 61, 62, 63, 66, 67, 75, 82, 83, 85, 92, 93,

94, 96, 99, 100, 101, 104, 106, 112, 113, 114, 123, 125, 126, 129, 130, 133, 140, 147, 164, 166, 167, 170, 173, 178, 182, 183, 188, 189, 191, 198, 201, 202, 204, 212, 213, 222, 236, 237, 240, 242, 244, 249, 251, 258, 259, 260, 263, 275, 277, 278, 279, 283, 289, 297, 298, 300, 301, 305, 306, 309, 311, 323, 333, 336, 349
Wildberger, Hans, 141
Williamson, H. G. M., 6, 8, 17, 18, 49, 77–79, 83, 141, 144, 188, 193, 219, 241, 261, 272, 273, 287
Witherington III, Ben, 227, 314, 317, 318, 319
Wolterstorff, Nicholas, 314
Wyschogrod, Michael, 50, 53, 54

# Scripture Index

HEBREW BIBLE

Genesis, 352
  1, 70, 132
  1:14–18, 288
  1:2, 31, 63, 279
  2, 132
  2–3, 198
  2:4, 356
  2:7, 131
  2:9–16, 198
  3, 279
  3:14, 338
  6:17, 93
  9:16, 244
  12, 54
  12:3, 54
  15:1, 199
  15:8, 166
  17:7, 174, 175
  17:13, 174, 175
  17:17–18, 196
  17:19, 174, 175
  18:12–15, 196
  18:23, 167
  18:23–33, 323
  19:1, 323
  19:11, 323
  19:13, 323
  19:16, 323
  19:21, 323
  19:24, 93
  22, 166, 196
  22:17, 166
  25:4, 289
  25:13, 289
  25:22, 159
  25:25, 310
  25:26, 103
  27:29, 144
  27:36, 103
  27:42–45, 144
  28–33, 144
  28:9, 289
  30:2, 161
  32, 166
  32:3, 75
  32:12, 166
  32:28, 103, 145, 159
  32:32 (Heb: 32:33), 159, 161
  34:3, 26
  34:5, 36
  36:1, 310
  36:3, 289
  37:36, 250
  39:1, 250
  39:4, 290
  40:2, 250
  40:4, 290
  40:7, 250
  44:18, 161
  46–50, 144
  46:3, 199
  46:3–4, 144
  50:21, 26
  50:29–33, 144
Exodus, 166, 183, 315
  2:15–22, 288
  3:7, 291
  4:14, 161

# 364 *Scripture Index*

**Exodus (cont.)**
5:6, 291
5:10, 291
5:13, 291
5:14, 291
7:3, 325
9:27, 167
14:14, 36
14:21, 323
15, 96
15:1, 324
15:1–18, 96
15:5, 324
15:6, 85
15:8, 324
15:11, 85
19:5–6, 50
22:23, 161
28:41, 301
30:30, 301
32:9, 160
32:10, 161
32:11, 161
32:19, 161
32:22, 161
33:3, 160
34:6–7, 317

**Leviticus**
2, 260, 345
2:16, 345
6, 260
6:20, 301
8:12, 301
9:18, 345
10:1–2, 93
11:7, 333
15:19–24, 325
16:29, 271
16:31, 271
16:32, 301
17:11, 333
20:2–5, 261
21:20, 252
22:25, 253
23:13, 260
23:18, 260
23:27, 271
23:29, 271
23:32, 271
24, 345
25:9, 209, 270

**Numbers**
3:3, 301
5:21, 335
11:1, 161
11:1–3, 93
11:12, 181
22, 288
35:19, 312
35:22–28, 312

**Deuteronomy, 54**
1:7, 289
3:25, 289
7:6, 50
7:7, 53
7:7–11, 50
10:8, 290
11:24, 289
14:2, 50
14:8, 333
17:1, 345
17:12, 290
18:11, 333
23:1 (Heb: 23:2), 252
25:1, 167
26:18, 50
28:30, 336
28:30–31, 307
28:33, 307, 336
28:36, 82
28:54, 149
28:56, 25–149
29:20 (Heb: 29:19), 335
32, 103
32:18, 196
32:22, 93
33, 103

**Joshua**
1:4, 289
6:4, 209
9:1, 289
11:4, 166
11:17, 289
12:7, 289
24:25, 174

**Judges**
1:8, 93
3:3, 289
3:27, 209
6–9, 288, 289
6:34, 209
7:12, 166

# Scripture Index

9:15, 93
14:15, 93
15:5, 93
19:3, 26
Ruth
2:13, 26
4:16, 181
1 Samuel
8:15, 250
8:20, 290
10:1, 301
13:5, 166
15:1, 301
16, 242
16:13, 301
17:43, 259
24:14, 259
2 Samuel, 242
2:4, 301
2:28, 209
6:15, 209, 270
7, 242
11:1, 290
13:17, 290
17:11, 166
18:16, 209
18:18, 251
22:35, 160
22:51, 242
23:1, 301
23:1–7, 242
23:2, 242, 301
23:3, 301
23:4, 301
23:5, 242, 301
23:6, 301
23:7, 301
24:22, 48
1 Kings
1:34, 204, 297
1:39, 209
4:20, 166
5:1–12, 289
8:11, 290
8:32, 167
10, 288
10:10, 289
11:7, 261
14:23, 333
16:31, 250
19:16, 301

21:25–26, 250
22:9, 250
22:31, 290
22:42, 305
2 Kings
8:6, 250
8:13, 254, 259
9:3, 301
9:13, 209
9:32, 250
10:1, 181
10:5, 181
14:7, 76
16:4, 261
17:10, 261
20:18, 251
21:1, 305
23:10, 261
24:12, 250
24:15, 250
1 Chronicles
1:29, 289
1:33, 289
2:46–47, 289
21:23, 48
28:1, 246
2 Chronicles
25:12, 76
36:23, 41
Ezra
1:3, 41
3:7, 41
6:4, 41
Nehemiah, 299
13:25, 190
Esther
1:10, 250, 251, 290
1:15, 250, 251
2:3, 250
2:14, 250
2:15, 250
2:21, 250, 251
4:4, 250
4:5, 250
6:2, 250, 251
6:14, 250, 251
7:9, 250
Job
18:17, 335
20:16, 279
20:24, 160

366                                        *Scripture Index*

Job (cont.)
  26:12, 202
  27:20, 93
  30:26, 287
  32:21–22, 104
  40:18, 160
Psalms, 70, 113, 322
  1:6, 167
  7:10 (Heb: 7:9), 167
  11:6, 93
  18:34, 160
  19:1a, 164
  21:9 (Heb: 21:10), 192
  22, 225, 227
  27:1, 287
  37:17, 167
  51:17, 348
  69, 228
  69:2 (Heb: 69:3), 93
  72:3, 291
  74:13, 202
  74:20, 174
  75:8, 210
  81:3 (Heb: 81:4), 270
  88:17 (Heb: 88:18), 93
  89, 242
  89:10 (Heb: 89:11), 202
  89:46 (Heb: 89:47), 192
  93:1, 202
  97:11, 287
  98:6, 209
  102:8 (Heb: 102:9), 335
  120:5, 288
  124:4–5, 93
  137, 75
  137:7, 310
  139:18, 166
  150:3, 209
Proverbs
  26:18, 193
Ecclesiastes
  4:1, 203
Isaiah, 11–12, 14, 15, 17, 25, 40, 48, 49, 77–79, 129,
    208, 245, 248, 274, 301, 310, 334, 347
  1, 278–279
  1–39, 6, 11–12, 14, 77–78, 87, 141, 182, 241, 249,
    258, 261, 265–267, 334, 345
  1–55, 78
  1:1–2:4, 351

1:3, 86
1:4, 129
1:7, 93, 192
1:10–20, 269
1:11, 253
1:11–15, 278
1:11–17, 346, 350
1:12–17, 253
1:15, 277
1:16, 253
1:17, 253
1:18, 86
1:19, 87, 241
1:19–20, 241, 274
1:20, 274
1:21, 260
1:23, 261
1:24, 129
1:28–30, 350
1:29, 261, 333
2, 245, 287
2:2–3, 287, 288
2:2–4, 287
2:5, 261, 287
2:6–21, 261
2:10, 86, 290
2:11, 261
2:12–13, 48, 49, 245
2:12–17, 245
2:13, 246
2:17, 261
2:18, 261
2:19, 86, 290
2:20, 261
2:21, 290
3:12, 291
3:13, 262
3:15, 262
4:2, 290
5:8, 129
5:11, 129
5:20, 129
5:21, 129
5:22, 129
5:23, 167
5:30, 192
6, 83, 219, 221
6:1, 261
6:9, 83

## Scripture Index

6:9–10, 261
6:9–13, 86
6:10, 262
6:12–13, 49
6:13, 246
7:22, 291
7:23–25, 246
8, 86
8:16, 188, 261, 326
8:17, 326
8:19, 326, 333
8:22–9:1, 192
9:1–4, 287
9:6–7, 301
9:10, 246
9:18–19, 110
9:29, 192
10, 86
10:20, 68
11, 266, 337–338
11:5, 318
11:6, 337
11:7, 337
11:8, 279
11:9, 337
13, 64
13:8, 81
13:16, 86
14:2, 288
14:4, 291
14:8, 246
14:11, 47
14:13–14, 154
16:5, 301
17:14, 86
21, 75–76
21:3, 81
21:10, 48
21:16, 288
21:17, 288
22:16, 181
24:8, 290
24:11, 290
24:14, 290
25, 334
25:6, 334, 335
25:7–8, 336
25:8, 336
26:1–2, 292

26:10, 167
27:12–13, 48
28:7, 93
28:15, 261
30:8, 181, 261, 326
30:9–10, 326
30:9–14, 87, 241
30:18, 326
30:22, 261
30:25–26, 49
30:26, 262
31:6, 261
31:7, 261
32:13, 290
32:14, 290
33:23, 86
34, 311
34:2, 310
34:3, 310
34:5, 310
34:6, 310
34:7, 310
34:8, 312
35, 49
35:1–2, 49
35:6–7, 49
37:24, 246
39, 6, 25
39:2, 124
39:7, 251
40, 2, 6, 33, 35, 38, 45, 81, 103, 105, 164, 171, 211, 244, 300, 307, 347, 350, 351
40–48, 33, 116, 143
40–55, 4, 6–10, 11, 12, 13, 14, 15, 17, 30, 33, 45, 49, 56, 57, 58, 59, 65, 68, 70, 74, 77–79, 88, 89, 95, 105, 115, 116, 118, 133, 136, 165, 174, 182, 184, 185, 189, 199, 204, 213, 218, 226, 229, 234, 241, 242, 245, 249, 253–254, 258, 260, 264–267, 273, 290, 297, 322, 324, 327, 328, 331, 336, 338
40:1, 1, 34, 46, 137, 197, 262
40:1–31, 21–33
40:2, 6, 46, 211, 214, 220, 241, 298
40:3, 261, 263, 307
40:4, 81, 124, 244
40:5, 241, 274, 348
40:6, 105
40:6–7, 348
40:6–8, 171, 204, 223, 348

Isaiah (cont.)
40:7, 81, 105, 351
40:8, 105, 244
40:9, 199
40:12, 192
40:12–14, 38
40:13, 192
40:13–14, 199
40:14, 192
40:15, 40
40:18, 192
40:19, 38
40:21, 192
40:21–25, 240
40:21–26, 46
40:22, 261
40:23, 171
40:25, 192
40:25–28, 88
40:27, 9, 66, 133–134, 136, 153, 172, 173, 192, 197,
  201, 235, 238, 250, 272, 339, 340
40:27–31, 133
40:28, 111, 125
40:28–31, 188
40:29, 111
40:30–31, 347
40:31, 35, 40, 111, 171
41, 49, 67, 72, 82, 246
41:1, 85, 169
41:1–7, 40
41:2, 64, 132, 182
41:5, 40, 45, 49
41:8, 50, 68, 145, 175
41:8–16, 72
41:8–9, 65, 66, 68, 71
41:8–20, 42–50, 172, 265
41:9, 50, 71
41:10, 34, 64, 189, 199, 204
41:11, 62
41:12, 62
41:13, 34, 71, 123, 189, 204
41:14, 34, 68, 189, 204
41:15, 124
41:15–16, 123
41:17, 48, 340
41:18, 124
41:19, 246
41:21, 88
41:21–24, 109
41:21–26, 88
41:21–29, 64, 265

41:22, 58, 339
41:22–23, 72
41:23, 45
41:24, 72
41:25, 132
42, 83, 94, 175
42:1, 71, 299
42:1–4, 65–68, 71, 72, 172
42:1–9, 41
42:3, 299
42:4, 85, 299
42:5, 73, 105, 158, 195
42:5–9, 69–73, 75
42:6, 123, 132, 174, 241
42:6–7, 297
42:7, 132
42:8, 74
42:9, 58, 75, 76, 339
42:10, 40
42:10–13, 74–77, 269
42:11, 288
42:13, 80, 81, 351
42:14, 351
42:14–15, 183
42:14–20, 75, 79–84, 88
42:15, 49
42:15–16, 119, 124
42:16, 340
42:17, 86
42:18–25, 83, 137, 241
42:19, 94
42:20, 86, 88, 94
42:21–25, 84–88, 243
42:24, 137, 218, 220, 241
42:25, 89, 94
43, 83, 133, 144
43–45, 95
43:1, 68, 73, 104, 108, 116, 125, 130, 158,
  195, 199, 204
43:1–7, 137
43:1–21, 89–97
43:2, 34
43:3, 133
43:5, 199, 204
43:5–6, 34
43:6, 169
43:7, 116, 130
43:8–13, 109
43:9, 58, 192, 339
43:10, 242
43:11, 73, 74, 99, 109, 150

# Scripture Index

43:13, 99
43:14, 6, 108, 123
43:15, 74, 101
43:15–17, 74
43:16, 195
43:16–17, 158
43:18, 1, 58, 142, 165, 265, 339
43:19–20, 49
43:20, 50
43:21, 100, 116
43:22, 68
43:22–24, 137
43:22–28, 88, 97–102, 137, 199
43:23, 114–115, 253
43:25, 340
43:26, 340
43:27, 137
43:28, 89
44:1, 34
44:1–4, 137
44:1–5, 97, 102–105, 145
44:2, 73, 108, 130, 158, 189, 195, 199, 204
44:3–4, 49
44:6, 116
44:6–8, 150
44:6–22, 105–114
44:7, 192
44:7–8, 88
44:8, 192, 199, 204, 242
44:9, 116
44:9–20, 260
44:10, 116
44:12, 116
44:13, 114
44:14, 247
44:19, 247
44:21, 116, 130
44:22, 116
44:23, 114–115, 116, 117, 244, 247, 269
44:24, 130, 195
44:24–26, 158
44:24–28, 73, 115–119
44:26, 63, 73
44:27, 49
44:28, 39, 41, 122, 123, 273
45:1, 39, 41
45:1–8, 121–126, 265
45:2, 160
45:4, 50, 104
45:5, 74
45:5–6, 150

45:6, 74
45:7, 64, 74, 287
45:8, 169, 244
45:9, 88, 192
45:9–10, 88
45:9–11, 163, 166
45:9–19, 240
45:9–25, 126–136, 265
45:10, 192, 352
45:11, 116, 192
45:15, 136
45:18, 74, 195
45:19, 136, 165, 235
45:20, 247
45:21, 192
45:21–22, 150
45:22, 166
45:23, 73
46:1–13, 138–143, 159
46:3, 159
46:5, 192
46:5–13, 88, 240
46:9, 1, 58, 96, 150, 165, 265, 339
46:10, 273
46:11, 73, 164
46:12, 159
47, 152
47:1, 6, 152, 210–211
47:1–15, 88, 145–152
47:2, 211
47:2–3, 153
47:3, 153
47:5, 152
47:8, 159, 211
47:9, 153, 211
47:10, 211
47:14, 93, 152
47:15, 152
48:1–11, 137, 157–161, 243
48:3, 58, 339
48:4, 164
48:5, 260
48:6, 192
48:6–13, 240
48:8, 163
48:8–11, 137
48:9, 31
48:12–22, 161–167
48:14, 6, 273
48:16, 136
48:17, 74

Isaiah (cont.)
48:18, 263
48:19, 350
48:20, 6, 7, 263
48:22, 263
49, 1, 33, 175, 211, 236, 288, 291, 340, 349
49–55, 177
49–66, 153
49:1, 40
49:1–13, 68, 71, 72, 167–174
49:2, 187, 317, 318
49:3, 222
49:5, 69
49:7, 50, 299
49:8, 71, 174, 189
49:8–9, 297
49:11, 244
49:13, 26, 69, 178, 233, 269
49:14, 9, 136, 172, 187, 197, 201, 233, 235, 238,
243, 250, 272, 290, 339
49:14–15, 352
49:14–50:3, 175–184, 233
49:15, 136, 339, 352
49:15–16, 233, 235
49:16, 104
49:17, 288, 306
49:18, 236, 265, 299
49:18–21, 153
49:19–23, 137
49:21, 153, 211, 238, 265, 339, 349
49:22, 288
49:22–23, 144, 153, 265, 352
49:22–26, 312
49:23, 153, 191, 291, 349
49:25, 88, 191, 262
49:26, 25
49:28, 288
50:1, 192, 235, 238
50:1–3, 137
50:2, 49, 192
50:4, 196
50:4–5, 237
50:4–11, 186–193, 197
50:6, 218, 223
50:7, 218
50:8, 45, 237
50:8–9, 69, 197, 204
50:9, 202
50:11, 93
51, 191
51–52, 307

51:1–8, 193–199
51:3, 26, 262
51:5, 40
51:5–6, 203
51:6, 202
51:7, 199, 204
51:8, 202
51:9, 208–209, 214
51:9–16, 200–205, 208
51:9–52:12, 208
51:12, 25, 34, 137, 199, 223, 249
51:12–13, 109, 199
51:13, 204, 340
51:15, 74
51:17, 153
51:17–52:12, 205–215
51:21–23, 218
51:22–23, 153
52, 33
52–53, 228
52:1, 153, 265, 299
52:2, 153, 217
52:7, 209, 318
52:9, 26
52:10, 203
52:13, 262
52:13–53:12, 2, 69, 215–224, 225, 227, 228, 231
53, 9, 11, 87, 230, 262
53:1–6, 229
53:4–6, 233
53:7, 69, 228
53:7–8, 227
53:10, 254, 262, 273
53:11, 219
53:12, 69, 228
54, 1, 156, 177, 185, 244, 290, 299, 304–306, 328,
340, 341, 349
54–55, 350
54:1, 153, 265, 305, 349, 352, 353
54:1–3, 352
54:1–17, 231–238
54:4, 153, 199, 340
54:5, 153, 306
54:6, 34, 243, 290, 305, 340
54:7–8, 29, 136–137, 289, 340
54:8, 135, 136, 243, 328, 340
54:9, 306
54:10, 53, 241, 244
54:11, 34
54:11–12, 153, 185, 265
54:11–14, 34

## Scripture Index

54:11–17, 328, 335
54:13, 153, 188
54:14–17, 199
54:15–17, 290
54:16–17, 153
54:17, 185, 193, 238, 253, 299, 328
55, 241, 246, 251, 252, 266, 338
55–66, 219
55:1, 48, 129, 291, 335
55:1–13, 238–245
55:2, 349
55:3, 175, 301
55:4, 242
55:5, 144, 288
55:7, 263, 340, 341
55:7–9, 280
55:8, 263
55:9, 263
55:10–11, 274
55:11, 73, 273
55:12, 247
55:12–13, 251
55:13, 245, 246, 247, 250, 251, 300, 301
56, 265, 266
56–66, 6–8, 10–11, 12, 14, 15, 17, 33, 59, 73,
    78–79, 137, 172, 185, 226, 229–230, 253–255,
    264–267, 286, 292–295, 313–319, 324, 328,
    332, 334, 341, 345, 346
56:1, 73
56:1–8, 247–253, 266
56:3, 10, 253, 292
56:3–8, 53, 295
56:4, 254, 346, 347
56:5, 7, 260, 347, 350
56:7, 7
56:6, 254
56:8, 7, 10, 73
56:9–57:21, 255–264, 266
56:11, 259, 292
56:12, 10
57, 220, 251, 313
57–59, 292, 302
57:1–10, 254
57:5, 247
57:6, 26
57:8, 251, 259
57:15, 254, 295
57:17, 137, 254, 292, 347
57:18, 26, 34, 137
57:18–21, 265
58, 279, 313, 341, 346, 348

58:1–2, 341
58:1–14, 57, 266, 267–274
58:3, 11
58:3–4, 346
58:4, 348
58:6–14, 295
58:7, 348
58:10, 286
58:13, 292
58:14, 144
59, 308, 313, 318
59:1–21, 266, 274–283
59:2, 137
59:4, 292
59:4–8, 254
59:7, 319
59:9, 286, 287
59:9–15, 11
59:13, 273
59:14, 292
59:15–16, 313
59:15–21, 312
59:16–17, 311, 318
59:17, 265, 312, 318
60–62, 286, 312
60:1–22, 292, 283–292
60:4, 349
60:4–13, 10
60:5, 314
60:6, 315
60:9, 40
60:10, 300
60:11, 300
60:13, 246, 247
60:14, 315
60:16, 265, 300, 349, 352
60:17, 300
60:18, 265
60:19–20, 265
60:22, 73
61:1, 242
61:1–11, 295–302
61:8, 74
62:1–12, 302–308
62:2, 335
62:3, 265
62:4–5, 153
62:6, 322
62:6–7, 335
62:7, 10
62:10, 10

372          *Scripture Index*

Isaiah (cont.)
  63, 278, 316, 317
  63–66, 255
  63:1–6, 308–313
  63:3, 278, 317
  63:7–64:12, 65, 266, 319–328
  63:17, 334
  64:1, 336
  64:5, 295, 341
  64:7, 137, 341
  64:7 (Heb: 64:6), 333
  64:8, 334
  64:9, 334, 341
  64:9 (Heb: 64:8), 334
  64:10–12, 10
  64:12 (Heb: 64:11), 333
  65, 266, 346, 351
  65–66, 266, 317, 351
  65:1–25, 254, 266, 328–338
  65:2, 254, 292
  65:3, 346
  65:3–5, 254
  65:4, 346
  65:5, 334, 346
  65:9, 50
  65:11, 341
  65:12, 254, 346
  65:13, 186
  65:13–15, 265, 292
  65:14, 341
  65:15, 50
  65:16, 341
  65:17, 58, 265, 341, 344
  65:20–22, 34
  65:22, 50
  65:24, 137
  65:25, 266
  66:1–2, 265
  66:1–24, 254, 266, 341–351
  66:3, 292
  66:3–6, 265
  66:7, 352
  66:7–8, 265, 353
  66:7–9, 353
  66:8, 153
  66:8–14, 265
  66:10–11, 265
  66:11, 33, 353
  66:12–13, 265
  66:13, 26, 33, 353
  66:14, 186

  66:14–16, 293
  66:15–16, 93
  66:15–17, 265
  66:19, 40
  66:20, 10
  66:24, 47, 93, 265
Jeremiah, 180, 189, 204
  2:10, 288
  2:20, 261, 333
  3:3, 160
  3:6, 261, 333
  3:13, 261
  4:19, 270
  6:17, 209
  8:17, 279
  13:16, 287
  13:23, 188
  17:9, 103
  25:15–29, 210
  29:4, 336
  29:21–23, 335
  31:15, 315
  32:5, 82
  32:35, 261
  33:22, 166
  48:26, 210
  49:7–22, 75, 310
  49:22, 81
  49:28, 75
Lamentations, 7, 9, 13, 26, 27, 149, 152–155,
    156, 163, 178–179, 180, 182, 184–185, 189,
    203, 210, 211–215, 222–223, 234, 240, 242,
    266, 322, 331, 338
  1:1, 149, 152–153, 181
  1:1–3, 180
  1:2, 26, 190, 211
  1:4, 180
  1:5, 220
  1:6, 152
  1:7, 327
  1:8, 220
  1:9, 26, 324, 325
  1:10, 327
  1:11, 240, 327
  1:11b–22, 178
  1:13, 152, 192
  1:14, 220
  1:15, 311
  1:16, 152, 223
  1:17, 26, 324
  1:17–19, 152

# Scripture Index

1:19, 240
1:21, 26, 152, 311
2:1, 152
2:4, 327
2:8, 152
2:10, 152
2:12, 153, 240
2:13, 152
2:13–19, 67
2:15, 152
2:18, 67
2:19, 67, 153, 211, 212, 240
2:20, 182
3, 69, 185, 187, 189–191, 221, 222–223
3:1, 190, 222
3:1–18, 220
3:1–20, 185
3:2, 82, 192, 287
3:23, 189
3:26, 189
3:27–30, 223
3:30, 189, 190
3:34, 223
3:39, 220, 221
3:42, 220
3:42–43, 220
3:46, 223
3:49, 220
3:49–51, 190
3:54, 93
3:56, 190
4, 210, 278
4:1, 212
4:1–2, 211, 236
4:2, 212, 236
4:2–4, 179
4:3–4, 290, 353
4:4, 73, 182, 240
4:5, 240, 335
4:9, 240
4:10, 182
4:11, 192
4:13–14, 213, 278
4:14, 278, 281, 311
4:15, 213
4:17, 311
4:21, 311
4:21–22, 310
5, 235, 240, 341
5:4, 240
5:6, 240

5:9, 240, 335
5:10, 240
5:20, 178, 235, 339, 340
5:21–22, 327
5:22, 322
Ezekiel, 40, 198, 260
3:7, 160
4:1, 181
23:31–35, 210
27:21, 288
27:6, 246
31:3, 246
32:8, 287
33:3–6, 209, 270
36:5, 310
36:35, 198
Daniel
1:3, 250, 251
1:7, 250, 251
1:8, 250, 251
1:9, 250, 251
1:10, 250, 251
1:11, 250, 251
1:18, 250, 251
11, 220
Hosea, 159, 260
2, 31
2:16, 26
5:10, 93
6:8, 103
12, 100, 144
12:2–4, 100
12:4, 145
Joel
2:2, 287
2:3, 198
Amos
1:3, 211
1:4, 93
1:6, 211
1:7, 93
1:9, 211
1:10, 93
1:11, 211
1:12, 93
1:13, 211
1:14, 93
2:1, 211
2:4, 211
2:6–8, 211
3:6, 209

374                                                     *Scripture Index*

Amos (cont.)
  5, 281
  5:18, 129, 287
  5:18–19, 280–281
  5:20, 287
  6:1, 129
Obadiah, 75, 310
Jonah
  1:3, 289
Micah
  3:6, 287
  4:4, 274
  4:13, 160
Nahum, 212–213, 214
  1:15 (Heb: 2:1), 212
  3:7, 212
  3:10, 212
  3:11, 212
Zephaniah
  2:5, 130
  3:1, 130
Zechariah
  9:8, 291
Malachi
  3:18, 167

## NEW TESTAMENT

Matthew, 315–316
  2:1, 314
  2:2, 315
  2:11, 314
  8:17, 228
  26:55, 228
  28:5, 199

Mark
  15:1–20, 227
  15:28, 228
Luke
  1:30, 199
  4:16–20, 313
  9:23–26, 226
  22:37, 228
Acts
  8:30–35, 227–228
Romans
  9–11, 52
  11:25, 52
  11:28–29, 50
  11:33, 52
Ephesians, 318
  6:10–17, 318–319
Philippians
  2:5–12, 226
  4:8, 120
1 Peter
  2:20–25, 228
1 John
  4:8, 317
Revelation, 318
  19, 316–318
  19:5, 316
  19:9–10, 316
  19:11, 316
  19:13, 316
  19:14, 317
  19:15, 316
  21:1, 336
  21:4, 336

# Subject Index

Abraham, 44–45, 50, 52, 54–55, 145, 166, 194, 196, 197–198, 199, 242, 244, 323, 326
allusion, 4, 7, 9, 11, 45, 67, 78, 81, 85, 86, 87, 91, 123, 131, 132, 136, 141, 145, 164, 174, 178, 183, 185, 187, 189–191, 196, 202, 204, 211–213, 214, 224, 241, 242–243, 250–252, 261–262, 266, 274, 277–278, 279, 281, 283, 304–307, 314, 315, 322–325, 328
ambiguity, 4, 27, 28, 120, 130, 132, 134–135, 136, 163–166, 180, 192, 201, 219, 236, 237, 297, 298, 308, 309, 339, 347
attitude, 4, 5, 9, 14, 34, 57, 82, 120, 129, 189, 193, 194–195, 197, 198, 200, 217, 218–219, 221, 254, 263–264, 265, 293, 295, 345, 348, 357

Babylon, 6, 7–9, 41–42, 67, 76, 88, 96, 98, 123, 137, 140, 143, 147–157, 159, 167, 210–211, 214, 217, 237, 242, 246, 251, 290, 327, 336

canon/canonical, 6, 11–13, 40, 48, 77–79, 241, 253, 274, 301
clothing/garment imagery, 153, 197, 198, 202, 211, 265, 280, 281–282, 298–299, 309, 310–311, 312, 318–319, 324
comfort/comforter, 1, 4, 10, 12, 25–26, 29, 32, 33–34, 45–46, 47, 63, 68, 69, 73, 74, 76, 80, 81–82, 91, 97, 99, 101, 105, 132–133, 137, 141, 142, 148, 152, 172, 179, 180, 184, 185–186, 197–198, 203, 204, 213, 214–215, 224, 233–234, 236, 237, 240, 258, 261–262, 263, 264, 265, 292, 297, 298, 299, 345, 348–351, 353
consolation, 10, 13, 49, 88, 92, 141, 205, 247, 248, 265, 349, 350, 353

covenant, 29, 45, 50–52, 55, 68, 71, 73, 172–175, 241–242, 244, 250, 252, 253, 254, 255, 261, 283, 298, 301, 307, 337
Cyrus the Persian, 38, 41–42, 66, 68, 76, 104, 115, 118–119, 122–126, 127, 132, 133, 134, 140, 143, 154, 164

David, 48, 123, 242–243, 244, 251, 301–302
disjunction, 1, 78, 234
Divine Council, 27
double-entendre, 4, 101, 141

emotion, 1, 4, 5, 10, 14, 29, 30, 32, 44, 47, 60, 62, 81, 82, 89, 109, 129, 130, 132–133, 137, 180, 181, 185, 199, 227, 255, 258, 261, 262, 264, 283, 340
encounter, 1, 3, 4, 5, 10, 11, 13, 14, 25, 29, 34, 36, 44, 48, 61, 65, 80, 84, 89, 94, 97, 105, 115, 119, 129, 161, 162, 169, 177, 183, 184, 187, 190, 199, 200, 201, 222, 224, 226, 227, 229, 267, 286, 293–294, 297, 309, 313, 331
formational, 120–121
exile, 6–10, 82, 86, 144, 152, 159, 214, 328
  Babylonian, 1, 2, 6, 7, 9, 12, 69, 82, 98, 209, 214, 218, 220, 222, 226, 242, 251, 253, 290, 300, 311, 336
  contemporary migration, 58
exiles, 7, 13, 41, 45, 46, 48, 49, 56, 57, 63, 64, 68, 70, 71–72, 76, 83, 84, 92, 93, 96, 100, 108, 110, 115–116, 118, 119, 122, 123, 125, 126, 132, 133, 137, 140, 141, 143–145, 147–148, 149, 150, 152, 160, 161, 163, 164, 166, 167, 173, 190, 201, 202, 203, 205, 208, 209, 214, 219, 222, 224, 233, 237, 253, 260, 263, 265, 288, 290, 298, 336, 339, 349, 350

375

# Subject Index

experience
contemporary, 57, 60, 226, 229, 231, 294
poetic, 3, 4, 5, 14, 47, 84, 147, 158,
163, 166

fear, 9–10, 13, 35, 36, 40, 44–47, 49, 57, 63–65, 82,
92–94, 97–98, 102, 104, 108–110, 113, 120,
123, 144, 152, 157, 161, 171, 174, 197, 199–200,
204–205, 237, 249, 282, 292
formation
of Isaiah, 8, 17, 77–79
personal, 119–121

historical context, 2–3, 5, 6, 7, 8–11, 41–42, 58,
96, 328
hope, 14, 40, 58, 84, 180, 190, 255, 283, 292,
339, 353

idol/idolatry, 30, 38, 74, 77, 82–83, 86, 95, 98,
109–113, 114, 116, 134, 139–143, 148, 159–160,
161, 247, 254, 255, 259–264, 332, 333–335,
337, 347
imagination, 14, 40–41, 69, 104, 106, 114, 120,
125–126, 137, 163, 193, 221, 226, 260, 292,
295, 308, 309
inclusio, 29, 92, 355
irony, 26, 35, 36, 37, 38, 40, 45, 61–65, 83, 85, 96,
97, 99, 100, 101, 110–113, 114, 124–126,
130–131, 134, 135, 136, 140, 142–143, 148,
150–151, 218, 219, 222, 240, 270, 272–273, 334
Isaiah of Jerusalem, 6, 78, 79, 83, 86, 88, 141, 219,
251, 339

Jacob
House of, 141, 159, 270
Patriarch, 36, 54, 100, 103, 143–145, 159,
160–161, 166, 199
Jacob-Israel, 9, 26, 34, 45, 47–48, 65, 66, 68–69,
71, 72, 77, 83, 100, 101, 102–104, 116, 122, 123,
125, 134, 143–145, 158, 163, 171, 173, 189, 218,
220
Jerusalem, 2, 6, 7, 10, 26, 118, 119, 132, 149, 156,
179, 184, 196, 208, 210, 211, 213, 223, 225, 237,
246–247, 286, 287, 290, 304, 307, 310, 315,
327, 349, 353
Judah, 7, 8, 48, 196, 214, 262
justice, 11, 14, 30, 31, 33, 48, 65, 66–68, 213, 224,
226, 230–231, 249, 253, 254, 258, 263–264,
266, 267, 269, 271–273, 278–279, 280, 281,

283, 292, 295, 297, 299, 302, 309, 310,
311–313, 316–318, 341, 346
poetic, 113, 154
juxtaposition, 1, 4–5, 10, 11, 13, 26–27, 29, 30, 31,
32, 34, 38, 45, 46–47, 69, 71, 72, 74, 80–81,
82, 86, 89, 92, 94, 97, 100, 101, 124, 125, 129,
131–133, 135–137, 145, 149, 151, 158, 159, 160,
163–167, 172, 177, 178, 180, 184–186, 196, 197,
198, 201, 204, 208, 219, 236, 237, 238, 249,
254, 258, 260, 262, 264–265, 267, 271, 273,
277, 279, 282, 287, 298–299, 300, 305, 312,
313, 325, 331, 335, 336, 337, 340, 345, 346, 350,
351, 356

Lady Zion/Daughter Zion, 13, 148, 152, 155–157,
177–186, 188, 324
legal imagery, 36, 62, 97, 100, 183, 191, 279
lyric, 3, 4
lyrically informed poetic approach, 3–5

maternal imagery, 27, 34, 153, 156, 177–183, 265,
290–291, 305, 348–353
memory, 1, 45, 58, 96, 100, 113, 139, 142, 177, 178,
179–182, 204, 205, 233, 235, 265, 322–324,
334, 335, 336, 338–341, 352
merism, 94, 117, 125, 170, 198, 243, 356
metaphor, 1, 4–5, 13, 27, 28, 31, 38, 92, 104, 109,
126, 154, 155, 163, 173, 178, 180, 183, 185, 223,
234, 236, 237, 244, 260, 263, 277, 279, 291,
301, 305–306, 332, 348, 349
migration, 55–60

nationalism, 59, 290

paradox, 4, 29, 67, 83, 219, 220, 224, 338
parallelism, 16, 24, 27, 28, 37, 40, 61, 62, 70,
102–105, 106, 109, 121, 135, 139, 172, 179, 182,
195, 202, 206, 207, 216, 231, 232, 233, 243,
248, 269–270, 286, 304, 332, 335, 344, 345,
352, 355, 356, 357
parataxis, 5, 163, 356
Persia, 41–42, 93, 125, 251, 308
personification, 9, 35, 36, 39, 40, 152, 155, 173, 178,
201, 203, 240, 307, 356
Babylon, 148–152, 155–157
Servant, 13, 65–69, 71–72, 74, 85, 154, 157, 165,
169–174, 175, 177, 184–191, 193, 195, 196, 197,
198, 204, 217–224, 226, 229, 230, 236–237,
238, 253–255, 262, 297, 298, 301, 351, 353

# Subject Index

377

Zion, 13, 14, 26, 66–67, 69, 74, 104, 155–157,
177–186, 190, 191, 196, 208, 209, 210–215,
217, 233–238, 241, 254, 260, 265, 291,
298–299, 305, 308, 311, 324, 339, 340,
349–350, 351, 352–353
poetic persuasion, 4, 11, 14, 34, 89, 120, 169, 177,
187, 193, 203, 237, 253, 254, 262, 295
poetic style, 1, 7, 34, 36, 71, 98, 106, 251, 265, 267
possible world, 3, 4, 5, 13–14
prophecy, 5, 25, 49, 56, 58, 76, 81, 85, 86, 87, 88,
122, 129, 160, 183, 212, 225, 240, 241, 245,
246–247, 280, 288, 326
prophet, 6, 8–10, 11, 13, 25, 26, 27, 31, 68, 78, 79,
87, 92, 98, 103, 105, 129, 130, 141, 143, 144,
145, 170, 171–172, 182, 186, 196, 213, 218, 230,
241, 242, 244, 245, 258, 259, 260, 261, 266,
271, 272, 278, 281, 297, 300, 301, 305, 313,
326, 339, 347
prophetic poetry, 1–3, 7, 13, 120, 154, 234

reconciliation, 10, 11, 13, 14, 33, 34, 81, 89, 98, 101,
137, 185, 214, 234–237, 254, 261, 292, 294,
298, 299, 302
repetition, 5, 21, 27, 28, 29, 30, 31, 32, 35–36, 37,
45–46, 47, 62, 64, 67, 72, 83, 86, 92, 93, 97,
98, 99, 102, 109, 111–112, 116, 117, 118, 119,
122, 124, 125, 148, 150, 151, 167, 172, 178, 179,
181, 204, 243, 263, 270, 282, 300, 307, 312,
318, 324, 325, 326, 328, 335
rhetorical question, 29–32, 38, 39, 83, 86–89, 92,
95, 103, 109, 130–131, 135, 140, 142, 164, 181,
182, 183, 191–192, 205, 240, 270, 320
rhythm, 5

Sarah, 196
sarcasm, 30, 62, 64, 88–89, 109, 112, 148, 151, 183,
192, 351
servant, 1, 13, 40, 41, 65–69, 71–72, 74, 85, 99, 101,
118, 145, 154, 157, 165, 169–175, 177, 179,
184–193, 194, 195–196, 197, 198, 204,
217–231, 236–237, 238, 253–255, 262,
297–299, 301, 351, 353
  audience as, 44, 65, 68, 83, 88, 94, 99, 102–103,
  105, 113
  Suffering, 68, 219–224, 226–227, 229–231, 262
Servant Songs, 17, 68
servants, 13–14, 137, 185, 193, 220, 237, 245, 252,
253–255, 290, 293, 295, 299, 315, 316,
327–328, 332, 334–335, 337–338, 341, 345, 350

silence, 1, 12–13, 25–26, 27, 36, 148, 223, 228
sound play, 4, 5, 27, 31, 36, 62, 82, 83, 85, 95, 118,
130, 148, 160, 172, 208–210, 211, 259, 269,
271–272, 290, 299, 312, 323, 336, 346
supersessionism, 50–55
synecdoche, 28, 40, 357
synthesis, 78, 248, 264, 265–267, 293, 294–295

Temple, 7, 41, 98, 118, 251, 252, 288, 289, 290, 327,
342, 346, 347
tension, 1, 4, 10, 29, 33, 79, 82, 94, 98, 101, 129,
131, 136–138, 152, 165, 172, 185, 204, 218, 220,
221, 233, 235, 237, 246, 266, 295, 339–341,
345, 350
tone, 4, 10, 13, 25, 30, 33–36, 37, 61–63, 70, 71,
73–74, 80, 82–84, 88–89, 91–92, 96, 98–99,
100, 101, 109, 111, 113, 126, 129–130, 134,
135–136, 139–143, 148, 151–152, 158, 167, 171,
191, 204, 205, 209, 240, 265, 274, 298, 352,
357
trauma, 56–57, 152

uncertainty, 4–5, 9, 163, 166, 167, 199–200, 294

voice, 8, 12, 23, 27, 32, 36, 55, 60, 79, 84, 103, 110,
111, 114, 136, 152, 165, 178, 191–192, 201, 217,
219, 229, 231, 240, 286, 297, 298, 300, 301,
304, 308, 323, 324, 341, 348
  Divine, 1, 4, 10, 12–13, 23, 25–26, 27, 31, 32,
  33–34, 35, 37, 39, 40, 44, 45, 47, 57, 61, 62,
  64, 65–66, 67, 68, 70, 71, 72, 73–75, 80–83,
  84, 88–89, 91, 93, 94, 95, 96, 97, 99, 100, 101,
  102, 103, 105, 108, 110, 111, 112, 113, 115–116,
  117, 118, 119, 122, 124, 125–126, 127, 129, 130,
  131–132, 133, 134, 135, 136–137, 139, 141, 142,
  143, 148, 149, 150, 151–152, 155, 158–160,
  163–165, 169–171, 173, 177–183, 185, 187, 189,
  191–192, 194, 197, 200, 201, 203–205, 208,
  217, 222, 233, 234, 235, 236, 237, 238, 240,
  243, 248, 252, 253, 263, 265, 291, 297–299,
  301, 302, 306, 309, 311, 324, 327, 331, 332–333,
  336, 337, 338, 339–340, 350, 351–353
  Jacob-Israel, 66, 67, 136, 171, 172, 185, 201, 235,
  238, 243, 250, 339, 340, 341
  poetic voicing, 1, 4, 5, 9–10, 11, 27–29, 32, 133,
  171, 293, 299, 327, 332, 336, 340
  prophet, 203
  prophetic poet, 1, 6, 11, 84, 86, 115, 133, 165,
  201, 203, 243, 277, 279

## 378 Subject Index

voice (cont.)
    servant, 1, 40, 71, 74, 165, 169–172, 184–185, 187, 188–189, 191, 192, 195, 197, 218, 297, 298–299
    we, 218, 219, 222, 227, 229, 277, 280, 325
    Zion, 1, 74, 136, 153–154, 172, 177, 184–185, 188, 201, 212, 233, 235, 238, 243, 250, 299, 311, 339, 340

welcome, 58, 60

word play, 4, 31, 37, 82, 103, 110, 117, 131, 136, 145, 251, 269–273, 306, 312, 336

Zion, 1, 9, 12, 13, 14, 26, 59, 65, 66–67, 68, 69, 74, 104, 136, 148, 152, 153, 155–157, 172, 177–186, 187, 188, 190, 191, 196, 197–198, 201, 205, 208, 209, 210–215, 217, 219, 233–238, 241, 250, 254, 260, 265, 287, 290, 291, 298–299, 304, 305, 308, 310, 311, 312, 324, 334, 339, 340, 349–353